A Sequence for Academic Writing

A Sequence for Academic Writing

Second Edition

Laurence Behrens
University of California, Santa Barbara

Leonard J. Rosen
Bentley College

Bonnie Beedles

PEARSON
Longman

New York • San Francisco • Boston
London • Toronto • Sydney • Tokyo • Singapore • Madrid
Mexico City • Munich • Paris • Cape Town • Hong Kong • Montreal

Senior Vice President and Publisher: Joseph Opiela
Senior Acquisitions Editor: Lynn M. Huddon
Marketing Manager: Deborah Murphy
Development Editor: Susan Messer
Senior Supplements Editor: Donna Campion
Production Manager: Charles Annis
Project Coordination, Text Design, and Electronic Page Makeup: Pre-Press Co., Inc.
Cover Designer/Manager: John Callahan
Manufacturing Buyer: Dennis J. Para
Printer and Binder: R. R. Donnelly and Sons Co.
Cover Printer: Lehigh Press, Inc.

For permission to use copyrighted material, grateful acknowledgment is made to the copyright holders on pages 343–47, which are hereby made part of the copyright page.

Library of Congress Cataloging-in-Publication Data

Behrens, Laurence.
  A sequence for academic writing / Laurence Behrens, Leonard J. Rosen,
Bonnie Beedles.-- 2nd ed.
    p. cm.
  Rev. ed. of: A sequence for academic writing / Bonnie Beedles, Laurence Behrens,
Leonard J. Rosen.
   Includes bibliographical references and index.
   ISBN 0-321-20780-7
   1. English language--Rhetoric. 2. Academic writing. I. Rosen, Leonard J.
II. Beedles, Bonnie. III. Beedles, Bonnie. Sequence for academic writing. IV. Title.

  PE1408.B46926 2004
  808'.042--dc22

                                                                    2004002552

Please visit us at http://www.ablongman.com/Behrens

ISBN 0-321-20780-7

7 8 9 10—DOC—07 06

Brief Contents

Detailed Contents

Chapter 3
Writing as a Process   87

Chapter 4
Explanatory Synthesis   119

Chapter 5
Argument Synthesis   179

What Is an Argument Synthesis?   179

Demonstration: Developing an Argument Synthesis—Volunteering in America   187

Preface for Instructors

A Sequence for Academic Writing evolved out of another text, *Writing and Reading Across the Curriculum (WRAC).* Through eight editions over the last 23 years, *WRAC* has helped hundreds of thousands of students prepare for the writing done well beyond the freshman composition course. *WRAC* features a rhetoric in which students are introduced to the core skills of summary, critique, and synthesis, and a reader that presents readings in the disciplines to which students can apply the skills learned in the earlier chapters. Because the skills of summary, critique, and synthesis are so central to academic thinking and writing, many instructors—both those teaching writing-across-the-curriculum and those using other approaches to composition instruction—have found *WRAC* a highly useful introduction to college-level writing. We therefore decided to adapt the rhetoric portion of *WRAC* into a separate book that instructors could use apart from any additional reading content they chose to incorporate in their writing courses. *A Sequence for Academic Writing* is both an adaptation of *WRAC* and an expansion: We have added the core skill of *analysis* to the mix because it, too, is an assignment type often encountered throughout the curriculum and beyond.

We proceed through a sequence from "Summary, Paraphrase, and Quotation" to "Critical Reading and Critique," to "Explanatory Synthesis" and "Argument Synthesis" to "Analysis." The final chapter, "Locating, Mining, and Citing Sources," introduces students to the tools and techniques they will need to apply skills learned earlier to sources they gather themselves when conducting research. Students will find the coverage of citation form and the listing of reference materials, including useful Web sites, to be both comprehensive and current. (We have consulted closely with reference librarians and have summarized the latest citation formats from the MLA and APA manuals.) Students will find, as well, in Chapter 3 a discussion of the writing process that is reinforced throughout the text. We make a special effort in all chapters to address the issue of plagiarism: We offer techniques for steering well clear of the problem, at the same time encouraging students to live up to the highest ethical standards.

Key features in *A Sequence for Academic Writing* include *boxes,* which sum up important concepts in each chapter; brief writing *exercises,* which prompt individual and group activities; *writing assignments,* which put each chapter's skills into practice, and *model papers,* which provide example responses to writing assignments discussed in the text. An Instructor's Manual and Companion Website provide further resources for teaching with this text.

While we are keenly aware of the overlapping nature of the skills on which we focus and while we could all endlessly debate an appropriate order in which to cover these skills, a book is necessarily linear. We have chosen the sequence that makes the most sense to us, though individual instructors may choose to cover these skills in their own sequence. Teachers should feel perfectly free to use these chapters in whatever order they feel is most useful to their individual aims and philosophies. Understanding the material in a later chapter does not, in most cases, depend on students having read material in the earlier chapters.

A NOTE ON THE SECOND EDITION

Users of the first edition of *Sequence for Academic Writing* will notice numerous changes to almost all chapters in the current edition. Most of the model papers are new: These include the sample critique on Greg Critser's essay "Too Much of a Good Thing"; a new argument synthesis on volunteerism; a new comparison-contrast synthesis on film versions of *Hamlet*; and a new analysis paper, "The Coming Apart of a Dorm Society." The model explanatory synthesis paper on computer-mediated-communication has also been revised, with new sources on instant messaging. Chapter 6 on Analysis has been almost entirely rewritten, with new material on analyzing visual media. Chapters 1, 2, 3, 4, and 6 also feature new major writing assignments. As indicated above, Chapters 3 and 7 have been restructured, and the latter includes new research resources and updated citations.

ACKNOWLEDGMENTS

We would like to thank the following reviewers for their help in the preparation of this text: Cora Agatucci, Central Oregon Community College; Patricia Baldwin, Pitt Community College; Bruce Closser, Andrews University; Clinton R. Gardner, Salt Lake Community College; Margaret Graham, Iowa State University; Susanmarie Harrington, Indiana University and Purdue University Indianapolis; Georgina Hill, Western Michigan University; Jane M. Kinney, Valdosta State University; Susan E. Knutson, University of Minnesota–Twin Cities; Cathy Leaker, North Carolina State University; Lyle W. Morgan, Pittsburg State University; Joan Perkins, University of Hawaii; Catherine Quick, Stephen F. Austin State University; Emily Rogers, University of Illinois-Urbana Champaign; William Scott Simkins, University of Southern Mississippi; Doug Swartz, Indiana University Northwest; Marcy Taylor, Central Michigan University; Zach Waggoner, Western Illinois University; Heidemarie Z. Weidner, Tennessee Technological University; and Betty R. Youngkin, The University of Dayton; Terry Meyers Zawacki, George Mason University. And we are grateful to UCSB librarian Lucia Snowhill for helping us update the reference sources in Chapter 7.

Thanks to Lynn Huddon, our editor at Longman Publishers, for seeing this project through from conception to completion. We are also grateful to Gordon Laws, project manager at Pre-Press Co., and Sam Blake for careful and attentive handling of the manuscript throughout the production process. And a final thanks to our development editor, Susan Messer, an excellent critic who pushed us to refine and clarify. All have contributed mightily to this effort, and we extend our warmest appreciation.

Laurence Behrens

Leonard J. Rosen

Bonnie Beedles

Introduction

In your sociology class, you are assigned to write a paper on the role of peer groups in influencing attitudes toward smoking. Your professor expects you to read some of the literature on the subject as well as to conduct interviews with members of such groups. For an environmental studies course, you must write a paper on how one or more industrial plants in a particular area have been affecting the local ecosystem. In your film studies class, you must select a contemporary filmmaker—you are trying to decide between Martin Scorsese and Spike Lee—and examine how at least three of his films demonstrate a distinctive point of view.

These writing assignments are typical of those you will undertake during your college years. In fact, such assignments are also common for those in professional life: for instance, scientists writing environmental impact statements, social scientists writing accounts of their research for professional journals, and film critics showing how the latest effort by a filmmaker fits into the general body of his or her work.

Core Skills

To succeed in such assignments, you will need to develop and hone particular skills in critical reading, thinking, and writing. You must develop—not necessarily in this order—the ability to

- read and accurately *summarize* a selection of material on your subject;
- determine the quality and relevance of your sources through a process of *critical reading* and assessment;
- *synthesize* different sources by discovering the relationships among them and showing how these relationships produce insights about the subject under discussion;
- *analyze* objects or phenomena by applying particular perspectives and theories;
- develop effective techniques for (1) discovering and using pertinent, authoritative information and ideas and (2) presenting the results of your work in generally accepted disciplinary formats.

A Sequence for Academic Writing will help you to meet these goals. You will learn techniques for preparing and writing the summary, critique, analysis, and synthesis because we have found that these are the core skills you must master if you are to succeed as a college writer, regardless of your major. In conversations with faculty across the curriculum, time and again we have been struck by a shared desire to see students thinking and writing in subject-appropriate ways. Psychology, biology, and engineering teachers want you to think, talk, and write like psychologists, biol- ogists, and engineers. We set out, therefore, to learn the strategies writers use to en- ter conversations in their respective disciplines. We discovered that four readily learned strategies—summary, critique, synthesis, and analysis—provided the basis for the great majority of writing in freshman- through senior-level courses, and in courses across disciplines. We therefore made these skills the centerpiece of instruc- tion for this book.

Applications Beyond College

While summary, critique, synthesis, and analysis are primary critical thinking and writing skills practiced throughout the university, these skills are also crucial to the work you will do in your life outside the university. In the professional world, people write letters, memos, and reports in which they must summarize procedures, activities, and the like. Critical reading and critique are important skills for writing legal briefs, business plans, and policy briefs. In addition, these same types of documents—common in the legal, business, and political worlds, respec- tively—involve synthesis. A business plan, for example, will often include a syn- thesis of ideas and proposals in one coherent plan. Finally, the ability to analyze complex data, processes, or ideas, to apply theories or perspectives to particular subjects, and then to effectively convey the results of analysis in writing is integral to writing in medicine, law, politics, business—in short, just about any of the pro- fessions in which you may later find yourself.

Emphasis on Process

Our focus on these four core skills culminates in a chapter on research, in which you will find suggestions for locating, mining, and citing the source materials you gather during the process of research. You'll find the latest MLA and APA formats for citing sources as well as guidance on where to locate the most promising sources and how to use them effectively. Necessarily, Chapter 7 builds on the skills of summary, critique, synthesis, and analysis learned earlier. The chapter also en- courages you to think of research as a *process*, an approach to writing that you will be familiar with from Chapter 3.

Note that while we have divided the tasks of reading, thinking, and writing into steps, we don't mean to imply that there is only one way to approach these tasks. That's not so. Yet the techniques we offer in this text have helped many thousands of college students succeed as writers. Learn the techniques, then. Once you be- come proficient at writing summaries, syntheses, analyses, and critiques, you may want to adopt alternate approaches more suited to your needs and abilities.

Several features in *A Sequence for Academic Writing* should enhance your under- standing of the material. Throughout you will find brief writing *exercises*, as well as longer *writing assignments*. *Boxed* material provides useful summaries and hints re- lating to points covered at greater length in the text. *Model papers* provide specific examples of responses to writing assignments discussed in the text.

Students often view introductory college writing courses as unnecessary and ir- relevant distractions from their subject-oriented courses. But success in these disci- plinary courses is directly correlated to the ability to perform assigned reading and writing tasks. Professors in disciplinary courses generally do not teach reading and writing skills, though they do take such skills for granted in their students. (And if your college professors expect you to possess solid reading and writing skills, just imagine the expectations of your future employers, co-workers, and clients!) Beyond the need for developing your writing skills, however, don't underestimate the sense of satisfaction, even enjoyment, you will derive from becoming a more skillful reader and writer. You may not have chosen to enroll in your present writing course, but it could well become one of the most valuable—and interesting—of your college career.

1

Summary, Paraphrase, and Quotation

WHAT IS A SUMMARY?

The best way to demonstrate that you understand the information and the ideas in any piece of writing is to compose an accurate and clearly written summary of that piece. By a *summary* we mean a *brief restatement, in your own words, of the content of a passage* (a group of paragraphs, a chapter, an article, a book). This restatement should focus on the *central idea* of the passage. The briefest of all summaries (one or two sentences) will do no more than this. A longer, more complete summary will indicate, in condensed form, the main points in the passage that support or explain the central idea. It will reflect the order in which these points are presented and the emphasis given to them. It may even include some important examples from the passage. But it will not include minor details. It will not repeat points simply for the purpose of emphasis. And it will not contain any of your own opinions or conclusions. A good summary, therefore, has three central qualities: *brevity, completeness,* and *objectivity.*

CAN A SUMMARY BE OBJECTIVE?

Of course, the last quality mentioned above, objectivity, might be difficult to achieve in a summary. By definition, writing a summary requires you to select some aspects of the original and leave out others. Since deciding what to select and what to leave out calls for your personal judgment, your summary really is a work of interpretation. And, certainly, your interpretation of a passage may differ from another person's. One factor affecting the nature and quality of your interpretation is your *prior knowledge* of the subject. For example, if you're attempting to summarize an anthropological article and you're a novice in that field, then your summary of the article will likely differ from that of your professor, who has spent 20 years studying this particular area and whose judgment about what is more or less significant is undoubtedly more reliable than your own. By the same token, your personal or professional *frame of reference* may also affect your interpretation. A union representative and a management representative attempting to summarize the latest management offer would probably come up with two very different accounts. Still, we believe that in most cases it's possible to produce a reasonably objective summary of a passage if you make a conscious, good-faith effort to be unbiased and to prevent your own feelings on the subject from distorting your account of the text.

USING THE SUMMARY

In some quarters, the summary has a bad reputation—and with reason. Summaries often are provided by writers as substitutes for analyses. As students, many of us have summarized books that we were supposed to *review critically*. All the same, the summary does have a place in respectable college work. First, writing a summary is an excellent way to understand what you read. This in itself is an important goal of academic study. If you don't understand your source material, chances are you won't be able to refer to it usefully in an essay or research paper. Summaries help you understand what you read because they force you to put the text into your own words. Practice with writing summaries also develops your general writing habits, since a good summary, like any other piece of good writing, is clear, coherent, and accurate.

Second, summaries are useful to your readers. Let's say you're writing a paper about the McCarthy era in America, and in part of that paper you want to discuss Arthur Miller's *Crucible* as a dramatic treatment of the subject. A summary of the plot would be helpful to a reader who hasn't seen or read—or who doesn't remember—the play. Or perhaps you're writing a paper about the politics of recent American military interventions. If your reader isn't likely to be familiar with American actions in Kosovo and Afghanistan, it would be a good idea to summarize these events at some early point in the paper. In many cases (an exam, for instance), you can use a summary to demonstrate your knowledge of what your professor already knows; when writing a paper, you can use a summary to inform your professor about some relatively unfamiliar source.

Third, summaries are required frequently in college-level writing. For example, on a psychology midterm, you may be asked to explain Carl Jung's theory of the collective unconscious and to show how it differs from Sigmund Freud's theory of the personal unconscious. You may have read about this theory in your textbook or in a supplementary article, or your in-

---

WHERE DO WE FIND WRITTEN SUMMARIES?

Here are just a few of the types of writing that involve summary:

Academic Writing

- **Critique papers.** Summarize material in order to critique it.
- **Synthesis papers.** Summarize to show relationships between sources.
- **Analysis papers.** Summarize theoretical perspectives before applying them.
- **Research papers.** Note-taking and reporting research require summary.
- **Literature reviews.** Overviews of work presented in brief summaries.
- **Argument papers.** Summarize evidence and opposing arguments.
- **Essay exams.** Demonstrate understanding of course materials through summary.

Workplace Writing

- **Policy briefs.** Condense complex public policy.
- **Business plans.** Summarize costs, relevant environmental impacts, and other important matters.
- **Memos, letters, and reports.** Summarize procedures, meetings, product assessments, expenditures, and more.
- **Medical charts.** Record patient data in summarized form.
- **Legal briefs.** Summarize relevant facts of cases.

structor may have outlined it in his or her lecture. You can best demonstrate your understanding of Jung's theory by summarizing it. Then you'll proceed to contrast it with Freud's theory—which, of course, you must also summarize.

THE READING PROCESS

It may seem to you that being able to tell (or retell) in summary form exactly what a passage says is a skill that ought to be taken for granted in anyone who can read at high school level. Unfortunately, this is not so: For all kinds of reasons, people don't always read carefully. In fact, it's probably safe to say that usually they don't. Either they read so inattentively that they skip over words, phrases, or even whole sentences, or, if they do see the words in front of them, they see them without registering their significance.

When a reader fails to pick up the meaning and implications of a sentence or two, usually there's no real harm done. (An exception: You could lose credit on an exam or paper because you failed to read or to realize the significance of a crucial direction by your instructor.) But over longer stretches—the paragraph, the section, the article, or the chapter—inattentive or haphazard reading interferes with your goals as a reader: to perceive the shape of the argument, to grasp the central idea, to determine the main points that compose it, to relate the parts of the whole, and to note key examples. This kind of reading takes a lot more energy and determination than casual reading. But, in the long run, it's an energy-saving method because it enables you to retain the content of the material and to use that content as a basis for your own responses. In other words, it allows you to develop an accurate and coherent written discussion that goes beyond summary.

Given the often large quantity of reading they are asked to do in college, many students skim their assignments. Skimming can be a useful way of managing some kinds of course material. For example, textbooks that outline broad concepts that a professor elaborates upon in a lecture might be skimmed before the lecture, then read more carefully later to fill in gaps in your understanding. However, for the most part you should carefully read and understand the material you are assigned.

One effective strategy with which to approach course readings is to ask yourself how the reading fits into the course—in terms of both theme and *purpose*. Why is the reading assigned? How do different readings relate to one another? For example, many college courses require you to read chapters from a textbook as well as articles selected from a reader or anthology. Textbooks usually provide general overviews, laying out and defining important concepts. Articles often follow up by narrowing the focus, showing the concepts in action, critiquing them, or providing more in-depth discussion of some key concept or issue. When you understand the purpose of the reading you're doing, you will benefit more from it.

A useful way to approach reading assignments is to think of reading as a process, and try to enjoy it as you're doing it, rather than focusing entirely on the result and just powering through to the end. Try to think of reading as a circular movement through a text rather than a linear movement. In other words, when you start at the beginning of an article or chapter, rather than moving through it in a straight, uninterrupted path to the end of the reading, stop reading periodically to sum up in your mind, flag difficult passages with notes or question marks in the margin, and circle back to reread those passages after you've read further and gained more understanding. Use paraphrase (see pp. 36–42) to sum up difficult points in your own words and record them in the margins or in reading notes.

As you read, pay attention to the stages of thought contained in a piece. Some readings are separated into sections with subheadings, which specifically identify the stages of thought. Other readings won't be sectioned off in this way, and you'll have to be alert to the shifts in focus that occur. If you're reading a difficult piece and find yourself confused, ask yourself not only what the author is *saying*, but also what he or she is *doing* in that portion of the reading. In other words, why is the author discussing this now? Is the writer providing examples, discussing opposing arguments, further elaborating an earlier point? By looking at what an author seems to be doing as well as saying, you'll have a better sense of how the parts of a reading make up the whole. Paying close attention to transitional words and phrases such as *on the other hand, for example, therefore,* and *conversely* will also help you locate the shifts in thought that occur in a piece of writing.

Read actively: Stop and think, question, and (if you own the book or if you're working with a photocopy) write notes of agreement, disagreement, confusion, or identification in the margin. Underline key points, but try not to go crazy with the highlighter as you read. Often the first time you read something, every point strikes you as a potentially key idea. You end up with pages that are almost entirely covered in fluorescent yellow or pink, and this can be distracting later on when you review your reading. (And of course, overmarking defeats the whole purpose of highlighting.) Underlining with a pencil, or making marks in the margin, can be more effective, for several reasons. First, when you underline with a pencil, you have to focus on the words more than you do when you quickly whisk a highlighter over them; therefore, you'll be further comprehending the ideas as you underline them. Second, your first impression of which points are important is likely to be a little off the mark. If you use a pencil, you can erase the underlining of less crucial passages after you've read the entire piece.

These tips are meant to help you get the most out of reading, whether or not your main purpose is to summarize. We've included more suggestions for critical reading and summary in the box on Critical Reading for Summary, on the next page. Now we turn to the next step: how you take what you've read and condense and rephrase it.

HOW TO WRITE SUMMARIES

Every article you read will present a unique challenge as you work to summarize it. As you'll discover, saying in a few words what has taken someone else a great many can be difficult. But like any other skill, the ability to summarize improves with practice. Here are a few pointers to get you started. They represent possible stages, or steps, in the process of writing a summary. These pointers are not meant to be ironclad rules; rather, they are designed to encourage habits of thinking that will allow you to vary your technique as the situation demands.

CRITICAL READING FOR SUMMARY

- **Examine the context.** Note the credentials, occupation, and publications of the author. Identify the source in which the piece originally appeared. This information helps illuminate the author's perspective on the topic he or she is addressing.
- **Note the title and subtitle.** Some titles are straightforward, whereas the meanings of others become clearer as you read. In either case, titles typically identify the topic being addressed, and often reveal the author's attitude toward that topic.
- **Identify the main point.** Whether a piece of writing contains a thesis statement in the first few paragraphs or builds its main point without stating it up front, look at the entire piece to arrive at an understanding of the overall point being made.
- **Identify the subordinate points.** Notice the smaller subpoints that make up the main point, and make sure you understand how they relate to the main point. If a particular subpoint doesn't clearly relate to the main point you've identified, you may need to modify your understanding of the main point.
- **Break the reading into sections.** Notice which paragraph(s) make up a piece's introduction, body, and conclusion. Break up the body paragraphs into sections that address the writer's various subpoints.
- **Distinguish between points, examples, counterarguments.** Critical reading requires careful attention to what a writer is *doing* as well as what he or she is *saying*. When a writer quotes someone else, or relays an example of something, ask yourself why this is being done. What point is the example supporting? Is another source being quoted as support for a point, or as a counterargument that the writer sets out to address?
- **Watch for transitions within and between paragraphs.** In order to follow the logic of a piece of writing, as well as to distinguish between points, examples, and counterarguments, pay attention to the transitional words and phrases writers use. Transitions function like road signs, preparing the reader for what's next.
- **Read actively and recursively.** Don't treat reading as a passive, linear progression through a text. Instead, read as though you are engaged in a dialogue with the writer: Ask questions of the text as you read, make notes in the margin, underline key ideas in pencil, put question or exclamation marks next to passages that confuse or excite you. Go back to earlier points once you finish a reading, stop during your reading to recap what's come so far, and move back and forth through a text.

GUIDELINES FOR WRITING SUMMARIES

- *Read the passage carefully.* Determine its structure. Identify the author's purpose in writing. (This will help you distinguish between more important and less important information.) Make a note in the margin when you get confused or when you think something is important; highlight or underline points sparingly, if at all.
- *Reread.* This time divide the passage into sections or stages of thought. The author's use of paragraphing will often be a useful guide. *Label,* on the passage itself, each section or stage of thought. *Underline* key ideas and terms. Write notes in the margin.
- *Write one-sentence summaries,* on a separate sheet of paper, of each stage of thought.
- *Write a thesis—a one- or two-sentence summary of the entire passage.* The thesis should express the central idea of the passage, as you have determined it from the preceding steps. You may find it useful to follow the approach of most newspaper stories—naming the *what, who, why, where, when,* and *how* of the matter. For persuasive passages, summarize in a sentence the author's conclusion. For descriptive passages, indicate the subject of the description and its key feature(s). *Note:* In some cases, *a suitable thesis may already be in the original passage.* If so, you may want to quote it directly in your summary.
- *Write the first draft of your summary* by (1) combining the thesis with your list of one-sentence summaries or (2) combining the thesis with one-sentence summaries *plus* significant details from the passage. In either case, eliminate repetition and less important information. Disregard minor details or generalize them (e.g., George H. W. Bush, and Bill Clinton might be generalized as "recent presidents"). Use as few words as possible to convey the main ideas.
- *Check your summary against the original passage* and make whatever adjustments are necessary for accuracy and completeness.
- *Revise your summary,* inserting transitional words and phrases where necessary to ensure coherence. Check for style. *Avoid a series of short, choppy sentences.* Combine sentences for a smooth, logical flow of ideas. Check for grammatical correctness, punctuation, and spelling.

DEMONSTRATION: SUMMARY

To demonstrate these points at work, let's go through the process of summarizing a passage of expository material—that is, writing that is meant to inform and/or persuade. Read the following selection carefully. Try to identify its parts and understand how they work together to create an overall point.

The Future of Love: Kiss Romance Goodbye, It's Time for the Real Thing
*Barbara Graham**

Author of the satire Women Who Run With Poodles: Myths and Tips for Honoring Your Mood Swings *(Avon, 1994), Barbara Graham has written articles for* Vogue, Self, Common Boundary, *and other publications. She regularly contributes articles to the* Utne Reader, *from which this essay was taken.*

1   Freud and his psychoanalytic descendants are no doubt correct in their assessment that the search for ideal love—for that one perfect soulmate—is the futile wish of not fully developed selves. But it also seems true that the longing for a profound, all-consuming erotic connection (and the heightened state of awareness that goes with it) is in our very wiring. The yearning for fulfillment through love seems to be to our psychic structure what food and water are to our cells.

2   Just consider the stories and myths that have shaped our consciousness: Beauty and the Beast, Snow White and her handsome prince, Cinderella and Prince Charming, Fred and Ginger, Barbie and Ken. (Note that, with the exception of the last two couples, all of these lovers are said to have lived happily ever after—even though we never get details of their lives after the weddings, after children and gravity and loss have exacted their price.) Still, it's not just these lucky fairy tale characters who have captured our collective imagination. The tragic twosomes we cut our teeth on—Romeo and Juliet, Tristan and Iseult, Launcelot and Guinevere, Heathcliff and Cathy, Rhett and Scarlett—are even more compelling role models. Their love is simply too powerful and anarchic, too shattering and exquisite, to be bound by anything so conventional as marriage or a long-term domestic arrangement.

3   If recent divorce and remarriage statistics are any indication, we're not as astute as the doomed lovers. Instead of drinking poison and putting an end to our love affairs while the heat is still turned up full blast, we expect our mar-

---

*Barbara Graham, "The Future of Love: Kiss Romance Goodbye, It's Time for the Real Thing," *Utne Reader* Jan.–Feb. 1997: 20–23.

riages and relationships to be long-running fairy tales. When they're not, instead of examining our expectations, we switch partners and reinvent the fantasy, hoping that this time we'll get it right. It's easy to see why: Despite all the talk of family values, we're constantly bombarded by visions of perfect romance. All you have to do is turn on the radio or TV or open any magazine and check out the perfume and lingerie ads. "Our culture is deeply regressed," says Florence Falk, a New York City psychotherapist. "Everywhere we turn, we're faced with glamorized, idealized versions of love. It's as if the culture wants us to stay trapped in the fantasy and does everything possible to encourage and expand that fantasy." Trying to forge an authentic relationship amidst all the romantic hype, she adds, makes what is already a tough proposition even harder.

4   What's most unusual about our culture is our feverish devotion to the belief that romantic love and marriage should be synonymous. Starting with George and Martha, continuing through Ozzie and Harriet right up to the present day, we have tirelessly tried to formalize, rationalize, legalize, legitimize, politicize and sanitize rapture. This may have something to do with our puritanical roots, as well as our tendency toward oversimplification. In any event, this attempt to satisfy all of our contradictory desires under the marital umbrella must be put in historical context in order to be properly understood.

5   "Personal intimacy is actually quite a new idea in human history and was never part of the marriage ideal before the 20th century," says John Welwood, a Northern California–based psychologist and author, most recently, of *Love and Awakening.* "Most couples throughout history managed to live together their whole lives without ever having a conversation about what was going on within or between them. As long as family and society prescribed the rules of marriage, individuals never had to develop any consciousness in this area."

6   In short, marriage was designed to serve the economic and social needs of families, communities, and religious institutions, and had little or nothing to do with love. Nor was it expected to satisfy lust.

7   In *Myths To Live By,* Joseph Campbell explains how the sages of ancient India viewed the relationship between marriage and passion. They concluded that there are five degrees of love, he writes, "through which a worshiper is increased in the service and knowledge of his God." The first degree has to do with the relationship of the worshiper to the divine. The next three degrees of love, in order of importance, are friendship, the parent/child relationship, and marriage. The fifth and highest form is passionate, illicit love. "In marriage, it is declared, one is still possessed of reason," Campbell adds. "The seizure of passionate love can be, in such a context, only illicit, breaking in upon the order of one's dutiful life in virtue as a devastating storm."

8   No wonder we're having problems. The pressures we place on our tender unions are unprecedented. Even our biochemistry seems to militate against long-term sexual relationships. Dr. Helen Fisher, an anthropologist at Rutgers University and author of *Anatomy of Love,* believes that human pair-bonds originally evolved according to "the ancient blueprint of serial monogamy and clandestine adultery" and are originally meant to last around four years—at

least long enough to raise a single dependent child through toddlerhood. The so-called seven-year-itch may be the remains of a four-year reproductive cycle, Fisher suggests.

9   Increasingly, Fisher and other researchers are coming to view what we call love as a series of complex biochemical events governed by hormones and enzymes. "People cling to the idea that romantic love is a mystery, but it's also a chemical experience," Fisher says, explaining that there are three distinct mating emotions and each is supported in the brain by the release of different chemicals. Lust, an emotion triggered by changing levels of testosterone in men and women, is associated with our basic sexual drive. Infatuation depends on the changing levels of dopamine, norepinephrine, and phenylethylamine (PEA), also called the "chemicals of love." They are natural—addictive—amphetamine-like chemicals that stimulate euphoria and make us want to stay up all night sharing our secrets. After infatuation and the dizzying highs associated with it have peaked—usually within a year or two—this brain chemistry reduces, and a new chemical system made up of oxytocin, vasopressin, and maybe the endorphins kicks in and supports a steadier, quieter, more nurturing intimacy. In the end, regardless of whether biochemistry accounts for cause or effect in love, it may help to explain why some people—those most responsive to the release of the attachment chemicals—are able to sustain a long-term partnership, while thrillseekers who feel depressed without regular hits of dopamine and PEA are likely to jump from one liaison to the next in order to maintain a buzz.

10   But even if our biochemistry suggests that there should be term limits on love, the heart is a stubborn muscle and, for better or worse, most of us continue to yearn for a relationship that will endure. As a group, Generation Xers—many of whom are children of divorce—are more determined than any other demographic group to have a different kind of marriage than their parents and to avoid divorce, says Howard Markman, author of *Fighting for Your Marriage*. What's more, lesbians and gay men who once opposed marriage and all of its heterosexual, patriarchal implications, now seek to reframe marriage as a more flexible, less repressive arrangement. And, according to the U.S. National Center for Health Statistics, in one out of an estimated seven weddings, either the bride or the groom—or both—are tying the knot for at least the third time—nearly twice as many as in 1970. There are many reasons for this, from the surge in the divorce rate that began in the '70s, to our ever-increasing life span. Even so, the fact that we're still trying to get love right—knowing all we know about the ephemeral nature of passion, in a time when the stigmas once associated with being divorced or single have all but disappeared—says something about our powerful need to connect.

11   And, judging from the army of psychologists, therapists, clergy, and other experts who can be found dispensing guidance on the subject, the effort to save—or reinvent, depending on who's doing the talking—love and marriage has become a multimillion dollar industry. The advice spans the spectrum. There's everything from *Rules*, by Ellen Fein and Sherrie Schneider, a popular new book which gives 90's women 50's-style tips on how to catch and keep their man, to Harville Hendrix's *Getting the Love You Want*, and other guides to "conscious love." But regardless of perspective, this much is clear: Never before have our

most intimate thoughts and actions been so thoroughly dissected, analyzed, scrutinized and medicalized. Now, people who fall madly in love over and over are called romance addicts. Their disease, modeled on alcoholism and other chemical dependencies, is considered "progressive and fatal."

12   Not everyone believes the attempt to deconstruct love is a good thing. The late philosopher Christopher Lasch wrote in his final (and newly released) book, *Women and the Common Life:* "The exposure of sexual life to scientific scrutiny contributed to the rationalization, not the liberation, of emotional life." His daughter, Elisabeth Lasch-Quinn, an historian at Syracuse University and the editor of the book, agrees. She contends that the progressive demystification of passionate life since Freud has promoted an asexual, dispassionate and utilitarian form of love. Moreover, like her father, she believes that the national malaise about romance can be attributed to insidious therapeutic modes of social control—a series of mechanisms that have reduced the citizen to a consumer of expertise. "We have fragmented life in such a way," she says, "as to take passion out of our experience."

13   Admittedly, it's a stretch to picture a lovesick 12th century French troubadour in a 12-step program for romance addicts. Still, we can't overlook the fact that our society's past efforts to fuse together those historically odd bedfellows—passionate love and marriage—have failed miserably. And though it's impossible to know whether all the attention currently being showered on relationships is the last gasp of a dying social order—marriage—or the first glimmer of a new paradigm for relating to one another, it's obvious that something radically different is needed.

Read, Reread, Underline

Let's consider our recommended pointers for writing a summary.

As you reread the passage, note in the margins of the essay important points, shifts in thought, and questions you may have. Consider the essay's significance as a whole and its stages of thought. What does it say? How is it organized? How does each part of the passage fit into the whole? What do all these points add up to?

Here is how the first few paragraphs of Graham's article might look after you had marked the main ideas, by highlighting and by marginal notations.

psychic impor-tance of love   Freud and his psychoanalytic descendants are no doubt correct in their assessment that the search for ideal love—for that one perfect soulmate—is the futile wish of not fully developed selves. But it also seems true that the longing for a profound, all-consuming erotic connection (and the heightened state of awareness that goes with it) is in our very wiring. The yearning for fulfillment through love seems to be to our psychic structure what food and water are to our cells.

Just consider the stories and myths that have shaped our consciousness: Beauty and the Beast, Snow White and her handsome prince, Cinderella and Prince Charming, Fred and Ginger, Barbie and Ken. (Note that,

fictional, sometimes tragic examples of ideal love

with the exception of the last two couples, all of these lovers are said to have lived happily ever after—even though we never get details of their lives after the weddings, after children and gravity and loss have exacted their price.) Still, it's not just these lucky fairy tale characters who have captured our collective imagination. The tragic twosomes we cut our teeth on—Romeo and Juliet, Tristan and Iseult, Launcelot and Guinevere, Heathcliff and Cathy, Rhett and Scarlett—are even more compelling role models. Their love is simply too powerful and anarchic, too shattering and exquisite, to be bound by anything so conventional as marriage or a long-term domestic arrangement.

If recent divorce and remarriage statistics are any indication, we're not as astute as the doomed lovers. Instead of drinking poison and putting an end to our love affairs while the heat is still turned up full blast, we expect our marriages and relationships to be long-running fairy tales. When they're not, instead of examining our expectations, we switch partners and reinvent the fantasy, hoping that this time we'll get it right. It's easy to see why: Despite all the talk of family values, we're constantly bombarded by visions of perfect romance. All you have to do is turn on the radio or TV or open any magazine and check out the perfume and lingerie ads. "Our culture is deeply regressed," says Florence Falk, a New York City

difficulty of having a real relationship in a culture that glamorizes ideal love

psychotherapist. "Everywhere we turn, we're faced with glamorized, idealized versions of love. It's as if the culture wants us to stay trapped in the fantasy and does everything possible to encourage and expand that fantasy." Trying to forge an authentic relationship amidst all the romantic hype, she adds, makes what is already a tough proposition even harder.

What's most unusual about our culture is our feverish devotion to the belief that romantic love and marriage should be synonymous. Starting with George and Martha, continuing through Ozzie and Harriet right up to the present day, we have tirelessly tried to formalize, rationalize, legalize, legitimize, politicize and sanitize rapture. This may have something to do with our puritanical roots, as well as our tendency toward oversimplification. In any event, this attempt to satisfy all of our contradictory desires under the marital umbrella must be put in historical context in order to be properly understood.

contradictions of ideal love and marriage

"Personal intimacy is actually quite a new idea in human history and was never part of the marriage ideal before the 20th century," says John Welwood, a Northern California–based psychologist and author, most recently, of *Love and Awakening.* "Most couples throughout history managed to live together their whole lives without ever having a conversation about what was going on within or between them. As long as family and society prescribed the rules of marriage, individuals never had to develop any consciousness in this area."

"personal intimacy" never considered part of marriage before 20th century

In short, marriage was designed to serve the economic and social needs of families, communities, and religious institutions, and had little or nothing to do with love. Nor was it expected to satisfy lust.

Divide into Stages of Thought

When a selection doesn't contain sections with thematic headings, as is the case with "The Future of Love," how do you determine where one stage of thought ends and the next one begins? Assuming that what you have read is coherent and unified, this should not be difficult. (When a selection is unified, all of its parts pertain to the main subject; when a selection is coherent, the parts follow one another in logical order.) Look, particularly, for transitional sentences at the beginning of paragraphs. Such sentences generally work in one or both of the following ways: (1) they summarize what has come before; (2) they set the stage for what is to follow.

For example, look at the sentence that opens paragraph 10: "But even if our biochemistry suggests that there should be term limits on love, the heart is a stubborn muscle, and for better or worse, most of us continue to yearn for a relationship that will endure." Notice how the first part of this sentence restates the main idea of the preceding section. The second part of the transitional sentence announces the topic of the upcoming section: three paragraphs devoted to the efforts people make to attain, save, or reinvent romantic relationships.

Each section of an article generally takes several paragraphs to develop. Between paragraphs, and almost certainly between sections of an article, you will usually find transitions that help you understand what you have just read and what you are about to read. For articles that have no subheadings, try writing your own section headings in the margins as you take notes. Then proceed with your summary.

The sections of Graham's article may be described as follows:

> **Section 1:** *Introduction*--a yearning for "fulfillment through love" pervades our culture, and that yearning is shaped by myths and romantic fantasies. (paragraphs 1-3).
>
> **Section 2:** *Marriage and love*--we expect passionate love to lead to happy, lifelong marriage. This is a relatively new and unique practice in human history (paragraphs 4-7).
>
> **Section 3:** *Biochemistry and love*--love has a biochemical component, which complicates our abilities to sustain long-term relationships (paragraphs 8-9).
>
> **Section 4:** *Marriage and love revisited*--many people are currently trying to preserve and/or reinvent marriage and love (paragraphs 10-12).

Section 5: *Conclusion*--the fusion of passionate love with the institution of marriage hasn't worked very well, and we need something "radically different" to replace it (paragraph 13).

Write a One- or Two-Sentence Summary of Each Stage of Thought

The purpose of this step is to wean you from the language of the original passage, so that you are not tied to it when writing the summary. Here are one-sentence summaries for each stage of thought in "The Future of Love" article's five sections:

Section 1: Introduction—a yearning for "fulfillment through love" pervades our culture, and that yearning is shaped by myths and romantic fantasies. (paragraphs 1–3).

Most members of American culture crave romantic love, but we have unreal expectations based upon idealized images of love we learn from fantasies and fairy tales.

Section 2: Marriage and love—we expect passionate love to lead to happy, lifelong marriage. This is a relatively new and unique practice in human history (paragraphs 4–7).

We expect the passionate love of fairy tales to lead to "happily ever after" in the institution of marriage, and when this fails, we move on and try it again. Ironically, the idea that marriage should be based on love--rather than upon social and economic concerns--is a relatively recent practice in Western history.

Section 3: Biochemistry and love—love has a biochemical component, which complicates our abilities to sustain long-term relationships (paragraphs 8–9).

Biochemists are discovering that love and lust have hormonal causes, and their evidence suggests that our biological makeup predisposes us to seek the excitement of short-term relationships.

Section 4: Marriage and love revisited—many people are currently trying to preserve and/or reinvent marriage and love (paragraphs 10–12).

```
Despite all the difficulties, we spend a lot of
time analyzing the elements of relationships in
order to preserve or perhaps reinvent marriage.
We clearly want to make it work.
```

Section 5: Conclusion—the fusion of passionate love with the institution of marriage hasn't worked very well, and we need something "radically different" to replace it (paragraph 13).

```
Because confining passionate love to the
institution of marriage hasn't worked very well, we
need to revise our model for human relationships.
```

Write a Thesis: A One- or Two-Sentence Summary of the Entire Passage

The thesis is the most general statement of a summary (or any other type of academic writing—see Chapter 3 for a more complete discussion of thesis statements). It is the statement that announces the paper's subject and the claim that you or—in the case of a summary—another author will be making about that subject. Every paragraph of a paper illuminates the thesis by providing supporting detail or explanation. The relationship of these paragraphs to the thesis is analogous to the relationship of the sentences within a paragraph to the topic sentence. Both the thesis and the topic sentences are general statements (the thesis being the more general) that are followed by systematically arranged details.

To ensure clarity for the reader, *the first sentence of your summary should begin with the author's thesis, regardless of where it appears in the article itself.* Authors may locate their thesis at the beginning of their work, in which case the thesis operates as a general principle from which details of the presentation follow. This is called a *deductive* organization: thesis first, supporting details second. Alternately, an author may locate his or her thesis at the end of the work, in which case the author begins with specific details and builds toward a more general conclusion, or thesis. This is called an *inductive* organization—an example of which you see in "The Future of Love."

A thesis consists of a subject and an assertion about that subject. How can we go about fashioning an adequate thesis for a summary of "The Future of Love"? Probably no two proposed thesis statements for this article would be worded identically, but it is fair to say that any reasonable thesis will indicate that the subject is the current state of love and marriage in American society. How does Graham view the topic? What *is* the current state of love and marriage, in her view? Looking back over our section summaries, Graham's focus on the illusions of fairy tales and myths, the difference between marriage in the present day and its earlier incarnations, and the problems of divorce and "romance addiction" suggest she does not view the current state of affairs in an altogether positive light. Does she make a statement anywhere that pulls all this together? Her conclusion, in paragraph 13, contains her main idea: "our society's past efforts to fuse together those historically odd bedfellows—passionate love and marriage—have failed miserably." Moreover, in the next sentence, she says "it's obvious that something radically different is needed." Further evidence of Graham's main point can be found in the complete title of the essay: "The Future of Love: Kiss Romance Goodbye, It's Time for the Real Thing." Mindful of Graham's subject and the assertion she makes about it, we can write a thesis statement *in our own words* and arrive at the following:

> The contemporary institution of marriage is in trouble, and this may be due to our unrealistic expectations that passionate love leads to lasting union; it may be time to develop a new model for love and relationships.

To clarify for our readers the fact that this idea is Graham's and not ours, we'll qualify the thesis as follows:

> In her article "The Future of Love: Kiss Romance Goodbye--It's Time for the Real Thing," Barbara Graham describes how our unrealistic expectations that passionate love leads to lasting union may be partly causing the troubled state of marriage today; thus she suggests we develop a new model for love and relationships.

The first sentence of a summary is crucially important, for it orients readers by letting them know what to expect in the coming paragraphs. In the example above, the sentence refers directly to an article, its author, and the thesis for the upcoming summary. The author and title reference also could be indicated in the summary's title (if this were a freestanding summary), in which case their mention could be dropped from the thesis. And lest you become frustrated too quickly, keep in mind that writing an acceptable thesis for a summary takes time—in this case, it took three drafts, or roughly seven minutes to compose one sentence and another few minutes of fine-tuning after a draft of the entire summary was completed. The thesis needed revision because the first draft was too vague and incomplete; the second draft was more specific and complete, but left out the author's point about correcting the problem; the third draft was more complete, but was cumbersome.

> **Draft 1:** Barbara Graham argues that our attempts to confine passionate love to the institution of marriage have failed.
> *(too vague—the problem isn't clear enough)*

Draft 2: Barbara Graham ~~argues that our attempts to confine passionate love to the institution of marriage have failed.~~ describes how the contemporary institution of marriage is in trouble, and this may be due, she thinks, to our unrealistic expectations that passionate love will lead to lasting union.
(Incomplete—what about her call for a change?)

Draft 3: In her article "The Future of Love: Kiss Romance Goodbye, It's Time for the Real Thing," Barbara Graham describes how ~~the contemporary institution of marriage is in trouble, and this may be due, she thinks, to~~ our unrealistic expectations that passionate love will lead to lasting union may be causing the troubles in the contemporary institution of marriage today, so she argues that perhaps it's time to develop a new model for love and relationships.
(Wordy)

Final: In her article "The Future of Love: Kiss Romance Goodbye, It's Time for the Real Thing," Barbara Graham describes how our unrealistic expectations that passionate love leads to lasting union may be partly causing the troubled state of ~~in the contemporary institution of~~ marriage today; thus she suggests we develop a new model for love and relationships.
(Add 'partly.' Cut out wordiness. Replace 'so' with 'thus')

Write the First Draft of the Summary

Let's consider two possible summaries of the example passage: (1) a short summary, combining a thesis with one-sentence section summaries, and (2) a longer summary, combining thesis, one-sentence section summaries, and some carefully chosen details. Again, realize that you are reading final versions; each of the following summaries is the result of at least two full drafts.

SUMMARY 1: COMBINE THESIS SENTENCE WITH ONE-SENTENCE SECTION SUMMARIES

In her article "The Future of Love: Kiss Romance Goodbye, It's Time for the Real Thing," Barbara Graham describes how our unrealistic expectations that passionate love leads to lasting union may

be partly causing the troubled state of marriage
today; thus she suggests we develop a new model
for love and relationships. The existing model,
and our craving for romantic love, is based
heavily upon idealized images of love we learn
from fantasies and fairy tales.

  We expect the passionate love of fairy
tales to lead to "happily ever after" in the
institution of marriage, and when this fails, we
move on and try it again. Ironically, the idea
that marriage should be based on love--rather
than upon social and economic concerns--is a
relatively recent practice in Western history.
While the romantic marriage ideal doesn't fit
with tradition, biological evidence is mounting
against it as well. Biochemists are discovering
that love and lust have hormonal causes, and
their evidence suggests that our biological
makeup predisposes us to seek the excitement of
short-term relationships.

  Nonetheless, despite all the difficulties, we
spend a lot of time analyzing the elements of
relationships in order to preserve or perhaps
reinvent marriage. We clearly want to make it
work. Because confining passionate love to the
institution of marriage hasn't worked very well,
Graham ends by suggesting that we ought to revise
our model for human relationships.

Discussion   This summary consists essentially of a restatement of Graham's thesis plus the section summaries, altered or expanded a little for stylistic purposes. The first sentence encompasses the summary of Section 1 and is followed by the summaries of Sections 2, 3, 4, and 5. Notice the insertion of a transitional sentence (highlighted) between the summaries of Sections 2 and 3, helping to link the ideas more coherently.

SUMMARY 2: COMBINE THESIS SENTENCE, SECTION SUMMARIES, AND CAREFULLY CHOSEN DETAILS

The thesis and one-sentence section summaries also can be used as the outline for a more detailed summary. Most of the details in the passage, however, won't be necessary in a summary. It isn't necessary even in a longer summary of this passage to discuss all of Graham's examples—specific romantic fairy tales, ancient Indian views of love and passion, the specific hormones involved with love and lust, or the examples of experts who examine and write about contemporary relationships. It would be appropriate, though, to mention one example of fairy tale romance, to refer to the historical information on marriage as an economic institution, and to explain some of the biological findings about love's chemical basis.

None of these details appeared in the first summary, but in a longer summary, a few carefully selected details might be desirable for clarity. How do you decide which details to include? First, since the idea that love and marriage are not necessarily compatible is the main point of the essay, it makes sense to cite some of the most persuasive evidence supporting this idea. For example, you could mention that for most of Western history, marriage was meant "to serve the economic and social needs of families, communities, and religious institutions," not the emotional and sexual needs of individuals. Further, you might explain the biochemists' argument that serial monogamy based on mutual interests, and clandestine adultery—not lifelong, love-based marriage—are the forms of relationships best serving human evolution.

You won't always know which details to include and which to exclude. Developing good judgment in comprehending and summarizing texts is largely a matter of reading skill and prior knowledge (see pages 1–2). Consider the analogy of the seasoned mechanic who can pinpoint an engine problem by simply listening to a characteristic sound that to a less experienced person is just noise. Or consider the chess player who can plot three separate winning strategies from a board position that to a novice looks like a hopeless jumble. In the same way, the more practiced a reader you are, the more knowledgeable you become about the subject, and the better able you will be to make critical distinctions between elements of greater and lesser importance. In the meantime, read as carefully as you can and use your own best judgment as to how to present your material.

Here's one version of a completed summary, with carefully chosen details. Note that we have highlighted phrases and sentences added to the original, briefer summary.

(Thesis)   In her article "The Future of Love: Kiss Romance Goodbye, It's Time for the Real Thing," Barbara Graham describes how our unrealistic expectations that passionate love leads to lasting union may be partly causing the troubled state of marriage today; thus she suggests we develop a new model for love and relationships.

     Most members of American culture crave romantic love, but we have unreal expectations based upon idealized images of love we learn from fantasies and fairy tales such as Beauty and the Beast and Cinderella. Tragedies such as Romeo and Juliet teach us about the all-consuming nature of "true love," and these stories are tragic precisely because the lovers never get to fulfill

(Section 1, what we've been taught is the ideal: living

¶s 1-3) happily ever after, in wedded bliss. The idea

that romantic love should be confined to marriage is perhaps the biggest fantasy to which we subscribe. When we are unable to make this fantasy real--and it seems that this is often the case--we end that marriage and move on to the next one. The twentieth century is actually the first century in Western history in which so much was asked of marriage. In earlier eras, marriage was designed to meet social and economic

(Section 2, purposes, rather than fulfill individual
¶s 4-7) emotional and sexual desires.

Casting further doubt on the effectiveness of the current model of marriage, biochemists are discovering how hormones and enzymes influence feelings of love and lust. It turns out that the "chemistry" a person newly in love often feels for another has a basis in fact, as those early feelings of excitement and contentment are biochemical in nature. When people jump from one relationship to the next, they may be seeking that chemical "rush." Further, these biochemical discoveries fit with principles of evolutionary

(Section 3, survival, because short-term relationships--and
¶s 8-9) even adulterous affairs--help to more quickly propagate the species.

Nonetheless, despite such historical and biological imperatives, we don't seem interested in abandoning the pursuit of love and marriage. In order to preserve or perhaps reinvent marriage, we spend a lot of time scrutinizing and dissecting the dynamics of relationships.

(Section 4, Self-help books on the subject of love and
¶s 10-12) relationships fill bookstore shelves and top best-seller lists.

While some argue that such scrutiny ruins rather than reinvigorates love, perhaps our efforts to understand relationships can help us

(Section 5, to invent some kind of revised model for human
¶ 13) relationships--since trying to confine passionate love to the institution of marriage clearly hasn't worked very well.

Discussion   The final two of our suggested steps for writing summaries are (1) to check your summary against the original passage, making sure that you have included all the important ideas, and (2) to revise so that the summary reads smoothly and coherently.

The structure of this summary generally reflects the structure of the original—with one notable departure. As we noted earlier, Graham uses an inductive approach, stating her thesis at the end of the essay. The summary, however, states the thesis right away, then proceeds deductively to develop that thesis.

Compared to the first, briefer summary, this effort mentions fairy tales and tragedy; develops the point about traditional versus contemporary versions of marriage; explains the biochemical/evolutionary point; and refers specifically to self-help books and their role in the issue.

How long should a summary be? This depends on the length of the original passage. A good rule of thumb is that a summary should be no longer than one-fourth of the original passage. Of course, if you were summarizing an entire chapter or even an entire book, it would have to be much shorter than that. The summary above is about one-fourth the length of the original passage. Although it shouldn't be very much longer, you have seen (pp. 17–18) that it could be quite a bit shorter.

The length as well as the content of the summary also depends on its *purpose.* Let's suppose you decided to use Graham's piece in a paper that dealt with the biochemical processes of love and lust. In this case, you might summarize *only* Graham's discussion of Fisher's findings, and perhaps the point Graham makes about how biochemical discoveries complicate marriage. If, instead, you were writing a paper in which you argued against attempts to redefine marriage, you would likely give less attention to the material on biochemistry. To help support your view, you might summarize Graham's points in paragraph 10 about the persistent desire for lasting union found among members of Generation X and evidenced in the high numbers of marriages and remarriages. Thus, depending on your purpose, you would summarize either selected portions of a source or an entire source, as we will see more fully in the chapters on syntheses.

EXERCISE **1.1**

Individual and Collaborative Summary Practice

Turn to Chapter 2 and read Brent Staples's essay "Driving Down the Highway, Mourning the Death of American Radio" (pp. 85–86). Follow the steps for writing summaries outlined above—read, underline, and divide into stages of thought. Write down a one- or two-sentence summary of each stage of thought in Staples's essay. Then, gather in groups of three or four classmates, and compare your summary sentences. Discuss the differences in your sentences, and come to some consensus about the divisions in Staples's stages of thought—and the ways in which to best sum these up.

As a group, write a one- or two-sentence thesis statement summing up the entire passage. You could go even further, and, using your individual summary sentences—or the versions of these your group revised—put together a brief summary of Staples's essay, modeled upon the brief summary of Graham's essay, on pages 17–18.

SUMMARIZING A NARRATIVE OR PERSONAL ESSAY

Narratives and personal essays differ from expository essays in that they focus on personal experiences and/or views, they aren't structured around an explicitly stated thesis, and their ideas are developed more through the description of events or ideas than through factual evidence or logical explanation. A *narrative* is a story, a retelling of a person's experiences. That person and those experiences may be imaginary, as is the case with fiction, or they may be real, as in biography. In first-person narratives, you can't assume that the narrator represents the author of the piece, unless you know the narrative is a memoir or biography. In a *personal essay*, on the other hand, the narrator is the author. And while the writer of a personal essay may tell stories about his or her experiences, usually writers of such essays discuss thoughts and ideas as much as or more than telling stories. Personal essays also tend to contain more obvious points than do narratives. Summarizing personal essays or narratives presents certain challenges—challenges that are different from those presented by summarizing expository writing.

You have seen that an author of an expository piece (such as Graham's "The Future of Love") follows assertions with examples and statements of support. Narratives, however, usually are less direct. The author relates a story—event follows event—the point of which may never be stated directly. The charm, the force, and the very point of the narrative lie in the telling; generally, narratives do not exhibit the same logical development of expository writing. They do not, therefore, lend themselves to summary in quite the same way. Narratives do have a logic, but that logic may be emotional, imaginative, or plot-bound. The writer who summarizes a narrative is obliged to give an overview—a synopsis—of the story's events and an account of how these events affect the central character(s). The summary must explain the significance or *meaning* of the events.

Similarly, while personal essays sometimes present points more explicitly than do narratives, their focus and structure link them to narratives. Personal essays often contain inexplicit main points, or multiple points; they tend to *explore* ideas and issues, rather than make explicit *assertions* about those ideas. This exploratory character often means that personal essays exhibit a loose structure, and they often contain stories or narratives within them. While summarizing a personal essay may not involve a synopsis of events, an account of the progression of thoughts and ideas is necessary and, as with a narrative, summaries of personal essays must explain the significance of what goes on in the piece being summarized.

In the following excerpt, Jeanne Wakatsuki and James D. Houston offer a powerful account of Wakatsuki's personal experience of being relocated to the Manzanar internment camp. You might need to provide a summary of this account for a paper dealing with some aspect of the Japanese–American experience during this historical period.

Arrival at Manzanar
Jeanne Wakatsuki and James D. Houston

The following passage is excerpted from Farewell to Manzanar *(1973), Jeanne Wakatsuki's account of her family's experience at Manzanar, an internment camp where Americans of Japanese ancestry living on the West Coast were forcibly relocated after the attack on Pearl Harbor in December 1941. Shortly before the family's relocation, Wakatsuki's father had been arrested because, as an alien as well as a commercial fisherman, he was falsely suspected of having made contact with enemy ships off the California coast. Born in 1935, Wakatsuki lived at Manzanar from age 7 to age 11.* Farewell to Manzanar *was written with her husband, James D. Houston, a novelist, whom she met while studying sociology and journalism at San Jose State University.*

1   In December of 1941 Papa's disappearance didn't bother me nearly so much as the world I soon found myself in.

2   He had been a jack-of-all-trades. When I was born he was farming near Inglewood. Later, when he started fishing, we moved to Ocean Park, near Santa Monica, and until they picked him up, that's where we lived, in a big frame house with a brick fireplace, a block back from the beach. We were the only Japanese family in the neighborhood. Papa liked it that way. He didn't want to be labeled or grouped by anyone. But with him gone and no way of knowing what to expect, my mother moved all of us down to Terminal Island. Woody already lived there, and one of my older sisters had married a Terminal Island boy. Mama's first concern now was to keep the family together; and once the war began, she felt safer there than isolated racially in Ocean Park. But for me, at age seven, the island was a country as foreign as India or Arabia would have been. It was the first time I had lived among other Japanese, or gone to school with them, and I was terrified all the time.

3   This was partly Papa's fault. One of his threats to keep us younger kids in line was "I'm going to sell you to the Chinaman." When I had entered kindergarten two years earlier, I was the only Oriental in the class. They sat me next to a Caucasian girl who happened to have very slanted eyes. I looked at her and began to scream, certain Papa had sold me out at last. My fear of her ran so deep I could not speak of it, even to Mama, couldn't explain why I was screaming. For two weeks I had nightmares about this girl, until the teachers finally moved me to the other side of the room. And it was still with me, this fear of Oriental faces, when we moved to Terminal Island.

4   In those days it was a company town, a ghetto owned and controlled by the canneries. The men went after fish; and whenever the boats came back—day or night—the women would be called to process the catch while it was fresh. One in the afternoon or four in the morning, it made no difference. My mother had to go to work right after we moved there. I can still hear the whistle—two toots

for French's, three for Van Camp's—and she and Chizu would be out of bed in the middle of the night, heading for the cannery.

5   The house we lived in was nothing more than a shack, a barracks with single plank walls and rough wooden floors, like the cheapest kind of migrant workers' housing. The people around us were hardworking, boisterous, a little proud of their nickname, *yo-go-re*, which meant literally uncouth one, or roughneck, or dead-end kid. They not only spoke Japanese exclusively, they spoke a dialect peculiar to Kyushu, where their families had come from in Japan, a rough, fisherman's language, full of oaths and insults. Instead of saying *baha-ta-re*, a common insult meaning stupid, Terminal Islanders would say *ba-ka-ya-ro*, a coarser and exclusively masculine use of the word, which implies gross stupidity. They would swagger and pick on outsiders and persecute anyone who didn't speak as they did. That was what made my own time there so hateful. I had never spoken anything but English, and the other kids in the second grade despised me for it. They were tough and mean, like ghetto kids anywhere. Each day after school I dreaded their ambush. My brother Kiyo, three years older, would wait for me at the door, where we would decide whether to run straight home together, or split up, or try a new and unexpected route.

6   None of these kids ever actually attacked. It was the threat that frightened us, their fearful looks, and the noises they would make, like miniature Samurai, in a language we couldn't understand.

7   At the time it seemed we had been living under this reign of fear for years. In fact, we lived there about two months. Late in February the navy decided to clear Terminal Island completely. Even though most of us were American-born, it was dangerous having that many Orientals so close to the Long Beach Naval Station, on the opposite end of the island. We had known something like this was coming. But, like Papa's arrest, not much could be done ahead of time. There were four of us kids still young enough to be living with Mama, plus Granny, her mother, sixty-five then, speaking no English, and nearly blind. Mama didn't know where else she could get work, and we had nowhere else to move to. On February 25 the choice was made for us. We were given forty-eight hours to clear out.

8   The secondhand dealers had been prowling around for weeks, like wolves, offering humiliating prices for goods and furniture they knew many of us would have to sell sooner or later. Mama had left all but her most valuable possessions in Ocean Park, simply because she had nowhere to put them: She had brought along her pottery, her silver, heirlooms like the kimonos Granny had brought from Japan, tea sets, lacquered tables, and one fine old set of china, blue and white porcelain, almost translucent. On the day we were leaving, Woody's car was so crammed with boxes and luggage and kids we had just run out of room. Mama had to sell this china.

9   One of the dealers offered her fifteen dollars for it. She said it was a full setting for twelve and worth at least two hundred. He said fifteen was his top price. Mama started to quiver. Her eyes blazed up at him. She had been packing all night and trying to calm down Granny, who didn't understand why were moving again and what all the rush was about. Mama's nerves were shot, and now

navy jeeps were patrolling the streets. She didn't say another word. She just glared at this man, all the rage, and frustration channeled at him through her eyes.

10   He watched her for a moment and said he was sure he couldn't pay more than seventeen fifty for that china. She reached into the red velvet case, took out a dinner plate and hurled it at the floor right in front of his feet.

11   The man leaped back shouting, "Hey! Hey, don't do that! Those are valuable dishes!"

12   Mama took out another dinner plate and hurled it at the floor, then another and another, never moving, never opening her mouth, just quivering and glaring at the retreating dealer, with tears streaming down her cheeks. He finally turned and scuttled out the door, heading for the next house. When he was gone she stood there smashing cups and bowls and platters until the whole set lay in scattered blue and white fragments across the wooden floor.

13   The name Manzanar meant nothing to us when we left Boyle Heights. We didn't know where it was or what it was. We went because the government ordered us to. And, in the case of my older brothers and sisters, we went with a certain amount of relief. They had all heard stories of Japanese homes being attacked, of beatings in the streets of California towns. They were as frightened of the Caucasians as Caucasians were of us. Moving, under what appeared to be government protection, to an area less directly threatened by the war seemed not such a bad idea at all. For some it actually sounded like a fine adventure.

14   Our pickup point was a Buddhist church in Los Angeles. It was very early, and misty, when we got there with our luggage. Mama had bought heavy coats for all of us. She grew up in eastern Washington and knew that anywhere inland in early April would be cold. I was proud of my new coat, and I remember sitting on a duffel bag trying to be friendly with the Greyhound driver. I smiled at him. He didn't smile back. He was befriending no one. Someone tied a numbered tag to my collar and to the duffel bag (each family was given a number, and that became our official designation until the camps were closed), someone else passed out box lunches for the trip, and we climbed aboard.

15   I had never been outside Los Angeles County, never traveled more than ten miles from the coast, had never even ridden on a bus. I was full of excitement, the way any kid would be, and wanted to look out the window. But for the first few hours the shades were drawn. Around me other people played cards, read magazines, dozed, waiting. I settled back, waiting too, and finally fell asleep. The bus felt very secure to me. Almost half its passengers were immediate relatives. Mama and my older brothers had succeeded in keeping most of us together, on the same bus, headed for the same camp. I didn't realize until much later what a job that was. The strategy had been, first, to have everyone living in the same district when the evacuation began, and then to get all of us included under the same family number, even though names had been changed by marriage. Many families weren't as lucky as ours and suffered months of anguish while trying to arrange transfers from one camp to another.

16   We rode all day. By the time we reached our destination, the shades were up. It was late afternoon. The first thing I saw was a yellow swirl across a blurred, reddish setting sun. The bus was being pelted by what sounded like splattering rain. It wasn't rain. This was my first look at something I would soon know very well, a billowing flurry of dust and sand churned up by the wind through Owens Valley.

17   We drove past a barbed-wire fence, through a gate, and into an open space where trunks and sacks and packages had been dumped from the baggage trucks that drove out ahead of us. I could see a few tents set up, the first rows of black barracks, and beyond them, blurred by sand, rows of barracks that seemed to spread for miles across this plain. People were sitting on cartons or milling around, with their backs to the wind, waiting to see which friends or relatives might be on this bus. As we approached, they turned or stood up, and some moved toward us expectantly. But inside the bus no one stirred. No one waved or spoke. They just stared out the windows, ominously silent. I didn't understand this. Hadn't we finally arrived, our whole family intact? I opened a window, leaned out, and yelled happily. "Hey! This whole bus is full of Wakatsukis!"

18   Outside, the greeters smiled. Inside there was an explosion of laughter, hysterical, tension-breaking laughter that left my brothers choking and whacking each other across the shoulders.

19   We had pulled up just in time for dinner. The mess halls weren't completed yet. An outdoor chow line snaked around a half-finished building that broke a good part of the wind. They issued us army mess kits, the round metal kind that fold over, and plopped in scoops of canned Vienna sausage, canned string beans, steamed rice that had been cooked too long; and on top of the rice a serving of canned apricots. The Caucasian servers were thinking the fruit poured over rice would make a good dessert. Among the Japanese, of course, rice is never eaten with sweet foods; only with salty or savory foods. Few of us could eat such a mixture. But at this point no one dared protest. It would have been impolite. I was horrified when I saw the apricot syrup seeping through my little mound of rice. I opened my mouth to complain. My mother jabbed me in the back to keep quiet. We moved on through the line and joined the others squatting in the lee of half-raised walls, dabbing courteously at what was, for almost everyone there, an inedible concoction.

20   After dinner we were taken to Block 16, a cluster of fifteen barracks that had just been finished—a day or so earlier—although finished was hardly the word for it. The shacks were built of one thickness of pine planking covered with tarpaper. They sat on concrete footings, with about two feet of open space between the floorboards and the ground. Gaps showed between the planks, and as the weeks passed and the green wood dried out, the gaps widened. Knotholes gaped in the uncovered floor.

21   Each barracks was divided into six units, sixteen by twenty feet, about the size of a living room, with one bare bulb hanging from the ceiling and an oil stove for heat. We were assigned two of these for the twelve people in our family group; and our official family "number" was enlarged by three digits—16

plus the number of this barracks. We were issued steel army cots, two brown army blankets each, and some mattress covers, which my brothers stuffed with straw.

22   The first task was to divide up what space we had for sleeping. Bill and Woody contributed a blanket each and partitioned off the first room: one side for Bill and Torni, one side for Woody and Chizu and their baby girl. Woody also got the stove, for heating formulas.

23   The people who had it hardest during the first few months were young couples like these, many of whom had married just before the evacuation began, in order not to be separated and sent to different camps. Our two rooms were crowded, but at least it was all in the family. My oldest sister and her husband were shoved into one of those sixteen-by-twenty-foot compartments with six people they had never seen before—two other couples, one recently married like themselves, the other with two teenage boys. Partitioning off a room like that wasn't easy. It was bitter cold when we arrived, and the wind did not abate. All they had to use for room dividers were those army blankets, two of which were barely enough to keep one person warm. They argued over whose blanket should be sacrificed and later argued about noise at night—the parents wanted their boys asleep by 9:00 p.m.—and they continued arguing over matters like that for six months, until my sister and her husband left to harvest sugar beets in Idaho. It was grueling work up there, and wages were pitiful, but when the call came through camp for workers to alleviate the wartime labor shortage, it sounded better than their life at Manzanar. They knew they'd have, if nothing else, a room, perhaps a cabin of their own.

24   That first night in Block 16, the rest of us squeezed into the second room—Granny, Lillian, age fourteen, Ray, thirteen, May, eleven, Kiyo, ten, Mama, and me. I didn't mind this at all at the time. Being youngest meant I got to sleep with Mama. And before we went to bed I had a great time jumping up and down on the mattress. The boys had stuffed so much straw into hers, we had to flatten it some so we wouldn't slide off. I slept with her every night after that until Papa came back.

If you have read the book *Farewell to Manzanar,* you may have done so because you were interested in the subject or because someone recommended it to you. Or you may have encountered this passage during the process of research or as an assigned reading for a course in history, Asian-American studies, or cultural anthropology. In any case, you could draw upon this passage for a number of purposes: to demonstrate the effects of racism or xenophobia, especially in times of war (remember the backlash against Arab-Americans in the months following the attack on the World Trade Center on September 11, 2001); to illustrate how individuals and individual families coped with the hardships of being uprooted and imprisoned in this fashion; or to explore a particular historical period in the experience of an ethnic group. Having established your purpose, you decide to

---

HOW TO SUMMARIZE PERSONAL ESSAYS AND NARRATIVES

- Your summary will *not* be a narrative, but rather the synopsis of a narrative or personal account. Your summary will likely be a paragraph at most.
- You will want to name and describe the principal character(s) of the narrative and describe the narrative's main actions or events; or, in the case of the personal essay, identify the narrator and his or her relationship to the discussion.
- You should seek to connect the narrative's character(s) and events: describe the significance of events for (or the impact of events on) the character(s), and/or the narrator.

---

use the events recounted in this passage to support one or more points you intend to make.

When you summarize narrative or a personal essay, bear in mind the principles that follow, as well as those listed in the box above.

To summarize events, reread the narrative and make a marginal note each time you see that an action advances the story from one moment to the next. The key here is to recall that narratives take place *in time.* In your summary, be sure to re-create for your reader a sense of time flowing. Name and describe the character(s) as well. (For our purposes, *character* refers to the person, real or fictional, about whom the narrative is written.) The trickiest part of the summary will be describing the connection between events and characters. Earlier (pp. 1–2) we made the point that summarizing any selection involves a degree of interpretation, and this is especially true of summarizing narratives and personal essays. What, in the case of Wakatsuki, is the significance of her narrative—or of any particular event she recounts? For example, what is the significance of the fact that the family was given almost no notice to prepare for their removal to an internment camp? Or of her mother's smashing the china set? Or of the "dessert" served by the American cooks during the family's first night at Manzanar? Each of these events may be used to illustrate a particular point, and the events on which you choose to focus while summarizing a narrative will depend entirely on your purpose in using the narrative in the first place.

The general principles of summarizing narratives are similar to those of summarizing expository or persuasive passage. Make sure that you cover the major events, in the order in which they occurred (in line with your overall purpose, of course). Bring in details only to the extent that they support your purpose.

Here is a three-paragraph summary of the passage from Wakatsuki's book. (The draft is the result of two prior drafts.)

In this section from her book <u>Farewell to Manzanar,</u> Jeanne Wakatsuki (writing with her husband James D. Houston) describes her extended family's experiences following the attack on Pearl Harbor in December 1941, including their forcible relocation to an internment camp for Japanese-American families. Originally, the Wakatsuki family lived in Ocean Park, a largely white community near Santa Monica, California. When Jeanne's father was arrested, she and her family moved to Terminal Island. There, the men would catch fish; the women processed them. A child at the time, Wakatsuki recalls being intimidated by the other kids in the neighborhood, who regularly insulted and chased her and her brother.

Two months after their arrival at Terminal Island, all Japanese were ordered to relocation camps away from the coast. Wakatsuki's family was given forty-eight hours to leave. Since they could take with them little more than what they could carry, they were forced to sell most of their possessions at a fraction of their value. Wakatsuki describes how one of the secondhand dealers, "wolves" as she terms them, offered her mother fifteen dollars for a valuable set of china, expecting that the woman would have little choice but to accept his terms. Rather than sell it to the dealer at this price, her mother smashed the china on the ground, one piece at a time.

The family was taken to the Manzanar camp in buses with blinds over the windows for most of the trip. On arrival, they were served their first meal in the camp. Wakatsuki provides some idea of the culture gap between the Japanese internees and their Caucasian guards by describing how the servers, with the best of intentions, poured sweet canned apricots over steamed rice--an unheard of combination for Japanese--thinking to give the prisoners "a good dessert." Following the meal, the family was assigned to new but ill-constructed barracks. Wakatsuki's family of twelve lived in two rooms in one of the barracks. Each person was given two blankets, though often one of these had to be given up to provide partitions within a room. For the young Wakatsuki, the only advantage of this

> arrangement was that she got to sleep every night
> with her mother.

Of course, depending upon how you use Wakatsuki and Houston's passage, you may not need as many details as are provided in the preceding summary. A briefer version would treat only the major events—the father's arrest, the family's move from Ocean Park to Terminal Island, the order to relocate, the bus trip to Manzanar, and the events that followed. In a briefer summary, you might reduce the incident of Wakatsuki's mother smashing to dishes to a single sentence (or eliminate it entirely). You may also decide that the incident with the "dessert," while interesting, has no bearing on your purpose and so can be safely left out. (This particular incident would be more relevant if you were writing a paper on cultural anthropology, one that focused on cultural differences among ethnic groups.)

Here is a briefer summary of the passage:

> In this section from her book <u>Farewell to
> Manzanar,</u> Jeanne Wakatsuki (writing with her
> husband James D. Houston) describes her extended
> family's experiences following the attack on
> Pearl Harbor in December 1941, including their
> forcible relocation to an internment camp for
> Japanese-American families. After her father's
> arrest, she and her family moved from a largely
> white community, Ocean Park, near Santa Monica,
> to a largely Japanese community in Terminal
> Island. But only two months after the family's
> arrival at Terminal Island, all Japanese were
> ordered to relocation camps away from the coast.
> Wakatsuki's family was given forty-eight hours
> to leave. They were allowed to carry only a
> few personal items; the rest had to be sold.
> Wakatsuki recalls how her mother smashed a costly
> set of china dishes rather than sell them at a
> fraction of their value to one of the "wolves,"
> or secondhand dealers, who preyed on those being
> forcibly relocated. Along with other families,
> they were driven to Manzanar in a bus with blinds
> drawn over the windows. At the camp, Wakatsuki's
> family of twelve lived in two rooms in an ill-
> constructed barracks. Each person was given two
> blankets, though one of these had to be given up
> for partitioning within a room. For the young
> internee, the only advantage of this arrangement
> was that she got to sleep every night with her
> mother.

Of course, the passage could be made briefer still: your purpose in your paper might be served by a one sentence reference to Wakatsuki and Houston's narrative:

> In <u>Farewell to Manzanar</u>, Jeanne Wakatsuki offers a dramatic and poignant account of the difficulties-- including forcible relocation to an internment camp with only 48 hours' notice--faced by Japanese-Americans after the bombing of Pearl Harbor.

Here, only the major events are treated. The only detail offered—the 48 hours' notice—is retained to emphasize the arbitrary and brutal nature of the internment order.

SUMMARIZING FIGURES AND TABLES

In your reading in the sciences and social sciences, often you will find data and concepts presented in nontext forms—as figures and tables. Such visual devices offer a snapshot, a pictorial overview of material that is more quickly and clearly communicated in graphic form than as a series of (often complicated) sentences. Note that in essence, figures and tables are themselves summaries. The writer uses a graph, which in an article or book is labeled as a numbered "figure," to present the quantitative results of research as points on a line or a bar, or as sections ("slices") of a pie. Pie charts show relative proportions, or percentages. Graphs, especially effective in showing patterns, relate one variable to another: for instance, income to years of education, or a college student's grade point average to hours of studying.

In the following sections, we present a number of figures and tables from two different sources, all related to romance and relationships. Figures 1.1, 1.2, and 1.3 and Table 1.1 come from a study of the criteria used by participants on television dating shows in the United States and Israel to pick dating partners.* The categories are self-explanatory, although we should note that the category "physical appearance" denotes features of height, weight, facial features, and hair, while "sexual anatomy and bedroom behavior" refers to specifically sexual features of physical appearance, as well as to "kissing technique," "foreplay tactics," and the like. Figure 1.1 shows the criteria 266 American and Israeli men chose as most important in selecting a dating partner. Study this pie chart.

Here is a summary of the information presented:

> Males rated the categories of "physical
> appearance" and "sexual anatomy and bedroom

---

*Amir Hetsroni, "Choosing a Mate in Television Dating Games: The Influence of Setting, Culture, and Gender," *Sex Roles* 42.1–2 (2000): 90–97.

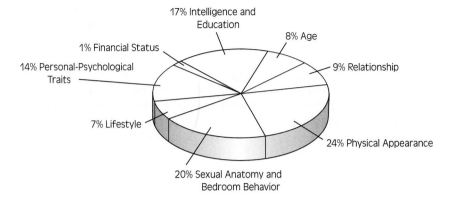

17% Intelligence and Education

8% Age

1% Financial Status

14% Personal-Psychological Traits

9% Relationship

7% Lifestyle

24% Physical Appearance

20% Sexual Anatomy and Bedroom Behavior

Figure 1.1   Categories Used by American and Israeli Males to Screen Dating Candidates

behavior" as most important to them. Nearly half the males in the sample, or 44%, rated these two categories, which both center on external rather than internal characteristics, as the most important ones for choosing a dating partner. Internal characteristics represented by the categories of "personal-psychological traits" and "intelligence and education" account for the next most important criteria, with a combined 31%. Males rated "relationship," "lifestyle," and "age" as nearly equal in their priorities; interestingly, a negligible 1% rated "financial status" as an important criterion when selecting a dating candidate.

Figure 1.2 shows, in percentages, how women rate dating criteria.

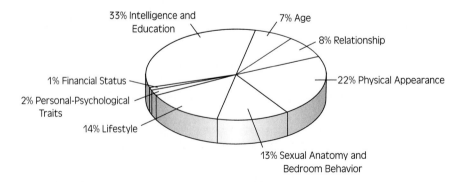

33% Intelligence and Education

7% Age

8% Relationship

1% Financial Status

22% Physical Appearance

2% Personal-Psychological Traits

14% Lifestyle

13% Sexual Anatomy and Bedroom Behavior

Figure 1.2   Categories Used by American and Israeli Females to Screen Dating Candidates

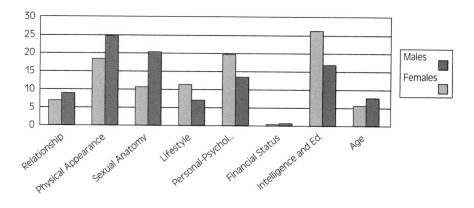

Figure 1.3 Comparison of Categories Used by American and Israeli Males and Females to Screen Dating Candidates

---

EXERCISE **1.2**

Summarizing Charts

Write a brief summary of the data in Figure 1.2. Use our summary of Figure 1.1 as a model, but structure and word your own summary differently.

Bar graphs are useful for comparing two sets of data. Figure 1.3 illustrates this with a comparison of categories males and females use to select dating partners.

Here is a summary of the information in Figure 1.3:

> Males clearly differ from females in the criteria
> they use to select dating partners. Males in this
> sample focused on external characteristics such
> as "physical appearance" and especially "sexual
> anatomy and bedroom behavior" at significantly
> higher rates than did females. Conversely,
> females selected the internal characteristics of
> "lifestyle," "personal-psychological traits," and
> "intelligence and education" at much higher
> rates than did males. However, less significant
> differences exist between males and females
> when rating the importance of "relationship,"
> "financial status," and "age"; both male and
> female participants rated these three criteria as
> of lesser importance when selecting a dating
> partner.

A table presents numerical data in rows and columns for quick reference. If the writer chooses, tabular information can be converted to graphic

Table 1.1 Categories Used by American and Israeli Males and Females to Screen Dating Candidates

Category	American Males (%) (n = 120)	Israeli Males (%) (n = 146)	American Females (%) (n = 156)	Israeli Females (%) (n = 244)
Relationship	9.5	8.0	9.5	5.0
Physical appearance	18.5	30.0	12.0	22.0
Sexual anatomy and bedroom behavior	11.5	27.5	4.5	15.0
Lifestyle	9.0	6.0	11.0	11.5
Personal-psychological traits	20.0	8.0	27.0	15.0
Financial status	1.5	–	–	1.0
Intelligence and education	22.5	12.5	29.0	24.0
Age	7.5	8.0	7.0	6.0
Total	100.0	100.0	100.0	100.0

information. Charts and graphs are preferable when the writer wants to emphasize a pattern or relationship; tables are used when the writer wants to emphasize numbers. While the previous charts and graphs combined the Israeli with the American data collected in the TV dating show study, Table 1.1 breaks down the percentages by sex and nationality, revealing some significant differences between the nationality groups. (Note: *n* refers to the total number of respondents in each category.)

Sometimes a single graph presents information on two or more populations, or data sets, all of which are tracked with the same measurements. Figure 1.4 comes from a study of 261 college students—93 males and 168 females. The students were asked (among other things) to rate the acceptability of a hypothetical instance of sexual betrayal by both a male and a female heterosexual romantic partner who has agreed to be monogamous. The graph plots the ways in which gender of the transgressor played into the acceptability ratings given by male and female respondents. The researchers established mean values of 1 to 4 (indicating ratings of "totally unacceptable" to "totally acceptable"). A *mean* indicates the average of the ratings or scores given by a population or, in numerical terms, the sum of the scores divided by the number of scores. When respondents in the study were asked to assign a numerical rating of acceptability to instances of sexual betrayal, they chose numbers on a scale from 1 to 4, and these choices were averaged into mean acceptability ratings. None of the scores given by respondents in this study surpassed a mean acceptability rating of 2, but differences are evident between male and female ratings. The male respondents were more accepting of betrayal than the females, with an overall mean acceptability score of 1.63, whereas the females' mean score was 1.31.

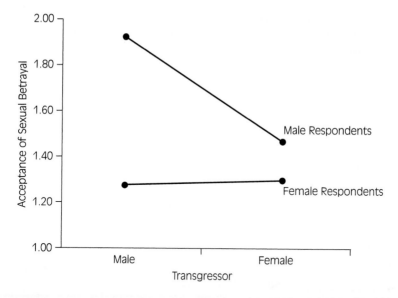

Figure 1.4 The Interaction of Sex of Respondent and Sex of Transgressor on the Acceptance of Sexual Betrayal

A complete, scientific understanding of these findings would require more data, and statistical analysis of such data would yield precise information such as the exact amount of difference between male and female ratings. For example, in the original text of this study, the authors note that males were 11.6 times more accepting of sexual betrayal by male transgressors than were females. Even without such details, it is possible to arrive at a basic understanding of the data represented in the graph, and to summarize this information in simple terms. Here is a summary of the information reported in this graph:

> While males and females both rated sexual betrayal as unacceptable, males (with a mean rating of 1.63) were significantly more accepting overall than were females (with a mean rating of 1.31). Even more dramatic, however, is the difference between male and female ratings when the gender of the transgressor is factored in. Males rated male transgression as markedly more acceptable than female transgression, with approximate means of 1.90 for male transgressions and 1.43 for female transgressions. The males' ratings contrast sharply with those of females, who indicated a mean acceptability rating of approximately 1.25 for male transgressors, and

> 1.30 for female transgressors. Therefore, while both sexes found transgression by members of their own sex more acceptable than transgressions by the opposite sex, men were more accepting overall than women, and men believed male transgressors were significantly more acceptable than female transgressors. On the other hand, women found transgression overall less acceptable than males did, and women indicated far less difference in their ratings of male versus female transgressors than did the male respondents.

PARAPHRASE

In certain cases, you may want to *paraphrase* rather than summarize material. Writing a paraphrase is similar to writing a summary: It involves recasting a passage into your own words, so it requires your complete understanding of the material. The difference is that while a summary is a shortened version of the original, the paraphrase is approximately the same length as the original.

Why write a paraphrase when you can quote the original? You may decide to offer a paraphrase of material written in language that is dense, abstract, archaic, or possibly confusing. For example, suppose you were writing a paper on some aspect of human progress and you came across the following passage by the Marquis de Condorcet, a French economist and politician, written in the late eighteenth century:

> If man can, with almost complete assurance, predict phenomena when he knows their laws, and if, even when he does not, he can still, with great expectations of success, forecast the future on the basis of his experience of the past, why, then, should it be regarded as a fantastic undertaking to sketch, with some pretense to truth, the future destiny of man on the basis of his history? The sole foundation for belief in the natural science is this idea, that the general laws directing the phenomena of the universe, known or unknown, are necessary and constant. Why should this principle be any less true for the development of the intellectual and moral faculties of man than for the other operations of nature?

You would like to introduce Condorcet's idea on predicting the future course of human history, but you also don't want to slow down your narrative with this dense and somewhat abstract quotation. You may decide to attempt a paraphrase, as follows:

> The Marquis de Condorcet believed that if we can predict such physical events as eclipses and

> tides, and if we can use past events as a guide
> to future ones, we should be able to forecast
> human destiny on the basis of history. Physical
> events, he maintained, are determined by natural
> laws that are knowable and predictable. Since
> humans are part of nature, why should their
> intellectual and moral development be any less
> predictable than other natural events?

Each sentence in the paraphrase corresponds to a sentence in the original. The paraphrase is somewhat shorter, owing to the differences of style between eighteenth- and twentieth-century prose (we tend to be more brisk and efficient, although not as eloquent). But the main difference is that we have replaced the language of the original with our own language. For example, we have paraphrased Condorcet's "the general laws directing the phenomena of the universe, known or unknown, are necessary and constant" with "Physical events, he maintained, are determined by natural laws that are knowable and predictable." To contemporary readers, "knowable and predictable" might be clearer than "necessary and constant" as a description of natural (i.e., physical) laws. Note that we added the specific examples of eclipses and tides to clarify what might have been a somewhat abstract idea. Note also that we included two attributions to Condorcet within the paraphrase to credit our source properly.

When you come across a passage that you don't understand, the temptation is strong to skip over it. Resist this temptation! Use a paraphrase as a tool for explaining to yourself the main ideas of a difficult passage. By translating another writer's language into your own, you can clarify what you understand and pinpoint what you don't. The paraphrase therefore becomes a tool for learning the subject.

The pointers below will help you write paraphrases.

HOW TO WRITE PARAPHRASES

- Make sure that you understand the source passage.
- Substitute your own words for those of the source passage; look for synonyms that carry the same meaning as the original words.
- Rearrange your own sentences so that they read smoothly. Sentence structure, even sentence order, in the paraphrase need not be based on that of the original. A good paraphrase, like a good summary, should stand by itself.

Let's consider some other examples. If you were investigating the ethical concerns relating to the practice of in vitro fertilization, you might conclude that you should read some medical literature. You might reasonably want to hear from the doctors who are themselves developing, performing, and questioning the procedures that you are researching. In professional journals and bulletins, physicians write to one another, not to the general public. They use specialized language. If you wanted to refer to a technically complex selection, you might need to write a paraphrase for the following selection.

In Vitro Fertilization: From Medical Reproduction to Genetic Diagnosis

Dietmar Mieth

[I]t is not only an improvement in the success-rate that participating research scientists hope for but, rather, developments in new fields of research in in-vitro gene diagnosis and in certain circumstances gene therapy. In view of this, the French expert J. F. Mattei has asked the following question: "Are we forced to accept that in vitro fertilization will become one of the most compelling methods of genetic diagnosis?" Evidently, by the introduction of a new law in France and Sweden (1994), this acceptance (albeit with certain restrictions) has already occurred prior to the application of in vitro fertilization reaching a technically mature and clinically applicable phase. This may seem astonishing in view of the question placed by the above-quoted French expert: the idea of embryo production so as to withhold one or two embryos before implantation presupposes a definite "attitude towards eugenics." And to destroy an embryo merely because of its genetic characteristics could signify the reduction of a human life to the sum of its genes. Mattei asks: "In face of a molecular judgment on our lives, is there no possibility for appeal? Will the diagnosis of inherited monogenetic illnesses soon be extended to genetic predisposition for multi-factorial illnesses?"*

Like most literature intended for physicians, the language of this selection is somewhat forbidding to an audience of nonspecialists, who have trouble with phrases such as "predisposition for multi-factorial illnesses." As a courtesy to your readers and in an effort to maintain a consistent tone and level in your essay, you could paraphrase this paragraph of the medical newsletter. First, of course, you must understand the meaning of the passage, perhaps no small task. But, having read the material carefully (and perhaps consulting a dictionary), you might eventually prepare a paraphrase like this one:

---

*Dietmar Mieth, "In vitro Fertilization: From Medical Reproduction to Genetic Diagnosis," *Biomedical Ethics: Newsletter of the European Network for Biomedical Ethics* 1.1 (1996): 45.

> Writing in the <u>Newsletter</u> <u>of</u> <u>the</u> <u>European</u> <u>Network</u> <u>for</u> <u>Biomedical</u> <u>Ethics</u>, Dietmar Mieth reports that fertility specialists today want not only to improve the success rates of their procedures but also to diagnose and repair genetic problems before they implant fertilized eggs. Since the result of the in vitro process is often more fertilized eggs than can be used in a procedure, doctors may examine test-tube embryos for genetic defects and "withhold one or two" before implanting them. The practice of selectively implanting embryos raises concerns about eugenics and the rights of rejected embryos. On what genetic grounds will specialists distinguish flawed from healthy embryos and make a decision whether or not to implant? The appearance of single genes linked directly to specific, or "monogenetic," illnesses could be grounds for destroying an embryo. More complicated would be genes that predispose people to an illness but in no way guarantee the onset of that illness. Would these genes, which are only one factor in "multi-factorial illnesses" also be labeled undesirable and lead to embryo destruction? Advances in fertility science raise difficult questions. Already, even before techniques of genetic diagnosis are fully developed, legislatures are writing laws governing the practices of fertility clinics.

We begin our paraphrase with the same "not only/but also" logic of the original's first sentence, introducing the concepts of genetic diagnosis and therapy. The next four sentences in the original introduce concerns of a "French expert." Rather than quoting Mieth, quoting the expert, and immediately mentioning new laws in France and Sweden, we decided (first) to explain that in vitro fertilization procedures can give rise to more embryos than needed. We reasoned that nonmedical readers would appreciate our making explicit the background knowledge that the author assumes other physicians possess. Then we quote Mieth briefly ("withhold one or two" embryos) to provide some flavor of the original. We maintain focus on the ethical questions and wait until the end of the paraphrase before mentioning the laws to which Mieth refers. Our paraphrase is roughly the same length as the original, and it conveys the author's concerns about eugenics. As you can see, the paraphrase requires a writer to make some decisions about the presentation of material. In many, if not most, cases, you will need to do more than simply "translate" from the original, sentence by sentence, to write your paraphrase.

Finally, let's consider a passage written by a fine writer that may, nonetheless, best be conveyed in paraphrase. In "Identify All Carriers," an article on AIDS, editor and columnist William F. Buckley makes the following statement:

> I have read and listened, and I think now that I can convincingly crystallize the thoughts chasing about in the minds of, first, those whose concern with AIDS victims is based primarily on a concern for them, and for the maintenance of the most rigid standards of civil liberties and personal privacy, and, second, those whose anxiety to protect the public impels them to give subordinate attention to the civil amenities of those who suffer from AIDS and primary attention to the safety of those who do not.

In style, Buckley's passage is more like Condorcet's than the medical newsletter: It is eloquent, balanced, and literate. Still, it is challenging, consisting of another lengthy sentence, perhaps a bit too eloquent for some readers to grasp. For your paper on AIDS, you decide to paraphrase Buckley. You might draft something like this:

```
Buckley finds two opposing sides in the AIDS
debate: those concerned primarily with the civil
liberties and the privacy of AIDS victims, and
those concerned primarily with the safety of the
public.
```

Paraphrases are generally about the same length as (sometimes shorter than) the passages on which they are based. But sometimes clarity requires that a paraphrase be longer than a tightly compacted source passage. For example, suppose you wanted to paraphrase this statement by Sigmund Freud:

> We have found out that the distortion in dreams which hinders our understanding of them is due to the activities of a censorship, directed against the unacceptable, unconscious wish-impulses.

If you were to paraphrase this statement (the first sentence in the Tenth Lecture of his *General Introduction to Psychoanalysis*), you might come up with something like this:

```
It is difficult to understand dreams because they
contain distortions. Freud believed that these
distortions arise from our internal censor, which
attempts to suppress unconscious and forbidden
desires.
```

Essentially, this paraphrase does little more than break up one sentence into two and somewhat rearrange the sentence structure for clarity.

Like summaries, then, *paraphrases* are useful devices, both in helping you to understand source material and in enabling you to convey the essence of this source material to your readers. When would you choose to write a summary instead of a paraphrase (or vice versa)? The answer to this question depends on your purpose in presenting your source material. As we've said, summaries are generally based on articles (or sections of articles) or books. Paraphrases are generally based on particularly difficult (or important) paragraphs or sentences. You would seldom paraphrase a long passage, or summarize a short one, unless there were particularly good reasons for doing so. (For example, a lawyer might want to paraphrase several pages of legal language so that his or her client, who is not a lawyer, could understand it.) The purpose of a summary is generally to save your reader time by presenting him or her with a brief and quickly readable version of a lengthy source. The purpose of a paraphrase is generally to clarify a short passage that might otherwise be unclear. Whether you summarize or paraphrase may also depend on the importance of your source. A particularly important source—if it is not too long—may rate a paraphrase. If it is less important, or peripheral to your central argument, you may choose to write a summary instead. And, of course, you may choose to summarize only part of your source—the part that is most relevant to the point you are making.

EXERCISE `1.3`

Summarizing and Paraphrasing

The following passage is excerpted from an article written in 1866 by Frederick Douglass, entitled "Reconstruction." In this piece the famed advocate for African-American rights appeals to the Second Session of the Thirty-ninth United States Congress, as it considered issues of state and federal rights in the aftermath of the Civil War. Read this passage and write both a summary and a paraphrase.

> Fortunately, the Constitution of the United States knows no distinction between citizens on account of color. Neither does it know any difference between a citizen of a State and a citizen of the United States. Citizenship evidently includes all the rights of citizens, whether State or national. If the Constitution knows none, it is clearly no part of the duty of a Republican Congress now to institute one. The mistake of the last session was the attempt to do this very thing, by a renunciation of its power to secure political rights to any class of citizens, with the obvious purpose to allow the rebellious States to disfranchise, if they should see fit, their colored citizens. This unfortunate blunder must now be retrieved, and the emasculated citizenship given to the negro supplanted by that contemplated in the Constitution of the United States, which declares that the citizens of each

State shall enjoy all the rights and immunities of citizens of the several States,—so that a legal voter in any State shall be a legal voter in all the States.*

More Paraphrasing

Locate three relatively complex, but brief, passages from readings currently assigned in your other courses. Paraphrase these passages, making the language more readable and understandable.

QUOTATIONS

A *quotation* records the exact language used by someone in speech or writing. A *summary*, in contrast, is a brief restatement in your own words of what someone else has said or written. And a *paraphrase* also is a restatement, although one that is often as long as the original source. Any paper in which you draw upon sources will rely heavily on quotation, summary, and paraphrase. How do you choose among the three?

Remember that the papers you write should be your own—for the most part: your own language and certainly your own thesis, your own inferences, and your own conclusion. It follows that references to your source materials should be written primarily as summaries and paraphrases, both of which are built on restatement, not quotation. You will use summaries when you need a *brief* restatement, and paraphrases, which provide more explicit detail than summaries, when you need to follow the development of a source closely. When you quote too much, you risk losing ownership of your work: more easily than you might think, your voice can be drowned out by the voices of those you've quoted. So *use quotation sparingly,* as you would a pungent spice.

Nevertheless, *quoting just the right source at the right time can significantly improve your papers.* The trick is to know when and how to use quotations.

Choosing Quotations

You'll find that using quotations can be particularly helpful in several situations.

QUOTING MEMORABLE LANGUAGE

Assume you're writing a paper on Napoleon Bonaparte's relationship with the celebrated Josephine. Through research you learn that two days after

---

*Frederick Douglass, "Reconstruction," *The Atlantic Monthly*, 18. 1866: 761–65.

```
┌─────────────────────────────────────────────┐
│                            WHEN TO QUOTE      │
└─────────────────────────────────────────────┘
```
WHEN TO QUOTE

- Use quotations when another writer's language is particularly memorable and will add interest and liveliness to your paper.
- Use quotations when another writer's language is so clear and economical that to make the same point in your own words would, by comparison, be ineffective.
- Use quotations when you want the solid reputation of a source to lend authority and credibility to your own writing.

their marriage, Napoleon, given command of an army, left his bride for what was to be a brilliant military campaign in Italy. How did the young general respond to leaving his wife so soon after their wedding? You come across the following, written by Napoleon from the field of battle on April 3, 1796:

> I have received all your letters, but none has such an impact on me as the last. Do you have any idea, darling, what you are doing, writing to me in those terms? Do you not think my situation cruel enough without intensifying my longing for you, overwhelming my soul? What a style! What emotions you evoke! Written in fire, they burn my poor heart!*

A summary of this passage might read as follows:

> On April 3, 1796, Napoleon wrote to Josephine, expressing how sorely he missed her and how passionately he responded to her passionate letters.

You might write the following as a paraphrase of the passage:

> On April 3, 1796, Napoleon wrote to Josephine that he had received her letters and that one among all others had had a special impact, overwhelming his soul with fiery emotions and longing.

How feeble this summary and paraphrase are when compared with the original! Use the vivid language that your sources give you. In this case, quote Napoleon in your paper to make your subject come alive with memorable detail:

---

*Francis Mossiker, trans. *Napoleon and Josephine* (New York: Simon and Schuster, 1964), 437.

> On April 3, 1796, a passionate, lovesick Napoleon
> responded to a letter from Josephine; she had
> written longingly to her husband, who, on a
> military campaign, acutely felt her absence. "Do
> you have any idea, darling, what you are doing,
> writing to me in those terms? . . . What emotions
> you evoke!" he said of her letters. "Written in
> fire, they burn my poor heart!"

Quotations can be direct or indirect. A *direct* quotation is one in which you record precisely the language of another, as we did with the sentences from Napoleon's letter. An *indirect* quotation is one in which you report what someone has said, although you are not obligated to repeat the words exactly as spoken (or written):

Direct quotation: Franklin D. Roosevelt said, "The only thing we have to fear is fear itself."

Indirect quotation: Franklin D. Roosevelt said that we have nothing to fear but fear itself.

The language in a direct quotation, which is indicated by a pair of quotation marks (" "), must be faithful to the language of the original passage. When using an indirect quotation, you have the liberty of changing words (although not changing meaning). For both direct and indirect quotations, *you must credit your sources,* naming them either in (or close to) the sentence that includes the quotation or in a parenthetical citation. (Note: We haven't included parenthetical citations in our examples here; see Chapter 7, pp. 309–332 for specific rules on citing sources properly.)

QUOTING CLEAR AND CONCISE LANGUAGE

You should quote a source when its language is particularly clear and economical—when your language, by contrast, would be wordy. Read this passage from a text by Patricia Curtis on biology:

> The honeybee colony, which usually has a population of 30,000 to 40,000 workers, differs from that of the bumblebee and many other social bees or wasps in that it survives the winter. This means that the bees must stay warm despite the cold. Like other bees, the isolated honeybee cannot fly if the temperature falls below 10°C (50°F) and cannot walk if the temperature is below 7°C (45°F). Within the wintering hive, bees maintain their temperature by clustering together in a dense ball; the lower the temperature, the denser the cluster. The clustered bees produce heat by constant muscular movements of their wings, legs, and abdomens. In very cold weather, the bees on the outside of the cluster keep moving toward the center, while those in the core of the cluster move to the colder outside periphery. The entire

cluster moves slowly about on the combs, eating the stored honey
from the combs as it moves.*

A summary of this paragraph might read as follows:

```
Honeybees, unlike many other varieties of bee,
are able to live through the winter by
"clustering together in a dense ball" for body
warmth.
```

A paraphrase of the same passage would be considerably more detailed:

```
Honeybees, unlike many other varieties of bee
(such as bumblebees), are able to live through
the winter. The 30,000 to 40,000 bees within a
honeybee hive could not, individually, move about
in cold winter temperatures. But when "clustering
together in a dense ball," the bees generate heat
by constantly moving their body parts. The
cluster also moves slowly about the hive, those
on the periphery of the cluster moving into the
center, those in the center moving to the
periphery, and all eating honey stored in the
combs. This nutrition, in addition to the heat
generated by the cluster, enables the honeybee to
survive the cold winter months.
```

In both the summary and the paraphrase we've quoted Curtis's "clustering
together in a dense ball," a phrase that lies at the heart of her description of
wintering honeybees. For us to describe this clustering in any language
other than Curtis's would be pointless since her description is admirably
brief and precise.

QUOTING AUTHORITATIVE LANGUAGE

You will also want to use quotations that lend authority to your work. When
quoting an expert or some prominent political, artistic, or historical figure,
you elevate your own work by placing it in esteemed company. Quote respected figures to establish background information in a paper, and your
readers will tend to perceive that information as reliable. Quote the opinions
of respected figures to endorse some statement that you've made, and your
statement becomes more credible to your readers. For example, in an essay
on the importance of reading well, you could make use of a passage from
Thoreau's *Walden:*

---

*Patricia Curtis, "Winter Organization," *Biology,* 2nd ed. (New York: Worth, 1976), 822–23.

> Reading well is hard work and requires great skill and training. It "is a noble exercise," writes Henry David Thoreau in <u>Walden</u>, "and one that will task the reader more than any exercise which the customs of the day esteem. . . . Books must be read as deliberately and reservedly as they were written."

[See below, pp. 49–50 for a discussion of when to use ellipses within quotations.]

By quoting a famous philosopher and essayist on the subject of reading, you add legitimacy to your discussion. Not only do *you* regard reading to be a skill that is both difficult and important, so too does Henry David Thoreau, one of our most influential thinkers. The quotation has elevated the level of your work.

You can also quote to advantage well-respected figures who have written or spoken about the subject of your paper. Here is a discussion of space flight. Author David Chandler refers to a physicist and a physicist-astronaut:

> A few scientists—notably James Van Allen, discoverer of the Earth's radiation belts—have decried the expense of the manned space program and called for an almost exclusive concentration on unmanned scientific exploration instead, saying this would be far more cost-effective.
>
> Other space scientists dispute that idea. Joseph Allen, physicist and former shuttle astronaut, says, "It seems to be argued that one takes away from the other. But before there was a manned space program, the funding on space science was zero. Now it's about $500 million a year."

Note that in the first paragraph Chandler has either summarized or used an indirect quotation to incorporate remarks made by James Van Allen into the discussion on space flight. In the second paragraph, Chandler directly quotes his next source, Joseph Allen. Both quotations, indirect and direct, lend authority and legitimacy to the article, for both James Van Allen and Joseph Allen are experts on the subject of space flight. Note also that Chandler provides brief but effective biographies of his sources, identifying both so that their qualifications to speak on the subject are known to all:

> James Van Allen, *discoverer of the Earth's radiation belts . . .*
>
> Joseph Allen, *physicist and former shuttle astronaut . . .*

The phrases in italics are called *appositives.* Their function is to rename the nouns they follow by providing explicit, identifying detail. Any information about a person that can be expressed in the following sentence pattern can be made into an appositive phrase:

> James Van Allen is the *discoverer of the Earth's radiation belts.*

He has decried the expense of the manned space program.

James Van Allen, *discoverer of the Earth's radiation belts,* has decried the expense of the manned space program.

Appositives (in the example above, "discover of the Earth's radiation belts") efficiently incorporate identifying information about the authors you quote, while adding variety to the structure of your sentences.

Incorporating Quotations into Your Sentences

QUOTING ONLY THE PART OF A SENTENCE OR PARAGRAPH THAT YOU NEED

We've said that a writer selects passages for quotation that are especially *vivid and memorable, concise,* or *authoritative.* Now put these principles into practice. Suppose that while conducting research on college sports, you've come across the following, written by Robert Hutchins, former president of the University of Chicago:

> If athleticism is bad for students, players, alumni, and the public, it is even worse for the colleges and universities themselves. They want to be educational institutions, but they can't. The story of the famous halfback whose only regret, when he bade his coach farewell, was that he hadn't learned to read and write is probably exaggerated. But we must admit that pressure from trustees, graduates, "friends," presidents, and even professors has tended to relax academic standards. These gentry often overlook the fact that a college should not be interested in a fullback who is a half-wit. Recruiting, subsidizing and the double educational standard cannot exist without the knowledge and the tacit approval, at least, of the colleges and universities themselves. Certain institutions encourage susceptible professors to be nice to athletes now admitted by paying them for serving as "faculty representatives" on the college athletic board.*

Suppose that in this entire paragraph you find a gem, a sentence with quotable words that will enliven your discussion. You may want to quote part of the following sentence:

> These gentry often overlook the fact that a college should not be interested in a fullback who is a half-wit.

INCORPORATING THE QUOTATION INTO THE FLOW OF YOUR OWN SENTENCE

Once you've selected the passage you want to quote, work the material into your paper in as natural and fluid a manner as possible. Here's how we would quote Hutchins:

---

*Robert Hutchins, "Gate Receipts and Glory," *The Saturday Evening Post* 3 Dec. 1983: 38.

> Robert Hutchins, former president of the
> University of Chicago, asserts that "a college
> should not be interested in a fullback who is a
> half-wit."

Note that we've used an appositive to identify Hutchins. And we've used only the part of the paragraph—a single clause—that we thought memorable enough to quote directly.

AVOIDING FREESTANDING QUOTATIONS

A quoted sentence should never stand by itself—as in the following example:

> Various people associated with the university
> admit that the pressures of athleticism have
> caused a relaxation of standards. "These gentry
> often overlook the fact that a college should not
> be interested in a fullback who is a half-wit."
> But this kind of thinking is bad for the
> university and even worse for the athletes.

Even if it includes a parenthetical citation, a freestanding quotation would have the problem of being jarring to the reader. Introduce the quotation with a *signal phrase* that attributes the source not in a parenthetical citation, but in some other part of the sentence—beginning, middle, or end. Thus, you could write:

> As Robert Hutchins notes, "These gentry often
> overlook the fact that a college should not be
> interested in a fullback who is a half-wit."

Here's a variation with the signal phrase in the middle:

> "These gentry," asserts Robert Hutchins, "often
> overlook the fact that a college should not be
> interested in a fullback who is a half-wit."

Another alternative is to introduce a sentence-long quotation with a colon:

> But Robert Hutchins disagrees: "These gentry
> often overlook the fact that a college should not
> be interested in a fullback who is a half-wit."

Use colons also to introduce indented quotations (as in the cases when we introduce long quotations in this chapter).

When attributing sources in signal phrases, try to vary the standard *states, writes, says,* and so on. Other, stronger verbs you might consider: *asserts, argues, maintains, insists, asks,* and even *wonders.*

Return to the passage by Jeanne Wakatsuki and James Houston, "Arrival at Manzanar," pages 23–27, and find some sentences that you think make interesting points. Imagine you want to use these points in an essay you're writing on the effects of racism and xenophobia. Write five different sentences that use a variety of the techniques discussed thus far to incorporate whole sentences as well as phrases from the "Manzanar" passage.

USING ELLIPSIS MARKS

Using quotations becomes somewhat complicated when you want to quote the beginning and end of a passage but not its middle—as was the case when we quoted Henry David Thoreau. Here's part of the paragraph in *Walden* from which we quoted a few sentences:

> To read well, that is to read true books in a true spirit, is a noble exercise, and one that will task the reader more than any exercise which the customs of the day esteem. It requires a training such as the athletes underwent, the steady intention almost of the whole life to this object. Books must be read as deliberately and reservedly as they were written.*

And here was how we used this material:

```
Reading well is hard work, writes Henry David
Thoreau in Walden, "that will task the reader
more than any exercise which the customs of the
day esteem. . . . Books must be read as
deliberately and reservedly as they were
written."
```

Whenever you quote a sentence but delete words from it, as we have done, indicate this deletion to the reader with three spaced periods—called an "ellipsis mark"—in the sentence at the point of deletion. The rationale for using an ellipsis mark is that a direct quotation must be reproduced *exactly* as it was written or spoken. When writers delete or change any part of the quoted material, readers must be alerted so they don't think the changes were part of the original. When deleting an entire sentence or sentences from a quoted paragraph, as in the example above, end the sentence you have quoted with a period, place the ellipsis, and continue the quotation.

---

*Henry David Thoreau, *Walden* (New York: Signet Classic, 1960): 72.

If you are deleting the middle of a single sentence, use an ellipsis in place of the deleted words:

> ```
> "To read well . . . is a noble exercise, and one
> that will task the reader more than any exercise
> which the customs of the day esteem."
> ```

If you are deleting material from the end of one sentence through to the beginning of another sentence, add a sentence period before the ellipsis:

> ```
> "It requires a training such as the athletes
> underwent. . . . Books must be read as
> deliberately and reservedly as they were
> written."
> ```

If you begin your quotation of an author in the middle of his or her sentence, you need not indicate deleted words with an ellipsis. Be sure, however, that the syntax of the quotation fits smoothly with the syntax of your sentence:

> ```
> Reading "is a noble exercise," writes Henry David
> Thoreau.
> ```

USING BRACKETS TO ADD OR SUBSTITUTE WORDS

Use brackets whenever you need to add or substitute words in a quoted sentence. The brackets indicate to the reader a word or phrase that does not appear in the original passage but that you have inserted to avoid confusion. For example, when a pronoun's antecedent would be unclear to readers, delete the pronoun from the sentences and substitute an identifying word or phrase in brackets. When you make such a substitution, no ellipsis marks are needed. Assume that you wish to quote either of the underlined sentences in the following passage by Jane Yolen:

> Golden Press's *Walt Disney's Cinderella* set the new pattern for America's Cinderella. This book's text is coy and condescending. (Sample: "And her best friends of all were—guess who—the mice!") The illustrations are poor cartoons. And Cinderella herself is a disaster. She cowers as her sisters rip her homemade ball gown to shreds. (Not even homemade by Cinderella, but by the mice and birds.) <u>She answers her stepmother with whines and pleadings. She is a sorry excuse for a heroine, pitiable and useless.</u> She cannot perform even a simple action to save herself, though she is warned by her friends, the mice. She does not hear them because she is "off in a world of dreams." Cinderella begs, she whimpers, and at last has to be rescued by—guess who—the mice!*

---

*Jane Yolen, "America's 'Cinderella,'" *Children's Literature in Education* 8 (1977): 22.

In quoting one of these sentences, you would need to identify to whom the pronoun *she* refers. You can do this inside the quotation by using brackets:

```
Jane Yolen believes that "[Cinderella] is a sorry
excuse for a heroine, pitiable and useless."
```

If the pronoun begins the sentence to be quoted, you can identify the pronoun outside the quotation and simply begin quoting your source one word later:

```
Jane Yolen believes that in the Golden Press
version, Cinderella "is a sorry excuse for a
heroine, pitiable and useless."
```

Here's another example of a case where the pronoun needing identification occurs in the middle of the sentence to be quoted. Newspaper reporters must use brackets in these cases frequently when quoting sources, who in interviews might say something like the following:

After the fire they did not return to the station house for three hours.

If the reporter wants to use this sentence in an article, he or she needs to identify the pronoun:

An official from City Hall, speaking on the condition that he not be identified, said, "After the fire [the officers] did not return to the station house for three hours."

You also will need to add bracketed information to a quoted sentence when a reference essential to the sentence's meaning is implied but not stated directly. Read the following paragraphs from physicist Robert Jastrow's "Toward an Intelligence Beyond Man's":

These are amiable qualities for the computer; it imitates life like an electronic monkey. As computers get more complex, the imitation gets better. Finally, the line between the original and the copy becomes blurred. In another 15 years or so—two more generations of computer evolution, in the jargon of the technologists—we will see the computer as an emergent form of life.

The proposition seems ridiculous because, for one thing, computers lack the drives and emotions of living creatures. But when drives are useful, they can be programmed into the computer's brain, just as nature programmed them into our ancestors' brains as a part of the equipment for survival. For example, computers, like people, work better and learn faster when they are motivated. Arthur Samuel made this discovery when he taught two IBM computers how to play checkers. They polished their game by playing each other, but they learned slowly. Finally, Dr. Samuel programmed in the will to win by forcing the computers to try harder—and to think out more moves in advance—when they were losing. Then the computers learned very quickly. One of them beat Samuel and went on to defeat a champion player who had not lost a game to a human opponent in eight years.*

If you wanted to quote only the underlined sentence, you would need to provide readers with a bracketed explanation; otherwise, the words *the proposition* would be unclear. Here is how you would manage the quotation:

> According to Robert Jastrow, a physicist and former official at NASA's Goddard Institute, "The proposition [that computers will emerge as a form of life] seems ridiculous because, for one thing, computers lack the drives and emotions of living creatures."

EXERCISE 1.6

Using Brackets

Write your own sentences incorporating the following quotations. Use brackets to clarify information that isn't clear outside of its original context—and refer to the original sources to remind yourself of this context.

From the Robert Jastrow piece on computers and intelligence:
(a) Arthur Samuel made *this discovery* when he taught two IBM computers how to play checkers.
(b) *They* polished their game by playing each other, but *they* learned slowly.

From the Jane Yolen excerpt on Cinderella:
(c) *This book's* text is coy and condescending
(d) *She* cannot perform even a simple action to save herself, though she is warned by her friends, the mice.
(e) She does not hear *them* because she is "off in a world of dreams."

Remember that when you quote the work of another, you are obligated to credit—or cite—the author's work properly; otherwise, you may be guilty of plagiarism. See pages 309–332 for guidance on citing sources.

---

*Robert Jastrow, "Toward an Intelligence Beyond Man's," *Time* 20 Feb. 1978: 35.

```
┌─────────────────────────────────────────────────────────┐
│ ┌───────────────────────────────────────────────────┐   │
│ │   WHEN TO SUMMARIZE, PARAPHRASE, AND QUOTE        │   │
│ └───────────────────────────────────────────────────┘   │
```

Summarize:
- To present main points of a lengthy passage (article or book)
- To condense peripheral points necessary to discussion

Paraphrase:
- To clarify a short passage
- To emphasize main points

Quote:
- To capture another writer's particularly memorable language
- To capture another writer's clearly and economically stated language
- To lend authority and credibility to your own writing

AVOIDING PLAGIARISM

Plagiarism is generally defined as the attempt to pass off the work of another as one's own. Whether born out of calculation or desperation, plagiarism is the least tolerated offense in the academic world. The fact that most plagiarism is unintentional—arising from ignorance of conventions rather than deceitfulness—makes no difference to many professors.

The ease of cutting and pasting whole blocks of text from Web sources into one's own paper makes it tempting for some to take the easy way out and avoid doing their own research and writing. But apart from the serious ethical issues involved, the same technology that makes such acts possible also makes it possible for instructors to detect them. Software marketed to instructors allows them to conduct Web searches, using suspicious phrases as keywords. The results often provide irrefutable evidence of plagiarism.

Of course, plagiarism is not confined to students. Recent years have seen a number of high profile cases—some of them reaching the front pages of newspapers—of well-known scholars who were shown to have copied passages from sources into their own book manuscripts, without proper attribution. In some cases, the scholars maintained that these appropriations were simply a matter of carelessness, and that in the press and volume of work, they had lost track of which words were theirs and which were the words of their sources. But such excuses sounded hollow: These careless acts inevitably embarrassed the scholars professionally, disappointed their many admirers, and tarnished their otherwise fine work and reputations.

You can avoid plagiarism and charges of plagiarism by following the basic rules provided on page 56.

Following is a passage of text, along with several student versions of the ideas represented. (The passage is from Richard Rovere's article on Senator Joseph P. McCarthy, titled "The Most Gifted and Successful Demagogue This Country Has Ever Known.")

> McCarthy never seemed to believe in himself or in anything he had said. He knew that Communists were not in charge of American foreign policy. He knew that they weren't running the United States Army. He knew that he had spent five years looking for Communists in the government and that—although some must certainly have been there, since Communists had turned up in practically every other major government in the world—he hadn't come up with even one.*

One student version of this passage reads as follows:

> McCarthy never believed in himself or in anything he had said. He knew that Communists were not in charge of American foreign policy and weren't running the United States Army. He knew that he had spent five years looking for Communists in the government, and although there must certainly have been some there, since Communists were in practically every other major government in the world, he hadn't come up with even one.

Clearly, this is intentional plagiarism. The student has copied the original passage almost word for word.

Here is another version of the same passage:

> McCarthy knew that Communists were not running foreign policy or the Army. He also knew that although there must have been some Communists in the government, he hadn't found a single one, even though he had spent five years looking.

This student has attempted to put the ideas into her own words, but both the wording and the sentence structure still are so heavily dependent on the original passage that even if it *were* cited, most professors would consider it plagiarism.

In the following version, the student has sufficiently changed the wording and sentence structure, and she uses a signal phrase (a phrase used to in-

---

*Richard Rovere, "The Most Gifted and Successful Demagogue This Country Has Ever Known," *New York Times Magazine* 30 Apr. 1967.

troduce a quotation or paraphrase, signaling to the reader that the words to follow come from someone else) to properly credit the information to Rovere, so that there is no question of plagiarism:

> According to Richard Rovere, McCarthy was fully aware that Communists were running neither the government nor the Army. He also knew that he hadn't found a single Communist in government, even after a lengthy search (192).

And although this is not a matter of plagiarism, as noted above, it's essential to quote accurately. You are not permitted to change any part of a quotation or to omit any part of it without using brackets or ellipses (see pp. 49–52).

RULES FOR AVOIDING PLAGIARISM

- Cite *all* quoted material and *all* summarized and paraphrased material, unless the information is common knowledge (e.g., the Civil War was fought from 1861 to 1865).
- Make sure that both the *wording* and the *sentence structure* of your summaries and paraphrases are substantially your own.

 Writing Assignment: Summary

Read "Landscape in the Classic Hollywood Western" by Stanley Solomon. Write a summary of the article, following the directions in this chapter for dividing the article into sections, for writing a one-sentence summary of each section, and then for joining section summaries with a thesis. Prepare for the summary by making notes in the margins. You may find it useful to recall that well-written pieces, like Solomon's, often telegraph clues to their own structure as a device for assisting readers. Such clues can be helpful when preparing a summary. Your finished product should be the result of two or more drafts.

Landscape in the Classic Hollywood Western
Stanley Solomon

Stanley Solomon, professor of film studies at Iona College, N.Y., has written or edited several books on film, including The Film Idea *(1972),* The Classic Cinema: Essays in Criticism *(1973), and* Beyond Formula: American Film Genres *(1976), from which the following passage is excerpted.*

1   The Western genre has been so prolific that several of its subgenres are no doubt larger than most of the other genres discussed in this book. What relates all these different categories—the unifying factor in our comprehension of hundreds of films as a genre—is a sense of place. The Western is primarily a genre of location, but richer than other such genres because the location—which varies from vast landscapes of rocky ridges to forts to Indian reservations to towns seemingly built on a single street—immediately circumscribes the kind of action that will occur. The location with almost equal rigidity suggests not only plot but characterization. If we are shown, for instance, a barren, craggy terrain, we assume that the people who ride over it triumphantly must themselves be fairly rugged. At the same time, we can also assume that others less rugged will be victimized by the same environment (by robbers of stage-

coach or train, perhaps) and will be forced to accept or actively seek the protection of those who will defend them (a cavalry escort, for example). If the environment expresses a kind of toughness and primitiveness that seems to foster a law of survival of the fittest, then we normally would expect some Western characters to present a bullying aggressiveness and criminality.

2   The rural locales, furthermore, are generally sparsely populated, except in films where cavalry hordes converge on a tribe of outnumbered Indians. Lack of population and the accompanying lack of industry make the sources of wealth few: banks, cattle ranches, and stagecoaches, for instance. These sources are constant temptations to that portion of the populace prone to live by violence because, banded together, these people represent enough power to grab up the wealth through daring or force. In defense, the citizenry forms a nominal, usually weak-spirited opposition group. This group gathers around the solitary defender, the sheriff or marshal who, in any Western environment, performs his duties despite numerically greater opponents but nevertheless manages to survive on strength of character as well as ability. Similarly, as an outpost of civilization, the fort, surrounded by gathering tribes, occupies in a broad sense the same position in a film about cowboys and Indians as the sheriff does in a lawless town.

3   The nature of Western locations tends to breed an environment of threat and counterthreat, in which conflict along sharply delineated moral lines is all but inevitable. To some, the moral issues joined in such an atmosphere are too simplistic, especially since they are seldom explored at length. It is true that right and wrong are meant to be apparent, and the characteristic laconic dialogue is hardly likely to lead to the articulation of moral problems. But the Western is a great genre because the issues it deals with are clearly embedded in the cinematic qualities of the films. We see the given premises and they are hard to argue with. The constant challenge of the landscape urges a consistency of response to typical situations and chance meetings with strangers, for there is never time to calculate all the degrees of danger in an unfamiliar place. Naturally, Westerners tend to develop codes of behavior to cope with most of their ordinary interactions with those not well known to them. The codes are easily ascertained, since both heroes and villains seem to understand them. Indeed, sometimes the outmaneuvered or over-matched hero can taunt his otherwise unethical enemy into hand-to-hand combat—the democratic way—with the outlaw relinquishing an advantage because the code of the place seems to demand it. When codes are violated, when someone is shot in the back, the villain is quite aware of his vileness and his motives for it (cowardice, revenge, and so on). The location further determines the moral perspective by inviting sudden violence and the accompanying necessity of perpetual preparedness. Thus, one ought to know how to act in a perilous situation. And therefore, if one is so prepared, the probability is strong that his whole life is patterned in a certain way, evident in a certain style. We are continually impressed by the fatalistic, melancholy, and serene deportment of many of the Western heroes played by John Wayne, Randolph Scott, Gary Cooper, and James Stewart on their way to one more deadly encounter.

4   The environment, of course, suggests a good deal about the roles of women as well. Only a few notable films depict women in control of events (as Joan Crawford is in Nicholas Ray's *Johnny Guitar* [1954]) or in a position of command (as Marlene Dietrich has in Fritz Lang's *Rancho Notorious* [1952]). More typically, the action—raids, robberies, shootouts, and so on—is taken up with men's pursuits, almost as if women were ancillary to the plot. And sometimes the location can supply a sense so unduly masculine that the men seem to exist on an animal level. Thematically, the function of women in the Western is to humanize the situation by providing a necessarily feminine role—not primarily as victims requiring masculine help, but as bringers of civilized thinking to a brutalized environment, especially through an insistence on the value of human life. Although they frequently offer tenderness, consolation, and devotion, women are only attractive to the Western hero when they prove to have an independent toughness of their own.

5   The special qualities of the Western landscape often affect our awareness of main characters' personal histories. In the Eastern locale, the metropolitan existence allows characters to arrive and immediately be assimilated into the environment, their appearance often informing us of nothing more than their present occupations. But the arrival of the hero or villain in the Western setting immediately prompts discussion of who he is, where he came from, why he left. Sometimes no great mystery is implied, and yet much of the film is spent on speculation: is he a retired outlaw, a bounty hunter, a revenge seeker? The answer to such speculation supplied in the film is often nothing more than a hint that the hero has lost a loved one (wife, brother, father—less commonly, I think, a mother, though Jesse James in Henry King's *Jesse James* [1939] did lose his). But even this little biographical information seems quite necessary, for the individual stands out in the Western landscape—on the plain as he rides alone or in the bar when he asks for a whiskey (or a glass of milk).

6   For a simple contrast to this use of personal biography, consider a well-known urban film such as Alfred Hitchcock's *The 39 Steps* (1935). The film begins with the hero wandering the street of London for amusement and entering a music hall. We see that he is a visitor from the way he takes in the sights, and later we learn that he is a Canadian. We never learn anything else about him; he apparently knows no one in London, but for all we can tell he may not know anyone in Canada either. He's just one of million tourists. Hitchcock even omits any mention of his occupation, his interests, or his place in society (in the literary source he is an engineer). Nothing matters in regard to the hero past; life in the city demands only an intent awareness of the present.

7   Now of course it sometimes happens, in an urban film, that we need to know the hero's past. But in a Western we must have constant interest in it, for when we encounter him the character stands at a critical point in his career. He may have changed a good deal from what he was, and that change itself may have occurred a long time ago, but the plot line will force him to confront his former self. Henry King's *The Gunfighter* (1950) which Robert Warshow has examined in terms of this quality of the inescapable past, provides an archetypal example of the pattern of confrontation, as does Anthony Mann's *Bend of the River*

(1951), in which the reformed badman must evolve into the heroic good man or be drawn back to his old ways—a typical issue of many good Westerns. In the genre, nevertheless, character formation often seems to have been fixed before the film begins and what we are therefore introduced to is a rather grim, fully experienced, mature man confronting some crisis situation that is not entirely new to him. The landscape will establish the arena for the reenactment of certain events, but almost always the mere surface action is meaningless unless it has some bearing on what the character has been through, similar situations he faced earlier in his career, and whether he handles matters any better now. Similarly, there are the historical Westerns in which the predicaments grow out of larger social problems not solved in the past such as the relations between the Indians and the representatives of the government.

8   The interrelationships of landscape, characterization, and the past are natural to the genre. The basic locale is either a form of the primitive settlement (the town, the lonely ranch house) or the wilderness itself (the mesas and valleys), which includes the temporary encampments of cattlemen, as in Howard Hawks's *Red River* (1948), and pioneer wagons that represent mobile outposts of civilization, as in John Ford's *Wagonmaster* (1950). Both types of locale are associated with the endless attempts to overcome the hardship (sometimes brutality) connected with nature in its untamed form. Yet almost never is the elemental aspect of nature a primary threat to the humans playing out their dramas within it. Much more common is the essential neutrality or passivity of nature. In a common form of the showdown gunfight, both hero and villain find cover behind the mountains' massive rock formations. Nature, if not exactly indifferent, tends to be fair in its hostility. It represents the constant factor of life—eternal past, present, and future. With settings of this sort, the genre is readily susceptible to themes linking the individual's past and future to a present event.

9   Since the most elemental dramatic question posed visually by the genre has to do with the human ability to survive in this primitive environment, the particular battle of hero and villain is only one more piece of evidence of the eternal myth of humanity's struggle to bring civilization to the wilderness. Those virtues constantly needed for survival must therefore be part of the hero's characterization. Among those virtues are competence in the face of danger, courage, determination, and endurance, and so the past experience of the characters is often the crucial factor for their survival. The Western is not notable for visual surprises. We usually need to be prepared for the outcome of events, and this is another reason why the characters' past is put before us. In Mann's *Winchester '73* (1950) we may be surprised to learn, late in the film, that the hero and the villain are brothers, but it is an inevitable surprise, since we know that something in their past has made them enemies—a fact that is visually apparent from the beginning. It would have been a surprise for the genre if the evil brother had killed the good brother in the final shootout and gotten away scot-free, but the genre excludes that sort of possibility.

10   The possibilities really appropriate to the genre tend to be clear-cut, in keeping with the conventions of the landscape. Thus the dramatic conflict, though

it may contain finely shaded ambiguities of moral responsibility and guilt, is always overtly clear in the confrontation of good and bad characters. Refinements made by the best filmmakers usually affect the development of the conflict rather than the nature of the conflict. No filmmakers, presumably, would want to tamper with the landscape, and therefore the most suitable kinds of conflict for those locations seem to have been fixed long ago.

Beyond Formula: American Film Genres (New York: Harcourt Brace, 1976).

2

Critical Reading and Critique

CRITICAL READING

When writing papers in college, you are often called on to respond critically to source materials. Critical reading requires the abilities to both summarize and evaluate a presentation. As you have seen in Chapter 1, a *summary* is a brief restatement in your own words of the content of a passage. An *evaluation*, however, is a more difficult matter.

In your college work, you read to gain and *use* new information; but as sources are not equally valid or equally useful, you must learn to distinguish critically among them by evaluating them.

There is no ready-made formula for determining validity. Critical reading and its written equivalent—the *critique*—require discernment, sensitivity, imagination, knowledge of the subject, and above all, willingness to become involved in what you read. These skills cannot be taken for granted and are developed only through repeated practice. You must begin somewhere, though, and we recommend that you start by posing two broad categories of questions about passages, articles, and books that you read: (1) What is the author's purpose in writing? Does he or she succeed in this purpose? (2) To what extent do you agree with the author?

Question Category 1: What Is the Author's Purpose in Writing? Does He or She Succeed in This Purpose?

All critical reading *begins with an accurate summary*. Thus before attempting an evaluation, you must be able to locate an author's thesis and identify the selection's content and structure. You must understand the author's *purpose*. Authors write to

---

WHERE DO WE FIND WRITTEN CRITIQUES?

Here are just a few types of writing that involve critique:

Academic Writing

- **Research papers.** Critique sources in order to establish their usefulness.
- **Position papers.** Stake out a position by critiquing other positions.
- **Book reviews.** Combine summary with critique.
- **Essay exams.** Demonstrate understanding of course material by critiquing it.

Workplace Writing

- **Legal briefs and legal arguments.** Critique previous rulings or arguments made by opposing counsel.
- **Business plans and proposals.** Critique other, less cost-effective approaches.
- **Policy briefs.** Communicate failings of policies and legislation through critique.

---

inform, to persuade, and to entertain. A given piece may be primarily *informative* (a summary of the research on cloning), primarily *persuasive* (an argument on why the government must do something to alleviate homelessness), or primarily *entertaining* (a play about the frustrations of young lovers). Or it may be all three (as in John Steinbeck's novel *The Grapes of Wrath*, about migrant workers during the Great Depression). Sometimes, authors are not fully conscious of their purpose. Sometimes their purpose changes as they write. Also, more than one purpose can overlap: An essay may need to inform the reader about an issue in order to make a persuasive point. But if the finished piece is coherent, it will have a primary reason for having been written, and it should be apparent that the author is attempting primarily to inform, persuade, or entertain a particular audience. To identify this primary reason—this purpose—is your first job as a critical reader. Your next job is to determine how successful the author has been. As a critical reader, you bring different criteria, or standards of judgment, to bear when you read pieces intended to inform, persuade, or entertain.

Writing to Inform

A piece intended to inform will provide definitions, describe or report on a process, recount a story, give historical background, and/or provide facts and figures. An informational piece responds to questions such as the following:

What (or who) is _____ ?

How does _____ work?

What is the controversy or problem about?

What happened?

How and why did it happen?

What were the results?

What are the arguments for and against _____ ?

To the extent that an author answers these and related questions and the answers are a matter of verifiable record (you could check for accuracy if you had the time and inclination), the selection is intended to inform. Having determined this, you can organize your response by considering three other criteria: accuracy, significance, and fair interpretation of information.

EVALUATING INFORMATIVE WRITING

Accuracy of Information   If you are going to use any of the information presented, you must be satisfied that it is trustworthy. One of your responsibilities as a critical reader, then, is to find out if it is accurate. This means you should check facts against other sources. Government publications are often good resources for verifying facts about political legislation, population data, crime statistics, and the like. You can also search key terms in library databases and on the Web. Since material on the Web is essentially "self-published," however, you must be especially vigilant in assessing its legitimacy. In Chapter 7, on research, we provide a more detailed discussion of how you should approach Web sources. A wealth of useful information is now available on the Internet—but there is also a tremendous amount of misinformation, distorted "facts," and unsupported opinion.

Significance of Information   One useful question that you can put to a reading is "So what?" In the case of selections that attempt to inform, you may reasonably wonder whether the information makes a difference. What can the person who is reading gain from this information? How is knowledge advanced by the publication of this material? Is the information of importance to you or to others in a particular audience? Why or why not?

Fair Interpretation of Information   At times you will read reports, the sole function of which is to relate raw data or information. In these cases, you will build your response on the two questions in category 1, introduced on page 61: What is the author's purpose in writing? Does she or he succeed in this purpose? More frequently, once an author has presented information, he or she will attempt to evaluate or interpret it—which is only reasonable, since information that has not been evaluated or interpreted is of little use. One of your tasks as a critical reader is to make a distinction between the author's presentation of facts and figures and his or her attempts to evaluate them.

Watch for shifts from straightforward descriptions of factual information ("20% of the population") to assertions about what this information means ("*a mere* 20% of the population"), what its implications are, and so on. Pay attention to whether the logic with which the author connects interpretation with facts is sound. You may find that the information is valuable but the interpretation is not. Perhaps the author's conclusions are not justified. Could you offer a contrary explanation for the same facts? Does more information need to be gathered before firm conclusions can be drawn? Why?

Writing to Persuade

Writing is frequently intended to persuade—that is, to influence the reader's thinking. To make a persuasive case, the writer must begin with an assertion that is arguable, some statement about which reasonable people could disagree. Such an assertion, when it serves as the essential organizing principle of the article or book, is called a *thesis*. Here are two examples:

> Because they do not speak English, many children in this affluent land are being denied their fundamental right to equal educational opportunity.

> Bilingual education, which has been stridently promoted by a small group of activists with their own agenda, is detrimental to the very students it is supposed to serve.

Thesis statements such as these—and the subsequent assertions used to help support them—represent conclusions that authors have drawn as a result of researching and thinking about an issue. You go through the same process yourself when you write persuasive papers or critiques. And just as you are entitled to critically evaluate the assertions of authors you read, so your professors—and other students—are entitled to evaluate *your* assertions, whether they be encountered as written arguments or as comments made in class discussion.

Keep in mind that writers organize arguments by arranging evidence to support one conclusion and oppose (or dismiss) another. You can assess the validity of the argument and the conclusion by determining whether the author has (1) clearly defined key terms, (2) used information fairly, (3) argued logically and not fallaciously (see pp. 68–74).

EXERCISE **2.1**

Informative and Persuasive Thesis Statements

With a partner from your class, write one informative and one persuasive thesis statement for *three* of the topics listed in the last paragraph of this exercise. For example, for the topic of prayer in schools, your informative thesis statement could read this way:

Both advocates and opponents of school prayer frame their position as a matter of freedom.

Your persuasive thesis statement might be worded as follows:

As long as schools don't dictate what kinds of prayers students should say, then school prayer should be allowed and even encouraged.

Don't worry about taking a position that you agree with or feel you could support. The exercise doesn't require that you write an essay at this point. The topics:

school prayer
gun control
sex education in schools
grammar instruction in English class
violent lyrics in music
teaching computer skills in primary schools
curfews in college dormitories
course registration procedures

EVALUATING PERSUASIVE WRITING

Read the argument that follows: a recommendation to curtail the steep, recent rise in childhood obesity. We will illustrate our discussion on defining terms, using information fairly, and arguing logically by referring to Greg Critser's argument. The example critique that follows these illustrations will be based on this same argument.

Too Much of a Good Thing
Greg Critser

In an op-ed essay for the Los Angeles Times *(July 22, 2001), Greg Critser argues that, faced with a rising obesity epidemic, we should stigmatize overeating. Critser is careful to distinguish between stigmatizing the person and the act, but he makes no apologies for urging that we teach children that "[e]ating too much food is a bad thing." Critser has written a book on the obesity epidemic:* Fat Land: How Americans Became the Fattest People in the World *(Houghton Mifflin, 2003).*

1 Sometime over the next month or so, United Nations health and nutrition experts will convene in New York to begin discussing what many consider to be the pivotal medical issue of our day: obesity and its impact on children. For the UN, traditionally concerned with starvation and malnutrition, it is a historic first, following up on an alarm it sounded about obese adults in 1999. "Obesity," the

UN proclaimed, "is the dominant unmet global health issue, with Westernized countries topping the list."

2   Solid epidemiological data drives the effort. In Canada, Great Britain, Japan, Australia—even coastal China and Southeast Asia—the rate of childhood obesity has been soaring for more than a decade. Closer to home, at least 25% of all Americans under age nineteen are overweight or obese, a figure that has doubled over the last 30 years and a figure that moved the surgeon general to declare childhood obesity an epidemic. The cost in health care dollars to treat obesity's medical consequences—from diabetes to coronary heart disease to a variety of crippling bone conditions—will eventually make the battle against HIV/AIDS seem inexpensive. Yet in the U.S., the most important foot soldiers against obesity are increasingly paralyzed by years of media-induced food hysteria, over-generalized and outdated nutritional wisdom, and, truth be told, an unwillingness to set firm and sometimes unpopular food parameters. That infantry is the much-strained American family and its increasingly harried commandant, *Parentis americanus*. What it needs to promulgate is dietary restraint, something our ancestors knew simply as avoiding gluttony.

3   This is not to say that parents should be blamed for the nation's growing dietary permissiveness. They are wary of confronting their children's eating habits for a reason: For years, conventional wisdom held that food should never become a dinner table battleground. "Pressure causes tension," write Harvey and Marilyn Diamond, authors of the classic *Fit for Life*, which has sold more than 3 million copies. "Where food is concerned, tension is always to be avoided." The operative notion is that a child restrained from overeating will either rebel by secretly gorging when away from the table or, worse, will suffer such a loss of self-esteem that a lifetime of disastrous eating behavior will follow.

4   Of course, no one should be stigmatized for being overweight. But stigmatizing the unhealthful behaviors that cause obesity would conform with what we know about effective health messages. In both the campaign against unsafe sex and the campaign against smoking, stigmatizing such behaviors proved highly effective in reducing risk and harm. It's true, smokers—and homosexuals—may have experienced a modicum of stereotyping in the short run, but such is the price of every public health advance: short term pain for long term gain.

5   Another inhibition to imposing dietary restraint is the belief, promoted in handbook after handbook of parental advice, that 'kids know when they are full.' But perhaps not. In fact, new research suggests just the opposite: Kids don't know when they are full.

6   In a recent study, Pennsylvania State University nutritional scholar Barbara Rolls and her associates examined the eating habits of two groups of kids, one of three-year-olds, another of five-year-olds. The children were presented with a series of plates of macaroni and cheese. The first plate was a normal serving built around baseline nutritional needs; the second was slightly larger; and the third was what might be called "supersized."

7   What the researchers found is that the younger children consistently ate the same baseline amount, leaving more food on the plates with larger servings. The 5-year-olds, though, altered their eating behavior dramatically de-

pending on the amount they were served, devouring whatever was on the plate. Something had happened. The mere presence of an oversized portion had induced exaggerated eating. The authors concluded that "these early years may provide a unique opportunity for interventions that reduce the risk of developing overweight." Those interventions "should include clear information on appropriate portion sizes for children."

8   Theorizing aside, our disinclination to restrain eating flies in the face of overwhelming evidence that, of all age groups, children seem to be the ones who respond most positively to dietary advice. In four randomized studies of obese 6- to 12-year-olds, those who were offered frequent, simple behavioral advice were substantially less overweight 10 years later than kids who did not get the advice. In fact, 30% of those studied were no longer obese at all.

9   The case for early intervention has been further buttressed by new studies on another age-old medical injunction: never put a kid on a diet. (The concern was that under-nutrition could lead to stunted growth.) But as the authors of a study of 1,062 kids under age three concluded in the journal *Pediatrics*, "a supervised, low-saturated-fat and low-cholesterol diet has no influence on growth during the first three years of life." Overweight kids who were put on such a diet ended up with better, more moderate eating habits.

10   Changing the eating habits of children, though, is antithetical to some notions many parents hold dear. And to some it seems a relic of an earlier, more religious era of moral certainties when gluttony was vilified as one of the seven deadly sins. Many boomer parents believe, as one parent and nutritionist said at a recent summit on childhood obesity, that "kids have the right to make bad nutrition decisions." That may be true. But ours is a world where at least a billion dollars a year is spent by just one fast-food chain to convince families to visit a crazy-looking clown with his own playground and purchase a thousand supersize calories for a mere $2.50. McDonald's official line today is that three meals a week at its restaurants are perfectly acceptable for an average kid. That's three meals a week of grease, refined flour, and a jumbo shot of sugar.

11   Given today's bounty of cheap and unhealthful food alternatives, and given the inconvenience that goes with making good nutritional choices, one might wonder if a campaign against over-consumption, a campaign advocating restraint, could work. On this point, we might take a cue from the French. In the early 20th century France, in response to its first experiences with widespread child obesity, launched the puericulture movement, which focused on excessive weight gain in early childhood and adolescence. Its prescription: All meals should be adult-supervised; all portions should be moderate, with 'seconds' a rare treat. All but an occasional small snack were forbidden. As its historian Peter N. Stearns writes in *Fat History*, puericulture's message was simple: Eating too much food is a bad thing.

12   Therein lies at least part of the explanation for the legendary leanness of the French: They were taught in childhood not to overeat. And it didn't seem to do much harm to their self-esteem.

Critical Reading Practice

Before continuing with the chapter's reading, look back at the Critical Reading for Summary box on page 6 of Chapter 1. Use each of the guidelines listed there to examine the essay by Critser. Note in the margins of the selection, or on a separate sheet of paper, the essay's main point, subpoints, and use of examples.

PERSUASIVE STRATEGIES

Clearly Defined Terms   The validity of an argument depends to some degree on how carefully an author has defined key terms. Take the assertion, for example, that American society must be grounded in "family values." Just what do people who use this phrase mean by it? The validity of their argument depends on whether they and their readers agree on a definition of "family values"—as well as what it means to be "grounded in" family values. If an author writes that in the recent past, "America's elites accepted as a matter of course that a free society can sustain itself only through virtue and temperance in the people" (Charles Murray, "The Coming White Underclass," *Wall Street Journal*, 20 Oct. 1993), readers need to know what, exactly, the author means by "elites" and by "virtue and temperance" before they can assess the validity of the argument. In such cases, the success of the argument—its ability to persuade—hinges on the definition of a term. So, in responding to an argument, be sure you (and the author) are clear on what exactly is being argued. Only then can you respond to the logic of the argument, to the author's use of evidence, and to the author's conclusions.

Critser supports his argument for launching a campaign to end overconsumption by stating that efforts to stigmatize "unhealthful behaviors ... conform with what we know about effective health messages." While Critser does provide examples of what he considers "effective health messages," his definition of *effective* is open to debate. By what measures have "the campaign against unsafe sex and the campaign against smoking" been effective? The reader might well point to level HIV infection rates in the United States and continuing billion-dollar profits by tobacco companies and challenge Critser's definition of *effective*.

Fair Use of Information   Information is used as evidence in support of arguments. When you encounter such evidence, ask yourself two questions: (1) "Is the information accurate and up-to-date?" At least a portion of an argument becomes invalid if the information used to support it is inaccurate or out-of-date. (2) "Has the author cited *representative* information?" The evidence used in an argument must be presented in a spirit of fair play. An author is less than ethical who presents only evidence favoring his views when he is well aware that contrary evidence exists. For instance, it would be dishonest to argue that an economic recession is imminent and to cite only indicators of economic downturn while ignoring and failing to cite contrary (positive) evidence.

Critser uses the information he cites fairly and accurately: He presents statistics in paragraph 2 on the rise of childhood obesity; he refers to a published study in paragraph 6 to refute the assertion that "kids know when they are full"; and he cites studies again in paragraphs 8 and 9. However, Critser chooses not to use, let alone mention, other information that bears on the topic of weight gain. For exampler, he argues that we should create an antiobesity campaign that stigmatizes the behavior of those who lack the willpower to stop eating. The assumption: A lack of willpower is the primary reason people are obese. Whether or not this view is correct, a great deal of information (scientific studies included) suggests that other causes may be implicated in obesity. By not raising the possibility that genes or hormones, for instance, might play a role, information about which Critser is undoubtedly aware, he fails to present full and representative information on his chosen topic. True, the op-ed piece is a brief form, leaving not much room to develop an argument. Still, Critser leaves the impression that he has cited the most pertinent information on combating obesity when, in fact, he has disregarded a great deal of information.

Logical Argumentation: Avoiding Logical Fallacies

At some point, you will need to respond to the logic of the argument itself. To be convincing, an argument should be governed by principles of *logic*— clear and orderly thinking. This does *not* mean that an argument should not be biased. A biased argument—that is, an argument weighted toward one point of view and against others, which is in fact the nature of argument— may be valid as long as it is logically sound.

Several examples of faulty thinking and logical fallacies to watch for follow.

Emotionally Loaded Terms   Writers sometimes attempt to sway readers by using emotionally charged words—words with positive connotations to sway readers to their own point of view (e.g., "family values") or words with negative connotations to sway readers away from the opposing point of view. The fact that an author uses emotionally loaded terms does not necessarily invalidate the argument. Emotional appeals are perfectly legitimate and time-honored modes of persuasion. But in academic writing, which is grounded in logical argumentation, they should not be the *only* means of persuasion. You should be sensitive to *how* emotionally loaded terms are being used. In particular, are they being used deceptively or to hide the essential facts?

Critser's use of the word *gluttony* inserts an emotionally charged, moralizing tone into his argument. Gluttony is one of the "seven deadly sins" that, for centuries, people have been warned against committing, so destructive are they of character. Critser takes pains to say that he is no moralist ("no one should be stigmatized for being overweight"), but that claim is made false by his introduction of a "sin" into a discussion about public health. Critser operates with a value judgment that he does not fully want to own. Critical readers might legitimately object to the notion that overeating is a "sin" that ought to be stigmatized.

Ad Hominem Argument   In an *ad hominem* argument, the writer rejects opposing views by attacking the person who holds them. By calling opponents names, an author avoids the issue. Consider this excerpt from a political speech:

> I could more easily accept my opponent's plan to increase revenues by collecting on delinquent tax bills if he had paid more than a hundred dollars in state taxes in each of the past three years. But the fact is, he's a millionaire with a millionaire's tax shelters. This man hasn't paid a wooden nickel for the state services he and his family depend on. So I ask you: Is *he* the one to be talking about taxes to *us*?

It could well be that the opponent has paid virtually no state taxes for three years; but this fact has nothing to do with, and is a ploy to divert attention from, the merits of a specific proposal for increasing revenues. The proposal is lost in the attack against the man himself, an attack that violates the principles of logic. Writers (and speakers) must make their points by citing evidence in support of their views and by challenging contrary evidence.

Faulty Cause and Effect   The fact that one event precedes another in time does not mean that the first event has caused the second. An example: Fish begin dying by the thousands in a lake near your hometown. An environmental group immediately cites chemical dumping by several manufacturing plants as the cause. But other causes are possible: A disease might have affected the fish; the growth of algae might have contributed to the deaths; or acid rain might be a factor. The origins of an event are usually complex and are not always traceable to a single cause. So you must carefully examine cause-and-effect reasoning when you find a writer using it. In Latin, this fallacy is known as *post hoc, ergo propter hoc* ("after this, therefore because of this").

Critser claims in this argument that dietary restraint will help reduce childhood obesity. Readers familiar with the literature on obesity know that a debate exists concerning the causes of the condition. For instance, some obese people may eat as little as their thin friends do but still lose no weight. For them, it is clear, lack of willpower does not contribute to their weight problems. Genes and body chemistry may play causal roles, but Critser mentions no causes other than lack of willpower. Asserting that one cause

TONE

Related to "emotionally loaded terms" is *tone*. When we speak of the tone of a piece of writing, we refer to the overall emotional effect produced by the writer's choice of language.

- Were a film reviewer to repeatedly use such terms as "wonderful," "adorable," "magnificent performance," when discussing a film and its actors, we might call the tone "gushing."
- If a columnist, in referring to a politician's tax proposal, used such language as "obscene," "the lackeys of big business fat cats," and "sleazeball techniques," we would call the tone "angry."
- If another writer were to use language like "That's a great idea. Let's all give three cheers," when he clearly meant just the opposite, we would call the tone "sarcastic."

These are extreme examples of tone; but tone can be more muted, particularly if the writer makes a special effort *not* to inject emotion into the writing. Almost any adjective describing human emotion can be attached to *tone* to describe the mood that is conveyed by the writer and the writing: playful, objective, brutal, dispassionate, sly, apologetic, rueful, cynical, hopeful, gleeful.

As we've indicated above in "Emotionally Loaded Terms," the fact that a writer's tone is highly emotional does not necessarily mean that the writer's argument is invalid. Conversely, a neutral tone does not ensure an argument's validity. One who argues passionately is not necessarily wrong, any more than one who comes across as objective and measured is necessarily right. In either case, we have to examine the validity of the argument on its own merits. We should recognize that we may have been manipulated into agreeing or disagreeing largely through an author's tone, rather than through her or his arguments.

Keep in mind, also, that many college instructors are likely to be put off by student writing that projects a highly emotional tone, a quality they will often consider more appropriate for the op-ed page of the student newspaper than for academic or preprofessional work. (One giveaway indicator of inappropriate emotion is the exclamation mark, which should be used very sparingly.)

leads to an effect—or failing to assert that multiple causes do—gives readers the right to question the logic of an argument.

Either/Or Reasoning   Either/or reasoning also results from an unwillingness to recognize complexity. If an author analyzes a problem and offers only two courses of action, one of which he or she refutes, then you are entitled to object that the other is not thereby true. Usually, several other options (at the very least) are possible. For whatever reason, the author has chosen to overlook them. As an example, suppose you are reading a selection on genetic engineering and the author builds an argument on the basis of the following:

> Research in gene splicing is at a crossroads: Either scientists will be carefully monitored by civil authorities and their efforts limited to acceptable applications, such as disease control; or, lacking regulatory guidelines, scientists will set their own ethical standards and begin programs in embryonic manipulation that, however well intended, exceed the proper limits of human knowledge.

Certainly, other possibilities for genetic engineering exist beyond the two mentioned here. But the author limits debate by establishing an either/or choice. Such limitation is artificial and does not allow for complexity. As a critical reader, be on the alert for either/or reasoning.

Hasty Generalization   Writers are guilty of hasty generalization when they draw their conclusions from too little evidence or from unrepresentative evidence. To argue that scientists should not proceed with the human genome project because a recent editorial urged that the project be abandoned is to make a hasty generalization. This lone editorial may be unrepresentative of the views of most individuals—both scientists and laypeople—who have studied and written about the matter. To argue that one should never obey authority because Stanley Milgram's Yale University experiments in the 1960s show the dangers of obedience is to ignore the fact that Milgram's experiment was concerned primarily with obedience to *immoral* authority. Thus, the experimental situation was unrepresentative of most routine demands for obedience—for example, to obey a parental rule or to comply with a summons for jury duty—and a conclusion about the malevolence of all authority would be a hasty generalization.

False Analogy   Comparing one person, event, or issue to another may be illuminating, but it may also be confusing or misleading. Differences between the two may be more significant than the similarities, and conclusions drawn from one may not necessarily apply to the other. A writer who argues that it is reasonable to quarantine people with AIDS because quarantine has been effective in preventing the spread of smallpox is assuming an analogy between AIDS and smallpox that (because of the differences between the two diseases) is not valid.

Just so, Critser's comparison between a proposed campaign to stigmatize obesity and "highly effective" campaigns that stigmatize unsafe sex and smoking (paragraph 4) suggests that obesity is fundamentally similar to unsafe sex and smoking. Critser assumes that all three damaging behaviors have similar causes (i.e., lack of self-restraint) that can be addressed using similar means (campaigns to stigmatize). But if the analogy between obesity and smoking or unsafe sex breaks down because we find that their causes differ (and research is far from conclusive on the matter), then readers have no reason to agree with Critser that campaigns that reduce smoking and unsafe sex will help to reduce obesity.

Begging the Question   To beg the question is to assume as a proven fact the very thesis being argued. To assert, for example, that America is not in decline because it is as strong and prosperous as ever is not to prove anything: it is merely to repeat the claim in different words. This fallacy is also known as *circular reasoning*.

In one sense, in advocating restraint to lower the incidence of obesity, Critser does an admirable job. He raises and rebuts two arguments against urging restraint on those who weigh too much (in paragraphs 3–7) and then argues directly that restraint is a successful strategy in combating obesity (in paragraphs 8–9). But Critser also assumes that lack of restraint, alone, is primarily the cause of obesity. Given the volume of compelling evidence (which he does not mention) that genes and other factors may play a role in weight gain, he would do well to argue—and not assume—that lack of restraint is a primary reason people gain weight. But he assumes the validity of this important point instead of proving it. He also assumes the validity of two lesser points: (1) that the campaigns against unsafe sex and smoking have been effective; and (2) that obesity is a condition comparable to unsafe sex and smoking and, thus, a condition that would benefit from campaigns to stigmatize unhealthy behaviors.

Non Sequitur   *Non sequitur* is Latin for "it does not follow"; the term is used to describe a conclusion that does not logically follow from a premise. "Since minorities have made such great strides in the past few decades," a writer may argue, "we no longer need affirmative action programs." Aside from the fact that the premise itself is arguable (*have* minorities made such great strides?), it does not follow that because minorities *may* have made great strides, there is no further need for affirmative action programs.

Oversimplification   Be alert for writers who offer easy solutions to complicated problems. "America's economy will be strong again if we all 'buy American,'" a politician may argue. But the problems of America's economy are complex and cannot be solved by a slogan or a simple change in buying habits. Likewise, a writer who argues that we should ban genetic engineering assumes that simple solutions ("just say 'no'") will be sufficient to deal with the complex moral dilemmas raised by this new technology.

For example, as noted, Critser does consider how causes other than lack of willpower may contribute to obesity. This is not to say that a lack of restraint plays no valid or even major role in weight gain. People can and should learn to say "no" to supersized fries. But to the extent Critser does not acknowledge other causes of obesity, he leaves himself open to the charge of oversimplification. His proposed "campaign against over-consumption" is one solution. It will not, alone, solve the obesity problem.

Understanding Logical Fallacies

Make a list of the nine logical fallacies discussed in the last section. Briefly define each one in your own words. Then, in a group of three or four class-mates, refer to your definitions and the examples we've provided for each logical fallacy. Collaborate with your group to find or invent examples for each of the fallacies. Compare your examples with those generated by the other groups in your class.

Writing To Entertain

Authors write not only to inform and persuade but also to entertain. One response to entertainment is a hearty laugh, but it is possible to entertain without laughter: A good book or play or poem may prompt you to reflect, grow wistful, become elated, get angry. Laughter is only one of many possible reactions. As with a response to an informative piece or an argument, your response to an essay, poem, story, play, novel, or film should be precisely stated and carefully developed. Ask yourself some of the following questions (you won't have space to explore all of them, but try to consider some of the most important): Did I care for the portrayal of a certain character? Did that character (or a group of characters united by occupation, age, ethnicity, etc.) seem overly sentimental, for example, or heroic? Did his adversaries seem too villainous or stupid? Were the situations believable? Was the action interesting or merely formulaic? Was the theme developed subtly or powerfully, or did the work come across as preachy or shrill? Did the action at the end of the work follow plausibly from what had come before? Was the language fresh and incisive or stale and predictable? Explain as specifically as possible what elements of the work seemed effective or ineffective and why. Offer an overall assessment, elaborating on your views.

Question Category 2: To What Extent Do You Agree or Disagree with the Author?

When formulating a critical response to a source, try to distinguish your evaluation of the author's purpose and success at achieving that purpose from your agreement or disagreement with the author's views. The distinction allows you to respond to a piece of writing on its merits. As an unbiased, evenhanded critic, you evaluate an author's clarity of presentation, use of evidence, and adherence to principles of logic. To what extent has the author succeeded in achieving his or her purpose? Still withholding judgment, offer your assessment and give the author (in effect) a grade. Significantly, your assessment of the presentation may not coincide with your views of the author's conclusions: You may agree with an author entirely but feel that the presentation is superficial; you may find the author's logic and use of evidence to be rock solid but at the same time may resist certain conclusions. A critical evaluation works well when it is conducted in two parts. After evaluating the author's purpose and design for achieving that purpose, respond to the author's main assertions. In doing so, you'll want to identify points of agreement and disagreement and also evaluate assumptions.

IDENTIFY POINTS OF AGREEMENT AND DISAGREEMENT

Be precise in identifying points of agreement and disagreement with an author. You should state as clearly as possible what *you* believe, and an effective way of doing this is to define your position in relation to that presented in the piece. Whether you agree enthusiastically, disagree, or agree with reservations, you can organize your reactions in two parts: (1) summarize the author's position; and (2) state your own position and elaborate on your reasons for holding it. The elaboration, in effect, becomes an argument itself, and this is true regardless of the position you take. An opinion is effective when you support it by supplying evidence. Without such evidence, opinions cannot be authoritative. "I thought the article on inflation was lousy." Why? "I just thought so, that's all." This opinion is worthless because the criticism is imprecise: The critic has taken neither the time to read the article carefully nor the time to explore his own reactions carefully.

EXERCISE 2.4

Exploring Your Viewpoints—in Three Paragraphs

Go to a Web site that presents short persuasive essays on current social issues, such as reason.com, opinion-pages.org, drudgereport.com, or Speakout.com. Or go to an Internet search engine and type in a social issue together with the word "articles," "editorials," or "opinion," and see what you find. Locate a selection on a topic of interest that takes a clear, argumentative position. Write one paragraph summarizing the author's key argument. Write two paragraphs articulating your agreement or disagreement with the author. (Devote each paragraph to a *single* point of agreement or disagreement.) Be sure to explain why you think or feel the way you do and, wherever possible, cite relevant evidence—from your reading, experience, or observation.

EXPLORE THE REASONS FOR AGREEMENT AND DISAGREEMENT:
EVALUATE ASSUMPTIONS

One way of elaborating your reactions to a reading is to explore the underlying *reasons* for agreement and disagreement. Your reactions are based largely on assumptions that you hold and how these assumptions compare with the author's. An *assumption* is a fundamental statement about the world and its operations that you take to be true. A writer's assumptions may be explicitly stated; but just as often assumptions are implicit and you will have to "ferret them out," that is, to infer them. Consider an example:

> *In vitro* fertilization and embryo transfer are brought about outside the bodies of the couple through actions of third parties whose competence and technical activity determine the success of the procedure. Such fertilization entrusts the life and identity of the embryo into the power of doctors and biologists and establishes the domination of technology over the origin and destiny of the human person. Such a relationship of domination is in itself contrary to the dignity and equality that must be common to parents and children.*

This paragraph is quoted from the February 1987 Vatican document on artificial procreation. Cardinal Joseph Ratzinger, principal author of the document, makes an implicit assumption in this paragraph: No good can come of the domination of technology over conception. The use of technology to bring about conception is morally wrong. Yet thousands of childless couples, Roman Catholics included, have rejected this assumption in favor of its opposite: Conception technology is an aid to the barren couple; far from creating a relationship of unequals, the technology brings children into the world who will be welcomed with joy and love.

Assumptions provide the foundation on which entire presentations are built. If you find an author's assumptions invalid—that is, not supported by factual evidence—or if you disagree with value-based assumptions underlying an author's positions, you may well disagree with conclusions that follow from these assumptions. The author of a book on developing nations may include a section outlining the resources and time that will be required to industrialize a particular country and so upgrade its general welfare. Her assumption—that industrialization in that particular country will ensure or even affect the general welfare—may or may not be valid. If you do not share the assumption, in your eyes the rationale for the entire book may be undermined.

How do you determine the validity of assumptions once you have identified them? In the absence of more scientific criteria, you may determine va-

---

*From the Vatican document *Instruction on Respect for Human Life in Its Origin and on the Dignity of Procreation*, given at Rome, from the Congregation for the Doctrine of the Faith, 22 Feb. 1987, as presented in *Origins: N.C. Documentary Service* 16.40 (19 Mar. 1987): 707.

lidity by how well the author's assumptions stack up against your own experience, observations, reading, and values. A caution, however: The overall value of an article or book may depend only to a small degree on the validity of the author's assumptions. For instance, a sociologist may do a fine job of gathering statistical data about the incidence of crime in urban areas along the eastern seaboard. The sociologist also might be a Marxist, and you may disagree with the subsequent analysis of the data. Yet you may still find the data extremely valuable for your own work.

Readers will want to examine two assumptions at the heart of Critser's proposal to launch a campaign against overeating. The first is that lack of willpower alone causes, or primarily causes, obesity. While Critser does not directly assert this cause-and-effect relationship, he implies it by failing to mention other possible causes of obesity. If, for instance, genes or hormones are involved in the weight gain of some people, then it seems cruel to argue that their lack of willpower is somehow responsible—that if only they "tried harder" they could shed those unwanted pounds. Readers may also want to examine another of Critser's assumptions, that a moralizing tone is appropriate to a discussion of public health. Readers might take a different view, based on a very different assumption: that in combating problems in public health, one must deal with behaviors, not with attitudes and values associated with behaviors. Thus, in campaigns to reduce HIV infections, one would not speak of "sin" (as "gluttony" is a sin) but would instead focus strictly on reducing behaviors that spread infection. Readers are entitled to meet each of an author's assumptions with assumptions of their own; to evaluate the validity of those assumptions; and to begin formulating a critique, based on their agreement or disagreement.

CRITIQUE

In Chapter 1 we focused on summary—the condensed presentation of ideas from another source. Summary is key to much of academic writing because it relies so heavily on the works of others for support of claims. It's not going too far to say that summarizing is the critical thinking skill from which a majority of academic writing builds. However, most academic thinking and writing do not stop at summary; usually we use summary to restate our understanding of things we see or read. Then we put that summary to use. In academic writing, one typical use of summary is as a prelude to critique.

A *critique* is a *formalized, critical reading of a passage*. It also is a personal response, but writing a critique is considerably more rigorous than saying that a movie is "great," or a book is "fascinating," or "I didn't like it." These are all responses, and, as such, they're a valid, even essential, part of your understanding of what you see and read. But such responses don't illuminate the subject for anyone—even you—if you haven't explained how you arrived at your conclusions.

Your task in writing a critique is to turn your critical reading of a passage into a systematic evaluation in order to deepen your reader's (and your own) understanding of that passage. Among other things, you're interested in determining what an author says, how well the points are made, what assumptions underlie the argument, what issues are overlooked, and what implications can be drawn from such an analysis. Critiques, positive or negative, should include a fair and accurate summary of the passage; they also should include a statement of your own assumptions. It is important to remember that you bring to bear an entire set of assumptions about the world. Stated or not, these assumptions underlie every evaluative comment you make; you therefore have an obligation, both to the reader and to yourself, to clarify your standards by making your assumptions explicit. Not only do your readers stand to gain by your forthrightness, but you do as well: In the process of writing a critical assessment, you are forced to examine your own knowledge, beliefs, and assumptions. Ultimately, the critique is a way of learning about yourself—yet another example of the ways in which writing is useful as a tool for critical thinking.

How to Write Critiques

You may find it useful to organize your critiques in five sections: introduction, summary, assessment of the presentation (on its own terms), your response to the presentation, and conclusion.

The box opposite offers some guidelines for writing critiques. Note that they are guidelines, not a rigid formula. Thousands of authors write critiques that do not follow the structure outlined here. Until you are more confident and practiced in writing critiques, however, we suggest you follow these guidelines. They are meant not to restrict you, but rather to provide a workable sequence for writing critiques.

DEMONSTRATION: CRITIQUE

The critique that follows is based on Greg Critser's "Too Much of a Good Thing," which appeared in the *Los Angeles Times* as an op-ed piece on July 22, 2001 (see pages 65–67) and which we have to some extent already begun to examine. In this formal critique, you will see that it is possible to agree with an author's main point or proposal, at least provisionally, but disagree with his or her method of demonstration, or argument. Critiquing a different selection, you could just as easily accept the author's facts and figures but reject the conclusion he draws from them. As long as you carefully articulate the author's assumptions and your own, explaining in some detail your agreement and disagreement, the critique is yours to take in whatever direction you see fit.

Let's summarize the preceding sections by returning to the core questions that guide critical reading. You will see how, when applied to Greg Critser's argument, they help to set up a critique.

GUIDELINES FOR WRITING CRITIQUES

- *Introduce.* Introduce both the passage under analysis and the author. State the author's main argument and the point(s) you intend to make about it.

  Provide background material to help your readers understand the relevance or appeal of the passage. This background material might include one or more of the following: an explanation of why the subject is of current interest; a reference to a possible controversy surrounding the subject of the passage or the passage itself; biographical information about the author; an account of the circumstances under which the passage was written; or a reference to the intended audience of the passage.

- *Summarize.* Summarize the author's main points, making sure to state the author's purpose for writing.

- *Assess the presentation.* Evaluate the validity of the author's presentation, as distinct from your points of agreement or disagreement. Comment on the author's success in achieving his or her purpose by reviewing three or four specific points. You might base your review on one (or more) of the following criteria:

  Is the information accurate?

  Is the information significant?

  Has the author defined terms clearly?

  Has the author used and interpreted information fairly?

  Has the author argued logically?

- *Respond to the presentation.* Now it is your turn to respond to the author's views. With which views do you agree? With which do you disagree? Discuss your reasons for agreement and disagreement, when possible, tying these reasons to assumptions—both the author's and your own.

- *Conclude.* State your conclusions about the overall validity of the piece—your assessment of the author's success at achieving his or her aims and your reactions to the author's views. Remind the reader of the weaknesses and strengths of the passage.

What Is the Author's Purpose in Writing?

As is the case with most editorials, Greg Critser's "Too Much of a Good Thing" is an argument. He wants readers to accept his proposal for resolving the obesity epidemic among children. Parents, Critser argues, should supervise what and how much their kids eat. Those who learn lessons of dietary restraint early on can avoid weight problems later in life.

Does He or She Succeed in This Purpose?

Critser takes a behavioral approach to the problem of obesity. To the extent that obesity is caused by undisciplined eating habits, his proposal is logical and convincing. But other studies show that not all causes of obesity are rooted in poor eating habits. Genetic makeup and hormone imbalances may also be at work. Critser makes no mention of these, and his analysis and proposed solution therefore seem limited. In addition, he adopts an antifat, judgmental tone in the essay that will likely offend people who are trying to lose weight. In sum, Critser is only partially successful in his argument.

To What Extent Do You Agree or Disagree with the Author? Evaluate Assumptions.

Because Critser's analysis and proposed solution are based on the assumption that obesity has a single cause (poor eating habits), he opens himself to the objection that he has oversimplified the problem. Still, common sense suggests that overweight and obese people do contribute to their conditions by making unhealthy dietary choices. So Critser's suggestion that we teach children to eat moderately before they become obese is worth supporting—provided care is taken to acknowledge the nonbehavioral causes of obesity. Critser's moralistic tone gets in the way of an otherwise reasonable (if limited) argument. Of course, one might object to his tone but continue to find merit in his proposal.

The selections you will be likely to critique are those, like Critser's, that argue a specific position. Indeed, every argument you read is an invitation to agreement or disagreement. It remains only for you to speak up and justify your position.

MODEL CRITIQUE*

Critique of Greg Critser's "Too Much of a Good Thing"

1   Citing statistics on the alarming increase in the rates of childhood obesity, especially in the industrialized West, Greg Critser (L.A. Times Op-Ed, 22 July 2001) argues that parents can help avert obesity in their own homes by more closely supervising the diets of their children, serving reasonably sized portions, and limiting snacks. Critser, who has extensively researched obesity in his book Fat Land: How Americans Become the Fattest People in the World (Houghton Mifflin 2003), argues that through education we can create a leaner cultural norm, much as the French did earlier in the century when faced with a similar problem.

2   The stakes for maintaining a healthy body weight couldn't be higher. Fully one-quarter of American

*References to Critser are to his article as reprinted in *A Sequence for Academic Writing*.

children through the age of eighteen "are overweight or obese"--an "epidemic," according to the United States Surgeon General (66). Not only are obese individuals at increased risk for a wide range of medical problems, but the nation as a whole will absorb enormous costs for their obesity, "eventually mak[ing] the battle against HIV/AIDS seem inexpensive" (66). Clearly we have good reason to fight the rise of obesity, and Critser's suggestion that individual families become a battleground for that fight makes perfect sense, as long as we realize that there will be other battlegrounds (for example, the hospital, the pharmacy, and the genetics lab). We should also take care that in "stigmatizing the unhealthful behaviors that cause obesity" (66) we do not turn a public health campaign into a moral crusade.

3   It takes no advanced degree in nutrition to accept the claim that children (indeed, all of us) should learn to eat in moderation. Apparently, before the age of five the lesson isn't even needed. Younger children, entirely on their own, will limit how much food they eat at a meal regardless of the amounts served. By five, however, they will eat whatever is put before them. In a culture of the "supersized," high-fat, sugar-loaded, fast-food meal, such lack of restraint can lead to obesity. If we can teach children before their fifth birthday what counts as a reasonable portion, they might learn--for life--to eat in moderation. Critser cites other research to show that simple and yet profound dietary lessons, learned early, can make all the difference in averting a life spent battling the scale. He wisely gives parents an important role in teaching these lessons because parents, after all, teach all sorts of lessons. However, with statistics showing that roughly half of the adult population in this country is overweight or obese, Critser may want to urge parents to learn lessons about moderation themselves before attempting to become teachers for their children.

4   Critser's plan for combating the rise of childhood obesity through education is certainly reasonable, as far as it goes. But he focuses almost exclusively on behavioral factors when scientists have discovered that obesity has other, nonbehavioral causes (Gibbs). In labs across the world, researchers are identifying genes and hormones that influence weight gain. No one fully understands all the mechanisms by which overweight people, who may eat as little as their skinnier counter-parts, gain or shed pounds. But it is clear that being fat is <u>not</u> simply about lacking willpower--that is, about "unhealthful behaviors" (66) around food. Thus, we should not expect Critser's approach of teaching

dietary moderation to work in every case. For many people, solutions to weight gain will be found both in new dietary behaviors and in medicines that come from labs where researchers study how the body burns and stores fat. To the extent that obesity is the result of a child's inability to say "no" to a supersized meal, we should teach restraint just as Critser advises. But his behavioral fix will not work for everyone, and parents should be instructed on what to do when teaching restraint, alone, fails to keep their children reasonably trim.

5   A more serious problem with Critser's argument is his use (twice) of the word "gluttony" and the judgmental attitude it implies. Early in the essay Critser argues that American parents need "to promulgate . . . dietary restraint, something our ancestors knew simply as avoiding gluttony" (66). Gluttony was one of the seven deadly sins (along with pride, greed, envy, anger, lust, and sloth), which Christian theologians have been denouncing for nearly 1500 years (University) to little effect. While Critser insists that "no one should be stigmatized for being overweight," he advocates "stigmatizing the unhealthful behaviors that cause obesity" (66), assuming that people distinguish between the sin and the sinner. In practice, people rarely do. Critser does little to distance himself from anti-fat bias after introducing the bias-heavy term "gluttony" into the essay--which is a mistake: the overweight and obese have a hard enough time losing weight. They should not have to suffer the judgments of those who suggest "that thinness signals self-discipline and self-respect, whereas fatness signals self-contempt and lack of resolve" (Worley).

6   Given a proposal that is otherwise so sensible, Critser doesn't need to complicate matters by inviting moral judgments. He is at his most convincing when he makes a straightforward recommendation to change the behavior of children based on sound scientific research. Effective dietary strategies can be taught, and parents are the best teachers in this case as long as they realize that teaching restraint will be only one of several approaches and that judgments equating thinness with virtue should have no place in our efforts. We face a difficult challenge in meeting the growing problem of childhood obesity, and for the most part Greg Critser suggests a reasonable and workable place to begin.

Works Cited

Critser, Greg. "Too Much of a Good Thing." Editorial. Los Angeles Times 22 July 2001.

Gibbs, W. Wayt. "Gaining on Fat." <u>Scientific American</u> Aug.
  1996.
University of Leicester History of Art Department. "Seven
  Deadly Sins." <u>University of Leicester Web site</u> 20 Dec.
  2001. 2 Aug. 2002 <http://www.le.ac.uk/arthistory/
  seedcorn/faq-sds.html>.
Worley, Mary. "Fat and Happy: In Defense of Fat
  Acceptance." <u>National Association to Advance Fat
  Acceptance</u> 22 Aug. 2002 <http://www.naafa.org>.

EXERCISE 2.5

Informal Critique of Sample Essay

Before reading the discussion of this model critique, write your own informal response to the critique. What are its strengths and weaknesses? To what extent does the critique follow the general guidelines for writing critiques that we outlined on page 79? To the extent it varies from the guidelines, speculate on why. Jot down some ideas for a critique that take a different approach to Critser's essay.

Discussion

- Paragraph 1 of the model critique introduces the selection to be reviewed, along with the author, and summarizes the author's main claim.

- Paragraph 2 provides brief background information. It sets a context that explains why the topic of obesity is important. The paragraph ends with the writer's thesis, offering qualified support for the proposal that parents should teach children to eat moderately.

- Paragraph 3 summarizes the argument of Critser's editorial. Note that the topic sentence expresses approval of the editorial's main (argumentative) thesis: Children should learn to eat in moderation.

- Paragraph 4 raises the first objection to Critser's argument, that he misrepresents the complexity of obesity by discussing only behavioral causes and solutions. The paragraph expresses qualified support for his position, but suggests that other, nonbehavioral ways of viewing the problem and other, nonbehavioral solutions should be explored.

- Paragraph 5 raises a significant disagreement with Critser's moralistic tone. The paragraph lays out the ways in which Critser is inappropriately judgmental.

- Paragraph 6, the conclusion, summarizes the overall position of the critique—to accept Critser's basic recommendation that parents teach dietary restraint to children, but to reject the moral judgments that make obese people feel inadequate.

CRITICAL READING FOR CRITIQUE

- **Use the tips from Critical Reading for Summary on page 6:** Remember to examine the context; note the title and subtitle; identify the main point; identify the subpoints; break the reading into sections; distinguish between points, examples, and counterarguments; watch for transitions within and between paragraphs; and read actively.
- **Establish the writer's primary purpose in writing:** Is the piece primarily meant to inform, persuade, or entertain?
- **Evaluate informative writing. Use these criteria (among others):**
  Accuracy of information
  Significance of information
  Fair interpretation of information
- **Evaluate persuasive writing. Use these criteria (among others):**
  Clear definition of terms
  Fair use and interpretation of information
  Logical reasoning
- **Evaluate writing that entertains. Use these criteria (among others):**
  Interesting characters
  Believable action, plot, and situations
  Communication of theme
  Use of language
- **Decide whether you agree or disagree with the writer's ideas, position, or message:** Once you have determined the extent to which an author has achieved his or her purpose, clarify your position in relation to the writer's.

 Writing Assignment: Critique

Read and write a critique of the following lament on the demise of radio programming in America. In "Driving Down the Highway, Mourning the Death of American Radio," Brent Staples argues that his purchase of a CD player "symbolizes [his] despair that commercial radio . . . has become so bad as to be unlistenable." You might read such an essay in a sociology course, in the context of a semester-long focus on the homogenization of American culture. Is it true that regional differences in music, food, language, and even personality are dissolving, giving rise to a homogeneous country? Brent Staples's essay would offer one (discouraging) voice in such a discussion. The piece originally appeared in the *New York Times* on June 8, 2003.

Before reading, review the tips presented in the box *Critical Reading for Critique*. When you're ready to write your critique, start by jotting down notes in response to the tips for critical reading and the earlier discussions of evaluating writing in this chapter. Review the logical fallacies on pages 69–74 and identify any that appear in the essay by Staples. Work out your ideas on paper, perhaps producing an outline. Then write a rough draft of your critique. Review the reading and revise your rough draft at least once before considering it finished. You may want to look ahead to Chapter 3, Writing as a Process, to help guide you through writing your critique.

Driving Down the Highway, Mourning the Death of American Radio
Brent Staples

1   Brooklynites who park their cars on the streets sometimes post signs—"nothing of value" and my favorite, "no radio, no nothing"—pleading with thieves not to break in. The smash and grabs are less frequent than they once were. But those of us who live here are no longer surprised by the pools of shattered glass—known as "sidewalk diamonds"—left by the thieves who make off with air bags, radios and anything else they can carry.

2   My aging Volvo will be parked safely in a garage after getting the new compact disc player that I hope to install by summer's end. Burglar magnet that it is, the CD player symbolizes my despair that commercial radio in New York—and most other major markets—has become so bad as to be unlistenable and is unlikely to improve anytime soon. I listen religiously to the public radio station WBGO in Newark, the best jazz station in the country. Man does not live by jazz alone. If you want decent pop, rock or country, you pretty much have to spin it yourself.

3   Commercial stations in New York are too expensive to be anything but bland, repetitive and laden with ads and promotions. A station that could be had for a pittance 30 years ago can go for more than $100 million in a big market like New York. Congress increased the value of the stations in 1996, when it raised the cap on the number of stations that a single company could own; now, three corporate entities control nearly half of the radio listenership in the country.

4   I grew up glued to radio and was present at the creation of legendary album-format stations like WMMR in Philadelphia and WXRT in Chicago. These stations played rich blends of rock, pop and jazz, and sometimes featured local bands. (This wide-ranging format enriched the collective musical taste and paid dividends by producing ever more varied strains of popular music.) Commercials were typically kept to between 8 and 12 minutes per hour, and 20 minutes or more could pass before the announcer broke in to give the station's call letters.

5   This format was profitable, but not on the money-raining scale required since Wall Street got wise to the radio game. Faced with pressure from investors and more corporate debt than some nations, the megacompanies that

acquire a hundred stations each must squeeze every cent out of every link in the chain. They do this by dismissing the local staff and loading up squalling commercials and promotional spots that can take up as much as 30 minutes per hour during morning "drive time."

6   The corporate owners then put pressure on their remaining rivals—and often force them to sell out—by promoting national advertising packages that allow commercials to be broadcast on several stations, or all over the country, at once. Disc jockeys are often declared expendable and let go. Where they remain in place, they are figureheads who spin a narrow and mind-numbing list of songs that have been market-tested to death, leaving stations that sound the same from coast to coast.

7   Critics have focused on the way corporatized radio fails to cover local news and on free-speech issues, like the one that emerged when a country band, the Dixie Chicks, was booted from corporate air for criticizing the president over the war in Iraq. If the stations find the Dixie Chicks too challenging to tolerate, it's easy to imagine them marginalizing genuinely controversial news and programming.

8   Corporate radio's treatment of the Dixie Chicks argues against those who wish to remove all remaining federal limits on corporate ownership—not just of radio, but of television as well. The dangers posed by concentrated ownership go beyond news and censorship issues, to the heart of popular culture itself. By standardizing music and voices around the country, radio is slowly killing off local musical cultures, along with the diverse bodies of music that enriched the national popular culture.

9   Independent radio even 25 years ago was as important to a civic landscape as city hall or the local sports star who made good. The disc jockeys (or "on-air personalities," as they came to be called) embodied local radio to the public. You could hear their distinctive influences when you drove into Philadelphia, Chicago, Minneapolis or Wheeling, W.Va.; radio stations could be identified not just by the call letters but from the unique blend of music that was played in each place.

10   Pre-corporate radio commonly played established, nationally known musicians along with unknown locals and traveling bands. In town for a show, a young, unknown Elvis could swivel-hip down to the local station for airplay and some chat. This sort of thing was still possible in the early 1980's, when an unclassifiable band out of Athens, Ga., called R.E.M. became hugely popular while barnstorming the country in a truck. R.E.M. forced itself onto the air without conceding its weirdness and became one of the most influential bands of the late 20th century.

11   Radio stations where unknown bands might once have come knocking at the door no longer even have doors. They have become drone stations, where a once multifarious body of music has been pared down and segmented in bland formats, overlaid with commercials. As record companies scramble to replicate the music that gets airplay, pop music is turning in on itself and flattening out.

12   Those of us who are breaking with radio are saddened to leave the community of listeners to which we have belonged for most of our lives. But we realize as well that the vitality of the medium, like youth, is lost and forever behind us.

3

Writing as a Process

WRITING AS THINKING

Most of us regard writing as an activity that culminates in a product: a paper, a letter to a friend, study notes, and the like. We tend to focus on the result rather than on the process of getting there. But how *do* we produce that paper or letter? Does the thought that you write down not exist until it appears on the page? Does thought precede writing? If so, is writing merely a translation of prior thought? The relationship between thinking and writing is complex and not entirely understood. But it is worth reflecting on, especially as you embark on your writing-intensive career as a college student. Every time you take up a pen or sit down to a computer to write, you engage in a thinking process—and what and how and when you think both affects and is affected by your writing in a variety of ways. Consider the possibilities as you complete the following brief exercises:

A: You find yourself enrolled in a composition class at a particular school. Why are you attending this school and not another? Write for 5 minutes on the question.

B: Write for 5 minutes—no more, no less—on this question: What single moment in your freshman experience thus far has been most (a) humorous, (b) promising, (c) vexing, (d) exasperating? Choose *one* and write.

C: Select one page of notes from the presumably many you have taken in any of your classes. Reread the page and rewrite it, converting your first-pass notes into a well-organized study guide that would help you prepare for an exam. Devote 5 minutes to the effort.

Reflect on these brief exercises. Specifically, locate in your responses to each the points at which you believe your thinking took place. (Admittedly, this will be a difficult and approximate effort, but give it a try.) Before completing Exercise A, you probably gave considerable thought to *where* you are or would like to be attending college. Examine your writing and reflect on your thinking: Were you in any way rethinking your choice of school as you wrote? Or were you explaining a decision you've already made—that is, reporting on *prior* thinking? Some combination? Now turn to your work for Exercise B, for which you wrote (most likely) on a new topic. Where did thinking occur here? *As* you wrote? Moments prior to your writing, as you selected the topic and focused your ideas? Last, consider Exercise C. Where did your thinking take place? How did revision change your first-draft notes? What makes your second draft a better study guide than your first draft? Finally, consider the differences in the relationship between writing and thinking *across* Exercises A, B, and C as you wrote on a topic you'd previously thought (but not written) about, on a new topic, and on a topic you've written about and are revising. Note the changing relationship between writing and thinking. Note especially how rewriting is related to rethinking.

If you have completed and reflected on these exercises, you have glimpsed something of the marvelous complexity of writing. The job of this chapter is to help you develop some familiarity and comfort with a process that no one fully understands. It is a daunting task—and one for which you'll need to expect a certain amount of open-endedness. You will not learn to "solve" the process of writing as you learn to solve an equation. Your learning will be more circular and will never be definitive. Writers write for a lifetime without knowing, ultimately, where their words come from. This is not to say that writing is a mystical process; but neither is it mechanical or mastered absolutely. Twenty-year veterans work just as hard at their writing projects as do freshmen-level writers. Experts don't learn the process and then skip over it once they become proficient. It is more accurate to say that professional writers come to *trust the process* to lead them to desirable results. All writers, regardless of level, with every project, must begin somewhere. They must think and write, and—if they want to produce quality work—they must revise. There are no shortcuts.

If you apply yourself and learn the general approach to writing that we present in the pages that follow, you will improve. You will learn enough to write competently for most any occasion. The more you write, the more you will discover the particulars of your own writing process and the more comfortable you will become.

STAGES OF THE WRITING PROCESS

By breaking the process into stages, writers turn the sometimes overwhelming task of writing a paper into manageable pieces, each requiring different actions that, collectively, build to a final draft. Generally, the stages involve

---

THE WRITING PROCESS

Understanding the task: Read—or create—the assignment. Understand scope and audience.

Gathering data: Locate and review information—from sources and from your own experience—and formulate an approach.

Invention: Use various techniques (e.g., listing, outlining, freewriting) to generate a definite approach to the assignment. Gather more data if needed. Aim for a working thesis, a tentative (but well-reasoned and well-informed) statement of the direction you intend to pursue.

Drafting: Sketch the paper you intend to write and then write all sections necessary to support the working thesis. Stop if necessary to gather more data. Typically, you will both follow your plan and revise and invent a new (or slightly new) plan as you write. Expect to discover key parts of your paper as you write.

Revision: Rewrite in order to make the draft coherent and unified.

- Revise at the *global* level, reshaping your thesis and adding to, rearranging, or deleting paragraphs in order to support the thesis. Gather more data as needed to flesh out paragraphs in support of the thesis.

- Revise at the *local* level of paragraphs, ensuring that each is well reasoned and supports the thesis.

Editing: Revise at the *sentence* level for style and brevity. Revise for correctness: grammar, punctuation, usage, and spelling.

understanding the task, gathering data, invention, drafting, revision, and *editing*. You should realize at the outset of this discussion that no two writers work entirely alike, and over time (if you have not already done so) you will discover a process for writing that suits you uniquely. For the moment, we suggest that you regard the writing process in the broad stages that we outline here. Once you grow familiar with a general approach to sketching, writing, and refining your work, you will have a foundation on which to build your own approach.

Broadly speaking, the five stages of the writing process occur in the order we've listed. But writing is *recursive*; that is, the process tends to loop back on itself. You will not typically begin at the beginning and follow a lock-step, straight-line path to the end. Writing is messier than that. For example, you might find a number of sources during the data gathering stage of the process and, after reading and taking notes, you may feel ready to move on to the invention stage—perhaps listing your ideas about the subject. So far, so good. But once you sketch your ideas, perhaps in outline form, you may see gaps in the information you've collected, requiring you to circle back and gather more data before proceeding to the next step of first-draft writing. The circling can happen at any point. Perhaps you are writing a draft and your ideas take you in an unexpected direction. You stop to consider: Do I want to follow this through? If so, you will need to rethink the overall organization of your work, which is an earlier stage. You get the point: You will move forward as you write, toward a finished product. But moving forward is seldom a straight-line process.

STAGE I: UNDERSTANDING THE TASK

Papers in the Academic Disciplines

Although most of your previous experience with academic papers may have been in English classes, you should be prepared for instructors in other academic disciplines to assign papers with significant research components. Here, for example, is a sampling of topics that have been assigned recently in a broad range of undergraduate courses:

Art History: Discuss the main differences between Romanesque and Gothic sculpture, using the sculptures of Jeremiah (St. Pierre Cathedral) and St. Theodore (Chartres Cathedral) as major examples.

Environmental Studies: Choose a problem or issue of the physical environment at any level from local to global. Use both field and library work to explore the situation. Include coverage of the following: (1) the history of the issue or problem; (2) the various interest groups involved, taking note of conflicts among them; (3) critical facts and theories from environmental science necessary to understand and evaluate the issue or problem; (4) impact and significance of management measures already taken or proposed; (5) your recommendations for management of the solution.

History: Write a paper analyzing the history of a public policy (for example, the U.S. Supreme Court's role in undermining the civil rights of African-Americans between 1870 and 1896), drawing your sources from the best, most current scholarly histories available.

Physics: Research and write a paper on solar cell technology, covering the following areas: basic physical theory, history and development, structure and materials, types and characteristics, practical uses, state of the art, and future prospects.

Political Science: Explain the contours of California's water policy in the past few decades and then, by focusing on one specific controversy, explain and analyze the way in which this policy was adapted and why. Consider such questions as these: Where does the water come from? How much is there?

Who uses it? Who pays for it? How much does it cost? Should more water resources be developed?

Religious Studies: Select a particular religious group or movement present in the nation for at least 20 years and show how its belief or practice has changed since members of the group have been in America or, if the group began in America, since its first generation.

Sociology: Write on one of the following topics: (1) a critical comparison of two (or more) theories of deviance; (2) a field or library research study of those in a specific deviant career: thieves, drug addicts, prostitutes, corrupt politicians, university administrators; (3) portrayals of deviance in popular culture—e.g., television accounts of terrorism, incest, domestic violence; (4) old age as a form of deviance in the context of youth culture; (5) the relationship between homelessness and mental illness.

Some of these papers allow students a considerable range of choice (within the general subject); others are highly specific in requiring students to address a particular issue. Most of these papers call for some library or online research; a few call for a combination of online, library, and field research; others may be based entirely on field research. As with all academic writing, your first task is to make sure you understand the assignment. Remember to critically read and analyze the specific task(s) required of you in a paper assignment. One useful technique for doing so is to locate the assignment's key verb(s), which will stipulate exactly what is expected of you.

IMPORTANT WORD MEANINGS IN ESSAY ASSIGNMENTS

Good answers to essay questions depend in part upon a clear understanding of the meanings of the important directive words. These are the words such as *explain, compare, contrast,* and *justify,* which indicate the way in which the material is to be presented. Background knowledge of the subject matter is essential. But mere evidence of this knowledge is not enough. If you are asked to *compare* the British and American secondary school systems, you will get little or no credit if you merely *describe them.* If you are asked to *criticize* the present electoral system, you are not answering the question if you merely *explain* how it operates. A paper is satisfactory only if it answers directly the question that was asked.

The words that follow are frequently used in essay examinations:

summarize sum up; give the main points briefly. *Summarize the ways in which humans preserve food.*

(continued on next page)

(continued from previous page)

evaluate	give the good points and the bad ones; appraise; give an opinion regarding the value of; talk over the advantages and limitations. *Evaluate the contributions of teaching machines.*
contrast	bring out the points of difference. *Contrast the novels of Jane Austen and William Makepeace Thackeray.*
explain	make clear; interpret; make plain; tell "how" to do; tell the meaning of. *Explain how humans can, at times, trigger a full-scale rainstorm.*
describe	give an account of; tell about; give a word picture of. *Describe the Pyramids of Giza.*
define	give the meaning of a word or concept; place it in the class to which it belongs and set it off from other items in the same class. *Define the term "archetype."*
compare	bring out points of similarity and points of difference. *Compare the legislative branches of the state government and the national government.*
discuss	talk over; consider from various points of view; present the different sides of. *Discuss the use of pesticides in controlling mosquitoes.*
criticize	state your opinion of the correctness or merits of an item or issue; criticism may approve or disapprove. *Criticize the increasing use of alcohol.*
justify	show good reason for; give your evidence; present facts to support your position. *Justify the American entry into World War II.*
trace	follow the course of; follow the trail of; give a description of progress. *Trace the development of television in school instruction.*
interpret	make plain; give the meaning of; give your thinking about; translate. *Interpret the poetic line, "The sound of a cobweb snapping is the noise of my life."*
prove	establish the truth of something by giving factual evidence or logical reasons. *Prove that in a full-employment economy, a society can get more of one product only by giving up another product.*
illustrate	use a word picture, a diagram, a chart, or a concrete example to clarify a point. *Illustrate the use of catapults in the amphibious warfare of Alexander.*

Source: Andrew Moss and Carol Holder, Improving Student Writing: A Guide for Faculty in All Disciplines *(Dubuque, IA: Kendall/Hunt, 1988) 17–18.*

In addition to understanding the major task of the assignment, you should also note guidelines on expected length and documentation method. Length requirements help determine the extent of your data gathering and the scope of your thesis. What kinds of sources you use is also important information for proceeding at this stage. For later reference, you should clarify the documentation method you are asked to follow, such as standard MLA format, APA, CSE (formerly CBE), or some variant of these. In addition to documentation format, learn what kind of manuscript format your instructor prefers. Clarify these issues if they're not spelled out explicitly in the assignment, and be sure to attend to them before submitting your final draft.

EXERCISE 3.1

Analyze an Example Assignment

Read the assignments from across the disciplines, above, and complete the following for any *two*: (1) identify the key verb(s) in each; (2) list the type of print, interview, or graphical data you should gather to complete the assignment; and (3) reflect on your own experience to find some anecdote that might be appropriately included in a paper (or, absent that, a related experience that would provide a personal motivation for writing the paper).

EXERCISE 3.2

Analyze Your Own Assignment

Reread the instructions for a recent assignment from another course. Complete the three activities in Exercise 3.1 for this assignment.

STAGE 2: GATHERING DATA

When you begin a writing task, you will want to pose three questions:

1. What is the task?
2. What do I know about the subject?*
3. What do I need to know in order to begin writing?

These questions prompt you to reflect on the task and define what is expected. Taking stock of class notes, readings, and whatever resources are available, survey what you already know. Once you identify the gaps between what you know and what you need to know in order to write, you

---

*Note: The terms *subject* and *topic* are often used interchangeably. In this chapter, we use *subject* to mean a broad area of interest that, once narrowed to a *topic*, becomes the focus of a paper. Within a thesis (the major organizing sentence of the paper—see below), we speak of *topic*, not *subject*.

can begin to gather data—most likely in stages. You may gather enough, at first, to formulate initial ideas. You might begin to write and see new gaps and realize you need more data.

In an academic context, gathering data typically involves reading source materials and discovering among them the materials pertinent to your writing (also keeping careful track of sources so you can cite them accurately later and avoid any problems with plagiarism). But just as important, mine your own experience for material to include in your work or, less explicitly but perhaps more importantly, for a personal connection to the subject that will provide you with an enthusiasm for writing. In a sociology course you may be assigned a paper on the changes, over the past 50 years, in the living arrangements of seniors. Doubtless, you will be able to locate many (perhaps too many!) print sources on the subject. But you could also recall and gain powerful insights from personal experience. Perhaps you've seen a grandparent or elderly neighbor shuttled from one marginally satisfactory living arrangement to another. You are frustrated. Use that energy, informed by direct experience, to guide your research and to provide a motivation to write.

Think "large," therefore, when you focus on gathering data for your writing projects. Draw data from your life as well as from the library, and use both to inform your papers.

Types of Data

Data is a term used most often to refer to *quantitative* information, such as the frequencies or percentages of natural occurrences in the sciences or of social phenomena in the social sciences. But *data* also refers to *qualitative* information—the sort that is textual rather than numerical. For example, interviews or ethnographic field notes recorded by a social scientist, also considered to be *data*, are usually qualitative in nature, comprising in-depth interview responses or detailed observations of human behavior. In the humanities, the term *data* can refer to the qualitative observations one makes of a particular art object one is interpreting or evaluating. Generally, quantitative data encompasses issues of "how many," or "how often," whereas qualitative research accounts for such issues as "what kind?" and "why?"

PRIMARY AND SECONDARY SOURCES

When you collect either or both of these kinds of data, you are generating *primary* data—data that a researcher gathers directly by using the research methods appropriate to a particular field of study, such as experiments or observations in the sciences, surveys or interviews in the social sciences, and close reading and interpretation in the humanities. More commonly as an undergraduate, however, the types of data you will collect are *secondary* in nature: information and ideas collected or generated by others who have performed their own primary and/or secondary research. The data gathering for most undergraduate academic writing will consist of library research and, increasingly, research conducted online via Internet databases and resources; you will rely on secondary data more often than you will generate your own primary data.

Chapter 7 on research provides an in-depth discussion of locating and using secondary sources. Refer also to the material presented in Chapters 1 and 2 on summary, critical reading, and critique. The techniques of critical reading and assessment of sources will help you make the best use of your sources. And the material in Chapter 1 on avoiding plagiarism will help you conform to the highest ethical standards in your research and writing.

STAGE 3: INVENTION

Given an assignment and the fruits of preliminary data gathering, you are in a position to frame your writing project: to give it scope, to name your main idea, and to create conditions for productive writing. You must define what you are writing about, after all, and this you achieve—in a preliminary way—in the *invention* stage. This stage of the process can also be termed "brainstorming," or "predrafting." Regardless of the name, invention is an important part of the process that typically overlaps with data gathering. The preliminary data you gather on a topic will inform the choices you make in defining (that is, in "inventing" ideas for) your project. As you invent, you will often return to gather more data.

Writers sometimes skip over the invention stage, preferring to save time by launching directly from data gathering into writing a draft. But time spent narrowing your ideas to a manageable scope at the beginning of a project will pay dividends all through the writing process. Many, *many* efforts go wrong when writers choose too broad a topic, resulting in superficial treatment of subtopics, or when they choose too narrow a topic and then must "pad" their work to meet a length requirement.

THE MYTH OF INSPIRATION

Some students believe that good writing comes primarily from a kind of magical—and unpredictable—formation of ideas as one sits down in front of blank paper or a blank computer screen. According to the myth, a writer must be inspired in order to write, as if given his or her ideas from some mystical source, such as a muse. While some element of inspiration may inform your writing, most of the time it is hard work—especially in the invention stage—that gets the job done. The old adage attributed to Thomas Edison, "Invention is one part inspiration and ninety-nine parts perspiration," applies here.

Choosing and Narrowing Your Subject

Suppose you have been assigned an open-ended, ten-page paper in an introductory course on environmental science. Not only do you have to choose a subject, but you also have to narrow it sufficiently and formulate your thesis. Where will you begin? We take the unusual case of an essentially directionless assignment to demonstrate how you can use invention strategies to identify topics of interest and narrow the scope of your paper. Typically, your assignments will provide more guidance than "write a ten-page paper." In that case, you can still apply the techniques discussed here, though you will have less work to do.

So, how to begin thinking about your paper in environmental science? First, you need to select broad subject matter from the course and become knowledgeable about its general features. What if no broad area of interest occurs to you?

- Work through the syllabus or your textbook(s). Identify topics that sparked your interest.
- Review course notes and pay especially close attention to lectures that held your interest.
- Scan recent headlines for news items that bear on your coursework.

Usually you can make use of material you've read in a text or heard in a lecture. The trick is to find a subject that is important to you, for whatever reason. (For a paper in sociology, you might write on the subject of bullying because of your own experience with school bullies. For an economics seminar, you might explore the factors that threaten banks with collapse because your great-great-grandparents lost their life savings during the Great Depression.) Whatever the academic discipline, try to discover a topic that you'll enjoy exploring; that way, you'll be writing for yourself as much as for your instructor.

THE MYTH OF TALENT

Many inexperienced writers believe that either you have writing talent or you don't, and if you don't, then you are doomed to go through life as a "bad writer." But again, hard work, rather than talent, is the norm. Yes, some people have more natural verbal ability than others—we all have our areas of strength and weakness. But in any endeavor, talent alone can't ensure success, and with hard work, writers who do not yet have much confidence can achieve great results. Not everyone can be a brilliant writer. But without question, everyone can be a competent writer.

Assume for your course in environmental science that you've settled on the broad subject of energy conservation. At this point, the goal of your research is to limit this subject to a manageable scope. A subject can be limited in at least two ways. First, you can seek out a general article (perhaps an encyclopedia entry, though these are not typically accepted as sources in a college-level paper). A general article may do the work for you by breaking the larger topic down into smaller subtopics that you can explore and, perhaps, limit even further. Second, you can limit a subject by asking several questions about it:

Who?
Which aspects?
Where?
When?
How?
Why?

These questions will occur to you as you conduct your research and see the ways in which various authors have focused their discussions. Having read several sources on energy conservation and having decided that you'd like to use them, you might limit the subject by asking *which aspects,* and deciding to focus on energy conservation as it relates to motor vehicles.

Certainly, "energy-efficient vehicles" offers a more specific focus than does "energy conservation." Still, the revised focus is too broad for a ten-page paper. (One can easily imagine several book-length works on the subject.) So again you try to limit your subject by posing additional questions, from the same list. In this case, you might ask which aspects of energy-efficient vehicles are possible and desirable and how auto manufacturers can be encouraged to develop them. In response to these questions, you may jot down such preliminary notes. For example:

- Types of energy-efficient vehicles
  All-electric vehicles
  Hybrid (combination of gasoline and electric) vehicles
  Fuel-cell vehicles

- Government action to encourage development of energy-efficient vehicles
  Mandates to automakers to build minimum quantities of energy-efficient vehicles by certain deadlines
  Additional taxes imposed on high-mileage vehicles
  Subsidies to developers of energy-efficient vehicles

Focusing on any *one* of these aspects as an approach to encouraging use of energy-efficient vehicles could provide the focus of a ten-page paper, and you do yourself an important service by choosing just one. To choose more would obligate you to too broad a discussion that would frustrate you: Either the paper would have to be longer than ten pages, or assuming you kept to the page limit, the paper would be superficial in its treatment. In both instances, the paper would fail, given the constraints of the assignment.

A certain level of judgment is involved in deciding whether a topic is too big or too small to generate the right number of pages. Judgment is a function of experience, of course, and in the absence of experience you will have to resort, at times, to trial and error. Still the strategies offered above (locate an article that identifies parts of a topic or pose multiple questions and identify parts) can guide you. Ultimately, you will be able to tell if you've selected an appropriate topic as you reread your work and answer this question: *Have I developed all key elements of the thesis in depth, fully?* If you have skimmed the surface, narrow the topic and/or the claim of your thesis and redraft the paper. If you have added filler to meet the assignment's page requirements, broaden the topic and/or claim and redraft the paper. In general, you will do well to spend ample time gathering data, brainstorming, gathering more data, and then brainstorming again in order to limit your subject before attempting to write about it. Let's take an example. Assume that you settle on the following as an appropriately defined topic for a ten-page paper:

> Encouraging the development of fuel cell vehicles

The process of choosing an initial subject (invention) depends heavily on the reading you do (data gathering). The more you read, the deeper your understanding. The deeper your understanding, the likelier it will be that you can divide a broad and complex subject into manageable—that is, researchable—topics. In the example above, your reading in the online and print literature may suggest that the development of fuel cell technology is one of the most promising approaches to energy conservation on the highway. So reading allows you to narrow the subject "energy conservation" by answering the initial questions—those focusing on *which aspects* of the general subject. Once you narrow your focus to "energy efficient vehicles," you may read further and quickly realize that this is a broad subject that also should be limited. In this way, reading stimulates you to identify an appropriate topic for your paper. Your process here is recursive—you move back and forth between Stages 1 and 2 of the process, each movement bringing you closer to establishing a clear focus *before* you attempt to write your paper.

EXERCISE **3.3**

Practice Narrowing Subjects

In groups of three or four classmates, choose one of the following subjects, and collaborate on a paragraph or two that explores the questions we listed above for narrowing subjects: Who? Which aspects? Where? When? How? See if you can narrow the subject.

- Downloading music off the Internet
- Internet chat rooms
- College sports
- School violence
- America's public school system

Invention Strategies

Writers use a number of successful strategies for thinking through ideas in writing. You may already be familiar with a variety of invention strategies. Several methods are provided below.

DIRECTED FREEWRITING

To freewrite is to let your mind go and write spontaneously, often for a set amount of time or set number of pages. The process of "just writing" can often free up thoughts and ideas about which we aren't even fully conscious, or that we haven't articulated to ourselves. In *directed freewriting,* you focus on a subject, and let what you think and know about the subject flow out of you in a focused stream of ideas. As a first step in the invention stage, you might sit down with an assignment and write continuously for 15 minutes. Such efforts might seem sluggish at first, but if you stick with it and try to let yourself write spontaneously, you'll be surprised at what comes out. You might generate questions whose answers lead to an argument, or logical connections between ideas that you hadn't noticed before. If you write for 15 minutes, and only one solid idea comes through, you've succeeded in using freewriting to help "free up" your thinking. As a second step, you might take that one idea and freewrite about it, shift to a different invention strategy to explore that one idea, or even begin to draft a thesis and subsequent rough draft, depending on the extent to which your idea is well formed.

LISTING

Some writers find it helpful to make lists of their ideas, breaking significant ideas into sublists and seeing where they lead. Approach this strategy as a form of freewriting; let your mind go, and jot down words and phrases that are related. Create lists by pulling related ideas out of your notes or your course readings. A caution: The linear nature of lists can lead you to jump prematurely into planning your paper's structure before working out your ideas. Instead, list ideas as a way of brainstorming, and then generate another list that works out the best structure for your points in a draft.

OUTLINING

As a more structured version of a list, an outline groups ideas in hierarchical order, with main points broken into subordinate points, sometimes indicating evidence in support of these points. Use outlines as a first stage in generating ideas during your invention process, or use outlines as a second step in invention. After freewriting and/or listing, refine and build on your ideas by inserting them into an outline for a workable structure in which to discuss the ideas you've brainstormed.

CLUSTERING AND BRANCHING

These two methods of invention are more visual, nonlinear versions of list-ing and outlining. With both clustering and branching, you start with an as-signment's main topic, or with an idea generated by freewriting or thinking, and you brainstorm related ideas that flow from that main idea. Clustering involves writing an idea in the middle of a page and circling it. Then draw lines leading from that circle, or "bubble," to new bubbles in which you write subtopics of that central idea. Picking the subtopics that interest you most, draw lines leading to more bubbles wherein you note important as-pects of the subtopics. (See the accompanying illustration.) Branching fol-lows the same principle, but instead of placing ideas in bubbles, write them on lines that branch off to other lines that, in turn, contain the related subtopics of your larger topic.

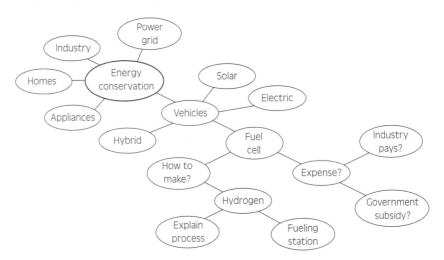

Clustering and branching are useful first steps in invention, for each helps isolate the topics about which you are most knowledgeable. As you branch off into the subtopics of a main paper topic, the number of ideas you generate in relation to these topics will help show where you have the most knowledge and/or interest.

DRAFTING

While drafting comprises the next full stage in the writing process, it's also possible to combine Stages 2 and 3; that is, in drafting a paper, you may dis-cover your ideas. Of course, this method requires that you have some notion of what you want to write about, and, as you begin your first draft, you can discover what you want to say *as* you write. This method may be viewed as a highly focused and directed form of freewriting. You might start drafting your body paragraphs first, or begin with the introduction. Typically, what you write at first will need to be heavily revised (or even discarded) later. Your first paragraph or so serves as a kind of pump priming or throat clearing, but as you proceed you can warm up and start to generate more useful material.

You can modify and combine invention techniques in a number of ways. There is no one right way to generate ideas—or to write a paper—and every writer will want to try different methods to find those that work best. The point to remember is that time spent on invention, regardless of method, creates the conditions in which to write a productive first draft.

EXERCISE **3.4**

Practice Invention Strategies

After completing the group exercise (Exercise 3.3, pages 98–99), in which you narrowed a subject, work individually to brainstorm ideas about the subject your group chose. Use one of the invention strategies listed above—preferably one that you haven't used before. After brainstorming on your own, meet with your group again to compare the ideas you each generated.

STAGE 4: DRAFTING

It's usually best to begin drafting a paper after you've settled on at least a working or preliminary thesis. While consulting the fruits of your efforts during invention (notes, lists, outlines, and so on), you face a number of choices about how to proceed with drafting your paper. Let's look at some of these, including the crucial step of drafting the thesis.

Strategies for Writing the Paper

Some writers can sit down very early in the process and put their ideas into an orderly form as they write. This drafting method results in a completed *rough draft*. Good writers rarely, if ever, produce an adequate piece of writing in one draft. Most need to plan the structure of a paper before they can sit down to a first draft. Even if this initial structure proves to be little more than a sketch that changes markedly as the paper develops, some sort of scaffolding usually helps in taking the step from planning to writing a first draft.

Ultimately, you will decide how best to proceed for you. And don't be surprised if you begin different writing projects differently. Whether you jump in without a plan, whether you plan rigorously, or whether you commit yourself to the briefest preliminary sketch, ask yourself the following:

- On what main point do I intend to focus my paper?
- What subpoints do I need to address in order to develop my main point?
- In what order should my points be arranged? (Do certain subpoints lead naturally to others?)

At Stage 3, as you clarify the direction in which you believe your paper is heading, you ought to be able to formulate at least a *preliminary thesis* (see below). Your thesis can be very rough, but if you don't have a sense of your main point, writing the first draft will be not be possible. In this case, you would have to consider what you've written a preliminary or a *discovery draft* (more of an invention strategy than an actual draft), a perfectly sensible way to proceed if you're having difficulty clarifying your thoughts. Even if you begin with what you regard as a clearly stated point, don't be surprised if by the end of the draft—just at the point where you are summing up—you discover that the paper you have in fact written differs from the paper you intended to write. However firmly your ideas may be when you begin, the act of writing a draft will usually clarify matters for you.

As you can see, the drafting and invention stages overlap. How much planning you do after working out your ideas and before drafting your paper is a matter of preference. Try different methods to see which work best for you, and keep in mind that different assignments may require new methods for invention and drafting.

Writing a Thesis

A thesis is a one-sentence summary of a paper's content. It is similar, actually, to a paper's conclusion, but it lacks the conclusion's concern for broad implications and significance. The thesis is the product of your thinking; it therefore represents *your* conclusion about the topic on which you're writing, and therefore you have to have spent some time thinking (that is, in the invention stage) in order to arrive at the thesis that governs your paper.

For a writer in the drafting stages, the thesis establishes a focus, a basis on which to include or exclude information. For the reader of a finished product, the thesis anticipates the author's discussion. *A thesis, therefore, is an essential tool for both writers and readers of academic papers.*

This last sentence is our thesis for this section. Based on it, we, as authors, have limited the content of the section; and you, as the reader, will be able to form certain expectations about the discussion that follows. You can expect a definition of a thesis; an enumeration of the uses of a thesis; and a discussion focused on academic material. As writers, we will have met our obligations to you only if in subsequent paragraphs we satisfy these expectations.

THE COMPONENTS OF A THESIS

Like any other sentence, a thesis includes a subject and a predicate, which consists of an assertion about the subject. In the sentence "Lee and Grant were different kinds of generals," "Lee and Grant" is the subject and "were different kinds of generals" is the predicate. What distinguishes a thesis from any other sentence with a subject and predicate is that *the thesis presents the controlling idea of the paper.* The subject of a thesis, and the assertion about it, must present the right balance between the general and the specific to allow for thorough discussion within the allotted length of the paper. The discussion might include definitions, details, comparisons, contrasts—whatever is needed to illuminate a subject and support the assertion. (If the sentence about Lee and Grant were a thesis, the reader would assume that the rest of the paper contained comparisons and contrasts between the two generals.)

Bear in mind when writing theses that the more general your subject and the more complex your assertion, the longer your paper will be. The broadest theses require book-length treatments, as in this case:

> Meaningful energy conservation requires a shrewd application of political, financial, and scientific will.

One could not write an effective ten-page paper based on this thesis. The topic alone would require pages merely to carefully define what is meant by "energy conservation" and then by "meaningful." Energy can be conserved in homes, vehicles, industries, appliances, and power plants, and each of these areas would need consideration. Having accomplished this task, the writer would then turn his or her attention to the claim, which entails a discussion of how politics, finance, and science individually and collectively influence energy conservation. Moreover, the thesis requires the writer to argue that "shrewd application" of politics, finance, and science is required. The thesis may very well be accurate and compelling. Yet it promises entirely too much for a ten-page paper.

To write an effective thesis and thus a controlled, effective paper, you need to limit your subject and your claims about it. We discussed narrowing your subject during the invention stage on pages 96–98; this narrowing process should help you arrive at a manageable topic for your paper. You will convert that topic to a thesis when you make an assertion about it—a *claim* that you will explain and support in the paper.

MAKING AN ASSERTION

As noted in the previous section, thesis statements constitute an assertion or claim you wish to make *about* your paper's topic. If you have spent enough time reading and gathering information, and brainstorming ideas about the assignment, you will be knowledgeable enough to have something to say based on a combination of your own thinking and the thinking of your sources.

If you have trouble making an assertion, devote more time to invention strategies: Try writing your subject at the top of a page and then listing everything you now know and feel about it. Often from such a list you will discover an assertion that you then can use to fashion a working thesis. A good way to gauge the reasonableness of your claim is to see what other authors have asserted about the same topic. In fact, keep good notes on the views of others. These notes will prove a useful counterpoint to your own views as you write and think about your claim, and you may want to use them in your paper. Next, make several assertions about your topic, in order of increasing complexity, as in the following:

1. Fuel cell technology has emerged as a promising approach to developing energy-efficient vehicles.
2. To reduce our dependence on nonrenewable fossil fuel, the federal government should encourage the development of fuel cell vehicles.
3. The federal government should subsidize the development of fuel cell vehicles as well as the hydrogen infrastructure needed to support them; otherwise, the United States will be increasingly vulnerable to recession and other economic dislocations resulting from our dependence on the continued flow of foreign oil.

Keep in mind that these are *working theses*. Because you haven't written a paper based on any of them, they remain *hypotheses* to be tested. You might choose one and use it to focus your initial draft. After completing a first draft, you would revise it by comparing the contents of the paper to the thesis and making adjustments as necessary for unity. The working thesis is an excellent tool for planning broad sections of the paper, but—again—don't let it prevent you from pursuing related discussions as they occur to you.

Starting with a Working Thesis

Professionals thoroughly familiar with a topic often begin writing with a clear thesis in mind—a happy state of affairs unfamiliar to most college students who are assigned papers. But professionals usually have an important advantage over students: experience. Because professionals know their material, are familiar with the ways of approaching it, are aware of the questions important to practitioners, and have devoted considerable time to study of the topic, they are naturally in a strong position to begin writing a paper. In addition, many professionals are practiced at invention; the time they spend listing or outlining their ideas helps them work out their thesis statements. Not only do professionals have experience in their fields, but also they have a clear purpose in writing; they know their audience and are comfortable with the format of their papers.

Experience counts—there's no way around it. As a student, you are not yet an expert and therefore don't generally have the luxury of beginning your writing tasks with a definite thesis in mind. But let's assume that you *do* have an area of expertise, that you are in your own right a professional (albeit not in academic matters). We'll assume that you understand some nonacademic subject—say, backpacking—and have been given a clear purpose for writing: to discuss the relative merits of backpack designs. Your job is to write a recommendation for the owner of a sporting-goods chain, suggesting which line of backpacks the chain should carry. Because you already know a good deal about backpacks, you may have some well-developed ideas on the subject before you start doing additional research.

Yet even as an expert in your field, you will find that crafting a thesis is challenging. After all, a thesis is a summary, and it is difficult to summarize a presentation yet to be written—especially if you plan to discover what you want to say during the process of writing. Even if you know your material well, the best you can do at the early stages is to formulate a working thesis—a hypothesis of sorts, a well-informed hunch about your topic and the claim to be made about it. Once you have completed a draft, you can evaluate the degree to which your working thesis accurately summarizes the content of your paper. If the match is a good one, the working thesis becomes the thesis. If, however, sections of the paper drift from the focus set out in the working thesis, you'll need to revise the thesis and the paper itself to ensure that the presentation is unified. (You'll know that the match between the content and thesis is a good one when every paragraph directly refers to and develops some element of the thesis.) Later in this chapter we'll discuss revision techniques that will be useful in establishing unity in your work.

This model works whether you are writing about a subject in your area of expertise—backpacking, for example—or one that is more in your professor's territory, such as government or medieval poetry. The difference is that when approaching subjects that are less familiar to you, you will have to spend more time gathering data and brainstorming. Such labor prepares you to make assertions about your subject.

USING THE THESIS TO PLAN A STRUCTURE

A working thesis will help you sketch the structure of your paper, since structure flows directly from the thesis. Consider, for example, the third thesis on fuel cell technology:

> The federal government should subsidize the development of fuel cell vehicles as well as the hydrogen infrastructure needed to support them; otherwise, the United States will be increasingly vulnerable to recession and other economic dislocations resulting from our dependence on the continued flow of foreign oil.

This thesis, compared to the mildly argumentative second statement and the explanatory first statement, is *strongly argumentative,* or *persuasive.* The economic catastrophes mentioned by the writer indicate a strong degree of urgency in the need for the solution recommended—federal subsidy of a national hydrogen infrastructure to support fuel cell vehicles. If a paper based on this thesis is to be well developed, the writer must commit him- or herself to explaining (1) why fuel cell vehicles are a preferred alternative to gasoline-powered vehicles; (2) why fuel cell vehicles require a hydrogen infrastructure (i.e., the writer must explain that fuel cells produce power by mixing hydrogen and oxygen, generating both electricity and water in the process); (3) why the government needs to subsidize industry in developing fuel cell vehicles; and (4) how continued reliance on fossil fuel technology could make the country vulnerable to economic dislocations. This thesis therefore helps the writer plan the paper, which should include a section on each of these four topics. Assuming that the paper follows the organizational plan we've proposed, the working thesis would become the final thesis, on the basis of which a reader could anticipate sections of the paper to come. In a finished product, the thesis becomes an essential tool for guiding readers.

Note, however, that this thesis is still provisional. It may turn out, as you research or begin drafting, that the paper to which this thesis commits you will be too long and complex. You may therefore decide to drop the second clause of the thesis dealing with the country's vulnerability to economic dislocations and focus almost exclusively on the need for the government to subsidize the development of fuel cell vehicles and of a hydrogen infrastructure, relegating the economic concerns to your conclusion (if at all). If you make this change, your final thesis would read as follows: "The federal government should subsidize the development of fuel cell vehicles, as well as the hydrogen infrastructure needed to support them."

This revised thesis makes an assertive commitment to the subject, although the assertion is not as complex as the original. Still, it is more assertive than the second proposed thesis:

> To reduce our dependence on nonrenewable fossil fuel energy sources, the federal government should encourage the development of fuel cell vehicles.

Here we have a *mildly argumentative* thesis that enables the writer to express an opinion. We infer from the use of the words "should encourage" that the writer endorses the idea of the government promoting fuel cell development. But a government that "encourages" development is making a lesser commitment than one that "subsidizes," which means that it allocates funds for a specific policy. So a writer who argues for mere encouragement takes a milder position than one who argues for subsidies. Note also the contrast between this second thesis and the first one, in which the writer is committed to no involvement in the debate and no government involvement whatsoever.

> Fuel cell technology has emerged as a promising approach to developing energy-efficient vehicles.

This first of the three thesis statements is *explanatory*, or *informative*. In developing a paper based on this thesis, the writer is committed only to ex-

---

HOW AMBITIOUS SHOULD YOUR THESIS BE?

Writing tasks vary according to the nature of the thesis.

- The *explanatory thesis* is often developed in response to short-answer exam questions that call for information, not analysis (e.g., "How does James Barber categorize the main types of presidential personality?").
- The *mildly argumentative thesis* is appropriate for organizing reports (even lengthy ones), as well as essay questions that call for some analysis (e.g., "Discuss the qualities of a good speech").
- The *strongly argumentative thesis* is used to organize papers and exam questions that call for information, analysis, *and* the writer's forcefully stated point of view (e.g., "Evaluate the proposed reforms of health maintenance organizations").

The strongly argumentative thesis, of course, is the riskiest of the three, since you must unequivocally state your position and make it appear reasonable—which requires that you offer evidence and defend against logical objections. But such intellectual risks pay dividends, and if you become involved enough in your work to make challenging assertions, you will provoke challenging responses that enliven classroom discussions and your own learning.

---

plaining how fuel cell technology works and why it is a promising approach to energy-efficient vehicles. Based on this particular thesis, then, a reader would *not* expect to find the author strongly recommending, for instance, that fuel cell engines replace internal combustion engines at some point in the near future. Neither does the thesis require the writer to defend a personal opinion; he or she need only justify the use of the relatively mild term "promising."

As you can see, for any topic you might explore in a paper, you can make any number of assertions—some relatively simple, some complex. It is on the basis of these assertions that you set yourself an agenda for your writing—and readers set for themselves expectations for reading. The more ambitious the thesis, the more complex will be the paper and the greater will be the readers' expectations.

To review: A thesis (a one-sentence summary of your paper) helps you organize your discussion, and it helps your reader anticipate it. Theses are distinguished by their carefully worded subjects and predicates, which should be just broad enough and complex enough to be developed within the length limitations of the assignment. Both novices and experts typically begin the initial draft of a paper with a working thesis—a statement that provides writers with structure enough to get started but with latitude enough to discover what they want to say as they write. Once you have completed a first draft, however, you test the "fit" of your thesis with the paper that follows. When you have a good fit, every element of the thesis is developed in the paper that follows. Discussions that drift from your thesis should be deleted, or the thesis changed to accommodate the new discussions. These concerns will be addressed more fully when we discuss the revision stage of the writing process.

EXERCISE   **3.5**

Drafting Thesis Statements

After completing the group exercise in which you narrowed a subject (Exercise 3.3, pages 98–99), and the individual invention exercise (Exercise 3.4, page 101), work individually or in small groups to draft three possible theses in relation to your earlier ideas. Draft one *explanatory thesis,* one *mildly argumentative thesis,* and one *strongly argumentative thesis.*

Writing Introductions and Conclusions

All writers, no matter how much they prepare, eventually face the task of writing their paper's introduction and conclusion. How to start? What's the best way to approach your topic? With a serious tone, a light touch, an anecdote? How to end? How best to make the connection from your work back to the reader's world?

Many writers avoid such decisions by putting them off—productively. Bypassing careful planning for the introduction and conclusion, they start by writing the body of the piece; only after they've finished the body do they go back to write the opening and closing paragraphs. There's a lot to be said for this approach. Because you have presumably spent more time thinking and writing about the topic itself than about how you're going to introduce or conclude it, you are in a better position to set out your ideas. And often, it's not until you've actually seen the piece on paper and read it over once or twice that a natural way of introducing or concluding it becomes apparent. You are generally in better psychological shape to write both the introduction and conclusion after the major task of writing is behind you and you know exactly what your major points are.

INTRODUCTIONS

The purpose of an introduction is to prepare the reader to enter the world of your paper. The introduction makes the connection between the more familiar world inhabited by the reader and the less familiar world of the writer's particular topic; it places a discussion in a context that the reader can understand. If you find yourself getting stuck on an introduction at the beginning of a first draft, skip over it for the moment. State your working thesis directly and move on to the body of the paper.

There are many strategies for opening a paper. We'll consider one here. You will find several others in the Appendix, on pages 333–37: historical review, review of a controversy, working from the general to the specific, working from the specific to the general (by providing an anecdote and illustration), posing a question, and directly stating the thesis.

Quotation   Here is an introduction to a paper on democracy:

> "Two cheers for democracy" was E. M. Forster's not-quite-wholehearted judgment. Most Americans would not agree. To them, our democracy is one of the glories of civilization. To one American in particular, E. B. White, democracy is "the hole in the stuffed shirt through which the sawdust slowly trickles . . . the dent in the high hat . . . the recurrent suspicion that more than half of the people are right more than half of the time" (915). American democracy is based on the oldest continuously operating written constitution in the world--a most impressive fact and a testament to the farsightedness of the founding fathers. But just how farsighted can mere humans be? In Future Shock, Alvin Toffler quotes economist Kenneth Boulding on the incredible acceleration of social change in our time: "The world of today . . . is as different from the world in which I was born as that world was from Julius Caesar's" (13). As we move into the twenty-first century, it seems legitimate to question the continued effectiveness of a governmental system that was devised in the eighteenth century; and it seems equally legitimate to consider alternatives.

The quotations by Forster and White help set the stage for the discussion of democracy by presenting the reader with provocative and well-phrased remarks. Later in the paragraph, the quotation by Boulding more specifically prepares us for the theme of change that will be central to the paper as a whole. Quoting the words of others offers you many points of departure for your paper. You can agree with the quotation. You can agree and expand. You can sharply disagree. You can use the quotation to set a context or tone. See pages 333–37 for six other strategies for introducing your work.

Drafting Introductions

Imagine that you are writing a paper using the topic, ideas, and thesis you developed in the exercises in this chapter. Choose one of the seven types of introductions we've discussed (one in this chapter and the remainder in the Appendix, 333–37)—preferably one you have never used before—and draft an introduction that would work to open a paper on your topic. Use our examples as models to help you draft your practice introduction.

Conclusions

One way to view the conclusion of your paper is as an introduction in reverse, a bridge from the world of your paper back to the world of your reader. A conclusion is the part of your paper in which you restate and (if necessary) expand on your thesis. Essential to many conclusions is the summary, which is not merely a repetition of the thesis but a restatement that takes advantage of the material you've presented. *The simplest conclusion is a summary of the paper, but you may want more than this.* Depending on your needs, you might offer a summary and then build onto it a discussion of the paper's significance or its implications for future study, for choices that individuals might make, for policy, and so on. You might also want to urge readers to change an attitude or modify behavior. Certainly, you are under no obligation to discuss the broader significance of your work (and a summary, alone, will satisfy the formal requirement that your paper have an ending); but the conclusions of better papers often reveal authors who are "thinking large" and want to connect their concerns with the broader concerns of society.

Two words of advice, however. First, no matter how clever or beautifully executed, a conclusion cannot salvage a poorly written paper. Second, by virtue of its placement, the conclusion carries rhetorical weight. It is the last statement a reader will encounter before turning from your work. Realizing this, writers who expand on the basic summary conclusion often wish to give their final words a dramatic flourish, a heightened level of diction. Soaring rhetoric and drama in a conclusion are fine as long as they do not unbalance the paper and call attention to themselves. Having labored long hours over your paper, you may be inclined at this point to wax eloquent. But keep a sense of proportion and timing. Make your points quickly and end crisply. Here we'll consider one strategy for expanding the basic summary-conclusion. (See the Appendix, pages 337–42, for other strategies: calling for further research; offering a solution; using an anecdote, quotation, or question; and ending with speculation.)

Statement of the Subject's Significance   One of the more effective ways to conclude a paper is to discuss the larger significance of what you have written, providing readers with one more reason to regard your work as a serious effort. When using this strategy, you move from the specific concern of your paper to the broader concerns of the reader's world. Often, you will need to choose among a range of significances: A paper on the Wright brothers might end with a discussion of air travel as it affects economies, politics, or families; a paper on contraception might end with a discussion of its effect on sexual mores, population, or the church. But don't overwhelm your reader with the importance of your remarks. Keep your discussion well focused.

The following paragraphs conclude an article on George H. Shull, a pioneer in the inbreeding and crossbreeding of corn:

> . . . Thus, the hybrids developed and described by Shull 75 years ago have finally dominated U.S. corn production.
>
> The adoption of hybrid corn was steady and dramatic in the Corn Belt. From 1930 through 1979 the average yields of corn in the U.S. increased from 21.9 to 95.1 bushels per acre, and the additional value to the farmer is now several billion dollars per year.
>
> The success of hybrid corn has also stimulated the breeding of other crops, such as sorghum hybrids, a major feed grain crop in arid parts of the world. Sorghum yields have increased 300 percent since 1930. Approximately 20 percent of the land devoted to rice production in China is planted with hybrid seed, which is reported to yield 20 percent more than the best varieties. And many superior varieties of tomatoes, cucumbers, spinach, and other vegetables are hybrids. Today virtually all corn produced in the developed countries is from hybrid seed. From those blue bloods of the plant kingdom has come a model for feeding the world.*

The first sentence of this conclusion is a summary, and from it the reader can infer that the paper included a discussion of Shull's techniques for the hybrid breeding of corn. The summary is followed by a two-paragraph discussion on the significance of Shull's research for feeding the world.

For examples of other types of conclusions, see the Appendix, pp. 337–42:

EXERCISE   3.7

Drafting Conclusions

Imagine that you have written a paper using the topic, ideas, and thesis you developed in the earlier exercises in this chapter. Choose one of the seven types of conclusions we've discussed (one in this chapter and the remainder in the Appendix, 337–42)—preferably one you have never used before—and draft a conclusion that would work to end your paper. Use our examples as models to help you draft your practice conclusion.

---

*William L. Brown, "Hybrid Vim and Vigor," *Science* Nov. 1984: 77–78.

STAGE 5: REVISION

Perhaps it's stating the obvious to say that rough drafts need revision, but as we've noted, too often students skimp on this phase of the writing process. The word *revision* can be used to describe all modifications one makes to a written document. However, it's useful to distinguish among three kinds of revision.

Global revisions focus on the thesis, the type and pattern of evidence employed, the overall organization, the match between thesis and content, and the tone. A global revision may also emerge from a change in purpose.

Local revisions focus on paragraphs: topic and transitional sentences; the type of evidence presented within a paragraph; evidence added, modified, or dropped within a paragraph; and logical connections from one sentence (or set of sentences) within a paragraph to another.

Surface revisions deal with sentence style and construction as well as word choice. Sentence editing involves correcting errors of grammar, mechanics, spelling, and citation form.

Global and local revisions fall within Stage 5 of the writing process, while surface revisions are covered in Stage 6, editing.

We advise separating large-scale (global and local) revision from later (sentence-editing) revisions as a way of keeping priorities in order. Different tasks require different cognitive functions. For example, when you are working on revising the structure and content of a paragraph within a paper, getting caught up in rewording an awkward sentence can distract you from the larger task at hand—a task that may prompt you to delete the very sentence you find awkward. Get the large pieces in place first: *content* (your ideas), *structure* (the arrangement of your paragraphs), and *paragraph structure* (the arrangement of ideas within your paragraphs). Then tend to the smaller elements, much as you would in building a house. You wouldn't lay the carpet before setting the floor joists.

Think of revision as re-vision, meaning "seeing anew." In order to re-see, it's often useful to set your paper aside for a time and come back later to view your rough draft with a fresh eye, from a new perspective. Doing so will better allow you to determine whether your work exhibits the characteristics of a good paper.

Characteristics of Good Papers

Apply the principles of *unity, coherence,* and *development* to the revision process. Let's start with unity, which we've already discussed somewhat in the context of the thesis.

UNITY

A paper is unified when focused on a main point. The chief tool for achieving paper unity is the thesis, as we've already noted: it's hard to achieve unity in a paper when a central point remains unstated. Unity, however, doesn't stop at the thesis; the body paragraphs that follow must clearly support and explain that thesis. Thus, the steps for determining unity are to first examine your introduction and make sure you have a clear, identifiable thesis. Next, check your paper's interior paragraphs to make sure your points all relate to that thesis. Ask yourself how your conclusion provides closure to your overall discussion.

COHERENCE

Coherence means "logical interconnectedness." When things cohere, separate elements hold together and make a whole. As applied to paper writing, coherence is very closely related to unity: Good papers cohere. They hold together logically and stay focused on a main point. All subordinate points addressed in the body of the paper clearly relate to the main point expressed in the thesis. Moreover, all those subpoints, examples, and supporting quotations are presented in a logical order so that connections between them are clear. You could write a highly unified paper, but if your points are discussed in a haphazard order, the reader will have a hard time following your argument or staying focused on your point. Lead readers along with your writing. Show them not only how sub-points relate to a main point, but also how they relate to one another.

DEVELOPMENT

Good papers are also well developed, meaning that their points are fully explained and supported. Readers do not live inside your head. They will not fully understand your points unless you adequately explain them. A reader also may not be persuaded that your paper's main point is valid unless you provide sufficient support for your arguments by using examples, the opinions of authorities on the subject, and your own sound logic to hold all together.

Use the three principles of unity, coherence, and development to analyze what you have written and make necessary revisions. Does your paper stay focused on the main point? Do your paper's points clearly relate to each other? Do you need better transitions between some paragraphs to help the ideas flow more logically and smoothly? Have you fully explained and given adequate support for all your points?

These three principles for good papers also apply to the composition of good paragraphs. Paragraphs are "mini-papers": they should stick to a main point (the topic sentence) and fully develop that point in an orderly fashion. Transitional words or phrases such as "however," "thus," "on the other hand," and "for example" help make clear to a reader how the sentences within individual paragraphs are related.

The Reverse Outline

The reverse outline is a useful technique for refining a working thesis and for establishing unity between your thesis statement and the body of your paper. When you outline a paper you intend to write, you do so *prospectively*—that is, before the fact of writing. In a reverse outline you outline the paper *retrospectively*—after the fact. The reverse outline is useful for spotting gaps in logic or development as well as problems with unity or coherence. Follow these steps to generate a reverse outline:

1. On a fresh sheet of paper (or electronic document), restate your thesis, making certain that the thesis you began with is the thesis that in fact governs the logic of the paper. (Look for a competing thesis in your conclusion. In summing up, you may have clarified for yourself what your *actual* governing idea is as opposed to the idea you thought would organize the paper.)

2. In the margin of your draft, summarize *each* paragraph in a phrase. If you have trouble writing a summary, place an asterisk by the paragraph as a reminder to clarify it later.

3. Beneath your thesis, write your paragraph-summary phrases, one to a line, in outline format.

4. Review the outline you have just created. Is the paper divided into readily identifiable major points in support of the thesis? Have you supported each major point sufficiently? Do the sections of the outline lead logically from one to the next? Do all sections develop the thesis?

5. Watch especially for uneven development. Add or delete material as needed to ensure a balanced presentation.

STAGE 6: EDITING

After revising a paper's large-scale elements—its unity, coherence, and development of its content; its overall structure; and its paragraph structure—you are ready to polish your paper by editing its sentences for style and correctness. At this stage you may be tired, and the temptation to merely correct a few glaring mistakes here and there may be strong. Resist that impulse: A paper with excellent ideas and structure can be ruined by mechanical, sentence-level errors. After all your work, you don't want readers to get distracted by sentence or punctuation errors.

Editing for Style

Developing an engaging writing style takes long practice. It's beyond the scope of this book to teach you the nuances of writing style, and you can consult many fine books for help. (See, for example, William Zinsser, *On*

Writing Well.) Here we'll focus on just one common stylistic problem: short, choppy sentences.

Perhaps out of fear of making sentence errors such as run-ons or comma splices, some writers avoid varying their sentence types, preferring strings of simple sentences. The result is usually unsatisfying. Compare, for instance, two versions of the same paragraph on study of the human genome:

> Scientists have finally succeeded in decoding the human genome. This accomplishment opens up a whole new field of study. Researchers now have new ways to understand human biological functioning. We may also be able to learn new perspectives on human behavior. For centuries people have wondered about how much we are shaped by genetics. They have also wondered how much environment shapes us. The age-old questions about nature vs. nurture may now be answered. Each individual's genetic heritage as well as his or her genetic future will be visible to geneticists. All of these discoveries may help us to improve and extend human life. Many diseases will be detectable. New treatments will be developed. These new discoveries open up a new area of ethical debate. Scientists and the public are going to have to decide how far to take this new genetic technology.

This paragraph illustrates the problems with choppy, repetitive sentences. First, the writer hasn't connected ideas, and sentences don't smoothly flow one to the next. Second, the same sentence structure (the simple sentence) appears repeatedly, each following the simple subject-verb-predicate form. The resulting repetition, while grammatically correct, taxes the reader's patience. Compare the preceding version to this revision (which represents just one way the paragraph could be rewritten):

> Scientists have opened a whole new field of study following their recent decoding of the human genome. Armed with new ways of understanding human biological and behavioral functioning, researchers may someday sort out the extent to which we are shaped by our genes and by our environment. When geneticists can examine an individual's genetic past and future, they may also be able to alter these things, with the goal of improving and extending human life through early disease detection and the development of new treatments. However, such promise is not without its pitfalls: genetic research must be scrutinized from an ethical standpoint, and scientists and the public will have to decide the uses and the limits of this new technology.

Not only is the edited version of this paragraph more pleasant to read, it's also more concise and clear, as well as more coherent. Sentences with related content have been combined. Brief sentences have been converted to clauses or phrases and incorporated into the structure of other sentences to form more complex units of meaning.

Guard against strings of short, choppy sentences in your own writing. Learn strategies for sentence-level revision by learning how different sentence structures work. You can link related ideas with subordinating conjunctions (*because, since, while, although,* etc.), commas and coordinating conjunctions (*for, and, nor, but, or, yet, so*), and semicolons and coordinating adverbs (*however, thus, therefore,* etc.).

Editing for Correctness

On matters of sentence style, there is no "correct" approach, per se. Each writer will have a different idea about what sentence structures, sentence lengths, and word choices sound best and best convey meaning. Often, personal style and taste influence sentence construction. Grammar and punctuation, on the other hand, follow more widely accepted, objective standards. Of these we (and your instructors) can speak in terms of "correctness"—of agreed-upon conventions, or rules, that people working in academic, professional, and business environments adopt as a standard of communication. You can find the rules (for comma placement, say, or the use of "amount" versus "number" or "affect" vesus "effect") in up-to-date writing handbooks. Review this list of common sentence-level errors, and eliminate such errors from your papers before submitting them.

COMMON SENTENCE-LEVEL ERRORS

Errors in Grammar

Sentence fragments—incomplete sentences missing a subject or predicate

Run-on sentences—two independent clauses joined together without the proper conjunctions (connecting words) or punctuation

Comma splices—two independent clauses joined with only a comma when they need stronger separation such as coordinating conjunctions, conjunctive adverbs, semicolons, or periods

Subject-verb agreement errors—the verb form doesn't match the plural or singular nature of the subject

Pronoun usage—pronoun reference errors, lack or clarity in pronoun reference, and errors of pronoun-antecedent agreement

Errors in Punctuation

Misplaced commas, missing commas, improper use of semicolons or colons, missing apostrophes, and the like

Errors in Spelling

Misspelled words

The Final Draft

When you have worked on a paper for days (or weeks), writing and revising multiple drafts, you may have trouble knowing when you're finished. With respect to poetry, the Pulitzer Prize–winning poet Henry Taylor once remarked that a writer is done when revisions begin to move the project laterally, instead of vertically. We think the same distinction applies to academic writing. Assuming you have revised at the sentence-level for grammar and punctuation, when you get the impression that your changes *do not actively advance* the main point with new facts or arguments or illustrations or supporting quotations, you are probably done. Stop writing and prepare a clean draft. Set it aside for a day or two (if you have that luxury), and read it one last time to catch remaining sentence-level errors.

Most difficult will be deciding when the paper is done stylistically, especially for the papers you care most deeply about. With respect to style, one could revise endlessly—and many writers do because there is no one correct way (stylistically speaking) to write a sentence. As long as a sentence is grammatical, you can write it numerous ways. Still, if a given sentence is dull, you will want to improve it, for an excessively dull style will bore the reader and defeat the paper as surely as a flawed argument or a host of grammatical errors. But having devoted time to polishing your sentences (for instance, to eliminating strings of short, choppy sentences—see p. 115), you will at some point need to pronounce yourself finished. Eventually, the time you invest will have diminishing returns. When your changes make your work merely different, not better, stop.

Your instructor will (likely) return the paper with comments and suggestions. Read these carefully. If you or the instructor feels that a revision is appropriate, think through the options for recasting the paper. Instructors generally respond well when you go into a conference with an action plan.

At some point, instructor's comments or no, the paper will be done and graded. Read it through one last time, and learn from it. Once you have determined what you did well and what you could improve for the next effort, it is time to move on.

Writing Assignment: Process

Choose either of the following writing assignments.

1. Write a paper following the process outlined in this chapter. As a guide, you may want to complete Exercises 3.1–7, which will serve as prompts. As you write, keep a log in which you record brief observations about each stage of the writing process. Share the log with your classmates and discuss the writing process with them.

2. In this chapter you have learned to approach writing as a task separated into stages that blend together and loop back on one another: data gathering, invention, drafting, revision, and editing. Write a one- or two-page statement in which you compare your writing process *prior* to taking a composition course to the process you've learned from this text and from your instructor. What are the salient differences? similarities? At the end of your statement, you may want to speculate on the ways you might eventually alter this process to better suit you.

4

Explanatory Synthesis

WHAT IS A SYNTHESIS?

A *synthesis* is a written discussion that draws on two or more sources. It follows that your ability to write syntheses depends on your ability to infer relationships among sources—essays, articles, fiction, and also nonwritten sources, such as lectures, interviews, and observations. This process is nothing new for you, since you infer relationships all the time—say, between something you've read in the newspaper and something you've seen for yourself, or between the teaching styles of your favorite and least favorite instructors. In fact, if you've written research papers, you've already written syntheses. In an *academic synthesis*, you make explicit the relationships that you have inferred among separate sources.

The skills you've already learned and practiced from the previous three chapters will be vital in writing syntheses. Clearly, before you're in a position to draw relationships between two or more sources, you must understand what those sources say; in other words, you must be able to *summarize* these sources. Readers will frequently benefit from at least partial summaries of sources in your synthesis essays. At the same time, you must go beyond summary to make judgments—judgments based, of course, on your *critical reading* of your sources: what conclusions you've drawn about the quality and validity of these sources, whether you agree or disagree with the points made in your sources, and why you agree or disagree.

Further, you must go beyond the critique of individual sources to determine the relationships among them. Is the information in source B, for example, an extended illustration of the generalizations in source A? Would it be useful to compare and contrast source C with source B? Having read and considered sources A, B, and C, can you infer something else—D (not a source, but your own idea)?

WHERE DO WE FIND WRITTEN SYNTHESES?

Here are just a few of the types of writing that involve synthesis:

Academic Writing

- **Analysis papers.** Synthesize and apply several related theoretical approaches.
- **Research papers.** Synthesize multiple sources.
- **Argument papers.** Synthesize different points into a coherent claim or position.
- **Essay exams.** Demonstrate understanding of course material through comparing and contrasting theories, viewpoints, or approaches in a particular field.

Workplace Writing

- **Newspaper and magazine articles.** Synthesize primary and secondary sources.
- **Position papers and policy briefs.** Compare and contrast solutions for solving problems.
- **Business plans.** Synthesize ideas and proposals into one coherent plan.
- **Memos and letters.** Synthesize multiple ideas, events, and proposals into concise form.
- **Web sites.** Synthesize information from various sources to present in Web pages and related links.

Because a synthesis is based on two or more sources, you will need to be selective when choosing information from each. It would be neither possible nor desirable, for instance, to discuss in a ten-page paper on the American Civil War every point that the authors of two books make about their subject. What you as a writer must do is select from each source the ideas and information that best allow you to achieve your purpose.

PURPOSE

Your purpose in reading source materials and then in drawing on them to write your own material is often reflected in the wording of an assignment. For instance, consider the following assignments on the Civil War:

American History: Evaluate the author's treatment of the origins of the Civil War.

Economics: Argue the following proposition, in light of your readings: "The Civil War was fought not for reasons of moral principle but for reasons of economic necessity."

Government: Prepare a report on the effects of the Civil War on Southern politics at the state level between 1870 and 1917.

Mass Communications: Discuss how the use of photography during the Civil War may have affected the perceptions of the war by Northerners living in industrial cities.

Literature: Select two twentieth-century Southern writers whose work you believe was influenced by the divisive effects of the Civil War. Discuss the ways this influence is apparent in a novel or a group of short stories written by each author. The works should not be *about* the Civil War.

Applied Technology: Compare and contrast the technology of warfare available in the 1860s with the technology available a century earlier.

Each of these assignments creates for you a particular purpose for writing. Having located sources relevant to your topic, you would select, for possible use in a paper, only those parts that helped you in fulfilling this purpose. And how you used those parts, how you related them to other material from other sources, would also depend on your purpose. For instance, if you were working on the government assignment, you might possibly draw on the same source as another student working on the literature assignment by referring to Robert Penn Warren's novel *All the King's Men*, about Louisiana politics in the early part of the twentieth century. But because the purposes of these assignments are different, you and the other student would make different uses of this source. Those same parts or aspects of the novel that you find worthy of detailed analysis might be mentioned only in passing by the other student.

USING YOUR SOURCES

Your purpose determines not only what parts of your sources you will use but also how you will relate them to one another. Since the very essence of synthesis is the combining of information and ideas, you must have some basis on which to combine them. *Some relationships among the material in your sources must make them worth synthesizing.* It follows that the better able you are to discover such relationships, the better able you will be to use your sources in writing syntheses. Notice that the mass communications assignment requires you to draw a *cause-and-effect* relationship between photographs of the war and Northerners' perceptions of the war. The applied technology assignment requires you to *compare and contrast* state-of-the-art weapons technology in the eighteenth and nineteenth centuries. The economics assignment requires you to *argue* a proposition. In each case, *your purpose will determine how you relate your source materials to one another.*

Consider some other examples. You may be asked on an exam question or in instructions for a paper to *describe* two or three approaches to prison reform during the past decade. You may be asked to *compare and contrast* one country's approach to imprisonment with another's. You may be asked to *develop an argument* of your own on this subject, based on your reading. Sometimes (when you are not given a specific assignment) you determine your own purpose: You are interested in exploring a particular subject; you are interested in making a case for one approach or another. In any event, your purpose shapes your essay. Your purpose determines which sources you research, which ones you use, which parts of them you use, at which points in your essay you use them, and in what manner you relate them to one another.

TYPES OF SYNTHESES: EXPLANATORY AND ARGUMENT

In this and the next chapter we categorize syntheses into two main types: *explanatory* and *argument*. The easiest way to recognize the difference between these two types may be to consider the difference between a newspaper article and an editorial on the same subject. Most likely, we'd say that the main purpose of the newspaper article is to convey *information*, and the main purpose of the editorial is to convey *opinion* or *interpretation*. Of course, this distinction is much too simplified: newspaper articles often convey opinion or bias, sometimes subtly, sometimes openly; and editorials often convey unbiased information, along with opinion. But as a practical matter, we can generally agree on the distinction between a newspaper article that primarily conveys information and an editorial that primarily conveys opinion.

We'll say, for the sake of convenience, that the newspaper article provides an explanation and that the editorial provides an argument. This is essentially the distinction we make between explanatory and argument syntheses.

As an example of the distinction, read the following paragraph:

> Researchers now use recombinant DNA technology to analyze genetic changes. With this technology, they cut and splice DNA from different species, then insert the modified molecules into bacteria or other types of cells that engage in rapid replication and cell division. The cells copy the foreign DNA right along with their own. In short order, huge populations produce useful quantities of recombinant DNA

molecules. The new technology also is the basis of genetic engineering, by which genes are isolated, modified, and inserted back into the same organism or into a different one.*

Now read this paragraph:

> Many in the life sciences field would have us believe that the new gene splicing technologies are irrepressible and irreversible and that any attempt to oppose their introduction is both futile and retrogressive. They never stop to even consider the possibility that the new genetic science might be used in a wholly different manner than is currently being proposed. The fact is, the corporate agenda is only one of two potential paths into the Biotech Century. It is possible that the growing number of anti-eugenic activists around the world might be able to ignite a global debate around alternative uses of the new science—approaches that are less invasive, more sustainable and humane and that conserve and protect the genetic rights of future generations.†

Both of these passages deal with the topic of biotechnology, but the two take quite different approaches. The first passage came from a biology textbook, while the second appeared in a magazine article. As we might expect from a textbook on the broad subject of biology, the first passage is explanatory and informative; it defines and explains some of the key concepts of biotechnology without taking a position or providing commentary about the implications of the technology. Magazine articles often present information in the same ways; however, many magazine articles take specific positions, as we see in the second passage. This passage is argumentative or persuasive. Its primary purpose is to convey a point of view regarding the topic of biotechnology.

While each of these excerpts presents a clear instance of writing that is either explanatory or argumentative, it is important to note that the sources for these excerpts—the textbook chapter and the magazine article—contain elements of both explanation and argument. The textbook writers, while they refrain from taking a particular position, do note the controversies surrounding biotechnology and genetic engineering. They might even subtly reveal a certain bias in favor of one side of the issue, through their word choice, tone, and perhaps through devoting more space and attention to one point of view. Explanatory and argumentative writing are not mutually exclusive. The overlap in the categories of explanation and argument is also found in the magazine article: In order to make his case against genetic engi-

---

*Cecie Starr and Ralph Taggart, "Recombinant DNA and Genetic Engineering," *Biology: The Unity and Diversity of Life* (New York: Wadsworth: 1998).

†Jeremy Rifkin, "The Ultimate Therapy: Commercial Eugenics on the Eve of the Biotech Century," *Tikkun* May–June 1998: 35.

neering, the writer has to explain certain elements of the issue. Yet, even while these categories overlap to a certain extent, the second passage clearly has argument as its primary purpose, whereas the first passage is primarily explanatory.

In Chapter 2 we noted that the primary purpose in a piece of writing is either informative, persuasive, or entertaining (or some combination of the three). Some scholars of writing argue that all writing is essentially persuasive, and even without entering into that complex argument, we've just seen how the varying purposes in writing do overlap. In order to persuade others of a particular position we typically must also inform them about it; conversely, a primarily informative piece of writing also must work to persuade the reader that its claims are truthful. Both informative and persuasive writing often include entertaining elements, and writing intended primarily to entertain also typically contains information and persuasion. For practical purposes, however, it is possible—and useful—to identify the *primary* purpose in a piece of writing as informative/ explanatory, persuasive/argumentative, or entertaining. Entertainment as a primary purpose is the one least often practiced in purely academic writing—perhaps to your disappointment!—but information and persuasion are ubiquitous. Thus, while recognizing the overlap between these categories, we distinguish in this and the following chapter between two types of synthesis writing: explanatory (or informative), and argument (or persuasive). Just as distinguishing the primary purpose in a piece of writing helps you to critically read and evaluate it, distinguishing the primary purpose in your own writing helps you to make the appropriate choices regarding your approach.

In this chapter we'll first present some guidelines for writing syntheses in general, then we'll proceed to focus on explanatory syntheses. In the next chapter, we'll discuss the argument synthesis.

HOW TO WRITE SYNTHESES

Although writing syntheses can't be reduced to a lockstep method, it should help you to follow the guidelines listed in the box on pages 125–126.

THE EXPLANATORY SYNTHESIS

Many of the papers you write in college will be more or less explanatory in nature. An explanation helps readers understand a topic. Writers explain when they divide a subject into its component parts and present them to the reader in a clear and orderly fashion. Explanations may entail descriptions that recreate in words some object, place, emotion, event, sequence of events, or state of affairs. As a student reporter, you may need to explain an event—

to relate when, where, and how it took place. In a science lab, you would observe the conditions and results of an experiment and record them for review by others. In a political science course, you might review research on a particular subject—say, the complexities underlying the debate over gay marriage—and then present the results of your research to your professor and the members of your class.

Your job in writing an explanatory paper—or in writing the explanatory portion of an argumentative paper—is not to argue a particular point, but rather *to present the facts in a reasonably objective manner*. Of course, explanatory papers, like other academic papers, should be based on a thesis. But the purpose of a thesis in an explanatory paper is less to advance a particular opinion than to focus the various facts contained in the paper.

GUIDELINES FOR WRITING SYNTHESES

- **Consider your purpose in writing.** What are you trying to accomplish in your essay? How will this purpose shape the way you approach your sources?
- **Select and carefully read your sources**, according to your purpose. Then reread the passages, mentally summarizing each. Identify those aspects or parts of your sources that will help you fulfill your purpose. When rereading, *label* or *underline* the sources for main ideas, key terms, and any details you want to use in the synthesis.
- **Take notes on your reading.** In addition to labeling or underlining key points in the readings, you might write brief one- or two-sentence summaries of each source. This will help you in formulating your thesis statement, and in choosing and organizing your sources later.
- **Formulate a thesis.** Your thesis is the main idea that you want to present in your synthesis. It should be expressed as a complete sentence. You might do some predrafting about the ideas discussed in the readings in order to help you work out a thesis. If you've written one-sentence summaries of the readings, looking these over will help you to brainstorm connections between readings and to devise a thesis.

  When you write your essay drafts, you will need to consider where your thesis fits in your paper. Sometimes the thesis is the first sentence, but more often it is *the final sentence of the first paragraph*. If you are writing an *inductively arranged* synthesis (see p. 221), the thesis sentence may not appear until the final paragraphs. (See Chapter 3 for more information on writing an effective thesis.)

  (continued)

- **Decide how you will use your source material.** How will the information and the ideas in the passages help you fulfill your purpose?
- **Develop an organizational plan**, according to your thesis. How will you arrange your material? It is not necessary to prepare a formal outline. But you should have some plan that will indicate the order in which you will present your material and that will indicate the relationships among your sources.
- **Draft the topic sentences for the main sections.** This is an optional step, but you may find it a helpful transition from organizational plan to first draft.
- **Write the first draft** of your synthesis, following your organizational plan. Be flexible with your plan, however. Frequently, you will use an outline to get started. As you write, you may discover new ideas and make room for them by adjusting the outline. When this happens, reread your work frequently, making sure that your thesis still accounts for what follows and that what follows still logically supports your thesis.
- **Document your sources.** You must do this by crediting them within the body of the synthesis—citing the author's last name and page number from which the point was taken and by providing full citation information in a list of "Works Cited" at the end. Don't open yourself to charges of plagiarism! (See pp. 53–56; see also Chapter 7 for more information on documenting sources.)
- **Revise your synthesis**, inserting transitional words and phrases where necessary. Make sure that the synthesis reads smoothly, logically, and clearly from beginning to end. Check for grammatical correctness, punctuation, spelling.

Note: The writing of syntheses is a recursive process, and you should accept a certain amount of backtracking and reformulating as inevitable. For instance, in developing an organizational plan (Step 6 of the procedure), you may discover a gap in your presentation that will send you scrambling for another source—back to Step 2. You may find that formulating a thesis and making inferences among sources occur simultaneously; indeed, inferences often are made before a thesis is formulated. Our recommendations for writing syntheses will give you a structure; they will get you started. But be flexible in your approach; expect discontinuity and, if possible, be comforted that through backtracking and reformulating you will eventually produce a coherent, well-crafted essay.

DEMONSTRATION: EXPLANATORY SYNTHESIS— COMPUTERS, COMMUNICATION, AND RELATIONSHIPS

To illustrate how the process of synthesis works, we'll begin with a number of short extracts from several articles on the same subject.

Suppose you were writing a paper on a matter that many computer users are discussing these days: the ways in which communication via computers (that is, computer mediated communication, or CMC) is changing human patterns of interaction and relationships. Some writers and thinkers are excited about the world of possibilities opened up by this technological medium, while others are skeptical about whether the Internet will lead to more interaction and connection between people, or will harm the quality of such connections. Still others argue that this new mode of communication is likely to further isolate us from each other, and "real" human contact will become a rare and precious thing.

EXERCISE ■ **4.1**

Exploring the Topic

Before reading what others have written on the subject of computers, communication, and relationships, write several paragraphs exploring what you know and what you think about this topic. You might focus your first paragraph on discussing your own experience with computer communication and relationships. How much have you used e-mail, instant messaging, and other Internet-related activity? How have these technologies affected your ability to communicate with others? What are some positive and negative impacts of such communication on relationships? In your second paragraph you might broaden the focus by discussing what you know about these issues in the world at large. What are some concerns people have about computers and their effects on communication? What do you think most interests journalists, professors, politicians, and businesspeople about computer communication and relationships?

Because this is a topic that bears upon a broader subject—the ways that computers and the Internet affect our lives—you decide to investigate what has been written on the subject, both in print and electronic texts. In the following pages we present excerpts from the kinds of articles your research might locate.

Note: To save space and for the purpose of demonstration, the following passages are brief excerpts only. In preparing your paper, naturally you would draw upon the entire articles from which these extracts were made. (The discussion of how these passages can form the basis of an explanatory synthesis resumes on page 138.)

Cyberspace: A New Frontier for Fighting Words
Sanjiv N. Singh

Sanjiv N. Singh holds a J.D. from the UCLA School of Law. The article from which this piece is excerpted appeared in the Rutgers Computer and Technology Law Journal, *in 1999.**

[T]he Internet has begun to transform the way in which people interact. Various mediums now exist that allow for cheap and almost instantaneous communication via computer. For example, e-mail is now an increasingly common way to communicate with family, friends, and acquaintances. In fact, more than fifteen percent of the U.S. adult population use e-mail. . . . Technology research firms estimate that by the year 2001, fifty percent of the U.S. population will communicate via e-mail. . . .

Many colleges and graduate schools routinely provide students with, and in some cases require, use of e-mail accounts. As a result, significant segments of our population are being socialized in an environment where cyberspace communication is an encouraged form of establishing and confirming social engagements or simply corresponding with friends.

Social Relationships in Electronic Forums: Hangouts, Salons, Workplaces and Communities
Rob Kling

Rob Kling is a professor of Information Systems and Information Science in the School for Library and Information Science at the University of Indiana at Bloomington. He has published numerous articles examining the impact of information technologies on organizations, the workplace, publishing and education, as well as on social life. His books include Computerization and Controversy: Value Conflicts and Social Choices *(1996), and* Computers and Politics: High Technology in American Local Governments *(1982). The following reading is excerpted from an essay that appeared in* CMC Magazine.†

---

*Sanjiv N. Singh, "Cyberspace: A New Frontier for Fighting Words," *Rutgers Computer and Technology Law Journal* 25.2 (1999): 283.

†Rob Kling, "Social Relationships in Electronic Forums: Hangouts, Salons, Workplaces and Communities," *CMC Magazine* 22 July 1996, 4 Feb. 2000 <http://www.december.com/cmc/mag/1996/jul/kling.html>.

Enthusiasts for [Internet] forums argue that they are building new forms of community life (Rheingold, 1993). But other analysts observe that not every collection of people who happen to talk (or write) to each other form the sense of trust, mutual interest, and sustained commitments that automatically deserve to be labeled as communities (Jones, 1995). . . .

In the United States, communities seem to be deteriorating from a complex combination of causes. In the inner cities of big urban centers, many people fear street crime and stay off the streets at night. In the larger suburban and post-suburban areas, many people hardly know their neighbors and "latch key" children often have little adult contact after school. An African proverb which says that "it takes a whole village to raise a child" refers to a rich community life with a sense of mutual responsibility that is difficult to find in many new neighborhoods. Some advocates believe that computer technology in concert with other efforts could play a role in rebuilding community life by improving communication, economic opportunity, civic participation, and education (Schuler, 1994; Civille, Fidelman, and Altobello, 1993).

Signs of Life in the USA
Sonia Maasik and Jack Solomon

Sonia Maasik is a member of the Writing Program faculty at UCLA, and Jack Solomon is an English professor at California State College, Northridge. In addition to their popular textbook (from which this excerpt comes) Signs of Life in the USA: Readings on Popular Culture for Writers *(3rd edition, 2000), the two have also collaborated on* California Dreams and Realities: Readings for Critical Thinkers and Writers *(1999).**

The emerging outlines of the Web's global village have some people very excited and others worried. The worried contingent are concerned that the relationships people are building on the Net lack an essential core of humanity. The unreal world of virtual culture, they believe, the world in which you can pretend to be just about anything, is being substituted for a social reality made up of real human beings. And such a world, based entirely on the transmission of electronic signals, is potentially a world in which human beings will be unable to conceive of others as human beings. When all interaction is electronic, they ask, where is the ground for true human empathy and relatedness?

---

*Sonia Maasik and Jack Solomon, eds., *Signs of Life in the USA* (Boston: Bedford Books, 1997), 701.

Life at High-Tech U
Deborah Branscum

A contributing editor to Newsweek, *a columnist for* Fortune.com's *"Valley Talk," and a free-lance technology writer, Deborah Branscum has written articles for a number of publications, including* Wired, The New York Times, Infoworld, *and* Yahoo Internet Life. *She operates a Web site called MonsterBuzz.com and founded its affiliated BUZZ executive conference.**

Some academics dismiss [e-mail] as an unhealthy substitute for human contact. But Stanford's Richard Holeton, who tracked e-mail discussions of first-year students in one dorm, found that 87 percent of their messages involved important social or critical dialogue. Those issues included "pornography, free speech, a potential grape boycott on campus and a sexual-harassment allegation," says Holeton. And the people who dominated dorm life in face-to-face encounters were not the same folks who ruled the e-mail debates. Electronic discourse, it seems, offered a voice to some students who might not otherwise be heard.

Instant Messaging Is In, Phones Out
Ellen Edwards

Ellen Edwards is a staff writer for The Washington Post. *This article appeared in* The Seattle Times *on June 16, 2003.*

In what may be a permanent shift, kids are communicating online rather than by phone. And as they get older, when they do use the phone, it's more likely to be a cell, and even that may be for text messaging rather than talking. "I'm absolutely certain instant messages will have a profound effect on relationships," says Georgetown University linguistics professor Deborah Tannen. "I just don't know what it will be. I think it will be as great or maybe greater than the invention of the telephone."

"The phone never rings in our home," says Gary Knell, the president and CEO of Sesame Workshop, which produces "Sesame Street." Knell has four children, ages 17, 15, 12 and 8. "I look, and they are holding IM conversations with 20 friends. All the arguments in our house are about computer access."

---

*Deborah Branscum, "Life At High-Tech U," *Newsweek* 27 Oct. 1997: 78–80.

The computer gives kids scope. As they get older and more independent, the cell gives them mobility.

America Online, which provides the most-used instant messaging service through AOL subscriptions and its free AOL Instant Messaging service (AIM), estimates that by 2005 IMs will surpass e-mail as the primary way of communicating online. Right now 1.6 billion AOL and AIM IMs are sent every day. AOL is of course fueling the fire by adding extras that kids love, taking the IM smiley face signs to new levels with customized signatures, instant greetings that flash and dance across the screen and personalized "away" messages.

The theory of "away" messages, for those times when you are on the Internet but away from your computer, says Tannen, "is that you're always supposed to be available." When you're not, she says, the "away" message is your apology. "When I come home from school, I get on the Internet right away," says Lucy Bascom, a seventh-grader at Bethesda, Md.'s, Westland Middle School. Homework questions still are left to the phone, not IMs, she says. IMs may be closing in on phone chat, but the mechanism hasn't killed it completely.

"Sometimes it's simultaneous," says Lucy's dad, John Bascom, who says his 13-year-old daughter multi-tasks pretty effectively between the two. But IMing got so all-consuming for Lucy several years ago that her parents installed software to limit her online time. When she's on the phone, she says, she's usually talking to someone with whom she is also IMing. "It's really convenient to say things you wouldn't have the confidence to say on the phone," says Lucy. "There are no long awkward pauses when you are trying to think of a word."

Teens Bare Their Hearts with Instant Messages
Stanley A. Miller II

Stanley A. Miller is a staff writer for the Milwaukee Journal Sentinel, *where this article first appeared on June 26, 2001.*

According to a study released late last week by the Pew Internet & American Life Project, a non-profit research group, 37% of teenagers said they have used instant messaging to write something they wouldn't have said in person.

"Sometimes it is easier to say what is in your heart online," a 17-year-old girl wrote in one of the study's online discussion groups. "You can type the words and hit send instead of freezing up in person. In the mornings I sometimes get love letters, and it makes me feel so good. I love hearing what my sweetie is thinking."

The report also found that 17% of teens using instant messaging said they used it to ask someone out, and 13% used it to break up with someone.

Sean Witzling, who will be a sophomore this fall at Shorewood High School, said he uses instant messaging every day, usually to coordinate social plans with his friends. Witzling said he's never asked a girl out using instant messaging, and he would never break up with one that way. "That would be too mean," he said.

Charles Giles Crosse IV, 15, thought it was mean when his girlfriend broke up with him about a year ago using instant messaging. The young couple were shooting messages back and forth about sports "when out of the blue she was like, 'oh yeah, by the way, I don't think we should see each anymore.' It came out of nowhere. I lost a lot of respect for that person."

Nick Eannelli, who will be a junior at Shorewood, said the method of communication is just too impersonal for that type of talk. Eannelli said he has never asked anyone out using instant messaging, but a friend of his did and was turned down. "I think it was more along the lines of my friend acting really strange," he said. "I think it was doomed to begin with. If you are going to do something personal, you should do it face to face."

The Pew study found there were no gender-based differences in who initiated instant-message breakups, with an equal number of boys and girls using the technology to end their relationships.

Teens' Instant-Messaging Lingo Is Evolving into a Hybrid Language
Stephanie Dunnewind

Stephanie Dunnewind is a staff writer for The Seattle Times, *where this article first appeared on April 12, 2003.*

As teens use it, instant messaging is full of acronyms (BRB equals "be right back"), words missing vowels and a complete lack of capitalization. It's like trying to read a sentence made of vanity license plates.

For example: "i wz gtin2d@ & now gota type it agen b patient!" equals, according to the Web site transL8it! (www.transl8it.com), "I was getting to that and now gotta type it again be patient!"

Instant messaging and chat lingo is shortened for speed since conversations are conducted in real time. If a friend is waiting for a response, you want to type it out as quickly as possible. For text messages on mobile devices, the number of characters that can fit in a transmission is limited, so the language is condensed.

"If your thumbs have got to carry the weight, you tend to do some abbreviations," explained Rob Mahowald, research manager for the Massachusetts-based IDC. "You quickly learn what shortcuts people are going to understand."

So the written language is stripped of everything unnecessary (punctuation, capitals, traditional spelling) until it's a bare, phonetic representation of how people talk.

'A Genuine Linguistic Revolution'

Some linguists argue that the Web language is a new entity, a hybrid of speech and writing. In an article on yourDictionary.com, one linguist called Net lingo "a genuine linguistic revolution." Others, however, note that it hasn't impacted language much outside the Internet yet. Teens say it's uncool to use IM acronyms in regular conversation.

"They are altering language to suit the technology," said David Silver, a University of Washington professor of communication who studies new media. Teens have also incorporated IM the same as teens have always used slang, as a way to separate themselves as a group, he said.

Nearly three-quarters of online teens use instant messaging, compared with less than half of adults, according to a 2000 survey by the Pew Internet & American Life Project.

"The strategic use of 'POS' 'parent over shoulder' is just brilliant," Silver said. "Say a teen is supposed to be doing homework but of course is on IM. A parent comes up and he quickly types 'POS' and sends it out. Suddenly everyone is talking about math homework."

Minding Your E-manners: Over-use of Instant Messaging Can Be a Major Breach of Netiquette
Michelle Slatalla

Michelle Slatalla is a staff writer for The Gazette *(Montreal, Quebec), where this article first appeared on September 25, 1999.*

Unlike E-mail messages, which wait patiently for you to open them, an instant message is the electronic equivalent of a ringing phone because it pops up on the recipient's screen right away.

But somebody apparently forgot to ask instant-message users what they thought. Many of the features that make the service so appealing to teenagers—its speed and the ability to see who else is online—has made it as welcome as a Friday afternoon meeting in many offices. . . .

Instant messages can be more annoying than other forms of electronic communication because they appear on screen as soon as they are sent. Recipients of voice mail, E-mail or faxes can acknowledge a message whenever it is convenient.

Just as you can turn off the ringer on your phone, you can turn off your instant messages, keeping everyone, or just certain people, from getting through. But just as with a phone that is never answered, people will wonder why you are not available for instant messages. Another strategy is to tell your computer to respond to instant messages by sending a message saying you will be back later, but that can also irritate people.

"It's the cyber-equivalent of someone walking into your office and starting up a conversation as if you had nothing better to do," said Jeanne Hinds, who publishes a Web page called Etiquette Hell, at www.thinds.com/jmh/ehell .

Hinds, whose site chronicles lapses in politeness, said instant messages violate the sense of private space.

"Even in the office, we think of our personal space as being a 5-foot radius around ourselves," she said. "Instant messages come blaring into the space, and it's an invasion."

Developing Personal and Emotional Relationships Via Computer-Mediated Communication
Brittney G. Chenault

Brittney G. Chenault holds a degree from the Graduate School of Library and Information Science at the University of Illinois, Urbana-Champaign. This article appeared in the online journal, CMC Magazine, *and has been widely read and quoted since its publication in 1998.**

> The idea of a community accessible only via my computer screen sounded cold to me at first, but I learned quickly that people can feel passionately about e-mail and computer conferences. I've become one of them. I care about these people I met through my computer . . . (Rheingold, 1993, p. 1). . . .

People meet via CMC every day, exchange information, debate, argue, woo, commiserate, and support. They may meet via a mailing list or newsgroup, and continue the interaction via e-mail. Their relationships can range from the cold, professional encounter, to the hot, intimate rendezvous. Rheingold describes people in virtual communities as using the words they type on screens to exchange pleasantries and argue, engage in intellectual discourse, conduct commerce, exchange knowledge, share emotional support, make plans, brainstorm, gossip, feud, fall in love, find friends and lose them, play games, flirt, create a little high art and a lot of idle talk.

---

*Brittney G. Chenault, "Developing Personal and Emotional Relationships Via Computer-Mediated Communication," *CMC Magazine* May 1998, 20 Mar. 2000 <http://www.december.com/cmc/mag/1998/may/chenault.html>.

Cyberspace Romances: Interview with Jean-François Perreault of *Branchez-vous*
John Suler

John Suler is a Professor of Psychology at Rider University in New Jersey and a practicing psychologist. His publications include Contemporary Psychoanalysis *and* Eastern Thought *(1993) as well as the online hypertext book (Web site)* The Psychology of Cyberspace. *This excerpt comes from that Web site and represents a comment by the interviewee, Jean-François Perreault, of the Quebec, Canada, based online magazine* Branchez-Vous.*

Perreault: My guess is that in a "true" romance on the Internet, the couple eventually will want to meet each other face-to-face. They may HAVE to meet each other for the relationship to fully develop and to be fully satisfying. For these people, the Internet simply was a way to meet each other. I say "simply" but this feature of the Internet shouldn't be underestimated. It is a POWERFUL way for people with compatible interests and personalities to find each other.

There are some people who may NOT want to meet the lover face-to-face. My guess is that these people prefer living with the fantasy that they have created (consciously or unconsciously) about the cyber-lover. . . . They may not want to meet each other face-to-face because the fantasy might be destroyed by the hard facts of reality. Who can say whether this is "wrong" or "dangerous"? Many people allow themselves the luxury of fantasy—either through books, or TV, or movies. And most people don't confuse this fantasy with reality. A cyber-lover is just another type of "escape fantasy"—only it's much more interactive, and therefore much more exciting, than the more usual methods.

Click Here for Romance
Jennifer Wolcott

A staff writer for The Christian Science Monitor, *Jennifer Wolcott writes on a wide range of topics, including social issues, the arts, and popular culture.†*

---

*John Suler, "Cyberspace Romances: Interview with Jean-François Perreault of Branchez-vous," *The Psychology of Cyberspace*, 11 Dec. 1996, 7 Apr. 2000 <http://www.rider.edu/users/suler/psycyber/psycyber.html>.

†Jennifer Wolcott, "Click Here for Romance," *The Christian Science Monitor* 13 Jan. 1999, 23 Feb. 2000 <http://www.csmonitor.com/durable/1991/01/13/fp11s1-csm.shtml>.

Online chat can sprout real-life romances that begin with surprisingly honest communication and realistic expectations, traits that many traditional relationships lack at first, according to an Ohio University sociologist who is studying relationships that begin in cyberspace. "I really feel the basis of these relationships is better and deeper than many real-life meetings because the couples are honest with each other in their writings," says Andrea Baker, assistant professor of sociology at Ohio University's Lancaster campus. . . . Baker's study suggests the written word tends to promote frank conversation in cyberspace, especially between couples who eventually want to meet face-to-face. Study participants said this immediate sincerity when meeting online was a pleasant switch from the typical blind date scenario. "Couples say this kind of honesty is absolutely necessary to forming a good relationship," Baker says. "In most cases, they are extremely honest and really cover the downsides as well as the upsides so there won't be any surprises when they meet." . . .

Honesty is what most appealed to California resident John Dwyer about the online approach. Disillusioned with the bar scene, he decided to give it a whirl. He posted a personal ad and photograph, got hundreds of responses, and eventually connected with Debbie. They married this past New Year's Eve—a year and a half after she answered his online ad. "If you are honest when talking online, you can strip away all the superficial stuff and really get to know someone," says Debbie. How did she know John was being honest? "I got a sense from the conversation whether it was real or contrived," she says. "I could tell after a while that he wasn't just someone trying to land a fish."

You've Got Romance! Seeking Love Online: Net-Based Services Change the Landscape, If Not the Odds, of Finding the Perfect Mate
Bonnie Rothman Morris

Bonnie Rothman Morris is a journalist and screenwriter who writes frequently for The New York Times, *which is the source for this excerpt. Morris's screenplays include the comedies "Guy and Doll" and "Taking the Leap."**

Tom Buckley didn't have much use for a dating service, or so he thought. "I didn't need to pay a company to help set me up to get a date, a girlfriend, a fiancée, a wife," said Buckley, 30, a steel broker in Portland, Ore., who plays rugby in his spare time. But after a lonely Thanksgiving dinner where he was the only single

*Bonnie R. Morris, "You've Got Romance! Seeking Love Online: Net-Based Services Change the Landscape, If Not the Odds, of Finding the Perfect Mate," *New York Times on the Web* 26 Aug. 1999, 23 Feb. 2000 <http://www.nytimes.com/library/tech/yr/mo/circuits/index.html>.

adult at the family dinner table, Buckley signed up for a free week on Match.com. What ensued on the matchmaking service was an e-mail romance with Terri Muir, a schoolteacher on Vancouver Island in British Columbia. "Anybody who knew us would never have thought we would have gone down that road," Buckley said in a telephone interview. Reflecting on the couple's instant attraction, he said, "e-mail made it easier to communicate because neither one of us was the type to walk up to someone in the gym or a bar and say, 'You're the fuel to my fire.'"

Thirteen months after their first feverish exchanges, Buckley and Ms. Muir lied to their families and friends and sneaked away to Vancouver to meet for the first time. At their wedding one year later, they finally told the tale of how they had met to their 100 guests. More and more single people, used to finding everything else on the Internet, are using it to search for love. More than 2,500 Web sites for adults are now devoted to matchmaking, said Daniel Bender, founder of Cupid's Network, an Internet portal for personals sites. . . .

[Robert Spradling] struck up an online romance with a Ukrainian woman whom he had met on American Singles. The woman immediately asked him for money to pay the agency she was using to translate and send her romantic e-mails back to him. There are many such agencies in the former Soviet Union, Spradling said. Next she told Spradling she wanted to start her own matchmaking agency. Spradling, 42, an employee in the development office at Morehead State University in Kentucky, footed the bill for that, too. After sending her about $8,000, Spradling asked her to marry him, via e-mail. She said yes and invited him to Kiev. "When you meet somebody and you think you're in love, you never see any faults," said Spradling, who said the couple had made wedding plans when he was visiting. After his return to the United States, Spradling never heard from her again. He's sworn off finding love through the Internet for now. . . . "I caution a lot of guys to be careful and keep their head and learn a lot about who they're dating online," Spradling said.

Online Dating Sheds Its Stigma as Losers.com
Amy Harmon

A graduate of the University of Michigan, Amy Harmon writes on technology issues for The New York Times, *where the article from which the following passage is excerpted first appeared on June 29, 2003.*

. . . Online dating, once viewed as a refuge for the socially inept and as a faintly disrespectable way to meet other people, is rapidly becoming a fixture of single life for adults of all ages, backgrounds and interests. More than 45 million Americans visited online dating sites last month, up from about 35 million at the end of 2002, according to comScore Media Metrix, a Web tracking service. Spending by subscribers on Web dating sites has soared, rising to a projected $100 million or more a quarter this year from under $10 million a quarter at the beginning of 2001, according to the Online Publishers Association.

And despite the Web's reputation as a meeting ground for casual sex, a majority of the leading sites' paying subscribers now say that what they are looking for is a relationship.

Stories of deception persist. Many online daters turn out to be married, and it is taken for granted that everybody lies a little. But they are more often trumped by a pervasive dissatisfaction with singles bars, dates set up by friends and other accepted ways of meeting prospective mates. . . .

Consider Your Purpose

Here, then, are brief selections from 13 sources on computer mediated communication. How do you go about synthesizing these sources?

First, remember that before considering the *how*, you must consider the *why*. In other words, what is your *purpose* in synthesizing these sources? You might use them for a paper dealing with a broader issue: the effects of computer technology on our daily lives. If this were your purpose, these sources would be used for only one section of your discussion, and the paper as a whole would advance an *argument* for a particular viewpoint about technology in modern society. Or, for a communications course you might consider the impact technology is having on communication, comparing this kind of communication with other forms of written communication and/or with face-to-face, verbal communication. The various excerpts would provide important examples of how communication is changing. Or, moving out of the academic world and into the commercial one, you might be a computer consultant preparing a brochure for a new Internet application or matchmaking Web site. In this brochure, you might want to address the personal uses to which people put these kinds of applications, or for the Web site, you would focus on the positive aspects of forming relationships on the Internet.

But for now let's keep it simple: You want to write a paper, or a section of a paper, that simply explains the impact the Internet is having on relationships between people so that those who may be interested, but who know little or nothing about these issues, will understand some aspects of the CMC phenomenon. Your job, then, is to write an *explanatory* synthesis—one that presents a focused overview of computer mediated communication but does not advance your own opinion on the *subject*.

EXERCISE **4.2**

Critical Reading for Synthesis

Look over the preceding readings and make a list of the ways they address the overall topics of computers, communication, and relationships. Make your list as specific and detailed as you can. Then write several lists grouping together the readings that deal with similar aspects of the overall topics. You might imagine that you were planning to write a very short synthesis on one small aspect of the broad topics; in this case, for different aspects of the topic, which readings would you use?

We asked one of our students, Alyssa Mellott, to read these passages and to use them as sources in a short paper on some of the issues surrounding CMC. We also asked her to write some additional comments describing the process of developing her ideas into a draft. We'll draw upon some of these comments in the following discussion.

Formulate a Thesis

The difference between a purpose and a thesis is a difference primarily of focus. Your purpose provides direction to your research and focus to your paper. Your thesis sharpens this focus by narrowing it and formulating it in the words of a single declarative statement. (Refer to Chapter 3 for additional discussion on formulating thesis statements.)

Since Alyssa's purpose in this case was to synthesize source material with little or no comment, her thesis would be the most obvious statement she could make about the relationship among these passages. By "obvious" we mean a statement that is broad enough to encompass the main points of all these readings. Taken as a whole, what do they *mean*? Here Alyssa describes the process she followed in coming up with a preliminary thesis for her explanatory synthesis:

> I began my writing process by looking over all the readings and noting the main point of each reading in a sentence on a piece of paper.
>
> Then I reviewed all of these points and identified the patterns in the readings. These I listed underneath my list of main points:--All the readings focus on Internet communication, or CMC.--The readings address several different kinds of relationships the authors believe are affected by CMC: communal relationships, relationships between long-distance friends, those between students and instructors, and love relationships.--Some authors discuss positive views, others negative views, of CMC and relationships.
>
> Looking over these points, I drafted a preliminary thesis. This thesis summed up the different issues in the sources and stated how these were interrelated.

> The Internet is changing the ways people interact and form relationships.

This was a true statement, but it sounded too vague and too obvious. I didn't feel it adequately represented the readings' points, since the readings explored a number of specific kinds of interactions and relationships impacted by CMC. I wanted my thesis to more fully reflect the complexity of people's concern regarding technology and relationships. My next version followed:

> Computers and the Internet add new ways for people to interact, but we have yet to see whether or not these new modes of communication will improve human interaction.

This thesis was more comprehensive, but it still didn't quite work. It was vague, and the last part seemed bland; it didn't reflect the strong feelings the writers expressed about the possible effects of CMC on different kinds of relationships. In my next attempt, I tried to be more specific and a little more dramatic:

> With so many computer users forming a variety of online relationships, no one can deny that this new technology is affecting our modes of communication; however, reactions to these changes range widely from excitement over our abilities to forge global connections, to fear that such connections will prove much less satisfying than old-fashioned human interactions.

This sentence was quite long, but I felt the second part of the sentence introduced the real point of my essay: that people have certain mixed reactions to how CMC will affect relationships. I thought this would be a good working thesis because it would help me structure my essay around specific views on CMC. Now I proceeded to the next step in writing--organizing my material.

Decide How You Will Use Your Source Material

The easiest way to deal with sources is to summarize them. But because you are synthesizing *ideas* rather than sources, you will have to be more selective than if you were writing a simple summary. You don't have to treat *all* the ideas in your sources, only the ones related to your thesis. Some sources might be summarized in their entirety; others, only in part. Look over your earlier notes or sentences discussing the topics covered in the readings, and refer back to the readings themselves. Focusing on some of the more subtle elements of the issues addressed by the authors, expand your earlier summary sentences. Write brief phrases in the margin of the sources, underline key phrases or sentences, or take notes on a separate sheet of paper or in a word processing file or electronic data filing program. Decide how your sources can help you achieve your purpose and support your thesis. For example, how, if at all, will you use the quotations by Rheingold contained in the passage by Chenault? How could you incorporate the personal experiences reported by some of the people who formed romantic attachments online?

Develop an Organizational Plan

An organizational plan is your map for presenting material to the reader. What material will you present? To find out, examine your thesis. Do the content and structure of the thesis (that is, the number and order of assertions) suggest an organizational plan for the paper? Expect to devote at least one paragraph of your paper to developing each section of this plan. Having identified likely sections, think through the possibilities of arrangement. Ask yourself: What information does the reader need to understand first? How do I build on this first section—what block of information will follow? Think of each section in relation to others until you have placed them all and have worked your way through to a plan for the whole paper.

Study your thesis, and let it help suggest an organization. Bear in mind that any one paper can be written—successfully—according to a variety of plans. Your job before beginning your first draft is to explore possibilities. Sketch a series of rough outlines: Arrange and rearrange your paper's likely sections until you develop a plan that both facilitates the reader's understanding and achieves your objectives as a writer. Think carefully about the logical order of your points: Does one idea or point lead to the next? If not, can you find a more logical place for the point, or are you just not clearly articulating the connections between the ideas?

Your final paper may well deviate from your final sketch, since in the act of writing you may discover the need to explore new material, to omit planned material, to refocus or to reorder your entire presentation. Just the same, a well-conceived organizational plan will encourage you to begin writing a draft.

Alyssa describes the process of organizing the material as follows.

Summary Statements

In reviewing my sources and writing summary
statements, I noted the most important aspects

of the computer interaction issue, according to the authors:

- An increasing number of people use the Internet to interact in new ways (Singh 128).
- In this era when community life is threatened by social and economic hardships, advocates of Internet communication believe this technology could help improve community life by "improving communication, economic opportunity, civic participation, and education" (Kling 129).
- Some fear the ways in which real human interaction is being taken over by "virtual culture" (Maasik and Solomon 129).
- One of the most popular and fastest-growing modes of CMC is the Instant Message. Teenagers especially love to "IM" one another. But others are less enthusiastic, viewing instant messages as frequently rude and intrusive (Edwards; Miller; Dunnewind; Slatalla 130–34).
- The Internet offers college students additional opportunities for meaningful "social or critical" discussions. It may be a useful outlet for otherwise quiet people (Branscum 130).
- Although the idea of interacting through the computer may sound impersonal, people who are involved in the many varieties of virtual communication come to form meaningful attachments to each other. (Rheingold qtd. in Chenault 134).
- Whether or not romances that begin over the Internet end up moving out into the real world, this form of communication has enormous potential for bringing together people with similar interests (Perreault qtd. in Suler 135).
- A sociologist studying Internet romances found that participants were generally quite honest and open with one another at the start of their relationships—perhaps

even more honest than people beginning relationships in more traditional ways. (Wolcott 136).

· A large number of Web sites offer matchmaking services, and people using such services report both positive and negative outcomes. People should be cautious, however, as some experiences show that it's easy to be duped by a potential partner via computer (Morris 137).

I tried to group some of these topics into categories that would have a logical order. The first thing that I wanted to communicate was the growing pervasiveness of the Internet in our everyday lives and the variety of relationships that can develop online, which has sparked a debate over their quality.

Next, I thought I should explain what Internet enthusiasts are so excited about. I wanted to discuss the idea of using the Internet to rebuild community life.

I also wanted to explain the position of those who feel that Internet relationships will prove to be less satisfying than old-fashioned human interactions. In opposition to that position, I wanted to explain that some people feel that the Internet can add additional qualities to communication that traditional human interaction lacks.

Next, I intended to counter this optimistic view with words of caution from Internet skeptics about romantic relationships that begin online.

Finally, I planned to conclude with a short summary of the debate.

I returned to my thesis:

> With so many computer users forming a variety of online relationships, no one can deny that this new technology is affecting our modes of communication; however, reactions to these changes range widely from excitement over our abilities to forge global connections, to fear that such connections will prove much less satisfying than old-fashioned human interactions.

Based on her thesis, Alyssa developed an outline for an eight-paragraph paper, including introduction and conclusion:

A. Introduction: explanation of the debate surrounding CMC.
B. Enthusiasm over the possibilities that the Internet provides for communication.
C. Skepticism about the quality of Internet relationships.
D. The growing popularity of instant messaging (IM).
E. Advantages of Internet relationships over old-fashioned relationships.
F. Specific example of a relationship formed online.
G. Words of caution and a negative example.
H. Conclusion: summing up.

Write the Topic Sentences

This is an optional step, but writing draft versions of topic sentences will get you started on each main idea of your synthesis and will help give you the sense of direction you need to proceed. Here are Alyssa's draft topic sentences for sections based on the thesis and organizational plan she developed. Note that when read in sequence following the thesis, these sentences give an idea of the logical progression of the essay as a whole.

· An increasing number of people are becoming Internet users every day.
· Using the Internet to strengthen community life may sound like a good idea; however, skeptics warn that the quality of relationships formed through the Internet is not up to par with those formed through face-to-face human interactions.
· One of the fastest-growing forms of CMC is the instant message, or IM, which is a kind of cross between a telephone and an e-mail conversation.
· Some contend that the Internet can provide certain advantages for communication that face-to-face human interactions cannot.
· Research indicates that at the start of a relationship, participants in Internet romances are often more honest and open with one another than their counterparts in traditional dating situations.

- With increasing numbers of people using
  Internet matchmaking services, skeptics
  remind us that people should exercise
  caution in getting to know people
  via CMC.

Write Your Synthesis

Here is the first draft of Alyssa's explanatory synthesis. Thesis and topic sentences are highlighted. Modern Language Association (MLA) documentation style, explained in Chapter 7, is used throughout. Note that for the sake of clarity, parenthetical references are to pages in *A Sequence for Academic Writing*.

Opposite each page of this first draft, we have included Alyssa's instructor's comments and suggestions for revision.

MODEL PAPER

Advantages and Disadvantages
of Computer Mediated
Communication
Alyssa Mellott

1   From the home, to the workplace, to the classroom, the Internet has clicked its way into our everyday lives. On any given day, research papers may be e-mailed to professors, ads are posted to sell just about anything, and arrangements to meet significant others for dinner and a movie can be made--all with the help of the Internet. In addition to providing us with such conveniences, computer mediated communication (CMC) provides a medium for fostering new relationships. Whether you are looking for a business partner, fellow political enthusiasts, or a future spouse, the Internet can be a powerful tool for uniting people with similar interests. With so many computer users forming a variety of online relationships, no one can deny that this new technology is affecting our modes of communication; however, reactions to these changes range widely from excitement over our abilities to forge global connections, to fear that such connections will prove much less satisfying than old-fashioned human interactions.

2   An increasing number of people are becoming Internet users every day. It is estimated that by the year 2001,

Discussion and Suggestions for Revision

The following section summarizes the key points and suggestions for revision made during Alyssa's conference with her instructor. (For purpose of demonstration, these comments are likely to be more comprehensive than the selective comments provided by most instructors.)

Title and Paragraph 1

Your title could be more interesting and less mechanical. Your first paragraph introduces the subject with some good, specific examples, but you sound a bit too much like a proponent of the new technology, rather than a writer who is objectively presenting various positions on CMC's potential.

Your thesis statement could be shortened and tightened up. While it's good that you aim to specifically characterize the two overall positions regarding CMC, you end up oversimplifying things a bit.

Suggestions for Revision: Make the current title more interesting and less focused on a clear-cut set of oppositions.

In order to maintain an objective stance—since this essay is meant to be explanatory rather than argumentative—you might cut some of your examples here and get to the point sooner. You could then follow your introduction with a paragraph in which you develop some of the background points you raise in your current introduction—that the Internet has enormous potential for "uniting people with similar interests," as you say. You could refer to points from the readings to make your discussion more objectively explanatory.

Shorten your thesis statement by separating the two ideas you've currently joined with a semicolon: the first clause introduces the thesis you state in the second clause, so separating these ideas will help emphasize your essay's main point. More important, rephrase your thesis so that it more accurately characterizes the positions offered in the readings. For example, none of the readings emphasize the "global" dimension to the connections forged on the Internet, nor does the

"fifty percent of the U.S. population will communicate via e-mail" (Singh 129). Is the growing popularity of the Internet as a form of communication and its effect on our modes of communication a positive trend? Champions of the Internet point out that in transforming the way people interact, the Internet has made communication faster, more efficient, and less expensive. Internet enthusiasts also feel that Internet forums "are building new forms of community life" (Kling 129). It has been suggested that CMC could play a role in "rebuilding [deteriorating] community life" in inner cities, suburban, and post-suburban areas of the United States. Kling quotes an African proverb "it takes a whole village to raise a child" to express the need for a "rich community life" based on "mutual responsibility" that seems to be lacking in our modern neighborhoods (129). Some observers feel CMC can improve "communication, economic opportunity, civic participation, and education" (Kling 129).

3 Using the Internet to strengthen community life may sound like a good idea; however, skeptics warn that the quality of relationships formed through the Internet is not up to par with those formed through face-to-face human interactions. Analysts have observed that not everyone who communicates via the

notion of "fear" that Internet relations will be "less satisfying than old-fashioned . . . interactions" adequately account for the negative views regarding CMC. Back up a bit and formulate a slightly less specific—and more comprehensive—statement.

Edit your use of passive voice—*who* e-mails papers to professors? Avoid clichéd phrases such as "on any given day. . . ."

Paragraph 2
This paragraph starts with a good background point about the prevalence of the Internet in our lives; then you shift to one of the key reasons some people are excited about CMC. The first idea does lead to the second, but could bear more development, as could your second point about CMC's community-building potential.

Suggestions for Revision: Consider splitting this paragraph in two. As suggested in the comments on paragraph 1, some of the points raised in your introduction could be moved to a background paragraph—and the first two sentences in this current paragraph 2 would fit there. Look back over the readings for more ideas that would help you develop points about CMC's pervasiveness and its general, positive potential. After discussing that, you could begin a third paragraph focused upon the point about the Internet's potential for building communities. Spend more time defining "community" and explaining how, according to its advocates, CMC could replace lost community.

Edit your sentences—you have some repetitive and choppy sentence structures and passive constructions that could be rephrased in the active voice.

Paragraph 3
Paragraph 3 follows logically from paragraph 2, and you make a clear transition in your topic sentence. However, this paragraph's points would be stronger if you had explained the arguments about the Internet's community-building potential in the last paragraph.

In your effort to paraphrase points from the Maasik and Solomon reading, and to intersperse their quoted words with your own, you end up producing

Internet forms "the sense of trust, mutual interest, and sustained commitments" that characterize communities (Kling 129). Others are concerned that the relationships people are building through the Internet "lack an essential core of humanity" (Maasik and Solomon 129). They feel that our social reality made up of real people is being taken over by a virtual culture. It is within this virtual culture that a danger exists for people to become "unable to conceive of others as human beings," resulting in an environment lacking in "human empathy and relatedness" (Maasik and Solomon 129). Similarly, some teachers consider e-mail to be "an unhealthy substitute for human contact" (Branscum 130).

4   One of the fastest-growing forms of CMC is the instant message, or IM, which is a kind of cross between a telephone and an e-mail conversation. Using IM, people carry on conversations in writing in real time. Increasingly, teenagers IM rather than phone or even e-mail one another (Edwards 130). America Online estimates that "by 2005 IMs will surpass e-mail as the primary way of communicating online" (Edwards 131). According to a recent study, "37% of teenagers said they have used instant messaging to write something they wouldn't have said in person" (Miller 131). The study re-

wordy and awkward sentences. Furthermore, when you paraphrase the authors in the sentence "They feel that our social reality . . . ," you haven't changed the wording enough to qualify as a legitimate paraphrase.

In the last sentence of this paragraph you throw in another reference that doesn't really add anything to your points. Why do you need this point?

Suggestions for Revision: Once you've developed your points further in paragraph 2, rework the points expressed by the "skeptics" in this paragraph to more clearly relate back to the ideas of community you've just discussed.

Consider dealing with the ideas from Maasik and Solomon in a block quote, or else rework your sentences to more smoothly incorporate their ideas without using their sentence structures and wording.

If you feel the added point in your last sentence is important, then clarify that importance; if it's really not necessary, then leave it out.

Paragraph 4
The sentences on breaking up romances by IM are interesting, but they seem to belong in a later part of the paper dealing with CMC romances. Here they may blur the focus. The same point applies to the sentences about IM lingo. While interesting, they don't directly relate to the thesis about the advantages and disadvantages of CMC communication.

Suggestions for revision: Either relocate or simply drop the sentences dealing with the breakup of e-romances via IM; also drop the following sentences on IM lingo. Otherwise, just fix up surface problems, making passive phrases ("it can also be seen as rude and intrusive" active).

ported that some even break up their romances through instant messages, though this is considered tacky. One youth said, "I lost a lot of respect for that person, after his girlfriend broke up with him by IM" (Miller 132). Teens have even created their own abbreviated lingo for IM communication: "I wz gtin2d@ & now gota type it agen b patient!" means "I was getting to that and now gotta type it again be patient!" BRB means "Be right back," and "POS" means "parent over shoulder," a phrase that is used just before the conversation changes direction to a more serious subject (Dunnewind 000). But while instant messaging is appealing and convenient, it can also be seen as rude and intrusive. According to reporter Michelle Slatalla, "Instant messages can be more annoying than other forms of electronic communication because they appear on the screen as soon as they are sent. Recipients of voice mail, E-mail, or faxes can acknowledge a message whenever it is convenient" (133). As Jeanne Hinds, publisher of a website on "netiquette," notes, "It's the cyber-equivalent of someone walking into your office and starting up a conversation as if you had nothing better to do"(qtd. in Slatalla 134).

5 Some contend that CMC can provide certain advantages to communication that

Paragraph 5
The topic sentence is confusing. You write, "The argument has been taken a step further . . . ," and this wording suggests that you're referring to the argument *against* CMC, since this is the last argument about which you've written. In actuality, however, you seem to be referring to the entire argument over CMC, not just one side of it. Other than that, this paragraph contains interesting points and good examples.

Suggestions for Revision: Change your opening sentence to more accurately reflect the paragraph's focus.

face-to-face human interactions cannot. In a study of first-year college students, Stanford's Richard Holeton found that students who were ordinarily reserved were often the most active participants in Internet discussions (Branscum 130). Similarly, the Internet can serve as a way for people who are having trouble dating to find romantic partners. For instance, Tom Buckley met his wife after signing up with Match.com. Buckley noted that the Internet helped him to meet his wife because "neither one of us was the type to walk up to someone in the gym or a bar and say, 'You're the fuel to my fire'" (qtd. in Morris 137). Holeton's research and Tom Buckley's experience suggest that the Internet may provide an avenue of expression and opportunity for otherwise quiet or timid individuals.

6   Research indicates that at the start of a relationship, participants in Internet romances are often more honest and open with one another than their counterparts in traditional dating situations. Andrea Baker, assistant professor of sociology at Ohio University's Lancaster campus who is studying romances that start over the Internet, reports that relationships that start online are "better and deeper" than traditional relationships because the couples are honest in the words they write

Paragraph 6
In paragraph 6 you do a nice job of extending the points in your last paragraph; however, your first sentence here doesn't make that relationship clear. By starting with "Research indicates . . ." you imply that you're moving on to a new element of CMC, rather than adding to the last point.

Suggestions for Revision: Write a topic sentence that spells out how your new points relate to the last ones. You also might add a sentence that sums up your overall point at the end of the paragraph to help improve the logical "flow" between this paragraph and paragraph 6.

(qtd. in Wolcott 136). Like the participants in Baker's study, California resident John Dwyer found the sincerity present in online communication to be a pleasant change from more traditional dating scenes (Wolcott 136). After posting a personal ad on the Internet, Dwyer met his future wife, Debbie, who commented, "'If you are honest when talking online, you can strip away all the superficial stuff and really get to know someone'" (Wolcott 136).

7   With increasing numbers of people using Internet matchmaking services, skeptics remind us that people should exercise caution in getting to know people via CMC. After having his heart broken and his wallet drained by a romantic partner he met online, Robert Spradling has sworn off using the Internet to find love and warns others to "be careful and keep their head and learn a lot about who they're dating online" (qtd. in Morris 137).

8   Wouldn't it be nice if the saying was "What you read is what you get"? Anyone who has spent even five minutes playing with e-mail cannot deny that the enthusiasm surrounding the possibilities posed for communication by the Internet is warranted. Nevertheless, we must constantly be reminded that the computer screen poses as an effective poker face for those with insincere intentions.

Paragraph 7
Again, you're lacking an effective transition here, one that makes clear the way these new points qualify or limit the positive assessments offered in paragraph 6. The Spradling story provides a nice counterpoint to the happy couple's experience in the last paragraph, but as a reader I don't get a complete picture of the actual events in Spradling's experience.

Suggestions for Revision: Write a better transitional sentence to open the paragraph. Slow down a little and tell Spradling's story more clearly. Review the reading by Suler: is there a way in which a cyberlove relationship might apply to Spradling's difficulties in moving his romance from the online to the offline realm?

Paragraph 8
Your conclusion focuses too much on the last issue raised in your essay, while failing to bring a sense of closure to the essay by pulling together all the points of the essay.

Suggestions for Revision: Think about what all these points add up to. Yes, as your current conclusion states, the Internet can help people hide malignant intentions—but is this the whole story? Are people able to lie and conceal things in real life as well as in the virtual world? And what about your earlier points about community-building and human connection? Try to wrap things up more comprehensively, rather than focusing narrowly on the one issue of deceit.

Works Cited

Branscum, Deborah. "Life At High-Tech U." <u>Newsweek</u> 27 Oct. 1997: 78–80.

Dunnewind, Stephanie. "Call Them 'Generation Text': Teens' Instant-Messaging Lingo Is Evolving into a Hybrid Language." <u>The Seattle Times</u> 12 Apr. 2003: E1+.

Edwards, Ellen. "IM Generation: Instant Messaging Is In, Phones Out." <u>The Seattle Times</u> 16 June 2003: E4.

Kling, Rob. "Social Relationships in Electronic Forums: Hangouts, Salons, Workplaces and Communities." <u>CMC Magazine</u> July 1996:4. Feb. 2000 <http://www.december.com/cmc/mag/1996/jul/kling.html>.

Maasik, Sonia, and Jack Solomon, eds. <u>Signs of Life in the USA</u>. Boston: Bedford Books, 1997. 701.

Miller, Stanley A. "Passing Notes: Teens Bare Their Hearts with Instant Messages." <u>Milwaukee Journal Sentinel</u> 26 June 2001: 1M+.

Morris, Bonnie R. "You've Got Romance! Seeking Love Online: Net-Based Services Change the Landscape, If Not the Odds, of Finding the Perfect Mate." <u>New York Times on the Web</u> 26 Aug. 1999. 23 Feb. 2000 <http://www.nytimes.com/library/tech/yr/mo/circuits/index.html>.

Singh, Sanjiv N. "Cyberspace: A New Frontier for Fighting Words." <u>Rutgers Computer and Technology Law Journal</u> 25.2 (1999): 283.

Slatalla, Michelle. "Minding Your Manners: Over-use of Instant Messaging Can Be a Major Breach of Etiquette." <u>The Gazette</u> (Montreal) 25 Sep. 1999: K2.

Wolcott, Jennifer. "Click Here for Romance." <u>The Christian Science Monitor</u> 13 Jan. 1999. 23 Feb. 2000 <http://www.csmonitor.com/durable/1991/01/13/fp11s1-csm.shtml>.

Robert Wright, "Will We Ever Log Off?" <u>Time</u> 21 Feb. 2000: 56–58.

Revise Your Synthesis: Global, Local, and Surface Revisions

Many writers find it helpful to plan for three types of revision: *global, local,* and *surface. Global revisions* affect the entire paper: the thesis, the type and pattern of evidence employed, the overall organization, the tone. A global revision may also emerge from a change in purpose. For example, the writer of this paper might decide to rewrite, focusing on the recent development of CMC, rather than on the advantages and disadvantages of this form of communication.

Local revisions affect paragraphs: topic and transitional sentences; the type of evidence presented within a paragraph; evidence added, modified, or dropped within a paragraph; logical connections from one sentence or set of sentences within a paragraph to another.

Surface revisions deal with sentence style and construction, word choice, and errors of grammar, mechanics, spelling, and citation form.

Most of the comments and suggestions for revision offered for the preceding draft focus on local revision strategies, though the instructor has suggested a few (relatively minor) global revisions for the first paragraph (e.g., "Your thesis statement could be shortened and tightened"). Subsequent revision suggestions focus on rewriting topic sentences for clarity, splitting long paragraphs into shorter ones, providing additional evidence to support the point made in the topic sentence, dropping evidence not sufficiently supporting the paper's thesis, clarifying a narrative, and changing the focus of the concluding paragraph. A few suggestions focus on surface elements: editing for repetitive and choppy sentence structure, replacing passive sentences with active ones.

EXERCISE   **4.3**

Revising the Sample Synthesis

Try your hand at creating a final draft of the paper on pages 146–52 by following the revision suggestions above, together with using your own best judgment about how to improve the first draft. Make global, local, and surface changes. After trying your own version of the paper, compare it to the revised version of our student–produced paper below.

REVISED MODEL PAPER

Computer Mediated Communication: New and Improved Human
Relations or the End of Real Interaction?
Alyssa Mellott

From the home, to the workplace, to the classroom,
the Internet has clicked its way into our everyday
lives. Today's students can e-mail as file attachments
their end-of-term papers to their professors and can
then turn around and use e-mail to gather a group
of friends for a party or to celebrate the term's
completion. These online exchanges, called CMC (or
computer mediated communication) sound fairly
commonplace at the turn of the millennium. But what
we have yet to discover is how CMC might change
both the ways we communicate and the quality of our
relationships. While many praise CMC's potential to
bridge barriers and promote meaningful dialogue, others
caution that CMC is fraught with dangers.

Very soon, half of America will communicate via
e-mail, according to analysts (Singh 129). We can only
assume that figure will grow--rapidly--as children who
have matured in the Internet era move on to college
and into careers. With e-mail becoming an increasingly
common form of communication, people are discovering
and conversing with one another in a variety of ways
that bring a new twist to old, familiar patterns. Using
e-mail, people meet "to exchange pleasantries and argue,
engage in intellectual discourse, conduct commerce,
exchange knowledge, share emotional support, make plans,
brainstorm, gossip, feud, [and] fall in love" (Rheingold
qtd. in Chenault 134). That is, through e-mail people do
what they have always done: communicate. But the medium
of that communication has changed, which excites some
people and concerns others.

Advocates argue that the Internet has not only made
existing types of communication faster, more convenient,
more efficient, and less expensive; it has also made
possible "new forms of community life," such as chat
rooms and discussion lists, in which people from
all over the country and the world gather to share
information and exchange points of view (Kling 129).
CMC is potentially so powerful a medium of exchange that
some believe it can promote dialogue within communities
that are declining. A community, after all, is built on
people acting in the interests of their neighbors for
the common good. Via e-mail, online newsgroups, and
e-forums, neighbors will have new ways of looking out
for one another (Kling 129).

Still, skeptics aren't convinced that electronic communication can provide the basis of lasting personal relationships, primarily because relationships initiated on a computer display lack immediacy and physical presence. What may be missing in the electronic village, say the critics, is "an essential core of humanity" (Maasik and Solomon 129):

> The unreal world of virtual culture . . . is being substituted for a social reality made up of real human beings. And such a world, based entirely on the transmission of electronic signals, is potentially a world in which human beings will be unable to conceive of others as human beings. When all interaction is electronic, [the critics] ask, where is the ground for true human empathy and related—ness? (Maasik and Solomon 129)

The fact that people communicate--via e-mail, snail (written) mail, or in person--does not guarantee that their exchanges lead to community. Members of a community trust and care for one another; they extend themselves and offer help (Kling 129). Critics of CMC argue that the supporters gloss over this important distinction when they assume that electronic forums are "building new forms of community life" (Kling 129). Talking, electronically or otherwise, marks only the beginning of a process. Community building is hard work and takes time.

One of the fastest-growing forms of CMC is the instant message, or IM, which is a kind of cross between a telephone and an e-mail conversation. Using IM, people carry on real time conversations in writing. Increasingly, teenagers IM rather than phone or even e-mail one another (Edwards 130). America Online estimates that "by 2003 IMs will surpass e-mail as the primary way of communicating online" (Edwards 131). According to a recent study, "37% of teenagers said they have used instant messaging to write something they wouldn't have said in person" (Miller 130). But while instant messaging is appealing and convenient, some users view it as potentially rude and intrusive. According to reporter Michelle Slatalla, "Instant messages can be more annoying than other forms of electronic communication because they appear on the screen as soon as they are sent. Recipients of voice mail, e-mail, or faxes can acknowledge a message whenever it is convenient" (133). As Jeanne Hinds, publisher of a website on "netiquette," notes, "It's the cyber-equivalent of someone walking into your office and starting up a conversation as if you had nothing better to do" (qtd. in Slalatta 134). Notwithstanding such concerns, proponents of CMC confidently point to examples in which the new technologies of communication bring people together in meaningful, healthy ways. In a study of first-year college students, researcher Richard Holeton of Stanford University found that students who were ordinarily reserved were often the most active participants in Internet discussions (Branscum 130). Similarly, the Internet can serve as a way for people who are having trouble dating to find partners. For instance, Tom Buckley of Portland, Oregon met his wife after signing up with Match.com. Buckley noted that the Internet helped him to meet his wife because "neither one of us was the type to walk up to someone in the gym or a bar and say, 'You're the fuel to my fire'" (qtd. in Morris 137). Holeton's research and Buckley's experience suggest that the Internet may provide a way for otherwise quiet or timid individuals to express themselves.

Beyond simply providing a safe and lower-stress place to meet, the Internet may actually promote honest communication. An Ohio University sociologist, Andrea Baker, concluded from her research that individuals who begin their romance online can be at an advantage: writing via e-mail can promote a "better and deeper" relationship than one begun in person because writing itself promotes a frank, honest exchange (qtd. in Wolcott 136). Certainly this was the experience of John Dwyer, a Californian who tired of meeting women in bars and decided instead to post an advertisement online. He eventually met the woman who would become his wife-- Debbie--who said: "'If you are honest when talking online, you can strip away all the superficial stuff and really get to know someone'" (Wolcott 136). When it works, CMC can promote a sincere exchange among those looking for lasting relationships.

Increasingly, Internet dating services are becoming an accepted way of meeting prospective romantic partners. As New York Times reporter Amy Harmon notes, "Online dating, once viewed as a refuge for the socially inept and as a faintly disrespectful way to meet other people, is rapidly becoming a fixture of single life for adults of all ages, backgrounds and interests" (137).

Skeptics are not so easily convinced, however. Show them an example of a relationship that blossomed online and they will point to another in which one party was betrayed emotionally or financially. Take, for instance, the experience of Robert Spradling. He met and formed a romantic attachment to a Ukrainian woman online. She encouraged the romance via e-mail and eventually asked for money to set up a business. He sent $8,000 and later, again online, asked her to marry him. She agreed, they met in Kiev, and after Spradling returned home, she disappeared--his money gone and his heart broken (Morris 136). Perhaps Spradling was one of the Internet romantics for whom it is wiser to avoid face-to-face meetings. That way, he could have enjoyed the interactive fantasy of a "cyber-lover" without ever having to ruin the fun with the uncomfortable truths of real life (Suler 135).

It is far from certain, then, that all or even most relationships begun online develop positively. Closer to the truth is that both online and offline, some relationships begin--and end--in deceit while others blossom. Experts do not yet know whether computer mediated communication, because of its electronic format, alters relationships as they are forming or, rather, simply offers a new territory in which to find others. Time will tell. In the meantime, the advice that loved ones give us when we set off to find new friends-- Be careful!--makes sense whether we are looking in the virtual world or down the street.

Works Cited

Branscum, Deborah. "Life at High-Tech U." Newsweek 27 Oct. 1997: 78-80.

Chenault, Brittney G. "Developing Personal and Emotional Relationships Via Computer-Mediated Communication." CMC Magazine May 1998. 20 Mar. 2000 <http://www.december.com/cmc/mag/1998/may/chenault.html>.

Edwards, Ellen. "IM Generation: Instant Messaging Is In, Phones Out." The Seattle Times 16 June 2003: E4.

Harmon, Amy. "Online Dating Sheds Its Stigma as Losers.com." New York Times 29 June 2003: A1+.

Kling, Rob. "Social Relationships in Electronic Forums: Hangouts, Salons, Workplaces and Communities." CMC Magazine 22 July 1996. 4 Feb. 2000 <http://www.december.com/cmc/mag/1996/jul/kling.html>.

Maasik, Sonia, and Jack Solomon, eds. Signs of Life in the USA. Boston: Bedford Books, 1997.

Miller, Stanley A. "Passing Notes: Teens Bare Their Hearts with Instant Messages." Milwaukee Journal Sentinel 26 June 2001: 1M+.

Morris, Bonnie R. "You've Got Romance! Seeking Love Online: Net-Based Services Change the Landscape, If Not the Odds, of Finding the Perfect Mate." New York Times on the Web 26 Aug. 1999. 23 Feb. 2000 <http://www.nytimes.com/library/tech/yr/mo/circuits/index.html>.

Singh, Sanjiv N. "Cyberspace: A New Frontier for Fighting Words." Rutgers Computer and Technology Law Journal 25.2 (1999): 283.

Slatalla, Michelle. "Minding Your Manners: Over-use of Instant Messaging Can Be a Major Breach of Etiquette." The Gazette (Montreal) 25 Sep. 1999: K2.

Suler, John. "Cyberspace Romances: Interview with Jean-Francois Perreault of Branchez-vous." The Psychology of Cyberspace 11 Dec. 1996. 7 Apr. 2000 <http://www.rider.edu/users/suler/psycyber/psycyber.html>.

Wolcott, Jennifer. "Click Here for Romance." The Christian Science Monitor 13 Jan. 1999. 23 Feb. 2000 <http://www.csmonitor.com/durable/1991/01/13/fp11s1-csm.shtml>.

CRITICAL READING FOR SYNTHESIS

- **Use the tips from Critical Reading for Summary on page 6.** Remember to examine the context; note the title and subtitle; identify the main point; identify the subpoints; break the reading into sections; distinguish between points, examples, and counterarguments; watch for transitions within and between paragraphs; and read actively and recursively.
- **Establish the writer's primary purpose.** Use some of the guidelines discussed in Chapter 2; is the piece primarily informative, persuasive, or entertaining? Assess whether the piece achieves its purpose.
- **Read to identify a key idea.** If you begin reading your source materials with a key idea or topic already in mind, read to identify what your sources have to say about the idea.
- **Read to discover a key idea.** If you begin the reading process without a key idea in mind yet, read to discover a key idea that your sources address.
- **Read for relationships.** Regardless of whether you already have a key idea, or whether you are attempting to discover one, your emphasis in reading should be on noting the ways in which the readings relate to each other, to a key idea, and to your purpose in writing the synthesis.

Writing Assignment:
The Music Downloading Controversy

Now we'll give you an opportunity to practice your skills in planning and writing an explanatory synthesis. On pages 160–78 we provide eight sources on the controversial issue of music downloading.

EXERCISE 4.4

Exploring Internet Sources

Since the topic of music downloading and file-sharing is so "cutting-edge"—and since the Internet itself provides a convenient forum for discussing these issues—many articles on the topic are available on the Internet. In addition to reading the sources we've provided, go to one of the search engines online (Google.com is a good one) and search for articles and discussions on file sharing. You will find all sorts of more recent pieces than those we've been able to collect here. If you end up using any of the sources you find on the Internet for the explanatory synthesis assignment, you should review our cautionary discussion of using Web-based sources in Chapter 7 on Evaluating Sources (pages 294–95).

In the past few years, young people have been enthusiastically downloading free music from the Internet from Web sites like Napster (now defunct) and Kazaa. The major recording companies and associations like the RIAA (Recording Industry Association of America), declaring that such downloading is essentially theft, have gone to court to stop the online file-sharing sites and have even threatened to sue individual users. Recently, Apple's iTunes Music Score, and America Online's MusicNet have offered subscription or fee-based alternatives to the free sites.

Read the following passages, then plan and write an explanatory synthesis dealing with some aspect of this subject. You don't have to draw upon *all* of the passages; conversely, as you plan your synthesis, you may want to research additional sources (for example, those covering more current methods of downloading, sharing, or swapping music files, or those that explore aspects of these subjects in greater detail).

A cautionary note: When writing syntheses, it is all-too-easy to become careless in properly crediting your sources. Before drafting your paper, please review the section on "Avoiding Plagiarism" in Chapter 1 (pp. 53–56) as well as the relevant sections on "Citing Sources" in Chapter 7 (pp. 309–332).

The Napster Challenge
Catherine Edwards

Catherine Edwards is a freelance writer. The following passage is an excerpt from an article that first appeared in Insight on the News *on January, 2001.*

A little computer program called Napster revolutionized the music industry last year and things don't look too different for 2001.

One year ago, 19-year-old Shawn Fanning was a freshman computer geek at Northeastern University in Boston. Now he is the very famous chief executive officer of Napster, the program that allows computer users to download music from other music-lovers' computers via the Internet for free—without going through a third-party provider.

Fanning wrote the program in his dormitory room and gave Napster the nickname he got as a kid from his bad haircuts. He had noticed that his roommates were downloading music from the World Wide Web using MP3 technology, which is the computer software that shrinks music and video files for easier Web transmission. He thought there could be a way music fans could share those music files over the Internet and went about writing the software to do just that. In September 1999, Napster went online and was an instant hit. Fanning got $15 million in seed money to start his corporation and has not looked back.

The recording industry hates Napster because it bypasses its income stream. Instead of the music lover taping songs off an audio source, now music files fly around in cyberspace and fans can download files and "burn" a perfect compact disc of all their favorite hits. Because of the stunning success of Napster, Fanning was sued last year by his favorite band, Metallica, as well as rapper Dr. Dre. "As an artist there are so many ways that we can be taken advantage of," says Dr. Dre. "To have yet one more way to strip an artist of making an honest living is just too much. That's why I sued."

But teen-agers' love Napster and, despite lawsuits, the recording industry is sure to be in a battle with America's teens in 2001. Record companies need teen-agers' business and they market products directly to them. But instead of buying CDs last year, 38 million cash-strapped fans switched their allegiance to Napster, at least on a casual basis, which has an estimated base of 900,000 hard-core users. And kids with tech savvy, which is nearly all of them, will figure out how to get the latest songs from Britney Spears and the Backstreet Boys for free regardless of whether Napster loses its legal battles in 2001.

The Recording Industry Association of America (RIAA) sued as well, claiming Napster infringed on record labels' copyrights. A California judge ordered Napster to shut down, but the order was stayed and Napster's case is on appeal. German music giant Bertelsmann AG, the owner of BMG Entertainment, decided it couldn't beat Napster so it joined them by striking a $50 million deal with the company in exchange for a new fee-based system for distributing BMG's music online.

MP3 and Me: How I Stopped Worrying and Learned to Love Online Music File-Sharing (sort of)
Lee Bockhorn

Lee Bockhorn is associate editor at The Weekly Standard. *The following passage is excerpted from an article that first appeared in* The Weekly Standard *on October 16, 2002.*

Among my twenty-something peers at *The Weekly Standard*, I'm thought to be a bit of a premature old fogy. Perhaps it's my stuffed-shirt sartorial choices, my TV preferences (Turner Classic Movies over the WB), or my taste in music (Duke Ellington over Eminem). What can I say? I'm a cranky old man trapped in a 26-year-old's body.

Another sign of this is my reluctance to embrace the world of online music file-sharing. First, let me stipulate that I'm no Luddite: I send e-mail and instant messages all the time, shop on Amazon and eBay, and buy my airline tickets online, too. But until recently, two things kept me from participating in the online music phenomenon. First, I missed the original wave of file-sharing madness (the use among college students of the now-defunct program Napster took off just after I graduated). More important, though, I've always had qualms about not paying an artist for their music, particularly since I was a music major in college.

Lately, however, I've succumbed to temptation. My descent into the world of downloading MP3s began innocently enough. Last spring, I saw the talented young singer Norah Jones perform on television. Bewitched by the fetching and honey-voiced Miss Jones, I bought her album, and also saw her play a concert here in June. (She sounds as good live as she does on the CD.) Jones ended her set with a heartbreaking encore rendition of "The Tennessee Waltz." So a few days later I visited her website and found an MP3 file, available for free, of Jones's performance of "Tennessee Waltz" recorded at an April concert in Chicago. I downloaded it, and got the free iTunes program for my Mac so I could play the song on my computer.

I felt no guilt about this—I'd bought the woman's album and paid to see her perform live, and she was offering the song on her website for free. But then I started to wonder what this MP3 file-sharing stuff was all about, so I downloaded LimeWire, one of the many successors (along with Kazaa and Morpheus) to Napster. Unlike Napster, these new "peer-to-peer" file-sharing programs are decentralized or operate overseas, making them less susceptible to legal challenges from the recording industry (for now, anyway).

My online music experience so far has been a mixed bag. I've acquired about 30 files via LimeWire from something called the Gnutella Network—everything from Mozart to the Beatles, Etta James to George Strait. The MP3 technology itself is unquestionably wonderful, and peer-to-peer file-sharing does offer some real perks: For example, I was able to get the few Stevie Wonder songs I wanted without having to drop $40 on a two-disc set of "greatest hits."

But there are also drawbacks. The availability of songs is dependent upon whether other people simultaneously on the network are sharing the types of music I want. Also, since I haven't yet bothered to get a broadband line, it can take a good 25 minutes to download a three-minute song over my slow-as-molasses modem connection. But even more nagging than these practical obstacles is my old-fogy notion that if I'm going to acquire someone's music, I should be willing to pay them for it. If I want to download "My Cherie Amour," Stevie Wonder should get a cut of whatever price a true market—not a market massively distorted by illegal sharing of copyrighted material—determines the song is worth. . . .

Figuring out the rights and wrongs of music file-sharing isn't easy. I've spent the last few weeks trying to decipher things like the Digital Millennium Copyright Act of 1998, the international Berne Convention for the Protection of Literary and Artistic Works, and the concept of "fair use" in copyright law. I hesitate to opine on all this for two reasons: one, I'm not a lawyer (praise God); and two, whatever I write is likely to be ground into hamburger by sharp lawyer-bloggers like (link-to) Glenn Reynolds.

But my bosses at *The Weekly Standard* don't pay me the big bucks to equivocate, so let me try to draw some tentative conclusions. Frankly, I find something to dislike about everyone involved in the debate over online music. Certainly, it is deeply amusing to see ads from the Recording Industry Association of America (RIAA) featuring "artists" like Britney Spears braying about protecting the value of their "intellectual property." I hold no brief for the record companies, either, most of whom produce an incredible amount of pure garbage with practically no redeeming social value. What's worse, the RIAA is now seeking powers to thwart file-sharing that are charitably described as distasteful. . . . [T]he record companies are [now] pushing legislation in Congress that would limit their liability when using software to flood peer-to-peer networks with dummy files, search public files on consumers' computers for illegally copied music, and block users from downloading files through "interdiction," which closes off a user's hard drive from others on the network. Finally, there's ample evidence that the recording industry has engaged in massive price-fixing over the years.

So it's tough to sympathize with pampered artists and greedy record companies in this fight. And yet, based on my layman's reading of the law, it's still clear to me that those who download and share copyrighted music online are doing something illegal. Unlike the old practice of copying analog tapes of music for friends (to which it is often compared), MP3 file-sharing among millions of people on peer-to-peer networks stretches the already nebulous concept of "fair use" to the point of absurdity. And while there's no direct evidence that file-sharing hurts CD sales, sales of pre-recorded CDs dropped 10 percent in 2001, and another 7 percent in the first half of 2002. That file-sharing diminishes the value of a certain type of intellectual property also seems to be at least a plausible argument.

In attempting to defend the illegal behavior of those who believe they never should have to pay for anything if it can be digitally transmitted and copied, some tech geeks have lauded file-sharing networks as a praiseworthy black market that's arisen to overcome the corrupt practices of the record companies. In the case of my Stevie Wonder example, for instance, they would argue that my acquisition of illegal copies of these songs via LimeWire is justified by the record companies' stubborn refusal to embrace technology that would allow me to acquire those songs "a la carte." Here, as always, two wrongs don't make a right.

But the specific "a la carte" argument has some merit: The desire of listeners to choose individual songs rather than entire albums is understandable, and nearly universal, since most albums have only one or two good songs and are padded with worthless dross. But even here, file-sharing has an unintended consequence: As Terry Teachout (link-to) predicts, the elevation of such "choice" is certain to lead to the eventual demise of the "album" as a unified artistic concept—you will no longer see such creations as Sinatra's "Only the Lonely" or the Beatles' "Sgt. Pepper's Lonely Hearts Club Band." (Teachout is quick to point out that this is not intrinsically a bad thing.)

My primary concern is whether file-sharing technology has permanently warped the moral sense of music consumers who've come of age using it, in two ways: by convincing them that acquiring illegal copies of music is the normal way to build one's music collection, and that "intellectual property" is merely a fig leaf used by Evil Record Companies to cover up their own greed.

Unfortunately, as we try to determine how to protect the viability of the concept of intellectual property in the digital age, the issue is being seen primarily through the prism of the music industry, where the side defending intellectual property happens to be a bunch of slimeballs.

The great unanswered question is whether the incredible popularity of sharing MP3s is due mostly to music lovers' desire for more choice in compiling their collections, or whether they simply prefer (rationally, if immorally and illegally) not to pay for something they can get just as easily for free. Based on my own limited experience with file-sharing, and my (perhaps naive) belief that most people want to do the right thing, I think the former is the case. That's why I hope the record companies will make a sincere effort to provide viable subscription sites, and that music consumers will give them a chance.

According to a recent article in the *New York Times*, it looks like this might finally be happening now with the growth of pay sites such as EMusic. For myself, I can only say that if the record companies allow me to subscribe monthly at a reasonable rate and download my half-dozen favorite Stevie Wonder songs, I wouldn't miss LimeWire at all. My conscience would certainly rest easier knowing that Stevie was getting a piece of the action.

I'm Just a Fan of Music (interview)
Terry McBride

The following is an excerpt from an interview by Researcher-Reporter John Intini of Terry McBride, who manages about 25 artists, including pop stars Avril Lavigne, Sarah McLachlan, the Barenaked Ladies, and Coldplay, and who is the co-founder and chief executive officer of the Vancouver-based Nettwerk Music Group. According to Intinu, "Terry McBride might have Canada's best ear for popular music." The interview appeared in Maclean's *on June 2, 2003.*

Intini: Does file-sharing concern you?

McBride: I have no issue with MP3 and file-sharing. I have an issue with the kids who burn CDs and sell them. That's wrong. The parties that are making the money are the cable and telephone companies and the manufacturers of blank CDs. It hurts the bands in the middle—the artists that could have sold platinum and made a living doing it disappear—the Dave Matthews-type bands. A kid hops in a taxi to the corner store where he steals a couple of six packs of pop and some junk food. Then he jumps back into the taxi and pays the fare even though the cabbie knew what was happening? The cab driver is party to the crime. Kids don't need to pay $50 a month for a high-speed connection just for e-mail or sending photos. They need it for music files. Cable companies know what's happening and should chip in. . . .

Digital Media: Don't Clamp Down Too Hard
Heather Green

Heather Green covers the Internet and e-commerce for Business Week, *where the article from which this passage is excerpted first appeared on October 14, 2002.*

It's hard to muster much concern about something that's likely to happen four years from now on TVs that few people own. But there's reason to make the effort. Right now, entertainment companies want the government to mandate technology that would control how digital TV shows are copied and distributed.

The goal is clear: To prevent the Napster-style pirating that has shaken the music industry. But the way the mandate is written, couch potatoes who make copies of the Super Bowl or *The West Wing* on the next generation of digital TV sets could find that an anti-pirating program erases them within 48 hours. "This battle is going to affect consumers for the next 50 years," says Joe Kraus, co-founder of DigitalConsumer.org, a public interest advocacy group.

And it's just the latest skirmish in the war over digital music, movies, and books. The entertainment industry's legal victory over Napster, the now-defunct file-sharing sensation, brought precious little relief. File sharers are installing Kazaa, a neo-Napster, at a rate of four copies per second, and they're swapping video- and computer-game software in addition to music. No wonder the music industry blames piracy, in part, for the drop in music sales—which during the first half of this year tumbled 6.7%, to $5.53 billion. And with the growth of broadband, bootleg movies are on the rise.

In congressional hearings on Sept. 26, entertainment industry execs pushed for powerful defenses. They want legislation to enable a host of new piracy protections. And they're pushing for greater leeway in launching cyberattacks against computers illegally transmitting copyrighted files. Congress and the Federal Communications Commission will hammer out a legislative approach to these issues through the rest of the year. "All of our enforcement efforts have been about supporting the value of the legitimate services," says Hilary Rosen, CEO of the Recording Industry Association of America.

These are tough times, and the entertainment industry is right to seek protection. Never before have media companies faced a technology that can make limitless perfect copies of their products and transmit them in a flash. But fear of this digital disaster is pushing the industry too far. From Hollywood to the publishing houses in New York, executives are weighing down their digital offerings with so much legal and technological armor that they could well scare away the public. Want to lend your college-bound daughter a dog-eared copy of *To the Lighthouse*? Go ahead. But if you try lending her the electronic book version, it's illegal. Dish out $16 for a CD, and you might get a new copyright-protected version that can't be copied onto your PC. So much for your MP3 player.

The risk is that the industry's strong defense will undermine its offense—its attempt to expand its audience with a vast array of digital offerings. Online music, for example, could pull the industry out of its slump, growing from $15 million to $540 million, or 5% of sales, by 2005, estimates Forrester Research Inc. But not many customers will pay for digital downloads if the music costs as much as a CD, or if a song can't be burned onto a recordable disk.

To win customers, companies have to steer a middle course. They must put aside some of their fears and their bent for control. Consumers have the freedom to lend and copy products such as books and CDs. They won't stand for anything less in the Digital Age. The challenge then is to provide freedoms without opening the door to massive, Napster-style ripoffs. Says David J. Farber, former chief technologist at the Federal Communications Commission: "If you made it convenient to buy material and added relatively bulletproof ways to protect it, you'd drum up a huge amount of business." Here are three steps that would help the industry do that:

(1) Loosen up on licensing. Web customers won't shop en masse until the selection on legal sites matches those of the file-swappers. For this, entertainment companies and artists need to ease up on licensing. The two industry sites, Pressplay, formed by Universal and Sony, and MusicNet, owned in part by AOL Time Warner and Bertelsmann, withhold licensing rights from each other. Together, the services dish up only 10% of the top Billboard songs. Kazaa provides far more for free.

Licensing woes also are dogging the nascent market for online movies. To be sure, cable programming companies such a Home Box Office and Showtime Networks Inc. have come up with innovative video-on-demand services. But at the movie studios, the zeal to control leads to tentative offerings. Before the end of the year, an online movie site backed by five studios called MovieLink will be launched with only some 150 movies. "This will be a great experiment," says Jack Valenti, president and CEO of the Motion Picture Association of America.

But independents feel boxed out. Last month, Intertainer Inc., an independent movie service, filed an antitrust suit against three studios that back the Movielink service. In time, the studio execs say they plan to license more to each other. A far better solution is to license to everyone. Blockbuster Inc. doesn't belong to one studio or another. But all of the studios benefit from a service that gets their products to customers.

(2) Come up with new products and pricing schemes. This means selling smaller pieces, such as songs, short stories, and shows, at low prices. Digital offerings cost virtually nothing to store and ship, and they occupy no shelf space. Companies should break free from the traditional packaging of CDs or books and sell cheaper bits and pieces. This process is under way. Over the summer, Warner Music, Sony, and Universal began offering consumers unlimited downloading of singles, either for subscription fees or 99 cents per song.

But online pricing is way off. The reason: Companies look at an online customer as a threat, someone who might stop buying CDs. So they try to set the price at nearly the CD level, even though the costs of online delivery are negligible.

The trick is to consider online as an opportunity, a chance to win back tens of millions of Napster-Kazaa users. This year, about 60 million copies of songs from Nirvana's 1991 Nevermind album will be downloaded from file-sharing networks, according to Web monitoring service Envisional Ltd. If even one-fifth of these people paid 25 cents a song, those downloads would net $3 million, or roughly a third of what the album made annually, says Envisional.

(3) **Embrace "fair use."** This means giving consumers the right to view or listen to a work any way they want, and on whatever device they choose. The industry fears that fair use will lead to billions of perfect copies circulating everywhere. To fend off this risk, publishers are adding lots of digital protection. This is inevitable and should help prevent piracy. But too much of it will discourage consumers.

At the same time, innovators also need fair use. Decades ago, they were free to tinker with televisions and radios. This produced inventions such as the videocassette recorder, which have benefited the industry. But since 1998, the Digital Millennium Copyright Act has prohibited inventors from unlocking copyright protection technology on digital products. Even to open the code on a DVD is a felony. The law should be amended so that thieves and pirates could be prosecuted, while inventors would have the freedom they need.

Debates rage about why consumers' rights should be protected in the digital age. The industry's rights deserve no less consideration. But until media companies give customers a taste of the old-fashioned freedoms from the analog world, the vast digital markets that promise riches will remain largely in the hands of pirates.

Paying to Play
Sarah Jones and Sarah Benzuly

The following is excerpted from an article that originally appeared in Mix *on May 1, 2003. The Sarahs are* Mix *editors.*

Has it really been three years since Napster appeared on computer screens worldwide? That can seem like an instant or a lifetime, depending on your view of "Internet time." Since then, illegal file-sharing music sites have spread through the Net like wildfire, igniting the most significant copyright debate our industry has seen in decades. There have been lawsuits and countersuits, injunctions and offshore servers, hacks and breakthroughs.

And all the while, consumers continued to swap their MP3s online, in effect determining how music was delivered through this medium. The media focused on illegal file sharing but largely ignored the other problem: There were no legitimate choices for those who wanted to download their favorite songs over the Web.

Reacting to widespread consumer demand for downloadable music, major-label-backed services such as pressplay and MusicNet launched last year—albeit without much fanfare. Initially, they offered little to attract customers: limited marketing push, limited content, limited flexibility and limited access—a limited business plan. According to a recent study, less than 1% of the general U.S. population had even heard of these sites, let alone visited them. It was a rocky start.

But today, the label and other subscription services offer a wide range of content to compete with the file-sharing sites.

Though this business model is still in its infancy, the services are ready for the mass market. A good majority of major-label content has been licensed; there are more options for what users can do with the music that they buy, whether they want unlimited streaming or a la carte downloads; and pricing plans are in place. All systems go.

$9.95: An Album or a Month?

In the physical world, music fans walk into a record store and know exactly what they're purchasing; whether on vinyl, cassette, CD or DVD, an album is an object—a collection of songs on a physical medium—that's theirs to keep. The same idea holds true in the online CD retail marketplace: A user can surf on over to Tower.com, Amazon.com, BestBuy.com, find the CDs that they want and proceed to the online checkout stand. But in the "invisible" universe of streaming and downloading, the concept of music as a physical product is undergoing a radical change.

"Consumers already understand how to download music on the Internet," explains Emusic.com's general manager Steve Grady. "What we have to do is give them a very good reason to pay for that as a service. If you think that's about selling units, then you're on the wrong track. It's not about how much you're making per unit, it's about how much you're making."

Music services are trying to get consumers used to the idea that $9.95—or any comparable monthly sum—can buy them a chunk of time, not a physical product. Most sites today offer unlimited streaming and/or "tethered" downloads [those that can only be played on the computer to which they were downloaded] or a la carte "portable" downloads, which, for about a dollar a song, consumers are free to copy to their portable devices and burn to CD. It's still too early to determine which combination of these services will work best, because no single model will work for all music fans: Some will appreciate the "discovery" aspect of unlimited downloading, while others will demand portable downloads so that they can take their music on a morning jog or weekday commute.

Even as this new music-by-the-month notion sinks in, a generation of Web-bred consumers is emerging with their own sense of what is valuable. "The generation that's there now is still relatively accustomed to buying CDs in a physical format," says Grady. "Those kids who are 10, 11 and 12 years old are growing up in a completely different world. It's not that they're not willing to pay for something, but they don't associate the same kind of value with something that they're downloading over the Internet as they do a CD that's bought in the store. That's just reality; let's accept it and build something around that.

"What you have to do is get people to pay for some service around the music that makes it easier for them to pay for it than it is to steal it," Grady continues. "That's the battle: adding value to the music, adding value to the whole experience of finding the music that they want. That's what people are ultimately going to pay for."

Forging a New Business

Subscription options average about $9.95 a month, a marketing decision based on the idea that a month of access will cost less than the price of a single CD. For example, Emusic began with two levels of service: $14.99 per month for a three-month subscription, or $9.99 per month for users willing to make a 12-month commitment. "We have a mixture of light, medium and heavy downloaders, and that mix has to ultimately be profitable," says Grady. "There are things that we can do that a peer-to-peer network could never do, such as guarantee the quality of a download. When you download a track from us, you're downloading it from our servers; you know what it's going to be, you know what the encoding rate is, you know that all of the tracks were encoded with a quality encoder.

"Just giving you the keys to a big warehouse full of music is not good enough," Grady continues. "And that's what the peer-to-peer networks do. If you know exactly what you're looking for, you don't really have a problem. A lot of what we're offering is a discovery service: a way for people to find new music that matches their interests at a low cost."

Some services position themselves as offering everything for everybody, from the casual shopper who might buy a handful of CDs a year to a new-music junkie who is scouting out the latest unknowns and obscure acts. Pressplay currently boasts 250,000 songs from the Big Five and 100 indies. "It's for the power user to the novice," says Seth Oster, Pressplay's VP of corporate communications and public affairs. "All of the music's in there, it's extremely easy to use, it's extremely easy to find, it's extremely easy to stream, download and burn." Added values include six decades' worth of Billboard chart data and pre-releases of exclusive tracks. "Right now, we're offering four songs exclusively from Celine Dion's new album," says Oster. "You cannot get them in stores right now, you cannot hear them on the radio, you can only go to Pressplay." Other features include permanent downloads for less than $1 and unlimited streaming for $9.95 a month.

As sites have developed during the past year, it has become obvious that the quantity of content is of prime importance. Why would consumers visit six different sites to get six different tracks when they could conveniently go to one site and get everything that they wanted? Possessing licensing deals with the major labels and indies has become an important selling point to attract consumers away from the free file-trading sites.

Listen.com's Rhapsody was the first online subscription service to host titles from the Big Five. It offers a variety of subscription options [including a seven-day free trial], with added features such as CD burning and Internet radio access. And to make the experience more user-friendly for paying consumers, sites are partnering up with other companies, i.e., hosting various players. RealNetworks recently invested in Rhapsody, offering its technology to bring the subscription beyond a user's PC. This strategy follows a year-long activity for Listen.com: partnering with consumer electronics companies to bring Rhapsody into consumer's homes, such as connecting a PC to a user's home-theater system. The key is convenience: Consumers want the ability to find music easily, go mobile with their music easily and pay easily.

MusicNet is unique among the services in that it is based on a business-to-business model, providing custom content and programming for its distributors via a software developer's kit; meaning, a site may "feature MusicNet," but MusicNet.com is not a destination for music shoppers. "We're responsible for acquiring content from the labels—the five majors—as well as key independents," explains MusicNet's general manager/executive VP Ellie Hirschhorn, "protecting it in DRM [digital rights management]; programming our service, not only making tracks available but also providing editorial; reporting back on the usage to our label partners, as well as our distribution partners—all this non-consumer-interface enablement of the business."

In what may be the biggest mass-market test of music services so far, MusicNet recently partnered with America Online. AOL's 27 million members are now offered "MusicNet on AOL" as a tier of service integrated into their AOL accounts. "That takes a deep level of customization, which our software developer kit approach allows us to take," says Hirschhorn. "We also are integrating into the trusted and familiar AOL customer service and billing." This way, MusicNet is built right into a monthly ISP statement, making payment for the service a relatively transparent [read: easy] experience.

MusicNet also works with individual labels to provide custom artist promotions for its partners. "Much of the content released by labels is proprietary but nonexclusive," says Hirschhorn. "So they give first looks, first listens, content that comes out before radio, or tracks that didn't make it onto an album. It's not always exclusive, but how we promote it may be very different than how other people do it. So, if AOL Music, for example, is doing an 'Artist of the Month' with Faith Hill, we may be able to extend the 'Artist of the Month' to an additional window of time [i.e., extending the promotion for an additional month] or we may be able to get related content that isn't available to other distribution partners." . . .

Now, Or in Five Years?

What will it take for music sites to succeed in such uncharted territory? In the future, will there be some monolithic, "getallyourmusichere.com" one-stop shop for the entire online music community? Or, will many sites thrive in a competitive marketplace that offers a variety of services for discriminating music fans? Will long-term anti-piracy campaigns ever make a big enough dent in the peer-to-peer file-swapping traffic? It's anyone's guess at this point. But most agree that someone will be cashing in. Pressplay's Oster says, "It's very early on, and once we start marketing, there'll be a much better sense of where our customers are. But we know they're out there, and they're out there in a very large number."

Emusic's Grady muses that this isn't the first time that an existing model's been challenged by new business, "and most of the time, the result is a new revenue stream; in many cases, it's bigger than the old revenue stream. I think that if you're optimistic and you believe for the most part that customers are willing to pay for things that offer them value, then there's a lot of money to be made out there by somebody. So we hope it's us, but I think it's not going to be just us. I think that there's going to be a lot of people that make a lot of money in this area, and consumers are ultimately going to benefit greatly."

The Media Likes What It Has Heard So Far from Apple's iTunes
Hugh Clifton

Hugh Clifton is a freelance writer. The following is excerpted from an article that originally appeared in PR Week *on May 13, 2003.*

Apple founder and CEO Steve Jobs thinks he has the solution to one of the biggest challenges facing the music industry—the loss of billions of dollars each year because of piracy from Napster-like file sharing.

Apple's proposal is its new iTunes Music Store, an idea that generated lots of media buzz even before it was formally revealed to the public in a glitzy, hyped-up unveiling worthy of the dot-com heyday.

Apple's ability to secure the backing of the five largest recording companies (Universal, Warner, EMI, Sony, and BMG) has been largely praised for finally delivering the new business model that the music industry needs to adapt to the times. Technology analyst P. J. McNealy told *The Boston Globe* (April 29), "This is the service we've been waiting for." In its marketing and promotion of iTunes, Apple apparently had numerous talking points it wanted to stress: ease of use, the fact that no subscription is required, the legal nature of the enterprise, the high quality of the downloads, its status as a cheaper alternative to more costly subscription sites, and the readily available catalog of 200,000 songs from all the biggest pop stars. All of these qualities help save time when searching for songs.

Of the aforementioned items, the media most frequently latched onto the notion that iTunes was easy to use. *Business Week* (April 28) reported that iTunes "exudes Apple's trademark elegance and simplicity."

Jobs advocated the a la carte strategy of downloads for 99 cents per song as an improvement on the subscription-based business model of rivals.

The New York Times (April 29) quoted Jobs as saying the latter 'treat you like a criminal (because of all the restrictions they put on you). We think subscriptions are the wrong path.'

About half of the coverage Media Watch analyzed reported that iTunes is only available for Mac users at the moment, but that plans are underway to offer these services to Windows users by the end of the year. Only a handful of these reported that the Mac user audience (about 4% of PC users) was too small for the service to make any impact.

Suggestions that iTunes would revolutionize the music industry came not only from Apple, but from music-industry executives and analysts as well.

Jobs made no attempt to understate expectations for iTunes as he boldly declared in a lengthy *Fortune* profile (May 12), "This will go down in history as a turning point for the music industry. This is landmark stuff. I can't overestimate it!"

Several media reports looked on approvingly, observing that the launch of iTunes, along with its iPod mp3 player, continues Apple's push to diversify its source of income beyond desktop computers. A technology analyst told the *San Francisco Chronicle* (April 29), 'Five or 10 years from now, we may look back and say this was the point when Apple changed from being a computer company to a digital media company.'

Since music is still readily available for free over the Internet, Apple will have its job cut out for it. However, the media and industry observers often highlighted Apple's reputation for successful marketing. *Billboard* magazine (May 3) cited the company's "reputation for savvy marketing" and its "ability to generate buzz among consumers" as reasons why iTunes could potentially be a huge success. The consensus appears to be that if anyone can make this business model work, it's Apple.

U.S. Labels to Sue Individuals for Net Music Piracy
David Teather

David Teather is a New York-based correspondent for The Guardian *of London, where this article first appeared on June 26, 2003.*

The American recording industry threatened yesterday to take legal action against thousands of people for illegally sharing music files, opening a new front in the war on online piracy.

The threat sends the message that the industry is no longer content to simply chase file-sharing services such as Napster and Kazaa and is going after individual users. The first cases may be brought as soon as August.

It shows that the industry has become desperate to staunch the flow of illegal downloads which is beginning to devastate CD sales. In 2000 the 10 top-selling albums in the US sold a total of 60 million copies. That dropped to 40 million in 2001 and 34 million last year.

The Recording Industry Association of America issued a statement with support from a coalition of artists including Peter Gabriel, Sheryl Crow, Missy Elliot, Eve, Shakira, Mandy Moore, the Dixie Chicks and Mary J Blige.

"Thievery is thievery," the singer Anastacia said. "If you dig an artist that much, then you should want to help keep that artist alive by purchasing the actual recording."

The RIAA cases will be confined to the US but are likely to prompt similar action by European music organizations.

Cary Sherman, president of the RIAA, said the industry had been trying for years to educate the public on the effects of illegal downloading, and had apparently failed.

The RIAA was compiling evidence for what could ultimately be thousands of cases of copyright infringement.

"The law is clear and the message to those who are distributing substantial quantities of music online should be equally clear—this activity is illegal, you are not anonymous when you do it, and engaging in it can have real consequences," he said.

"Once we begin our evidence-gathering process, any individual computer user who continues to offer music illegally to millions of others will run the very real risk of facing legal action."

The RIAA will gather evidence against "peer-to-peer" file sharers by scanning public directories, downloading the copyrighted files, issuing subpoenas against Internet service providers to find the individual's name and address.

The aim is to get people to start buying music again. The US industry's income fell from $14.6 billion in 1999 to $12.6 billion last year, and downloading from the Internet is blamed for most of the drop in sales.

The RIAA estimates that more than 2.6 billion song files are illegally downloaded every month and that about 5 million users are online offering an estimated 800 million files for copying through various peer-to-peer networks at any one time.

A number of legitimate services have been launched, including Apple's iTunes, which offers singles for 99 cents.

The most notorious file-sharing network was Napster, set up by a college dropout and hounded offline by the big record companies. A Silicon Valley software company recently bought the name and assets to revive it as a paid-for service.

In recent months the industry has sent millions of instant messages to people on the Kazaa and Grokster peer-to-peer file-sharing networks warning them that they are infringing copyright.

File Sharing Woes
Rob Rogers

ROB ROGERS—PITTSBURGH POST-GAZETTE

Tone Deaf to a Moral Dilemma?
John Healey and Jeff Leeds

John Healey and Jeff Leeds are staff writers for The Los Angeles Times, *where this article first appeared on September 2, 2003.*

Susan Philips has a conscience so sensitive to ethical failings that she feels guilty if she leaves her shopping cart adrift in the grocery store parking lot.

Her influence is reflected in her elder daughter's career choice: Miriam Philips, 22, wants to be a rabbi.

On at least one moral dilemma, though, mother and daughter are on opposite sides. To Susan, downloading music on the Internet without permission is wrong. To Miriam, it's just what you do when you go to college.

"My freshman year I was like, 'No, that isn't right.' I wouldn't do that at all," Miriam said at her family's kitchen table, two blocks from the sand in Seal Beach. But by her sophomore year at Brandeis University, she said, she was steering her iMac to free music, collecting enough songs to fill 150 CDs.

Philips' shift helps explain why the record industry has been losing its battle to shape the public's definition of theft in a digital society. Music labels have won a series of court rulings and poured millions of dollars into marketing the message that downloading free songs amounts to online shoplifting—but CD sales keep sinking.

Now the record companies are readying their most desperate bid yet to shake up the public psyche: The industry plans to bombard college students, parents of teenage downloaders and other Internet users with lawsuits alleging millions of dollars in copyright violations.

One goal is to persuade parents to crack down on their children's file sharing before an entire generation comes to expect music to be free. Unlike Susan Philips, many parents see no problem if their kids download tunes, and some actively encourage it for their own ends.

Some observers argue, however, that the effort is as futile as the federal government's attempt to ban booze 80 years ago. About half of the Internet users in the United States, some 60 million people, copy music, movies and other digital goodies from each other for free through online networks such as Kazaa and Morpheus—a statistic that suggests a culture of piracy already has solidified. Said one teenage Kazaa user, "It's hard for me to see it as wrong when so many people are doing it."

She reflects the view of many downloaders. They understand that what they're doing may break the rules of copyright law, but they don't see anything immoral about it. In fact, some even argue that copying a song online isn't "stealing" because the owner still has the original track and still can sell the CD.

Miriam Philips, for example, said that she and her friends at Brandeis knew that their music copying "was illegal and why it was illegal." Similarly, two recent surveys found that a growing number of people acknowledge it's wrong to download songs without permission, but that it doesn't stop many of them from doing it.

Like countless millions, Philips said she felt no guilt about downloading music from a shared campus folder. Not downloading "is the normal ethics of my life," she said, but at college her ethical meter was, well, recalibrated.

And she offered no sympathy for the record labels or well-known artists.

"They're big. They're rich. They can deal with it," she said, adding later: "You can argue that it's illegal but not unethical once they're rich."

Said Deborah Rhode, law professor and director of the Keck Center on Legal Ethics at Stanford University: "There's a view that no one's really harmed. And that turns out to be one of the major predictors of dishonest behavior, whether people can actually draw a connection between their actions and some concrete identifiable victim."

Plus, the ephemeral nature of online music makes it difficult for some to conceive of downloading as stealing. Philips, for instance, said she would never download a movie for free. That's not acceptable even by her college standards.

What makes music different?

"I guess I don't put as high a value on it," said Philips, whose tastes run from Aaron Copland and Stephen Sondheim to Barenaked Ladies and the Byrds.

Expressing a common view, she said music was "more of a background thing," providing flavor to her day but not a focus. As a result, she said, it's "something that doesn't feel quite as tangible" as a movie.

Jonathan Zittrain, director of the Berkman Center for Internet & Society at Harvard Law School, also noted that downloaders copy songs without taking them away from the people sharing them. "Normally, we think that sharing is a good thing," Zittrain said. "It's not just, 'Hey, we're all looting.' It's not a looter's mind-set."

File sharing networks are like groups of libraries that invite people to roll photocopiers from stack to stack. To "share" songs on a "peer-to-peer" network such as Kazaa, for example, users simply put them into a folder on their computer and open the folder to others on the network. Anyone searching for those songs can use Kazaa to find the computers where they're stored, then download copies onto his or her PC.

The Recording Industry Assn. of America argues that it's illegal to share or download music without permission because the labels' copyrights give them exclusive rights to distribute and make copies of their songs. That view is widely supported when it comes to users who copy hundreds of files, but some legal experts contend that downloading a few files may prove to be legal under the "fair use" doctrine in copyright law.

"It's far too early in the day to conclude that everything everyone does with peer-to-peer, even when it comes to copyrighted MP3 files, is conclusively infringing," said Peter Jaszi, a law professor at American University.

In addition, Philips and others argue that their downloading actually can benefit labels and artists. The free songs stoked her interest in pop music, Philips said, and prompted her to buy more CDs than she ever had before. She now owns about 50, many of them from artists she discovered through downloading.

"There's really no service that provides this," she said, adding that she doesn't usually fall in love with music unless she listens to it a lot. And buying a CD without knowing the songs "is too darn expensive."

It's a common refrain from downloaders—CDs are too expensive, new releases often contain only one or two good songs, and there's no other way to satisfy their curiosity about unfamiliar bands. Another familiar argument is that they support the artists whose music they copy for free by going to their shows and buying their T-shirts.

A college-bound 17-year-old named Amber, who asked that her last name not be used, said if she wanted only one song from a CD, she wouldn't buy the disc—she would just download the track from Kazaa. Amber's parents stopped buying music for her when she landed a part-time job, she said, so she has to make every dollar she spends on music count.

If she winds up downloading several songs from the same record and liking them, she said, she'll buy the CD—as she did with recent releases by Missy Elliott, Ludacris, Tyrese and Bow Wow.

"In that sense," Amber said, "I do have a conscience."

Cody Morrow, a 13-year-old Simi Valley skateboard fan, said he had used file sharing networks to locate music he couldn't find at his local record store, such as songs from punk band Operation Ivy. By his logic, his family is paying for the privilege of access to music when it pays for Internet access.

His mother, Maryann, an accountant, has drawn a clear line: Although reselling music downloaded from the Internet is against the rules, her son's practice of copying music for personal use is fine.

The notion that record labels would sue individual kids seems to generate more anger than worry. Taking families to court for behavior like her son's, she said, is outrageous. "I'm in America. [Suing] for personal use? I think that's crazy."

Parents, she suggested, are far more concerned their children may become involved with drugs or violence than with online music.

"I pick my battles," she said. "You don't want to be nagging and harping, or they're not going to listen to anything you say."

But the major record companies remain determined to force a shift in families' dynamics. Even as the RIAA prepares to seize parents' attention with lawsuits, music executives increasingly have been trying to call attention to the fact that file swapping networks also are frequently used to share child pornography and other X-rated images. Record executives say privately they're also aiming to use the proliferation of pornography as a means of persuading members of Congress and law enforcement officials to take a tougher stance against the file networks.

With the debate intensifying, many Internet-savvy parents are forecasting a tectonic shift for the $30-billion global music business. David Philips, Miriam's father, envisions a future "where the key to power is ownership of information and the movement of information." And Philips, a former rock 'n' roll roadie who has no love for the major record labels, worries that copyright holders' power is expanding while antitrust enforcement is diminishing.

"From the perspective of starving musicians, I think the file sharing networks are a huge plus," said Philips, a civil engineer. "It is theft, but it's probably in the public interest."

Yet he also says flatly, "If you take something without permission from someone who believes they ought to be paid for that thing, according to Jewish law, that's stealing. And you shouldn't do it . . . because to behave unethically is spiritually degrading. You are not as good a person as you were before."

Susan Philips also condemns unauthorized file sharing, but without any qualification.

"It's not just the artist who's getting cheated" by unauthorized downloading, but also songwriters and accompanying musicians, she said. And though it's probably true that the record companies are taking advantage of their artists, she said, the artists wouldn't get very far without the labels' support.

She vaguely remembers talking to Miriam about her music copying practices and telling her, "It doesn't seem ethical to me." Miriam says if the conversation did take place—she doesn't recall it—it wouldn't have affected her downloading.

After all, that's what she would expect her mother to say.

Other downloaders say their parents encourage their file sharing and CD burning, either directly or unwittingly. Amber said her mother didn't know a thing about computers, and her father didn't object to her using Kazaa. He even asked her to make a CD for him of songs from Body & Soul, a music channel on cable TV, so she dutifully downloaded a number of R&B classics and put them on a disc.

RIAA officials hope that the coming wave of lawsuits will prompt more parents to crack down on their teens' downloading. The RIAA plans to sue the people responsible for the Internet accounts used to share files, and not necessarily the file sharers themselves. If a Kazaa-crazed teen is targeted, his or her parents are the ones who'll be named as defendants.

The lawsuits probably will change some young downloaders' attitudes too. In a recent survey by Forrester Research of 1,170 12- to 22-year-olds, nearly 70% said they would stop downloading music if there was a "serious risk" of being fined or jailed.

But James DeLong, director of the Center for the Study of Digital Property at the Progress & Freedom Foundation, a conservative think tank, said enforcement won't be effective unless the music industry offers compelling legal alternatives to file sharing.

"If they have the stuff available legitimately, then they can make the moral case that people ought to be paying the artist," he said. "And I think people will accept that."

For Miriam Philips, free music is a thing of the past. Her ethics meter has been reset since college, she said. Of course, it helps to be back home, a couple of thousand miles away from the daily temptations of the Brandeis computer network.

"It's easier to refuse to do it," she said, "because you're not doing it on a daily basis."

AOL Poll Results on File Sharing

The following table documents results from user poll conducted by America Online and posted on June 30, 2003. AOL cautions that these poll results are not scientific (i.e., these responses may not be representative of music consumers or file sharers as a whole) and represent only a compilation of responses to posted questions received from subscribers.

Has the music industry's plan to sue individuals stopped you from swapping songs online?

54%	No	59,773
27%	I don't download songs	29,932
13%	I've cut back but haven't stopped	14,205
6%	Yes	7,039
	Total votes:	110,949

EXERCISE   4.5

Summary Statements

Go back over these passages and write one- or two-sentence summary statements about the main point in each reading. Use these statements to start brainstorming issues and subtopics you might like to focus on for the explanatory synthesis assignment.

5

Argument Synthesis

WHAT IS AN ARGUMENT SYNTHESIS?

The explanatory synthesis, as we have seen, is fairly modest in purpose. It emphasizes the sources themselves, not the writer's interpretation. Because your reader is not always in a position to read your sources, this kind of synthesis, if well done, can be very informative. But the main characteristic of the explanatory synthesis is that it is designed more to *inform* than to *persuade*. As we have said, rather than arguing a particular point, the thesis in an explanatory synthesis focuses on an objective presentation of facts or opinions. As the writer of an explanatory synthesis, you remain, for the most part, a detached observer.

Recall the thesis our student devised for her final draft of the explanatory synthesis on computer mediated communication in Chapter 4:

> While many praise CMC's potential to bridge barriers
> and promote meaningful dialogue, others caution that
> CMC is fraught with dangers.

This thesis summarizes the viewpoints people espouse in regard to CMC, neither arguing for or against any one viewpoint.

In contrast to an explanatory thesis, an argumentative thesis is *persuasive* in purpose. Writers working with the same source material might conceive of and support opposing theses. So the thesis for an argument synthesis is a claim about which reasonable people could disagree. It is a claim with which—given the right arguments—your audience might be persuaded to agree. The strategy of your argument synthesis is therefore to find and use convincing *support* for your *claim*.

The Elements of Argument: Claim, Support, Assumption

Let's consider the terminology we've just used. One way of looking at an argument is to see it as an interplay of three essential elements: claim, support, and assumption. A *claim* is a proposition or conclusion that you are trying to prove. You prove this claim by using *support* in the form of fact or expert opinion. Linking your supporting evidence to your claim is your *assumption* about the subject. This assumption, also called a *warrant*, is—as we've discussed in Chapter 2—an underlying belief or principle about some aspect of the world and how it operates. By nature, assumptions (which are often unstated) tend to be more general than either claims or supporting evidence.

For example, here are the essential elements of an argument advocating parental restriction of television viewing for their high school children:

Claim

```
High school students should be restricted to no
more than two hours of TV viewing per day.
```

Support

```
An important new study and the testimony of
educational specialists reveal that students who
watch more than two hours of TV a night have, on
average, lower grades than those who watch less TV.
```

Assumption

```
Excessive TV viewing adversely affects academic
performance.
```

As another example, if we converted the thesis for our explanatory synthesis into a claim suitable for an argument synthesis, it might read as follows:

```
CMC threatens to undermine human intimacy,
connection, and ultimately community.
```

Here are the other elements of this argument:

Support

```
While the Internet presents us with increased
opportunities to meet people, these meetings are
limited by geographical distance.
```

```
People are spending increasing amounts of time in
cyberspace: In 1998, the average Internet user
spent over four hours per week online, a figure
that has nearly doubled recently.
```

```
College health officials report that excessive
Internet usage threatens many college students'
academic and psychological well-being.
```

> New kinds of relationships fostered on the
> Internet often pose challenges to pre-existing
> relationships.

Assumptions

> The communication skills used and the connections
> formed during Internet contact fundamentally
> differ from those used and formed during face-to-
> face contact.
>
> "Real" connection and a sense of community are
> sustained by face-to-face contact, not by
> Internet interactions.

For the most part, arguments should be constructed logically, or rationally, so that assumptions link evidence (supporting facts and expert opinions) to claims. As we'll see, however, logic is only one component of effective arguments.

EXERCISE 5.1

Practicing Claim, Support, and Assumption

Devise two sets of claims with support and assumptions for each. First, in response to the example immediately above on computer-mediated communication and relationships, devise a one-sentence claim addressing the positive impact (or potentially positive impact) of CMC on relationships—whether you personally agree with the claim or not. Then list the support on which such a claim might rest, and the assumption that underlies these. Second, write a claim that states your own position on any debatable topic you choose. Again, devise statements of support and relevant assumptions.

The Three Appeals of Argument: *Logos, Ethos, Pathos*

Speakers and writers have never relied upon logic alone in advancing and supporting their claims. More than 2,000 years ago, the Athenian philosopher and rhetorician Aristotle explained how speakers attempting to persuade others to their point of view could achieve their purpose by relying on one or more *appeals*, which he called *logos, ethos,* and *pathos*.

Since we frequently find these three appeals employed in political argument, we'll use political examples in the following discussion. But keep in mind that these appeals are also used extensively in advertising, legal cases, business documents, and many other types of argument.

Logos

Logos is the rational appeal, the appeal to reason. If speakers expect to persuade their audiences, they must argue logically and must supply appropriate evidence to support their case. Logical arguments are commonly of two types (often combined). The *deductive* argument begins with a generalization, then cites a specific case related to that generalization, from which follows a conclusion. A familiar example of deductive reasoning, used by Aristotle himself, is the following:

> All men are mortal. (*generalization*)
>
> Socrates is a man. (*specific case*)
>
> Socrates is mortal. (*conclusion about the specific case*)

In the terms we've just been discussing, this deduction may be restated as follows:

> Socrates is mortal. (*claim*)
>
> Socrates is a man. (*support*)
>
> All men are mortal. (*assumption*)

An example of a more contemporary deductive argument may be seen in President John F. Kennedy's address to the nation in June 1963 on the need for sweeping civil rights legislation. Kennedy begins with the generalizations that it "ought to be possible . . . for American students of any color to attend any public institution they select without having to be backed up by troops" and that "it ought to be possible for American citizens of any color to register and vote in a free election without interference or fear of reprisal." Kennedy then provides several specific examples (primarily recent events in Birmingham, Alabama) and statistics to show that this was not the case. He concludes:

> We face, therefore, a moral crisis as a country and a people. It cannot be met by repressive police action. It cannot be left to increased demonstrations in the streets. It cannot be quieted by token moves or talk. It is time to act in the Congress, in your state and local legislative body, and, above all, in all of our daily lives.

Underlying Kennedy's argument is the following reasoning:

> All Americans should enjoy certain rights. (*assumption*)
>
> Some Americans do not enjoy these rights. (*support*)
>
> We must take action to ensure that all Americans enjoy these rights. (*claim*)

Another form of logical argumentation is *inductive* reasoning. A speaker or writer who argues inductively begins not with a generalization, but with several pieces of specific evidence. The speaker then draws a conclusion from this evidence. For example, in a 1990 debate on gun control, Senator Robert C. Byrd (D-VA) cites specific examples of rampant crime involving guns: "I read of young men being viciously murdered for a pair of sneakers, a leather jacket, or $20." He also offers statistical evidence of the increasing crime rate: "in 1951, there were 3.2 policemen for every felony committed in the United States; this year [1990] nearly 3.2 felonies will be committed per every police officer." He concludes, "Something has to change. We have to stop the crimes that are distorting and disrupting the way of life for so many innocent, law-respecting Americans. The bill that we are debating today attempts to do just that."

Senator Edward M. Kennedy (D–MA) also used statistical evidence in arguing for passage of the Racial Justice Act of 1990, designed to ensure that minorities were not disproportionately singled out for the death penalty. Kennedy points out that between 1973 and 1980, 17 defendants in Fulton County, Georgia, were charged with killing police officers, but the only defendant who received the death sentence was a black man. Kennedy also cites statistics to show that "those who killed whites were 4.3 times more likely to receive the death penalty than were killers of blacks," and that "in Georgia, blacks who killed whites received the death penalty 16.7 percent of the time, while whites who killed received the death penalty only 4.2 percent of the time."

Of course, the mere piling up of evidence does not in itself make the speaker's case. As Donna Cross explains in "Politics: The Art of Bamboozling,"* politicians are very adept at "card-stacking." And statistics can be selected and manipulated to prove anything, as demonstrated in Darrell Huff's landmark book *How to Lie with Statistics* (1954). Moreover, what appears to be a logical argument may, in fact, be fundamentally flawed. (See Chapter 2 for a discussion of logical fallacies and faulty reasoning strategies.) On the other hand, the fact that evidence can be distorted, statistics misused, and logic fractured does not mean that these tools of reason can be dispensed with or should be dismissed. It means only that audiences have to listen and read critically—perceptively, knowledgeably, and skeptically (though not necessarily cynically).

Sometimes, politicians can turn their opponents' false logic against them. Major R. Owens (D–NY), attempted to counter what he took to be the reasoning on welfare adopted by his opponents:

> Welfare programs create dependency and so should be reformed or abolished. (*assumption*)
>
> Aid to Families with Dependent Children (AFDC) is a welfare program. (*support*)
>
> AFDC should be reformed or abolished. (*claim*)

In his speech opposing the Republican welfare reform measure of 1995, Owens simply changes the specific (middle) term, pointing out that federal

---

*Donna Cross, *Word Abuse: How the Words We Use Use Us* (New York: Coward, 1979).

subsidies for electric power in the West and Midwest and farmers' low-rate home loan mortgages are, in effect, welfare programs. ("We are spoiling America's farmers by smothering them with socialism.") The logical conclusion—that we should reform or eliminate farmers' home loan mortgages—would clearly be unacceptable to many of those pushing for reform of AFDC. Owens thus suggests that opposition to AFDC is based less on reason than on lack of sympathy for its recipients.

EXERCISE 5.2

Using Deductive and Inductive Logic

Choose an issue currently being debated at your school, or a college-related issue about which you are concerned. Write down a claim about this issue. Then write two paragraphs addressing your claim—one in which you organize your points deductively, and one in which you organize them inductively. Some sample issues might include college admissions policies, classroom crowding, or grade inflation. Alternatively, you could base your paragraphs on a claim generated in Exercise 5.1.

ETHOS

Ethos, or the ethical appeal, is based not on the ethical rationale for the subject under discussion, but rather on the ethical nature of the person making the appeal. A person making an argument must have a certain degree of credibility: That person must be of good character, have sound sense, and be qualified to hold the office or recommend policy.

For example, Elizabeth Cervantes Barrón, running for senator as the peace and freedom candidate, begins her statement, "I was born and raised in central Los Angeles. I grew up in a multiethnic, multicultural environment where I learned to respect those who were different from me. . . . I am a teacher and am aware of how cutbacks in education have affected our children and our communities."

On the other end of the political spectrum, American Independent gubernatorial candidate Jerry McCready also begins with an ethical appeal: "As a self-employed businessman, I have learned firsthand what it is like to try to make ends meet in an unstable economy being manipulated by out-of-touch politicians." Both candidates are making an appeal to *ethos*, based on the strength of their personal qualities for the office they seek.

L. A. Kauffman is not running for office but rather writing an article arguing against socialism as a viable ideology for the future ("Socialism: No." *Progressive*, 1 April 1993). To defuse objections that he is simply a tool of capitalism, Kauffman begins with an appeal to *ethos*: "Until recently, I was executive editor of the journal *Socialist Review*. Before that I worked for the Marxist magazine, *Monthly Review*. My bookshelves are filled with books of

Marxist theory, and I even have a picture of Karl Marx up on my wall." Thus, Kauffman establishes his credentials to argue knowledgeably about Marxist ideology.

Conservative commentator Rush Limbaugh frequently makes use of the ethical appeal by linking himself with the kind of Americans he assumes his audiences to be (what author Donna Cross calls "glory by association"):

> In their attacks [on me], my critics misjudge and insult the American people. If I were really what liberals claim—racist, hatemonger, blowhard—I would years ago have deservedly gone into oblivion. The truth is, I provide information and analysis the media refuses to disseminate, information and analysis the public craves. People listen to me for one reason: I am effective. And my credibility is judged in the marketplace every day. . . . I represent America's rejection of liberal elites. . . . I validate the convictions of ordinary people.*

EXERCISE 5.3

Using Ethos

Return to the claim you used for Exercise 5.2, and write a paragraph in which you use an appeal to *ethos* to make a case for that claim.

PATHOS

Finally, speakers and writers appeal to their audiences by use of *pathos*, the appeal to the emotions. Nothing is inherently wrong with using an emotional appeal. Indeed, since emotions often move people far more powerfully than reason alone, speakers and writers would be foolish not to use emotion. And it would be a drab, humorless world if human beings were not subject to the sway of feeling, as well as reason. The emotional appeal becomes problematic only if it is the *sole* or *primary* basis of the argument. This imbalance of emotion over logic is the kind of situation that led, for example, to the internment of Japanese Americans during World War II or that leads to periodic political spasms to enact anti-flag-burning legislation.

President Reagan was a master of emotional appeal. He closed his first inaugural address with a reference to the view from the Capitol to the Arlington National Cemetery, where lie thousands of markers of "heroes":

> Under one such marker lies a young man, Martin Treptow, who left his job in a small-town barbershop in 1917 to go to France with the

---

*Rush Limbaugh, "Why I Am a Threat to the Left," *Los Angeles Times*, 9 Oct. 1994.

famed Rainbow Division. There, on the western front, he was killed trying to carry a message between battalions under heavy artillery fire. We're told that on his body was found a diary. On the flyleaf under the heading, "My Pledge," he had written these words: "America must win this war. Therefore, I will work, I will save, I will sacrifice, I will endure, I will fight cheerfully and do my utmost, as if the issue of the whole struggle depended on me alone." The crisis we are facing today does not require of us the kind of sacrifice that Martin Treptow and so many thousands of others were called upon to make. It does require, however, our best effort and our willingness to believe in ourselves and to believe in our capacity to perform great deeds, to believe that together with God's help we can and will resolve the problems which now confront us.

Surely, Reagan implies, if Martin Treptow can act so courageously and so selflessly, we can do the same. The logic is somewhat unclear, since the connection between Martin Treptow and ordinary Americans of 1981 is rather tenuous (as Reagan concedes); but the emotional power of Martin Treptow, whom reporters were sent scurrying to research, carries the argument.

A more recent president, Bill Clinton, also used *pathos*. Addressing an audience of the nation's governors about his welfare plan, Clinton closed his remarks by referring to a conversation he had held with a welfare mother who had gone through the kind of training program Clinton was advocating. Asked by Clinton whether she thought that such training programs should be mandatory, the mother said, "I sure do." When Clinton asked her why, she said:

> "Well, because if it wasn't, there would be a lot of people like me home watching the soaps because we don't believe we can make anything of ourselves anymore. So you've got to make it mandatory." And I said, "What's the best thing about having a job?" She said, "When my boy goes to school, and they say, 'What does your mama do for a living?' he can give an answer."

Clinton uses the emotional power he counts on in that anecdote to set up his conclusion: "We must end poverty for Americans who want to work. And we must do it on terms that dignify all of the rest of us, as well as help our country to work better. I need your help, and I think we can do it."

EXERCISE 5.4

Using Pathos

Return to the claim you used for Exercises 5.2 and 5.3, and write a paragraph in which you use an appeal to *pathos* to argue for that claim.

DEMONSTRATION: DEVELOPING AN ARGUMENT SYNTHESIS—VOLUNTEERING IN AMERICA

To demonstrate how to plan and draft an argument synthesis, let's consider another subject. If you were taking an economics or sociology course, you might at some point consider the phenomenon of volunteerism, the extent to which Americans volunteer—that is, give away their time freely—for causes they deem worthy. In a market economy, why would people agree to forgo wages in exchange for their labor? Are there other kinds of compensation for people who volunteer? Is peer pressure involved? Can a spirit of volunteerism be taught or encouraged? And, in light of the articles that follow and the example argument based on them, can the government—which has the constitutional right to compel military service—*compel* citizens to serve their communities (rendering their service something other than an act of volunteering)?

Suppose, in preparing to write a short paper on volunteering, you located the following sources:

"A New Start for National Service," John McCain and Evan Bayh

"A Time to Heed the Call," David Gergen

"Volunteering in the United States," US Department of Labor

"Americorps Mission Statement"

"National Service, Political Socialization, and Citizenship," Eric B. Gorham

"Calls for National Service," Landrum, Eberly, and Sherraden

"The Moral Equivalent of War," William James

"Crito," Plato

"Keeping Alive the Spirit of National Service," Richard North Patterson

"Rumsfeld: No Need For Draft; 'Disadvantages Notable,'" Kathleen T. Rhem

"Politics and National Service: A Virus Attacks the Volunteer Sector," Bruce Chapman

Read these sources (which follow) carefully, noting as you do the kinds of information and ideas you could draw upon to develop an *argument synthesis*.

Note: To save space and for the purpose of demonstration, several of the following passages are excerpts only. In preparing your paper, naturally you would draw upon entire articles and book chapters from which the extracts were made. (The discussion of how these passages can form the basis of an argument synthesis resumes on page 213.)

A New Start for National Service
John McCain and Evan Bayh

John McCain (R-AZ) and Evan Bayh (D-IN) are United States senators. This Op-ed piece ap-peared in the New York Times *on November 6, 2001, a few weeks after the terrorist attack of September 11th.*

1   Since Sept. 11, Americans have found a new spirit of national unity and purpose. Forty years ago, at the height of the cold war, President John F. Kennedy challenged Americans to enter into public service. Today, confronted with a challenge no less daunting than the cold war, Americans again are eager for ways to serve at home and abroad. Government should make it easier for them to do so.

2   That is why we are introducing legislation to revamp national service programs and dramatically expand opportunities for public service.

3   Many tasks lie ahead, both new and old. On the home front, there are new security and civil defense requirements, like increased police and border patrol needs. We will charge the Corporation for National Service, the federal office that oversees national volunteer programs, with the task of assembling a plan that would put civilians to work to assist the Office of Homeland Security. The military will need new recruits to confront the challenges abroad, so our bill will also improve benefits for our servicemembers.

4   At the same time, because the society we defend needs increased services, from promoting literacy to caring for the elderly, we expand AmeriCorps and senior service programs to enlarge our national army of volunteers.

5   AmeriCorps' achievements have been impressive: thousands of homes have been built, hundreds of thousands of seniors given the care they need to live independently and millions of children tutored.

6   Since its inception in 1993, nearly 250,000 Americans have served stints of one or two years in AmeriCorps. But for all its concrete achievements, AmeriCorps has been too small to rouse the nation's imagination. Under our bill, 250,000 volunteers each year would be able to answer the call—with half of them assisting in civil defense needs and half continuing the good work of AmeriCorps.

7   We must also ask our nation's colleges to promote service more aggressively. Currently, many colleges devote only a small fraction of federal work-study funds to community service, while the majority of federal resources are used to fill low-skill positions. This was not Congress's vision when it passed the Higher Education Act of 1965. Under our bill, universities will be required to promote student involvement in community activities more vigorously.

8   And for those who might consider serving their country in the armed forces, the benefits must keep pace with the times. While the volunteer military has been successful, our armed forces continue to suffer from significant recruitment challenges.

9   Our legislation encourages more young Americans to serve in the military by allowing the Defense Department to create a new, shorter-term enlistment option. This "18-18-18" plan would offer an $18,000 bonus—in addition to regular pay—for 18 months of active duty and 18 months of reserve duty. And we would significantly improve education payments made to service members under current law.

10   Public service is a virtue, and national service should one day be a rite of passage for young Americans. This is the right moment to issue a new call to service and give a new generation a way to claim the rewards and responsibilities of active citizenship.

A Time to Heed the Call
David Gergen

David Gergen is an editor-at-large for U.S. News & World Report, *in which this essay appeared on December 24, 2001. He has served as an advisor to Presidents Nixon, Ford, Reagan, and Clinton and currently directs the Center for Public Leadership at the John F. Kennedy School of Government.*

1   Leaving church on a Sunday several weeks ago, Seth Moulton posed a haunting question. Moulton is a clean-cut, good-looking young guy who graduated from Harvard last spring and represented his class as commencement speaker. "I have been planning to go to Wall Street for a while," he said, "Now with what's happened, I think I should give some time to the country. But tell me: Where should I sign up?"

2   Since September 11, a surge in patriotic sentiment has prompted thousands of others to ask themselves similar questions. People want to help and are trying to figure out how. Some 81 percent recently told surveyors from the firm Penn, Schoen & Berland Associates they would like the federal government to encourage increased community and national service. They strongly support college scholarships, similar to the GI Bill, for young people who serve as police officers, firefighters, or civil-defense workers, and they favor a dramatic expansion of the national service program.

3   So far, our political leaders have rightly focused on battling terrorists overseas, giving only scant attention to creating a new culture of service at home. But their very successes against Osama bin Laden are opening a second phase in this struggle. We now have a chance to step back and think longer term. How do we transform this new love of nation into a lasting mission? How do we keep the flame alive? With imagination, we could do just that if we boldly call millions of young Americans to give at least a year of service to the nation. Remember FDR's Civilian Conservation Corps and the magnificent parks all those young people built in the wilderness? There are many parallel responsibilities today. Beefing up border operations, teaching kids in poor schools, helping out in hospitals—

those are just a few. Add three months of physical training, with kids from Brooklyn mixing in with kids from Berkeley, and the results would be eye popping.

4   Giving something back. Voluntary service when young often changes people for life. They learn to give their fair share. Some 60 percent of alumni from Teach for America, a marvelous program, now work full time in education, and many others remain deeply involved in social change. Mark Levine, for example, has started two community-owned credit unions in Washington Heights, N.Y., for recent immigrants. Alumni of City Year, another terrific program, vote at twice the rates of their peers. Or think of the Peace Corps alumni. Six now serve in the House of Representatives, one (Christopher Dodd) in the Senate.

5   A culture of service might also help reverse the trend among many young people to shun politics and public affairs. Presidential voting among 18-to-29-year-olds has fallen over the past three decades from half to less than a third. In a famous poll of a year ago, some 47 percent said their regular source of political news was the late-night comedy shows. If the young were to sign up for national service, as scholar Bill Galston argues, that could lead to greater civic engagement.

6   President Bush clearly supports the idea. What is lacking, though, is a clarion call, a "certain trumpet" that breaks through, along with a sweeping plan for action. The best plan on offer today is one advanced by Sens. John McCain of Arizona, a Republican, and Democrat Evan Bayh of Indiana and given strong support by the Democratic Leadership Council. It would build on AmeriCorps, the volunteer program started by President Clinton, at first opposed and now embraced by many Republicans. AmeriCorps has achieved significant results but remains modest in size with about 50,000 volunteers. It has never enjoyed the panache of the Peace Corps—as many as 2 out of 3 Americans say they have never heard of the program. McCain and Bayh would expand AmeriCorps fivefold, to 250,000 volunteers a year, and channel half the new recruits into homeland-security efforts. The program would also open up more chances for seniors to serve—another important contribution.

7   With support from the president, this bill would become one of the first major accomplishments of Congress next year. Interest has been spiraling upward in recent weeks. Some oppose it because they would like all volunteer service to be directed to homeland security. That is a mistake. Our schools are as important to our future as are border patrols. Others dismiss voluntary service as patriotism on the cheap; they would like to see a full-scale restoration of the draft, providing manpower for both military and civilian purposes. There are powerful arguments for a universal draft, but the public isn't ready for that yet. It would be wiser to start here . . . and now.

8   September 11 was a seminal moment for America. Everyone who lived through it will remember exactly where he or she was when the terrible news came. But the moment will pass unless we seize it and give it more permanent meaning. Fortunately, some already hear the call. Leaving church on Sunday last, Seth Moulton said he had made his choice: He has volunteered for four years in the United States Marines. Now, let the trumpet sound for the rest of his generation.

Volunteering in the United States, 2003
Bureau of Labor Statistics, US Department of Labor

Every year, the Bureau of Labor Statistics collects and analyzes patterns of volunteering in the United States. Following is a summary of data collected from September 2002 to September 2003. Links to the various tables cited below can be found at the end of the article. Table 1 from the BLS report follows this selection.

1   Both the number of volunteers and the volunteer rate rose over the year ended in September 2003, the Bureau of Labor Statistics of the U.S. Department of Labor reported today. About 63.8 million people did volunteer work at some point from September 2002 to September 2003, up from 59.8 million for the similar period ended in September 2002. The volunteer rate grew to 28.8 percent, up from 27.4 percent.

2   These data on volunteering were collected through a supplement to the September 2003 Current Population Survey (CPS). Volunteers are defined as persons who did unpaid work (except for expenses) through or for an organization. The CPS is a monthly survey of about 60,000 households that obtains information on employment and unemployment among the nation's civilian noninstitutional population age 16 and over. For more information about the volunteer supplement, see the Technical Note.

Changes in Volunteer Rates

3   About 25.1 percent of men and 32.2 percent of women did volunteer work in the year ended in September 2003, increases of 1.5 and 1.2 percentage points from 2002, respectively. For teenagers, the volunteer rate jumped by 2.6 percentage points to 29.5 percent. In contrast, the volunteer rate for the group most likely to volunteer, 35- to 44-year olds, was little changed at 34.7 percent. (See Tables A and 1.)

4   The volunteer rate for whites rose from 29.2 percent for the year ended in September 2002 to 30.6 percent for the year ended in September 2003, while the rates for blacks and Hispanics were little changed. About 18.7 percent of Asians performed some sort of volunteer work through or for an organization over the year ended in September 2003. (Data for Asians were not tabulated in 2002.)

5   Among persons 25 years of age and over, the volunteer rates for those with at least some college education or a bachelor's degree or better rose over the year, while the rates for those whose education had not gone beyond high school graduation remained about the same.

Volunteering Among Demographic Groups

6   Almost 64 million persons, or 28.8 percent of the civilian noninstitutional population age 16 and over, volunteered through or for organizations at some point from September 2002 to September 2003. Women volunteered at a higher rate than did men, a relationship that held across age groups, education levels, and other major characteristics. (See Table 1.)

Table A. Volunteers by selected characteristics, September 2002 and 2003

(Numbers in thousands)

Characteristic	September 2002r			September 2003		
	Number	Percent of population	Median annual hours	Number	Percent of population	Median annual hours
Sex						
Total, both sexes	59,783	27.4	52	63,791	28.8	52
Men	24,706	23.6	52	26,805	25.1	52
Women	35,076	31.0	50	36,987	32.2	52
Age						
Total, 16 years and over	59,783	27.4	52	63,791	28.8	52
16 to 24 years	7,742	21.9	40	8,671	24.1	40
25 to 34 years	9,574	24.8	33	10,337	26.5	36
35 to 44 years	14,971	34.1	52	15,165	34.7	50
45 to 54 years	12,477	31.3	52	13,302	32.7	52
55 to 64 years	7,331	27.5	60	8,170	29.2	60
65 years and over	7,687	22.7	96	8,146	23.7	88
Race and Hispanic or Latino ethnicity						
White (1)	52,591	29.2	52	55,572	30.6	52
Black or African American (1)	4,896	19.1	52	5,145	20.0	52
Asian (1)	(2)	(2)	(2)	1,735	18.7	40
Hispanic or Latino Ethnicity	4,059	15.5	40	4,364	15.7	40

Educational attainment (3)

Less than a high school diploma	2,806	10.1	48	2,793	9.9	48
High school graduate, no college (4)	12,542	21.2	49	12,882	21.7	48
Less than a bachelor's degree (5)	15,066	32.8	52	15,966	34.1	52
College graduates	21,627	43.3	60	23,481	45.6	60

Employment status

Civilian labor force	42,773	29.3	48	45,499	30.9	48
Employed	40,742	29.5	48	43,138	31.2	48
Full time (6)	32,210	28.3	46	33,599	29.6	48
Part time (7)	8,532	35.4	52	9,539	38.4	52
Unemployed	2,031	25.1	50	2,361	26.7	48
Not in the labor force	17,010	23.7	72	18,293	24.6	66

(1) Beginning in 2003, persons who selected this race group only; persons who selected more than one race group are not included. Prior to 2003, persons who reported more than one race group were included in the group they identified as the main race.
(2) Data for Asians were not tabulated in 2002.
(3) Data refer to persons 25 yeas and over.
(4) Includes high school diploma or equivalent.
(5) Includes the categories, some college, no degree; and associate degree.
(6) Usually work 35 hours or more a week at all jobs.
(7) Usually work less than 35 hours a week at all jobs.
r = revised. Estimates for 2002 have been revised to reflect the use of Census 2000-based population controls. See the Technical Note for additional information.

NOTE: Estimates for the above race groups (white, black or African American, and Asian) do not sum to totals because data are not presented for all races. In addition, persons whose ethnicity is identified as Hispanic or Latino may be of any race and, therefore, are classified by ethnicity as well as by race.

7   By age, 35- to 44-year olds were the most likely to volunteer, closely followed by 45- to 54-year olds. Their volunteer rates were 34.7 percent and 32.7 percent, respectively. Teenagers also had a relatively high volunteer rate, 29.5 percent, perhaps reflecting an emphasis on volunteer activities in schools. Volunteer rates were lowest among persons age 65 years and over (23.7 percent) and among those in their early twenties (19.7 percent). Within the 65 years and over group, volunteer rates decreased as age increased.

8   Parents with children under age 18 were more likely to volunteer than persons with no children of that age, with volunteer rates of 37.5 percent and 25.0 percent, respectively. Volunteer rates were higher among married persons (34.0 percent) than among never-married persons (22.8 percent) and persons of other marital statuses (22.5 percent).

9   Whites volunteered at a higher rate (30.6 percent) than did blacks (20.0 percent) and Asians (18.7 percent). Among individuals of Hispanic or Latino ethnicity, 15.7 percent volunteered.

10   Overall, 31.2 percent of all employed persons had volunteered during the year ended in September 2003. By comparison, the volunteer rates of persons who were unemployed (26.7 percent) or not in the labor force (24.6 percent) were lower. Among the employed, part-time workers were more likely than full-time workers to have participated in volunteer activities—38.4 percent and 29.6 percent, respectively.

Total Annual Hours Spent Volunteering

11   Volunteers spent a median of 52 hours on volunteer activities during the period from September 2002 to September 2003, unchanged from the previous survey period. The median number of hours men and women spent volunteering was the same (52 hours). (See Table 2.)

12   Among the age groups, volunteers age 65 and over devoted the most time—a median of 88 hours—to volunteer activities. Those age 25 to 34 years spent the least time, volunteering a median of 36 hours during the year.

Number and Type of Organizations

13   Most volunteers were involved with one or two organizations—69.2 percent and 19.2 percent, respectively. Individuals with higher educational attainment were more likely to volunteer for multiple organizations than were individuals with less education. (See Table 3.)

14   The main organization—the organization for which the volunteer worked the most hours during the year—was either religious (34.6 percent of all volunteers) or educational/youth-service related (27.4 percent). Another 11.8 percent of volunteers performed activities mainly for social or community service organizations, and 8.2 percent volunteered the most hours for hospitals or other health organizations. This distribution is largely the same as in the prior year. (See Table 4.)

15   Older volunteers were more likely to work mainly for religious organizations than were their younger counterparts. For example, 46.5 percent of volunteers age 65 and over performed volunteer activities mainly through or for a reli-

gious organization, compared with 29.1 percent of volunteers age 16 to 24 years. Younger individuals were more likely to volunteer for educational or youth service organizations.

16   Among volunteers with children under 18 years, 47.2 percent of mothers and 36.1 percent of fathers volunteered mainly for an educational/youth-service related organization, such as a school or little league. Parents were more than twice as likely to volunteer for such organizations as persons with no children of that age. Conversely, volunteers with no children under 18 were about twice as likely as parents to volunteer for some other types of organizations, such as social or community service organizations.

Volunteer Activities for Main Organization

17   The activities of volunteers varied. Among the more commonly reported (volunteers could report more than one activity) were fundraising or selling items to raise money (28.8 percent); coaching, refereeing, tutoring, or teaching (28.6 percent); collecting, preparing, distributing, or serving food (24.9 percent); providing information, which would include being an usher, greeter, or minister (22.0 percent); and engaging in general labor (21.8 percent). (See Table 5.)

18   Some demographic groups were more likely to engage in certain activities than were others. For example, parents of children under 18 were much more likely to coach, referee, tutor, or teach than were persons with no children of that age. College graduates were more than four times as likely as those with less than a high school diploma to provide professional or management assistance.

19   The volunteer activity categories were redesigned for 2003 to be more consistent conceptually and to provide better information about the types of volunteer activities performed. The redesign eliminated a "catch-all" category used in 2002 that received over two-fifths of all responses to the question on the type of volunteer activities performed. As a result of the redesign, the 2003 data on volunteer activities performed are not comparable with the data for 2002.

How Volunteers Became Involved with Main Organization

20   Two in five volunteers became involved with the main organization for which they did volunteer work on their own initiative; that is, they approached the organization. Almost 44 percent were asked to become a volunteer, most often by someone in the organization. (See Table 6.)

Reasons for Not Volunteering

21   Among those who had volunteered at some point in the past, the most common reason given for not volunteering in the year ended September 2003 was lack of time (44.7 percent), followed by health or medical problems (14.7 percent) and family responsibilities or childcare problems (9.5 percent). Lack of time was the most common reason for all groups except those age 65 and over and for those with less than a high school diploma, or who were not in the labor force—both of which contained a relatively high proportion of older persons. For each of these three groups, health or medical problems was the primary reason for not volunteering. *(Text continued on page 198.)*

Table 1. Volunteers by selected characteristics, September 2003

(Numbers in thousands)

Characteristics in September 2003	Total, both sexes			Men			Women		
	Civilian noninstitutional population	Volunteers Number	Percent of population	Civilian noninstitutional population	Volunteers Number	Percent of population	Civilian noninstitutional population	Volunteers Number	Percent of population
Age									
Total, 16 years and over	221,779	63,791	28.8	106,744	26,805	25.1	115,035	36,987	32.2
16 to 24 years	35,979	8,671	24.1	18,079	3,782	20.9	17,900	4,888	27.3
16 to 19 years	16,131	4,758	29.5	8,176	2,098	25.7	7,955	2,661	33.4
20 to 24 years	19,848	3,912	19.7	9,903	1,685	17.0	9,945	2,228	22.4
25 years and over	185,800	55,121	29.7	88,665	23,022	26.0	97,135	32,098	33.0
25 to 34 years	39,072	10,337	26.5	19,375	3,976	20.5	19,697	6,360	32.3
35 to 44 years	43,691	15,165	34.7	21,440	6,308	29.4	22,251	8,857	39.8
45 to 54 years	40,692	13,302	32.7	19,863	5,829	29.3	20,828	7,474	35.9
55 to 64 years	28,003	8,170	29.2	13,437	3,569	26.6	14,566	4,602	31.6
65 years and over	34,342	8,146	23.7	14,550	3,341	23.0	19,792	4,806	24.3
Race and Hispanic or Latino ethnicity									
White	181,696	55,572	30.6	88,462	23,507	26.6	93,234	32,065	34.4
Black or African American	25,784	5,145	20.0	11,501	1,975	17.2	14,283	3,170	22.2
Asian	9,278	1,735	18.7	4,362	774	17.7	4,916	961	19.5
Hispanic or Latino ethnicity	27,808	4,364	15.7	14,233	1,702	12.0	13,575	2,662	19.6
Educational attainment (1)									
Less than a high school diploma	28,243	2,793	9.9	13,659	1,141	8.4	14,584	1,652	11.3
High school graduate, no college (2)	59,241	12,882	21.7	27,666	4,985	18.0	31,575	7,896	25.0
Less than a bachelor's degree (3)	46,786	15,966	34.1	21,341	6,146	28.8	25,444	9,819	38.6
College graduates	51,530	23,481	45.6	25,999	10,750	41.3	25,531	12,731	49.9

Marital status

Single, never married	60,017	13,670	22.8	31,962	5,953	18.6	28,055	7,718	27.5
Married, spouse present	118,986	40,486	34.0	59,925	18,155	30.3	59,061	22,331	37.8
Other marital status (4)	42,775	9,635	22.5	14,856	2,697	18.2	27,919	6,938	24.9

Presence of own children under 18 years (5)

Without own children under 18	155,359	38,907	25.0	77,121	16,969	22.0	78,238	21,938	28.0
With own children under 18	66,420	24,884	37.5	29,623	9,836	33.2	36,797	15,049	40.9

Employment status

Civilian labor force	147,322	45,499	30.9	78,854	21,231	26.9	68,468	24,268	35.4
Employed	138,477	43,138	31.2	74,155	20,247	27.3	64,322	22,890	35.6
Full time (6)	113,636	33,599	29.6	65,952	17,741	26.9	47,684	15,857	33.3
Part time (7)	24,841	9,539	38.4	8,203	2,506	30.5	16,638	7,033	42.3
Unemployed	8,844	2,361	26.7	4,699	983	20.9	4,146	1,378	33.2
Not in the labor force	74,457	18,293	24.6	27,890	5,574	20.0	46,567	12,719	27.3

1 Data refer to persons 25 years and over.
2 Includes high school diploma or equivalent.
3 Includes the categories, some college, no degree; and associate degree.
4 Includes divorced, separated, and widowed persons.
5 Own children include sons, daughters, stepchildren, and adopted children. Not included are nieces, nephews, grandchildren, and other related and unrelated children.
6 Usually work 35 hours or more a week at all jobs.
7 Usually work less than 35 hours a week at all jobs.

NOTE: Data on volunteers relate to persons who performed unpaid volunteer activities for an organization at any point from September 1, 2002, through the survey period in September 2003. Estimates for the above race groups (white, black or African American, and Asian) do not sum to totals because data are not presented for all races. In addition, persons whose ethnicity is identified as Hispanic or Latino may be of any race and, therefore, are classified by ethnicity as well as by race.

Changes in Volunteer Estimates

Estimates shown in this release for the years ended September 2002 and September 2003 are based on Census 2000 population controls. For this reason, the estimates for the year ended September 2002 appearing in this release may differ from those published earlier, which were based on population controls derived from the 1990 census.

- Table 1. Volunteers by selected characteristics, September 2003
- Table 2. Volunteers by annual hours of volunteer activities and selected characteristics, September 2003
- Table 3. Volunteers by number of organizations for which volunteer activities were performed and selected characteristics, September 2003
- Table 4. Volunteers by type of main organization for which volunteer activities were performed and selected characteristics, September 2003
- Table 5. Volunteer activities for main organization for which activities were performed and selected characteristics, September 2003
- Table 6. Volunteers by how they became involved with main organization for which volunteer activities were performed and selected characteristics, September 2003
- Table 7. Main reason for not volunteering last year as reported by non-volunteers who had volunteered in the past by selected characteristics, September 2003

AmeriCorps Mission Statement

"AmeriCorps is a network of national service programs that engage more than 50,000 Americans each year in intensive service to meet critical needs in education, public safety, health, and the environment. AmeriCorps members serve through more than 2,100 nonprofits, public agencies, and faith-based organizations. They tutor and mentor youth, build affordable housing, teach computer skills, clean parks and streams, run after-school programs, and help communities respond to disasters. Created in 1993, AmeriCorps is part of the Corporation for National and Community Service, which also oversees Senior Corps and Learn and Serve America. Together these programs engage more than 2 million Americans of all ages and backgrounds in service each year."[1] Following is the organization's mission statement from its Program Directory, Spring/Summer 1995.

1   AmeriCorps joins a long tradition of national programs such as the Civilian Conservation Corps, the GI Bill, and the Peace Corps that have encouraged and rewarded service to our country. Although each of the over 300 programs of the AmeriCorps National Service Network is designed to meet the special

needs of the community it serves, all AmeriCorps programs are united by a common mission:

2 **Getting Things Done**—AmeriCorps will help communities meet their education, public safety, human or environmental needs through direct and demonstrable service.

3 **Strengthening Communities**—AmeriCorps units individuals from many different backgrounds in the common effort to improve our communities.

4 **Encouraging Responsibility**—Through service and civic education, AmeriCorps enables Members to become problem-solvers, leaders, and more responsible members of their communities.

5 **Expanding Opportunity**—Members may receive job skills, educational benefits, and invaluable experience.

1. Institute for Future Work Force Development. "National AmeriCorps History." *Youth in Action AmeriCorps*, Northern Arizona University. 10 July 2003. 20 July 2003 <http://www4.nau.edu> Path: americorps; Americorps History.

National Service, Political Socialization, and Citizenship
Eric B. Gorham

This passage from the first chapter of Eric B. Gorham's National Service, Citizenship, and Political Education *(1992) provides a definition and brief overview of the history of national service in the United States. In the book, Gorham argues that the language government uses to promote programs for national service betrays an effort to "reproduce a postindustrial, capitalist economy in the name of good citizenship." Eric Gorham is associate professor of political science at Loyola University, New Orleans.*

1 Many politicians, academics, and planners define national service as a nationwide program of community work that citizens, mostly young people, enter for one or two years. It is either voluntary or coercive, and employs participants in public sector or "voluntary" sector jobs at subminimum wages. In the process, participants serve the needs of the nation, acquire job and life skills, and learn the essentials of American citizenship.

2   This definition has evolved from William James's conception of national service in the early part of this century. James argued that the "gilded youth" of America ought to be required to serve the nation in order to "toughen" their spirit, and help them recognize the poverty which afflicts their country. James proposed a "moral equivalent of war" in order that Americans may become more concerned with their communities, and in order that a "peaceful" alternative to

the military be offered to the public.[1] Individuals could then view their country from different perspectives and not merely conform their behavior to certain nonmilitary standards.

3   After James, a number of other prominent Americans accepted his idea on principle, but offered competing proposals for a service program. Franklin Delano Roosevelt proposed that programs were needed to put young people to work during the depression. On March 21, 1933, he announced his intention to create the Civilian Conservation Corps (CCC):

> We can take a vast army of these unemployed into healthful surroundings. We can eliminate, to some extent, at least, the threat that enforced idleness brings to spiritual and moral stability.[2]

For Roosevelt, the CCC was necessary to employ underprivileged youth, not James's "gilded youth," and to provide them with certain physical and moral standards by which they could improve their lot.

4   After World War II, James's theme of educating youth returned in the form of John F. Kennedy's Peace Corps proposal. An international "moral equivalent of war," the Peace Corps offered thousands of privileged youth the opportunity to work selflessly for their country and for others. A domestic program, Volunteers in Service to America (VISTA), was established to provide similar opportunities for work in the poorer regions of America. More recently, there have also been a number of university programs that promote service—like Campus Compact and the Campus Outreach Opportunity League (COOL).

5   At the same time, various administrations have experimented with employment programs for youth. The Johnson Administration instituted a National Job Corps program, and that program has had various incarnations throughout the past twenty-five years. Regional conservation programs were created; among the most prominent have been the California and Wisconsin conservation corps. Finally, cities have developed service programs for their young citizens—for example, the New York City Service Corps or Seattle's Program for Local Service. These programs are aimed at giving young people job skills while teaching them the values they will need to prosper as adults.

6   The apparent success of such programs has recently sparked interest in a national program of voluntary service. These programs would create a new institution—generally in the form of a national service foundation—to oversee a comprehensive program of citizen service for young people. The arguments for this program are generally threefold: (1) the nation has needs that remain unfulfilled, like environmental conservation, day care, health care, etc.; (2) young people need to develop themselves morally, and national service can help (here supporters commonly cite such problems as drug dependency, crime, idleness, and teenage pregnancy); and (3) Americans, especially young people, need to develop a stronger sense of citizenship. Proponents of national service believe that the program can enhance the well-being of the nation and restore a sense of community to American public life.

7   Since the late 1970s, national service has become a very important issue. Numerous bills have been introduced in Congress promoting versions of this proposal, new books have emerged on the subject almost every year, national politicians have endorsed the idea, and public and private conferences and commissions have been held every few years on the matter. The most publicized proposal has been the Sam Nunn–Dave McCurdy national service bill (SR3-1989), which ties federal education aid to service programs. On a smaller, less systematic scale, the [first] Bush administration has introduced the Youth Entering Service (YES) program, which earmarks twenty-five million dollars for voluntary service work for young people.

8   On November 16, 1990, President Bush [senior] signed into law the National and Community Service Act of 1990 (PL 101-610). This national service law differs from previous efforts in one very important way—it attempts to merge service programs for both "gilded" and underprivileged youth, in order to provide the youth of America with a common set of norms and opportunities. It is a comprehensive law which includes a variety of youth service schemes, and it is designed to test the feasibility of national service for a number of different socioeconomic groups.

9   All service programs, whether for rich or poor, have had one component in common. Proponents maintain that young people must learn citizenship, and either they argue that such programs inculcate this generally, or they have attached particular programs designed to increase the civic competence of young adults.[3] Indeed, the rhetoric of citizenship justifies the program ideologically; that is, it defends national service on moral and political grounds, rather than instrumental ones.

Notes

1. William James, "The Moral Equivalent of War," *International Conciliation*, no. 27 (Washington, D.C.: Carnegie Endowment for International Peace, 1910), pp. 8–20. [see pages 203–06.]
2. Quoted in John A. Salmond, *The Civilian Conservation Corps, 1933–1942: A New Deal Case Study* (Durham, N.C.: Duke University Press, 1967), p. 13.
3. The National and Community Service Act of 1990 states that its *primary* purpose is "to renew the ethic of civic responsibility in the United States" (section 2[1]). This purpose is also the primary justification given by Senator Edward Kennedy, its chief sponsor, in arguing for its passage. Press Release, on the Conference Report on the National and Community Service Act of 1990, Office of Senator Edward M. Kennedy, October 12, 1990.

Calls for National Service
Roger Landrum, Donald J. Eberly, and Michael W. Sherraden

The passage that follows introduces the work of William James (mentioned prominently in the Gorham selection), a Harvard philosopher whose speech "The Moral Equivalent of War" (1906, excerpted below, pages 203–06) helped set an agenda for the national service movement. The essay appears in a collection of scholarly commentaries on national service, edited by Sherraden and Eberly.

1   The first major call for a national service in the United States was by the social philosopher and psychologist William James. James' seminal essay "The Moral Equivalent of War," was given as a major address at Stanford University in 1906 and first published in 1910. The essay proposed national service as a pragmatic means by which a democratic nation could maintain social cohesiveness apart from the external threat of war. In his extraordinarily vivid language, James attacked a view he considered ingrained in Western civilization from Alexander the Great through Theodore Roosevelt: that war's "dreadful hammer is the welder of men into cohesive states, and nowhere but in such states can human nature adequately develop its capacity." James wasn't any easier on pacifists, suggesting that the "duties, penalties, and sanctions pictured in the utopias they paint are all too weak and tame to substitute for war's disciplinary function." The most promising line of conciliation between militarists and pacifists, James thought, was some "moral equivalent of war."

> Men now are proud of belonging to a conquering nation, and without a murmur they lay down their persons and their wealth, if by so doing they may fight off subjugation. But who can be sure that other aspects of one's country may not, with time and education and suggestion enough, come to be regarded with similarly effective feelings of pride and shame? Why should men not someday feel that it is worth a blood-tax to belong to a collectivity superior in any ideal respect? Why should they not blush with indignant shame if the community that owns them is vile in any way whatsoever?
>
> Individuals, daily more numerous, now feel this civic passion. It is only a question of blowing on the spark till the whole population gets incandescent, and on the ruins of the old morals of military honor, until a stable system of morals of civic honor builds itself up. What the whole community comes to believe in grasps the individual as in a vise. The war function has grasped us so far; but constructive interests may someday seem no less imperative, and impose on the individual a hardly lighter burden.
>
> If now—and this is my idea—there were, instead of military conscription, a conscription of the whole youthful population to form for a certain number of years a part of the army enlisted against *Nature*, the injustice would tend to be evened out, and numerous other goods to the commonwealth would follow. . . .

Such a conscription, with the state of public opinion that would have required it, and the many moral fruits it would bear, would preserve in the
midst of a pacific civilization the manly virtues which the military party is so
afraid of seeing disappear in peace.[1]

James argued that a permanently successful peace economy cannot be a simple pleasure economy. He proposed a conscription of the youthful population
of the United States into national service to provide a new sense of "civic discipline" outside the context of war. James also believed that national service
would benefit young people. They would experience "self-forgetfulness" rather
than "self-seeking." No one would be "flung out of employment to degenerate
because there is no immediate work for them to do." None would "remain blind,
as the luxurious classes now are blind, to man's relations to the globe he lives
on." The childishness would be "knocked out of them." The moral equivalent of
war would cultivate in youth "toughness without callousness, healthier sympathies and soberer ideas, ideals of hardihood and discipline, and civic temper."

2   The logic and rhetoric of James' call for national service have an antique ring
today. James was clearly thinking only of young men and the image of Ivy League
undergraduates seemed to be at the center of his thinking. He didn't consider
the issue of constitutional limits on involuntary servitude. His recommendation
of conscription was softened only by the concepts of collectivity and social sanctions: "What the whole community comes to believe in grasps the individual as in
a vise." He said nothing of cost and organization. Of course, there were half as
many young people in those days, only 15 percent of them in high school, and a
vastly different organization of the work force. Still, James succeeded in embed-
ding a phrase, "the moral equivalent of war," in the national consciousness; he
raised the fundamental issue of proper socialization of youth in the context of a
democracy at peace; and he planted the idea of national service.

Notes

1. William James, "The Moral Equivalent of War," *International Conciliation*, no. 27 (Washington, D.C.:
   Carnegie Endowment for International Peace, 1910), pp. 8–20. [See pages 203–06.]

The Moral Equivalent of War
William James

*William James (1842–1910), an influential philosopher, psychologist and professor at Harvard
University, is best known for his works* The Varieties of Religious Experience *(1902) and* The
Principles of Psychology *(1890). "The Moral Equivalent of War," first delivered in 1906 as a
speech at Stanford University and later published (1910), became a seminal document in the
national service movement. In the speech, James argues that the qualities of character that*

distinguish soldiers (for instance, self-discipline and regard for the common good) are impor-
tant to developing and maintaining a civil society. James believes these qualities "can be bred
without war" and lays out a "moral equivalent of war" for doing so. The essay, which is chal-
lenging but also rewarding, is central to any understanding of the national service movement.
We reproduce the final eight paragraphs (with some editing) here. For the full text of the
speech, go to <http://www.emory.edu/EDUCATION/mfp/moral.html>.

1   I will now confess my own utopia. I devoutly believe in the reign of peace and in the gradual advent of some sort of socialistic equilibrium. The fatalistic view of the war function is to me nonsense, for I know that war-making is due to definite motives and subject to prudential checks and reasonable criticisms, just like any other form of enterprise. And when whole nations are the armies, and the science of destruction vies in intellectual refinement with the science of production, I see that war becomes absurd and impossible from its own monstrosity. Extravagant ambitions will have to be replaced by reasonable claims, and nations must make common cause against them. I see no reason why all this should not apply to yellow as well as to white countries, and I look forward to a future when acts of war shall be formally outlawed as between civilized peoples.

2   All these beliefs of mine put me firmly into the anti-military party. But I do not believe that peace either ought to be or will be permanent on this globe, unless the states, pacifically organized, preserve some of the old elements of army-discipline. A permanently successful peace-economy cannot be a simple pleasure-economy. In the more or less socialistic future toward which mankind seems [to be] drifting we must still subject ourselves collectively to those severities which answer to our real position upon this only partly hospitable globe. We must make new energies and hardihoods continue the manliness to which the military mind so faithfully clings. Martial virtues must be the enduring cement; intrepidity, contempt of softness, surrender of private interest, obedience to command, must still remain the rock upon which states are built—unless, indeed, we wish for dangerous reactions against commonwealths, fit only for contempt, and liable to invite attack whenever a centre of crystallization for military-minded enterprise gets formed anywhere in their neighborhood.

3   The war-party is assuredly right in affirming and reaffirming that the martial virtues, although originally gained by the race through war, are absolute and permanent human goods. Patriotic pride and ambition in their military form are, after all, only specifications of a more general competitive passion. They are its first form, but that is no reason for supposing them to be its last form. Men are now proud of belonging to a conquering nation, and without a murmur they lay down their persons and their wealth, if by so doing they may fend off subjection. But who can be sure that *other aspects of one's country* may not, with time and education and suggestion enough, come to be regarded with similarly effective feelings of pride and shame? Why should men not some day feel that it is worth a blood-tax to belong to a collectivity superior in *any* respect? Why should they not blush with indignant shame if the community that owns them

is vile in any way whatsoever? Individuals, daily more numerous, now feel this civic passion. It is only a question of blowing on the spark until the whole population gets incandescent, and on the ruins of the old morals of military honor, a stable system of morals of civic honor builds itself up. What the whole community comes to believe in grasps the individual as in a vise. The war-function has grasped us so far; but the constructive interests may some day seem no less imperative, and impose on the individual a hardly lighter burden.

4   Let me illustrate my idea more concretely. There is nothing to make one indignant in the mere fact that life is hard, that men should toil and suffer pain. The planetary conditions once for all are such, and we can stand it. But that so many men, by mere accidents of birth and opportunity, should have a life of *nothing else* but toil and pain and hardness and inferiority imposed upon them, should have *no* vacation, while others natively no more deserving never get any taste of this campaigning life at all,—*this* is capable of arousing indignation in reflective minds. It may end by seeming shameful to all of us that some of us have nothing but campaigning, and others nothing but unmanly ease. If now— and this is my idea—there were, instead of military conscription, a conscription of the whole youthful population to form for a certain number of years a part of the army enlisted against *Nature*, the injustice would tend to be evened out, and numerous other goods to the commonwealth would remain blind as the luxurious classes now are blind, to man's relations to the globe he lives on, and to the permanently sour and hard foundations of his higher life. To coal and iron mines, to freight trains, to fishing fleets in December, to dishwashing, clotheswashing, and window washing, to road-building and tunnel-making, to foundries and stoke-holes, and to the frames of skyscrapers, would our gilded youths be drafted off, according to their choice, to get the childishness knocked out of them, and to come back into society with healthier sympathies and soberer ideas. They would have paid their blood-tax, done their own part in the immemorial human warfare against nature; they would tread the earth more proudly, the women would value them more highly, they would be better fathers and teachers of the following generation.

5   Such a conscription, with the state of public opinion that would have required it, and the many moral fruits it would bear, would preserve in the midst of a pacific civilization the manly virtues which the military party is so afraid of seeing disappear in peace. We should get toughness without callousness, authority with as little criminal cruelty as possible, and painful work done cheerily because the duty is temporary, and threatens not, as now, to degrade the whole remainder of one's life. I spoke of the "moral equivalent" of war. So far, war has been the only force that can discipline a whole community, and until an equivalent discipline is organized, I believe that war must have its way. But I have no serious doubt that the ordinary prides and shames of social man, once developed to a certain intensity, are capable of organizing such a moral equivalent as I have sketched, or some other just as effective for preserving manliness of type. It is but a question of time, of skilful propogandism, and of opinion-making men seizing historic opportunities.

6   The martial type of character can be bred without war. Strenuous honor and disinterestedness abound everywhere. Priests and medical men are in a fashion educated to it, and we should all feel some degree of its imperative if we were conscious of our work as an obligatory service to the state. We should be *owned*, as soldiers are by the army, and our pride would rise accordingly. We could be poor, then, without humiliation, as army officers now are. The only thing needed henceforward is to inflame the civic temper as past history has inflamed the military temper. H. G. Wells, as usual, sees the centre of the situation. "In many ways," he says, "military organization is the most peaceful of activities. When the contemporary man steps from the street, of clamorous insincere advertisement, push, adulteration, underselling and intermittent employment into the barrack-yard, he steps on to a higher social plane, into an atmosphere of service and cooperation and of infinitely more honorable emulations. Here at least men are not flung out of employment to degenerate because there is no immediate work for them to do. They are fed and drilled and trained for better services. Here at least a man is supposed to win promotion by self-forgetfulness and not by self-seeking. And beside the feeble and irregular endowment of research by commercialism, its little shortsighted snatches at profit by innovation and scientific economy, see how remarkable is the steady and rapid development of method and appliances in naval and military affairs! Nothing is more striking than to compare the progress of civil conveniences which has been left almost entirely to the trader, to the progress in military apparatus during the last few decades. The house-appliances of today, for example, are little better than they were fifty years ago. A house of today is still almost as ill-ventilated, badly heated by wasteful fires, clumsily arranged and furnished as the house of 1858. Houses a couple of hundred years old are still satisfactory places of residence, so little have our standards risen. But the rifle or battleship of fifty years ago was beyond all comparison inferior to those we now possess; in power, in speed, in convenience alike. No one has a use now for such superannuated things."

7   Wells adds that he thinks that the conceptions of order and discipline, the tradition of service and devotion, of physical fitness, unstinted exertion, and universal responsibility, which universal military duty is now teaching European nations, will remain a permanent acquisition when the last ammunition has been used in the fireworks that celebrate the final peace. I believe as he does. It would be simply preposterous if the only force that could work ideals of honor and standards of efficiency into English or American natures should be the fear of being killed by the Germans or the Japanese. Great indeed is Fear; but it is not, as our military enthusiasts believe and try to make us believe, the only stimulus known for awakening the higher ranges of men's spiritual energy.

Crito
Plato

This following passage, excerpted from one of Plato's famous dialogues, "Crito," is set in the prison cell of Socrates, who was condemned to die by the authorities of Athens for "corrupting" its youth through his teachings. Crito wishes to convince his friend and teacher to escape before the sentence (death by the drinking of hemlock, a poison) is to be carried out. Instead of running, Socrates (who is speaking in this excerpt) engages Crito in a classic dialogue about the obligations of a citizen to the State. His reference to "the laws" and to "we" and "us," is to the authorities of Athens—and, by extension, to any governing body to which people freely give their allegiance.

Socrates:

Then the laws will say: "Consider, Socrates, if this is true, that in your present attempt you are going to do us wrong. For, after having brought you into the world, and nurtured and educated you, and given you and every other citizen a share in every good that we had to give, we further proclaim and give the right to every Athenian, that if he does not like us when he has come of age and has seen the ways of the city, and made our acquaintance, he may go where he pleases and take his goods with him; and none of us laws will forbid him or interfere with him. Any of you who does not like us and the city, and who wants to go to a colony or to any other city, may go where he likes, and take his goods with him. But he who has experience of the manner in which we order justice and administer the State, and still remains, has entered into an implied contract that he will do as we command him. And he who disobeys us is, as we maintain, thrice wrong: first, because in disobeying us he is disobeying his parents; secondly, because we are the authors of his education; thirdly, because he has made an agreement with us that he will duly obey our commands; and he neither obeys them nor convinces us that our commands are wrong; and we do not rudely impose them, but give him the alternative of obeying or convincing us; that is what we offer and he does neither. These are the sort of accusations to which, as we were saying, you, Socrates, will be exposed if you accomplish your intentions; you, above all other Athenians." Suppose I ask, why is this? they will justly retort upon me that I above all other men have acknowledged the agreement. "There is clear proof," they will say, "Socrates, that we and the city were not displeasing to you. Of all Athenians you have been the most constant resident in the city, which, as you never leave, you may be supposed to love. For you never went out of the city either to see the games, except once when you went to the Isthmus, or to any other place unless when you were on military service; nor did you travel as other men do. Nor had you any curiosity to know other States or their laws: your affections did not go beyond us and our State; we were your especial favorites, and you acquiesced in our government of you; and this is the State in which you begat your children, which is a proof of your satisfaction. Moreover, you might, if you had liked, have fixed the penalty at banishment in the course of the trial—the State which refuses to let you go now would have let you go then. But you pretended that you preferred death to exile, and that you were not grieved at death. And now you have forgotten these fine sentiments, and pay no respect to us, the laws, of whom you are the destroyer; and are doing what only a miserable slave would do, running away and turning your back upon the compacts and agreements which you made as a citizen. And first of all answer this very question: Are we right in saying that you agreed to be governed according to us in deed, and not in word only? Is that true or not?" How shall we answer that, Crito? Must we not agree?

Keeping Alive the Spirit of National Service
Richard North Patterson

Richard North Patterson is a prolific novelist [his titles include Protect and Defend *(2001) and* Balance of Power *(2003)] who lives in San Francisco and Martha's Vineyard. This op-ed essay on national service appeared in the* Boston Globe *on August 1, 1999.*

1   I doubt that many of us are nostalgic for the Great Depression, global warfare, or the military draft. But one need not wish to reprise history to notice what has been lost to America's young people—a common experience, a chance to serve, which cuts across the barriers of race, class, and education.

2   In the 1930s, thousands joined the Civilian Conservation Corps, undertaking scores of needed projects while trading their adverse circumstances for a broader experience of the country's needs and promise. The compelling need to wage World War II reinforced the belief that common sacrifice for the common good is an incident of citizenship. It was this spirit which led many to join the Peace Corps—a governmental call to action—or to respond to the moral call of the civil rights movement. And, in the process, their vision of America and the world became less parochial and more compassionate.

3   But somewhere in the last few decades, we mislaid the idea that national service is either obligatory or enriching. As with many shifts in social attitudes, Vietnam serves as a fault line. One of the ugliest truths of the Vietnam draft—with its class biases and small corruptions—is that Americans who served (and died) were disproportionately poor, black, and less educated. And one of its ugliest legacies is the elitist notion that (the officer corps aside) military service is not for everyone but is a job and a training program for those without a better place to go.

4   The result is that all too often, we offer young people a vision of community which extends to the nearest shopping mall.

5   One byproduct is to exacerbate our growing division—the America of the inner city, the worst schools, the least hope versus the America of the designer label, the gated community, the best (and, sometimes, most isolated) education money can buy.

6   Yet anyone who spends time with the new generation is struck by how many —while corrosively cynical about politics and politicians—are passionate about and committed to helping others. From tutoring children to building houses through Habitat for Humanity, these young people eagerly seek chances to serve. All of which makes the recent proposal to expand AmeriCorps so refreshing.

7   This "domestic peace corps" engaged more than 40,000 people in intense service to communities around the country. It is not a wasteful bureaucracy, a program to redistribute dollars in return for a year of civic basketweaving and singing folk songs around the campfire.

8   Two-thirds of its money passes through governors to grass-roots community groups; the rest goes to traditional nonprofits. Volunteers spend a year living and working wherever they're needed. They mentor, tutor, and teach, ensuring that kids stay in school. They help build housing. They augment neighborhood safety programs. They combat drug abuse. They assist disaster relief efforts: In Oklahoma, more than 60 are now working with victims of the recent tornadoes.

9   In short, they fulfill Robert Kennedy's vision of the original VISTA program: that Americans "invest a year of their lives . . . under Spartan conditions, to help millions of their fellow citizens who, through no fault of their own, are denied the essentials of a decent life." And, at the end of their service, they receive a maximum stipend of $4,725 to pay off student loans or for graduate or postgraduate education.

10   Politicians across the political spectrum have recognized that this has been a good investment. Now, five years after its inception, AmeriCorps requires congressional reauthorization.

11   Those of us who believe in national service hope to make the program a continuing call to service that transcends the politics of the moment and that offers up to 100,000 Americans every year a focus for their energy and idealism.

12   This may fall short of a universal commitment to national service. But it's an important step in keeping alive something of universal value: the chance for our young to make their best contribution to a stronger country and a better society. We should take it.

Rumsfeld: No Need for Draft; 'Disadvantages Notable'
Kathleen T. Rhem

Kathleen Rhem is a reporter for the American Forces Press Service. This article was posted on the DefenseLINK Web site on January 7, 2003.

1   WASHINGTON, Jan. 7, 2003—The United States is not going to implement a military draft, because there is no need for it, Defense Secretary Donald Rumsfeld said today.

2   Rep. Charles Rangel said last week he was planning to introduce such legislation in the New Year. Rep. John Conyers Jr. has since expressed support.

3   "I believe that if those calling for war knew their children were more likely to be required to serve—and to be placed in harm's way—there would be more caution and a greater willingness to work with the international community in dealing with Iraq," Rangel wrote in a recent commentary in the New York Times.

4   Rumsfeld dismissed the notion out of hand during a Pentagon press briefing. "I don't know of anyone in this building or in the administration who thinks that anyone ought to go to war lightly," he said. "I know the president doesn't, and I know I don't."

5   The country doesn't need a draft because the all-volunteer force works—in fact, the United States has the most effective military in the world precisely because it is all-volunteer, Joint Chiefs Chairman Air Force Gen. Richard B. Myers said.

6   "[The all-volunteer force is] efficient; it's effective; it's given the United States of America, the citizens of this great country, a military that is second to none," Myers said.

7   "The people that are in the armed services today . . . are there because they want to be there and are ready and willing and, without any question, capable of doing whatever the president may ask," Rumsfeld added.

8   The secretary described "notable disadvantages" to having a conscripted force. He said people are involuntarily forced to serve, some for less than they could earn on the outside. There are many exemptions, which change all the time, thus providing for unfair situations. Troops are "churned" through training, serve the minimum amount of time and leave—thus causing more money to be spent to churn more draftees through the system.

9   He also dismissed the notion that the all-volunteer force leads to a disproportionate number of blacks and other minorities being killed in battle.

10   "I do not know that that's historically correct," Rumsfeld said. "And I do not know that, even if it were historically correct, that it's correct today."

11   He and Myers kept coming back to their bottom line: America is better off for the force it has today.

12   "We have people serving today—God bless 'em—because they volunteered," Rumsfeld said. "They want to be doing what it is they're doing. And we're just lucky as a country that there are so many wonderfully talented young men and young women who each year step up and say, 'I'm ready; let me do that.'"

Politics and National Service:
A Virus Attacks the Volunteer Sector
Bruce Chapman

Bruce Chapman, former U.S. Ambassador to the U.N. organizations in Vienna and former senior fellow at the Hudson Institute, currently serves as president of the Discovery Institute of Seattle, Washington, a public policy center for studying national and international affairs. An early proponent of the all-volunteer army who dedicated many years to public service (as secretary of state for the State of Washington, former director of the U.S. Census Bureau, and as aide to President Reagan), Chapman argues that volunteerism, "true service," is "corrupted" when it is in any way coerced or induced—through government programs, for instance, that pay stipends. The excerpted selection that follows appears in a collection of essays, National Service: Pro & Con *(1990).*

1   Proposals for government-operated national service, like influenza, flare up from time to time, depress the resistance of the body politic, run their course, and seem to disappear, only to mutate and afflict public life anew. Unfortunately, another epidemic may be on the way. The disease metaphor comes to mind not as an aspersion on the advocates of national service because, with good-natured patience, persistence, and seemingly relentless political invention, they mean well, but from the frustration of constantly combating the changing strains of a statist idea that one thought had been eliminated in the early 1970s, along with smallpox.

2   Why does the national service virus keep coming back? Perhaps because its romance is so easy to catch, commanding a nostalgic imagination and evoking times when Americans were eager to sacrifice for their country. Claiming to derive inspiration from both military experience and the social gospel—if we could only get America's wastrel youth into at least a psychic uniform we might be able to teach self-discipline again and revive the spirit of giving—it hearkens back to William James's call for a "moral equivalent of war." But at the end of the twentieth century should we be looking to war for moral guidance?

3   True service is one of the glories of our civilization in the West, especially in the great independent (or volunteer) sector of American society. Inspiration for service in the West comes from the Bible in parable and admonition and is constantly restated in the long historical tradition of Judeo-Christian faith. Personal service is a freewill offering to God. This is very different from performance of an obligation to government, which is a tax on time or money.

4   True service, then, has a spiritual basis, even for some outside the Judeo-Christian tradition per se. Fulfillment of an obligation to government, in contrast, has a contractual basis unless it is founded on an outright commitment to a coercive utopianism. Either way, it is not true service. Nor can enrollment in a government-funded self-improvement project or acceptance of a government job be called true service. Indeed, when coercion or inducements are

provided, as in the various national service schemes, the spirit of service is to that degree corrupted.

5   In practice the service in a federal program of national service would be contaminated by governmental determination of goals, bureaucratization of procedures, and, inevitably, government insistence on further regulating the independent sector with which it contracted. National service would tend to demoralize those citizens who volunteer without expectation of financial reward and stigmatize the honest labor of people whose fields were invaded by stipened and vouchered volunteers.

6   Government intervention is always a potential threat to the voluntary sector. When totalitarians have come to power in other Western countries, they have sought to absorb this sector, conferring official sponsorship on certain organizations and scorning others, thereby inculcating in the citizenry the government's valuation even on use of free time. Although in the United States totalitarianism is not a current danger to our liberal democracy, coercive utopianism is always a legitimate concern.

7   Alexis de Tocqueville saw in our own early history that the genius of voluntary association was America's superior answer to the leadership energy provided in other societies by aristocracies. But government, he warned, may seek to direct the voluntary sector in the same way it erroneously seeks to control industrial undertakings:

> Once it leaves the sphere of politics to launch out on this new task, it will, even without intending this, exercise an intolerable tyranny. For a government can only dictate precise rules. It imposes the sentiments and ideas which it favors, and it is never easy to tell the difference between its advice and its commands.[1]

---

1. Alexis de Tocqueville, *Democracy in America*, vol. 2, book 2, chap. 5, J. P. Mayer (New York: Doubleday and Co., 1969).

EXERCISE   5.5

Critical Reading for Synthesis

Having read the selections relating to national service, pages 188–212, take a sheet and write a one-sentence summary of each. On the same sheet, list two or three topics that you think are common to several of the selections. Beneath each topic, list the authors who have something to say and briefly note what they have to say. Finally, for each topic, jot down what *you* have to say. Now regard your effort. With each topic you have created a discussion point suitable for inclusion in a paper. (Of course, until you know the claim of such a paper, you would not know to what end you would put the discussion.) Write a paragraph or two in which you introduce the topic and then conduct a brief conversation among the interested parties (including yourself).

Consider Your Purpose

As with the explanatory synthesis, your specific purpose in writing an argument synthesis is crucial. What, exactly, you want to do will affect your claim, the evidence you select to support your claim, and the way you organize the evidence. Your purpose may be clear to you before you begin research, may emerge during the course of research, or may not emerge until after you have completed your research. (Of course, the sooner your purpose is clear to you, the fewer wasted motions you will make. On the other hand, the more you approach research as an exploratory process, the likelier that your conclusions will emerge from the sources themselves, rather than from preconceived ideas. For a discussion on locating and evaluating sources, see Chapter 7.)

Let's say that while reading these sources, your own encounters with a service organization (perhaps you help school children improve their literacy skills) have influenced your thinking on the subject. You find yourself impressed that so many people at the literacy center volunteer without being compelled to do so. You observe that giving time freely adds to the pleasures of volunteering, and to its significance as well. Meanwhile, perhaps your school is considering a service "requirement"—that is, a mandate that all students perform a given number of community service hours in order to graduate. The juxtaposition of "compelled" service with freely given service sparks in you an idea for a source-based paper.

On the one hand, you can understand and even sympathize with the viewpoints of educators who believe that while they have students in their clutches (so to speak), they have an opportunity to pass on an ethic of service. To students who would not volunteer time on their own, setting a graduation requirement makes sense. On the other hand, it seems to you that forced volunteerism, a contradiction in terms if ever there was one, defeats the essential quality of volunteering: that it is time given freely. The donation of time to meet the needs of others is an act of selflessness that brings you profound satisfaction. Your purpose in writing, then, emerges from these kinds of response to the source material.

Making a Claim: Formulate a Thesis

As we indicated in the introduction to this chapter, one useful way of approaching an argument is to see it as making a *claim*. A claim is a proposition, a conclusion that you are trying to prove or demonstrate. If your purpose is to demonstrate that the state should not compel people to serve their communities, then that is the claim at the heart of your argument. The claim is generally expressed in one-sentence form as a *thesis*. You draw *support* from your sources as you argue logically for your claim. At times, you may also argue by making appeals to *ethos* and *pathos* (see pp. 184–86).

Of course, not every piece of information in a source is useful for supporting a claim. By the same token, you may draw support for your claim from sources that make entirely different claims. You may use as support for your own claim, for example, a sentiment expressed in William James's "On the Moral Equivalent of War," that values such as selfless concern for the common good, learned through service, "are absolute and permanent human goods." Yet while James called for "a conscription of the whole youthful population" to nonmilitary service projects, you may believe that service should be voluntary. Still, you could cite James and comment, where you think appropriate, on where you and he diverge.

Similarly, you might use one source as part of a *counterargument*—an argument opposite to your own—so that you can demonstrate its weaknesses and, in the process, strengthen your own claim. On the other hand, the author of one of your sources may be so convincing in supporting a claim that you adopt it yourself, either partially or entirely. The point is that *the argument is in your hands*: you must devise it yourself and must use your sources in ways that will support the claim expressed in your thesis.

You may not want to divulge your thesis until the end of the paper, to draw the reader along toward your conclusion, allowing the thesis to flow naturally out of the argument and the evidence on which it is based. If you do this, you are working *inductively*. Or you may wish to be more direct and *begin* with your thesis, following the thesis statement with evidence to support it. If you do this, you are working *deductively*. In academic papers, deductive arguments are far more common than inductive arguments.

Based on your own experience and reactions to reading sources, you find yourself agreeing with Bruce Chapman's argument that compelled or monetarily induced service "corrupts" the experience of service. At the same time, you find yourself unwilling to take Chapman's extreme stance that even modest stipends such as the ones earned while working for AmeriCorps and other government programs constitute "corruption." While you believe that government programs encouraging service are beneficial, you certainly don't want to see the federal government create a nonmilitary version of compulsory national service. After a few tries, you develop the following thesis:

> The impulse to expand service through volunteer programs like AmeriCorps, VISTA, and the Peace Corps is understandable, even praiseworthy. But as volunteerism grows and gains public support, we should resist letting its successes become an argument for *compulsory* national service.

Decide How You Will Use Your Source Material

Your claim commits you to (1) discussing the benefits of service in government-sponsored programs like AmeriCorps and VISTA, and (2) arguing that, benefits notwithstanding, there are compelling reasons not to make national service compulsory. The sources provide plenty of information and ideas—that is, evidence—that will allow you to support your claim. (You might draw on one universally available source, the U.S. Constitution, not included in the materials here.) William James and Plato, backed by contemporary commentators Eric Gorham and Roger Landrum, Donald Eberly, and Michael Sherreden, provide a philosophical and historical foundation for the essay. The statistics generated by the Department of Labor offer current, accurate information on volunteerism in America. The selections by David Gergen, Richard North Patterson, and Senators McCain and Bayh provide pro-service arguments, while the essay by Chapman provides a negative one.

Develop an Organizational Plan

Having established your overall purpose and your claim, having developed a thesis (which may change as you write and revise the essay), and having decided how to use your source materials, how do you logically organize your essay? In many cases, including this one, a well-written thesis will suggest an overall organization. Thus, the first part of your argument synthesis will define volunteerism and set a broad context regarding its pervasiveness and history, along with mention of a possible early attempt to make national service compulsory. The second part will argue that national service should *not* be made compulsory. Sorting through your material and categorizing it by topic and subtopic, you might arrive at the following outline:

  I. Introduction. Pervasiveness of volunteerism in America. Use Bureau of Labor Statistics data.

 II. The desire to "make more of a good thing." The McCain/Bayh "Call to Service Act." *Thesis*.

III. Intellectual history of service:
    A. Recent history. Refer to William James. State that service need not be military.
    B. Ancient history. Refer to Plato. State that citizens owe the State an obligation.

 IV. Can the U.S. government compel citizens to service?
    A. Military service. Yes. Right granted by U.S. Constitution.
    B. Transition: military vs. civilian.
    C. Civilian service: No.
       1. Logical reason: public service is not analogous to military service.
       2. Legal reason: U.S. Constitution (Amendment XIII) forbids involuntary servitude.

3. Moral reason: compelled or induced
   service (that is, with money)
   "corrupts" spirit of service.
   a. Concede point that "less pure"
      forms of service that pay stipends,
      such as AmeriCorps and VISTA, are
      beneficial.
   b. But state forcefully that
      compulsory (as opposed to minimally
      compensated) service does corrupt
      the spirit of service.
V. Conclusion:
   A. Government should expand opportunities to
      serve *voluntarily* (even with pay).
   B. It should resist the impulse to compel
      young people to serve.

Argument Strategy

The argument represented by this outline will build not only on evidence drawn from sources but also on the writer's assumptions. Consider the bare-bones logic of the argument:

Voluntary service, paid or unpaid, promotes good citizenship and benefits the community. (assumption)

People who have worked in volunteer programs have made significant contributions to community and public life. (support)

We should support programs that foster volunteerism. (claim)

The crucial point about which reasonable people will disagree is the *assumption* that unpaid *and* paid volunteer service promote good citizenship. One source author, Bruce Chapman, makes a partial and extreme form of this assumption when he writes that financially rewarded service is "corrupted" (see p. 212). A less-extreme assumption—the one guiding the model paper—is possible: Citizenship can be learned in a minimally paid environment such as AmeriCorps. The writer of the model paper agrees with Chapman, however, about another assumption: that service should never be compelled.

   Writers can accept or partially accept an opposing assumption by making a *concession*, in the process establishing themselves as reasonable and willing to compromise. In our example, the writer does exactly this (see ¶ 10 in the sample synthesis that follows) and then uses as *supporting evidence* facts from David Gergen's report that many paid veterans of government-sponsored teaching programs learn about citizenship and continue to teach after their contracted time is up. By raising potential objections and making concessions, the writer blunts the effectiveness of *counterarguments*.

The *claim* of the example argument about service is primarily a claim about *policy*, about actions that should (or should not) be taken. An argument can also concern a claim about *facts* (Does X exist? Does X lead to Y? How can we define X?) or a claim about *value* (What is X worth?). You have seen that the present argument rests on an assumed definition of "service." Depending on how you define the term, you will agree—or not—with the writer. Among the source authors, Bruce Chapman defines service one way (it is neither rewarded with money nor compelled), while David Gergen and Senators McCain and Bayh define it another (as work done with or without minimal pay to help others and re-enforce core values). As you read the following paper, watch how these opposing views are woven into the argument.

A well-reasoned argument will involve a claim primarily about fact, value, *or* policy. Secondary arguments are sometimes needed, as in the present example, to help make a case.

Draft and Revise Your Synthesis

The final draft of a completed synthesis, based on the above outline, follows. Thesis, transitions, and topic sentences are highlighted; Modern Language Association (MLA) documentation style, explained in Chapter 7, is used throughout. Note that for the sake of clarity, references in the following synthesis are to pages in *A Sequence for Academic Writing*.

A cautionary note: When writing syntheses, it is all too easy to become careless in properly crediting your sources. Before drafting your paper, please review the section on "Avoiding Plagiarism" in Chapter 1 (pp. 53–55) as well as the relevant sections on "Citing Sources" in Chapter 7 (pp. 309–32).

MODEL SYNTHESIS

1
                    Keeping Volunteering Voluntary
        The spirit of volunteerism flourishes in America. In
2002-2003, 28.8 percent of Americans, 16 and older, some
63.8 million, freely gave time to their communities
(Bureau, "Volunteering" 196). Prompted by a desire to
serve others without thought of personal gain, more than
one-quarter of us donate 52 hours a year, more than one
full work-week, to building shelters, coaching Little
League, caring for the elderly, teaching literacy, and
countless other community minded pursuits (Bureau,
"Volunteering" 192; "Table 1" 196). Not included in
these numbers are the many tens of thousands who donate
time through less "pure" volunteer programs run by the
government, such as AmeriCorps, VISTA (Volunteers in
Service to America), and the Peace Corps, all of which
pay recruits a small stipend. Volunteerism is so

pervasive that it seems bred into the American character. A former director of the U.S. Census Bureau observes that "Alexis de Tocqueville saw in [America's] early history that the genius of voluntary association was [the country's] superior answer to the leadership energy provided in other societies by aristocracies" (Chapman 212).

2   Advocates claim that volunteerism builds character, teaches citizenship, and addresses unfulfilled national needs (Gorham 199). But if only one American in four volunteers, a percentage that surely could be improved, and if volunteerism is such a boon to communities, it is little wonder that from time to time politicians propose to make more of a good thing. In this spirit, in November 2001 Senators John McCain (R-AZ) and Evan Bayh (D-IN) introduced Bill S1274, the "Call to Service Act," which would dramatically increase the opportunities to serve in government-sponsored volunteer programs. "Public service is a virtue," write the senators in a New York Times op-ed piece not quite two months after the horrors of September 11, 2001. "[N]ational service should one day be a rite of passage for young Americans." The senators believe that this "is the right moment to issue a new call to service and give a new generation a way to claim the rewards and responsibilities of active citizenship." The impulse to expand service through volunteer programs like AmeriCorps, VISTA, and the Peace Corps is understandable, even praiseworthy. But as volunteerism grows and gains public support, we should resist letting its successes become an argument for compulsory national service.

3   Senators McCain and Bayh do not call for compulsory service. Nonetheless, one can hear an echo of the word "compulsory" in their claim that "national service should one day be a rite of passage for young Americans." The word "should" suggests nothing if not obligation, and the word "all" is clearly implied. It's not a stretch to imagine the senators and others at some point endorsing a program of compulsory service, an idea that has been around for nearly a century. In 1906, the philosopher William James called for "a conscription of the whole youthful population" to non-military projects that would improve character. James, whom many consider the intellectual father of national service, admired the discipline and sacrifice of soldiers but thought it absurd that such "[m]artial virtues" as "intrepidity, contempt of softness, surrender of private interest, [and] obedience to command" should be developed only in the service of war. He imagined a "reign of peace" in which these qualities would "remain the rock upon which"

peaceful states might be built. In a famous passage of
his talk at Stanford University, which he titled "The
Moral Equivalent of War," James urges on youth a hard
(but non-military) service:

> To coal and iron mines, to freight trains, to
> fishing fleets in December, to dishwashing,
> clothes-washing, and window washing, to road-
> building and tunnel-making, to foundries and
> stoke-holes, and to the frames of skyscrap-
> ers, would our gilded youths be drafted off,
> according to their choice, to get the child-
> ishness knocked out of them, and to come back
> into society with healthier sympathies and
> soberer ideas. They would have paid their
> blood-tax, done their own part in the immemo-
> rial human warfare against nature; they would
> tread the earth more proudly, the women would
> value them more highly, they would be better
> fathers and teachers of the following genera-
> tion. (205)

James's "gilded youths" were the (male) students of
elite colleges. In the early twentieth century, there
were not nearly as many young people as today, both in
absolute terms and in college (Landrum, Eberly, and
Sherraden 203), and so the logistics of compulsory
national service may have seemed manageable. A century
later we might regard his proposal as impractical or
even illegal, but at the time he struck an important
chord. His vision of learning the virtues and
disciplines of citizenship through a non-military
regimen in peace time (a "moral equivalent of war")
entered our national vocabulary and remains a part of it
today (Landrum, Eberly, and Sherraden 203).

4   The question of what sort of service, or obligation,
citizens owe a country is as old as the first gathering
of peoples into a collective for mutual safety and
comfort. In one of his famous dialogues, Plato records a
conversation between Socrates, whom Athens had imprisoned
and condemned to death for corrupting the city's youth
with his teachings, and a friend who urges that he escape
and save himself. Socrates argues that if he has accepted
and enjoyed the privileges of citizenship, then he must
also accept the judgment of the State, even if that
judgment calls for his execution:

> [A]fter having brought you into the world,
> and nurtured and educated you, and given you
> and every other citizen a share in every good
> that we [that is, the State] had to give, we
> further proclaim and give the right to every
> Athenian, that if he does not like us when he

has come of age and has seen the ways of the
city, and made our acquaintance, he may go
where he pleases and take his goods with him;
and none of us laws will forbid him or interfere with him. Any of you who does not like us
and the city, and who wants to go to a colony
or to any other city, may go where he likes,
and take his goods with him. But he who has
experience of the manner in which we order
justice and administer the State, and still
remains, has entered into an implied contract
that he will do as we command him. (207)

Citizens obligate themselves to the State when they
accept its bounties and protections. But how is that
obligation to be paid? Some twenty-four hundred years
after Socrates accepted his fate and drank his cup of
hemlock, Americans pay their obligations to the
government through taxes, jury duty, and obedience to
laws passed by elected representatives.

5   Can the government compel us to do more? Can it
compel us, for instance, to military or non-military
service? The U.S. Constitution grants Congress the right
to raise armies (Article 1, Section 8, Clause 14). The
way Congress chooses to do this, however, reflects the
needs of a particular time. During World War II and the
Vietnam War, the government implemented a military draft.
Today, for reasons of professionalism and morale, the
Department of Defense prefers an all-volunteer army to an
army of conscripts. The Chairman of the Joint Chiefs of
Staff was recently reported to have said that the
"country doesn't need a draft because the all-volunteer
force works--in fact, the United States has the most
effective military in the world precisely because it is
all-volunteer" (Rehm 210). Defense Secretary Rumsfeld
sees distinct disadvantages to the draft: "[P]eople are
involuntarily forced to serve, some for less than they
could earn on the outside. . . . Troops are 'churned'
through training, serve the minimum amount of time and
leave--thus causing more money to be spent to churn more
draftees through the system" (qtd. in Rehm 210).

6   Clearly the State has a constitutional right to
compel young people into military service in times of
military need, whether it chooses to exercise that right
through an all-volunteer or a conscripted army. Does the
State have an equivalent right to press citizens into
non-military service? For example, because our libraries
are understaffed, our parks ill-kept, and our youth
reading below grade level, should the State compel
citizens into service for the common good? No--for
logical, legal, and moral reasons.

7 Military need is not logically equivalent to non-military need, primarily because non-military needs are typically met through the normal operations of representative government and the market economy. When the State identifies work to be done for the common good, it taxes citizens and directs its employees to perform that work. Alternately, it may put out bids and pay contractors to perform the work. This is how highways and libraries get built. If the State does not adequately perform these basic functions, it fails in its responsibilities. The remedy to this failure should not be the drafting of America's youth into national service for one or two years. The State could not honestly or reasonably call for universal service as a means of upgrading the moral character of youth when its real need is to plug holes in its own leaky ship. Such disingenuous arguments would only call attention to the State's failures. If the State lacks the money or competence to do its work, then citizens should overhaul the system by electing a new, more efficient administration. If necessary, the legislature could raise taxes. But it should not make a bogus public "need" into an occasion to compel public service.

8 Nor does the State have a legal basis on which to press its citizens into national service. While the Constitution grants Congress the authority to raise armies, it expressly forbids forced service: "Neither slavery nor involuntary servitude, except as a punishment for crime whereof the party shall have been duly convicted, shall exist within the United States, or any place subject to their jurisdiction" (Amendment XIII). A program for compulsory national service, however noble its aims, would never withstand a legal challenge.

9 But even if advocates could circumvent the logical and legal obstacles to compulsory national service, they could not on moral grounds compel youth to serve against their will. Advocates argue, persuasively, that volunteerism builds character and promotes citizenship (Gorham 200). And, in fact, volunteer service does foster selflessness, a concern for community, and an appreciation of country (McCain and Bayh; Gergen; James; Patterson). Still, the essential quality of volunteerism is that it is time given freely. "True service," writes Bruce Chapman, "has a spiritual basis [rooted in the Judeo-Christian tradition]. . . . Fulfillment of an obligation to government, in contrast, has a contractual basis." Chapman argues that "performance of an obligation to government . . . is a tax on time and money." The spirit of service is "corrupted" when it is compelled or encouraged with stipends (211–12).

10   One need not agree, however, that volunteer programs that pay youth in room and board, health care, and tuition vouchers "corrupt" the spirit of giving. Chapman makes an extreme argument that ignores the financial realities of many young people. Were they to get no compensation, many would forgo volunteering and the possibility of learning from programs that encourage civic participation and patriotism. That would be a shame, for the members of AmeriCorps, the Peace Corps, and VISTA, all of whom are paid a small stipend, grow as individuals and as citizens, learning life-long lessons. David Gergen vividly makes this point:

> Voluntary service when young often changes people for life. They learn to give their fair share. Some 60 percent of alumni from Teach for America, a marvelous program, now work full time in education, and many others remain deeply involved in social change. Mark Levine, for example, has started two community-owned credit unions in Washington Heights, NY, for recent immigrants. Alumni of City Year, another terrific program, vote at twice the rates of their peers. Or think of the Peace Corps alumni. Six now serve in the House of Representatives, one [Christopher Dodd] in the Senate. (190)

Unquestionably, national programs for volunteers can benefit both the individuals serving and the communities served. For example, AmeriCorps sets goals lofty enough to ensure that all involved will benefit. The Corps helps communities when it places members in projects designed to have a positive educational, social, and environmental impact. Communities are also strengthened when culturally and racially diverse people work side by side to achieve project goals. Additionally, AmeriCorps seeks through its programming and its job- and educational benefits to improve the lives of members (Corporation 199). Both communities and individuals gain from AmeriCorps' efforts.

11   Still, as Chapman points out, volunteerism that is compelled in any way, that turns the impulse to serve into an obligation, would be a corruption. If the State instituted obligatory non-military service for the "good" of the individual (and recall that it could not reasonably or honestly do so for the social "needs" of the State), the act of service would no longer be rooted in generosity. And it is the spirit of generosity, of one person's freely giving to another, that underlies all the good that volunteering achieves. Convert the

essential generous impulse to an obligation, and the very logic for compelling service--to teach civic values--disappears. The State could no more expect the veterans of obligatory service to have learned the values of good citizenship or to feel special affection for the country than we could expect a child whose parents order him to "make friends with Johnny" to have learned anything useful about friendship or to feel a special kinship with Johnny. Affection, citizenship, and patriotism don't work that way. They are freely given, or they are coerced. And if coerced, they are corrupt. Compelled allegiance is a form of bullying that teaches nothing so much as resentment.

12   Without any inducement other than the good it would do their communities and their own hearts, 63.8 million Americans--more than one quarter of the country--volunteer. Could more people volunteer, specifically more young people? Yes, especially in light of the finding that young people in their early twenties volunteer the least, relative to all other age groups (Bureau, "Table 1" 196). The McCain/Bayh "Call to Service Act" deserves enthusiastic support, as does any government effort to encourage service by people younger than 25. Those who learn to serve while young turn out to be more involved with their communities over the course of their lives (Gergen; AmeriCorps), and such involvement can only benefit us all. Reasonable inducements such as tuition vouchers, minimal pay, health care, and room and board can give young people the safety net they need to experiment with serving others and in that way discover their own wellsprings of generosity.

13   So let's support McCain/Bayh and every such effort to encourage service. Ideally, enough programs will be in place one day to offer all high school and college graduates the option of serving their communities. "[T]oo often," writes Richard North Patterson, "we offer young people a vision of community which extends to the nearest shopping mall" (209). Government-sponsored programs for service can make us better than that, and we should promote volunteerism wherever and whenever we can. But we must guard against using the success of these programs as a pretext for establishing mandatory national or community service. Such a mandate would fail legal and logical tests and, most importantly, a moral test: Volunteerism is built on choice. To command someone to do good works, to make good works obligatory, is to poison the very essence of service.

Works Cited

Bureau of Labor Statistics. "Table 1: Volunteers by
    Selected Characteristics, September 2003." 17 Dec.
    2003. 17 Jan. 2004 <http://www.bls.gov/news.release/
    volun.t01.htm>.

---. "Volunteering in the United States, 2003." 18 Dec.
    2003. 17 Jan. 2004 <http://www.bls.gov/
    news.release/volun.nr0.htm>.

Chapman, Bruce. "Politics and National Service: A Virus
    Attacks the Volunteer Sector." National Service: Pro
    & Con. Ed. Williamson M. Evers. Stanford, CA: Hoover
    Institution P, 1990. 133-44.

"Constitution of the United States of America." The New
    York Public Library Desk Reference. New York:
    Webster's New World, 1989.

Corporation for National and Community Service.
    "AmeriCorps Mission." AmeriCorps: Getting Things
    Done. Program Directory, Spring/Summer 1995.
    Microfiche Y2N.21/29 10AM3. Washington, DC: GPO,
    1995.

Gergen, David. "A Time to Heed the Call." U.S. News &
    World Report 24 Dec. 2001: 60.

Gorham, Eric B. "National Service, Political
    Socialization, and Citizenship." National Service,
    Citizenship, and Political Education. Albany: SUNY
    P, 1992. 5-30.

James, William. "The Moral Equivalent of War."
    International Conciliation 27 (Washington, DC:
    Carnegie Endowment for International Peace, 1910):
    8-20.

Landrum, Roger, Donald J. Eberly, and Michael W.
    Sherraden. "Calls for National Service." National
    Service: Social, Economic and Military Impacts. Ed.
    Michael W. Sherraden and Donald J. Eberly. New York:
    Pergamon, 1982. 21-38.

McCain John and Evan Bayh. "A New Start for National
    Service." New York Times 6 Nov. 2001: Op-ed.

Patterson, Richard North. "Keeping Alive the Spirit of
    National Service." Boston Globe 1 Aug. 1999: Op-ed.

Plato, "Crito." Classic Literature Online Library. Trans.
    Benjamin Jowett. 17 July 2003 <http://
    www.greece.com/library/plato/crito_04.html>.

Rhem, Kathleen T. "Rumsfeld: No Need for Draft." American
    Forces Information Service 7 Jan. 2003. 17 July 2003
    <http://www.dod.gov/news/Jan2003/
    n01072003_200301074.html>.

Discussion

The writer of this argument synthesis on compulsory national service attempts to support a *claim*—one that favors national service but that insists on keeping it voluntary—by offering *support* in the form of facts (rates of volunteerism from the Bureau of Labor Statistics) and opinions (testimony of experts). However, since the writer's claim rests on a definition of "true service," its effectiveness depends partially upon the extent to which we, as readers, agree with the *assumptions* underlying that definition. (See our discussion of assumptions in Chapter 2, pages 76–77.) An assumption (sometimes called a *warrant*) is a generalization or principle about how the world works or should work—a fundamental statement of belief about facts or values. In this particular case, the underlying assumption is that "true service" to a community must be voluntary, never required. The writer makes this assumption explicit. Though you are under no obligation to do so, stating assumptions explicitly will clarify your arguments to readers.

Assumptions often are deeply rooted in people's psyches, sometimes deriving from lifelong experiences and observations and not easily changed, even by the most logical of arguments. People who learned the spirit of volunteerism early in life, perhaps through "required" activities in religious or public school, might not accept the support offered for the claim that required service would be illogical, illegal, and "corrupted." But others might well be persuaded and might agree that programs to expand opportunities for national service should be supported, though service itself should never be compelled. A discussion of the model argument's paragraphs, along with the argument strategy for each, follows. Note that the paper devotes one paragraph to developing every section of the outline on pages 215–216. Note also that the writer avoids plagiarism by careful attribution and quotation of sources.

- **Paragraph 1:** The writer uses statistics to establish that a culture of volunteerism is and has been alive and well in America from its earliest days.

  Argument strategy: In this opening paragraph, the writer sets up the general topic—volunteerism in America—and establishes that Americans volunteer in impressive numbers. The writer uses information from the Bureau of Labor Statistics, as well as the reference to volunteerism in early America, to anticipate and deflect possible criticism from those who might say: "So few of us volunteer that we should require national service in order to promote citizenship and to build character."

- **Paragraph 2:** Here the writer sets a context for and introduces the McCain/Bayh proposal to expand national service. The writer then presents the thesis.

  Argument strategy: This paragraph moves in one direction with an inspiring call to service by Senators McCain and Bayh and then takes a sharp, contrasting turn to the thesis. The first part of the thesis, "as volunteerism grows and gains public support," clearly follows from (and summarizes) the first part of paragraph 2. The transition "But" signals the contrast, which sets up the warning. A contrast generates interest by creating tension, in this case prompting readers to wonder: "Why *should* we resist compulsory service?"

- **Paragraphs 3 and 4:** In these paragraphs, the writer discusses the intellectual history of service: first, the writing of William James in the early years of the past century, and next, Plato's account of a dialogue between Socrates and a student. The writer quotes both authors at length and then discusses their relevance to the issue at the center of this essay: service to the greater community.

  Argument strategy: At this point, the writer is *preparing* to offer reasons for accepting the claim that we must resist compulsory service. The goal of paragraphs 3 and 4 is to set a deep historical context for the essay by establishing service as a significant cultural norm in America and, more broadly, by showing that the notion of obligation to the State is fundamental to civil societies. The end of paragraph 4 makes a transition to modern-day America and begins to move from the preparation for argument to argument.

- **Paragraph 5:** This paragraph opens with a question and sets up a key distinction in the essay between military and non-military service. After raising the distinction, the writer devotes the paragraph to establishing the right of the American government to draft citizens into the army. High-ranking military administrators are quoted to the effect that the all-volunteer army is a better fighting force than earlier, conscripted armies.

  Argument strategy: This paragraph begins moving the reader into the argument by introducing and discussing the first part of the distinction just presented: military service. The writer establishes that compelled military service is constitutional and in keeping with the historical obligations that citizens owe the State. But even here, in a case in which the State has the clear authority to conscript people, the writer quotes military officials to the effect that voluntary service is superior to compulsory service. The reader will find this strong preference for volunteerism continued in the second part of the essay devoted to non-military service.

- **Paragraph 6:** This transitional paragraph raises the core question on which the argument hangs: Does the State have the right, as it does in military matters, to press citizens into non-military, national service? The writer answers the question in the final sentence of this paragraph and, in so doing, forecasts the discussion to follow.

  Argument strategy: Here the writer sets up the second part of the essay, where reasons for accepting the claim will be presented. Up until this point, the writer has established that (1) volunteers can build character through service, (2) citizens owe a debt to the State, and (3) the State can legally collect on that debt by drafting citizens into the army in time of war. In this transition paragraph, the writer poses the question that will take the rest of the paper to answer. The question becomes an invitation to read.

- **Paragraphs 7–9:** In each of these three paragraphs, the writer answers—in the negative—the question posed in paragraph 6. The State does *not* have the right to press citizens into national service. Paragraph 7 offers a logical reason: that military and non-military service are not equivalent. Paragraph 8 offers a legal reason: that the Constitution prohibits "involuntary servitude." Paragraph 9 offers a moral reason: that coerced or compelled service is "corrupted."

  Argument strategy: These paragraphs lay out the main reasons for accepting the claim that we should resist letting the successes of volunteerism become an argument for compulsory national service. The writer argues on multiple grounds—logical, legal, and moral—in an effort to build a strong case.

- **Paragraph 10:** Here the writer concedes a problem with the view (expressed by Chapman) in paragraph 9 that service that is either compelled or financially rewarded is corrupted. Allowing that this extreme position does not take into account the financial needs of young people, the writer endorses an alternate view, that minimal payment for service is legitimate. To support this more moderate position, the writer quotes David Gergen at length and also refers to the AmeriCorps mission statement.

  Argument strategy: With this concession, the writer backs off an extreme view. The tactic makes the writer look both reasonable and realistic just prior to arguing very firmly, in the next paragraph, against compulsory service.

- **Paragraph 11:** Here the writer endorses one of Chapman's strongly held positions: forced service is not service at all and corrupts the spirit of volunteerism.

  Argument strategy: Here is the emotional core of the argument. The writer has previously argued that for logical (paragraph 7) and legal (paragraph 8) reasons compulsory service must be rejected. The writer devotes three paragraphs to developing moral reasons. In paragraph 11, the writer uses an analogy for the first time: compelling service is equivalent to compelling a child to like someone. Neither works. The value of service rests on the offering of oneself freely to those in need.

- **Paragraphs 12–13:** The writer concludes by re-stating the claim—in two paragraphs.

  Argument strategy: These concluding paragraphs parallel the two-part structure of the thesis: Part 1 (paragraph 12), that volunteerism has many benefits and deserves support; Part 2 (paragraph 13), that we must resist the any effort to make service compulsory.

Other approaches to an argument synthesis would be possible, based on the sources provided here. One could agree with Bruce Chapman and adopt the extreme view against both compulsory and paid service. Such an argument would make no concessions of the sort found in paragraph 10 of the model synthesis. Another approach would be to argue that young people must be taught the value of service before they take these values on themselves, and that the best way to teach an ethic of service is to require a year or two of "compulsory volunteering." That which is required, goes the logic of this argument, eventually becomes second nature. We might make a parallel case about teaching kids to read. Kids may not enjoy practicing thirty minutes every night, but eventually they come to realize the joys and benefits of reading, which last a lifetime. Still another argument might be to focus on the extent to which Americans meet (or fail to meet) their obligations to the larger community. This would be a glass-half-full/half-empty argument, beginning with the statistic that one-quarter of Americans regularly volunteer. The half-full argument would praise current efforts and, perhaps, suggest policies for ensuring continued success. The half-empty argument would cite the statistic with alarm, claim that we have a problem of shockingly low volunteer rates, and then propose a solution. Whatever your approach to the subject, in first *critically examining* the various sources and then *synthesizing* them to support a position about which you feel strongly, you are engaging in the kind of critical thinking that is essential to success in a good deal of academic and professional work.

DEVELOPING AND ORGANIZING THE SUPPORT FOR YOUR ARGUMENTS

Experienced writers seem to have an intuitive sense of how to develop and present supporting evidence for their claims; this sense is developed through much hard work and practice. Less experienced writers wonder what to say first, and having decided on that, wonder what to say next. There is no single method of presentation. But the techniques of even the most experienced writers often boil down to a few tried and tested arrangements.

As we've seen in the model synthesis in this chapter, the key to devising effective arguments is to find and use those kinds of support that most persuasively strengthen your claim. Some writers categorize support into two broad types: *evidence* and *motivational appeals*. Evidence, in the form of facts, statistics, and expert testimony, helps make the appeal to *logos* or reason. Motivational appeals—appeals to *pathos* and *ethos*—are employed to get people to change their minds, to agree with the writer or speaker, or to decide upon a plan of activity.

Following are some of the most common principles for using and organizing support for your claims.

Summarize, Paraphrase, and Quote Supporting Evidence

In most of the papers and reports you will write in college and the professional world, evidence and motivational appeals derive from summarizing, paraphrasing, and quoting material in the sources that either have been provided to you or that you have independently researched. (See Chapter 1 on when to summarize, paraphrase, and quote material from sources.) For example, in paragraph 10 of the model argument synthesis you will find a block quotation from David Gergen used to make the point that minimally paid volunteer programs can provide lifelong lessons. You will find two other block quotations in the argument and a number of brief quotations woven into sentences throughout. In addition, you will find summaries and a paraphrase. In each case, the writer is careful to cite sources.

Provide Various Types of Evidence and Motivational Appeals

Keep in mind the appeals to both *logos* and *pathos*. As we've discussed, the appeal to *logos* is based on evidence that consists of a combination of *facts, statistics, and expert testimony*. In the model synthesis, the writer uses all of these varieties of evidence: facts (from David Gergen's article on how "[v]oluntary service . . . often changes people for life"); statistics (the incidence of volunteering in the United States); and testimony (from Eric Gorham, Bruce Chapman, David Gergen, Roger Landrum, Donald Rumsfeld, and William James). The model synthesis makes an appeal to *pathos* by engaging the reader's self interest: Certainly if the federal government were to institute compulsory national service, the lives of readers would be touched. More explicitly, paragraph 11 makes a moral argument against compulsory service. Through analogy (compelling citizens to service is equivalent to ordering a child to like someone), the writer attempts to claim the reader's sympathy and respect for common sense. In effect, the writer says, responsible parents would never do such a thing; responsible governments shouldn't, either. (Of course, readers could reject the analogy and the assumption about good parenting on which it rests. Some parents might very well push their children into friendships and believe themselves justified for doing so.)

Use Climactic Order

Organize by climactic order when you plan to offer a number of categories or elements of support for your claim. Recognize that some elements will be more important—and likely more persuasive—than others. The basic principle here is that you should *save the most important evidence for the end*, since whatever you have said last is what readers are likely to most remember. A secondary principle is that whatever you say first is what they are *next* most likely to remember. Therefore, when you have several reasons to support your claim, an effective argument strategy is to present the second most important, then one or more additional reasons, and finally, the most important reason. Paragraphs 7–11 of the model synthesis do exactly this.

Use Logical or Conventional Order

Using logical or conventional order means that you use as a template a preestablished pattern or plan for arguing your case.

- One common pattern is describing or arguing a *problem/solution*. Using this pattern, you begin with an introduction in which you typically define the problem, then perhaps explain its origins, then offer one or more solutions, then conclude.

- Another common pattern is presenting *two sides of a controversy*. Using this pattern, you introduce the controversy and (if an argument synthesis) your own point of view or claim, then explain the other side's arguments, providing reasons why your point of view should prevail.

- A third common pattern is *comparison-contrast*. In fact, this pattern is so important that we will discuss it separately in the next section.

- The order in which you present elements of an argument is sometimes dictated by the conventions of the discipline in which you are writing. For example, lab reports and experiments in the sciences and social sciences often follow this pattern: *Opening* or *Introduction, Methods and Materials* [of the experiment or study], *Results, Discussion*. Legal arguments often follow the so-called IRAC format: *Issue, Rule, Application, Conclusion*.

Present and Respond to Counterarguments

When developing arguments on a controversial topic, you can effectively use *counterargument* to help support your claims. When you use counterargument, you present an argument *against* your claim, but then show that this argument is weak or flawed. The advantage of this technique is that you demonstrate that you are aware of the other side of the argument and that you are prepared to answer it.

Here is how a counterargument typically is developed:

    I. Introduction and claim

   II. Main opposing argument

    III. Refutation of opposing argument
    IV. Main positive argument

Use Concession

Concession is a variation of counterargument. As in counterargument, you present the opposing (or otherwise objectionable) viewpoint, but instead of demolishing that argument, you concede that it does have some validity and even some appeal, although your own argument is the stronger one. This concession bolsters your own standing—your own ethos—as a fair-minded person who is not blind to the virtues of the other side. See paragraphs 9 and 10 of the example synthesis for one version of the concession argument. You'll find that instead of making an *opposing* argument, the writer produces a supporting argument but views one part of it as flawed. The writer rejects that section (the extreme position that *any* form of compensation corrupts the spirit of volunteerism) and endorses the remaining sections. In terms of overall argument strategy, the result—the reader sees the writer as being reasonable—is the same as it would be if the writer used the more standard concession in which an opposing argument is viewed as having some merit. Here is an outline for a more typical concession argument:

    I. Introduction and claim
    II. Important opposing argument
    III. Concession that this argument has some validity
    IV. Positive argument(s)

Sometimes, when you are developing a counterargument or concession argument, you may become convinced of the validity of the opposing point of view and change your own views. Don't be afraid of this happening. Writing is a tool for learning. To change your mind because of new evidence is a sign of flexibility and maturity, and your writing can only be the better for it.

Avoid Common Fallacies in Developing and Using Support

In Chapter 2, in the section on "Critical Reading," we considered some of the criteria that, as a reader, you may use for evaluating informative and persuasive writing (see pp. 69–74). We discussed how you can assess the accuracy, the significance, and the author's interpretation of the information presented. We also considered the importance in good argument of clearly defined key terms and the pitfalls of emotionally loaded language. Finally, we saw how to recognize such logical fallacies as either/or reasoning, faulty cause-and-effect reasoning, hasty generalization, and false analogy. As a writer, no less than as a critical reader, be aware of these common problems and try to avoid them.

Be aware, also, of your responsibility to cite source materials appropriately. When you quote a source, double and triple check that you have done so accurately. When you summarize or paraphrase, take care to use your own language and sentence structures (though you can, of course, also quote within these forms). When you refer to someone else's idea—even if you are not quoting, summarizing, or paraphrasing—give the source credit. By maintaining an ethical stance with regard to the use of sources, you take your place in and perpetuate the highest traditions of the academic community.

EXERCISE   **5.6**

Practicing Arguments

Read, or reread, the articles on downloading music off the Internet, reproduced at the end of Chapter 4 (pp. 160–78). If you're inclined, locate other articles on the topic to supplement those selections. Then devise an argumentative claim and use an outline to sketch the strategies for an argument that develop this claim. What types of evidence—facts, statistics, and expert opinions—from the readings would you use to support the claim? What motivational appeals would be appropriate? Which counterarguments would you address, and how would you address them? Finally, what concessions would you make (if any)?

THE COMPARISON-AND-CONTRAST SYNTHESIS

A particularly important type of argument synthesis is built on patterns of comparison and contrast. Techniques of comparison and contrast enable you to examine two subjects (or sources) in terms of one another. When you compare, you consider *similarities*. When you contrast, you consider *differences*. By comparing and contrasting, you perform a multifaceted analysis that often suggests subtleties that otherwise might not have come to your (or the reader's) attention.

To organize a comparison-and-contrast argument, you must carefully read sources in order to discover *significant criteria for analysis*. A *criterion* is a specific point to which both of your authors refer and about which they may agree or disagree. (For example, in a comparative report on compact cars, criteria for *comparison and contrast* might be road handling, fuel economy, and comfort of ride.) The best criteria are those that allow you not only to account for obvious similarities and differences—those concerning the main aspects of your sources or subjects—but also to plumb deeper, exploring subtle yet significant comparisons and contrasts among details or subcomponents, which you can then relate to your overall thesis.

Organizing Comparison-and-Contrast Syntheses

Two basic approaches to organizing a comparison-and-contrast synthesis are available: organization by *source* and organization by *criteria*.

ORGANIZING BY SOURCE OR SUBJECT

You can organize a comparative synthesis by first summarizing each of your sources or subjects, and then discussing significant similarities and differences between them. Having read the summaries and become familiar with the distinguishing features of each source, your readers will most likely be able to appreciate the more obvious similarities and differences. In the discussion, your task is to focus on both the obvious and subtle comparisons and contrasts, focusing on the most significant, that is, on those that most clearly support your thesis.

Organization by source or subject is best saved for passages that can be briefly summarized. If the summary of your source or subject becomes too long, your readers might forget the points you made in the first summary as they are reading the second. A comparison-and-contrast synthesis organized by source or subject might proceed like this:

I. Introduce the paper; lead to thesis.

II. Summarize source/subject A by discussing its significant features.

III. Summarize source/subject B by discussing its significant features.

IV. Write a paragraph (or two) in which you discuss the significant points of comparison and contrast between sources or subjects A and B. Alternatively, begin comparison-contrast in section III upon introducing source or subject B.

End with a conclusion in which you summarize your points and, perhaps, raise and respond to pertinent questions.

ORGANIZING BY CRITERIA

Instead of summarizing entire sources one at a time with the intention of comparing them later, you could discuss two sources simultaneously, examining the views of each author point by point (criterion by criterion), comparing and contrasting these views in the process. The criterion approach is best used when you have a number of points to discuss or when passages or subjects are long and/or complex. A comparison-and-contrast synthesis organized by criteria might look like this:

I. Introduce the paper; lead to thesis.

II. Criterion 1

a. Discuss what author A says about this point.

b. Discuss what author B says about this point, comparing and contrasting B's treatment of the point with A's.

    III. Criterion 2

       a. Discuss what author A says about this point.

       b. Discuss what author B says about this point, comparing and contrasting B's treatment of the point with A's.

And so on. Proceed criterion by criterion until you have completed your discussion. Be sure to arrange criteria with a clear method; knowing how the discussion of one criterion leads to the next will ensure smooth transitions throughout your paper. End by summarizing your key points and, perhaps, raising and responding to pertinent questions.

However you organize your comparison-and-contrast synthesis, keep in mind that comparing and contrasting are not ends in themselves. Your discussion should point somewhere: to a conclusion, an answer to "So what— why bother to compare and contrast in the first place?" If your discussion is part of a larger synthesis, point to and support the larger claim. If you write a stand-alone comparison-and-contrast, though, you must by the final paragraph answer the "why bother?" question. The model comparison-and-contrast synthesis that follows does exactly this.

EXERCISE   **5.7**

Comparing and Contrasting

Refer back to the readings on the compulsory national service controversy. Select two that take opposing sides, such as Bruce Chapman's "Politics and National Service: A Virus Attacks the Volunteer Sector" (p. 211) and David Gergen's "A Time to Heed the Call" (p. 189). Identify at least two significant criteria for analysis—two specific points to which both authors refer, and about which they agree or disagree. Then imagine you are preparing to write a short comparison-and-contrast paper and devise two outlines: the first organized by source, and the second organized by criteria.

A Case for Comparison-Contrast: Two Ophelias in Two Filmed *Hamlets*

We'll see how these principles can be applied to a paper dealing with two film versions of Shakespeare's *Hamlet*. Students were shown segments of two versions of *Hamlet*—those directed by Franco Zeffirelli (1991) and Kenneth Branagh (1996). Videotapes of each film were available for viewing at the media lab. Students were then assigned to write a paper comparing and contrasting any two film versions of a particular scene. The student whose paper is presented below selected Ophelia's "mad scene."

COMPARISON-CONTRAST (ORGANIZED BY CRITERIA)

Here is a plan for the comparison-contrast synthesis, organized by *criteria*. The thesis (and the *claim*) is as follows:

> *Thesis:* These contrasting interpretations [just discussed in the preceding introduction], reinforced through the films' different approaches to the staging of the action, to the acting, and to the cinematography, are particularly evident during the scene showing Ophelia's loss of sanity.
>
> I. Introduction. Hamlet's tragedy often overshadows Ophelia's. This important character has been treated in two very different ways by Franco Zeffirelli and Kenneth Branagh in their film versions of Hamlet. Thesis.
> II. Summary of the action in the scene (Act IV, Scene 5)
> III. The dramatic significance of the "mad scene."
> IV. The staging of the scene in front of the camera.
>   A. Zeffirelli presents a relatively childlike Ophelia.
>   B. Branagh presents a more mature Ophelia.
> V. The actress's approach to Ophelia's character.
>   A. Helena Bonham Carter presents Ophelia as lost and overpowered.
>   B. Kate Winslet presents Ophelia as angry, but also as more in control of her fate.
> VI. Cinematography. By means of camera angle, camera movement, and framing of characters, Zeffirelli and Branagh reinforce these contrasting interpretations of Ophelia.
> VII. Conclusion. Neither director's approach is more valid than the other's. Each reflects a particular interpretation of the character as well as of the play as a whole.

Following is a comparison-contrast synthesis by criteria, written according to the preceding plan. (Thesis and topic sentences are highlighted.)

MODEL PAPER

Two Ophelias

1   Shakespeare's <u>Hamlet</u> is probably the most well known of tragic heroes. But Hamlet's love, the "fair Ophelia," who dies shortly before the prince, is often overlooked. In our fascination with and concern for Hamlet, we often give too little regard to the grief and pain that this innocent young woman suffers and the way that she deals with her sorrows. Some call Ophelia mad, others depressed; but regardless of how we classify her, we cannot deny that she is a complex character who deserves our fuller attention. Franco Zeffirelli and Kenneth Branagh each chose to tackle the enormous task of directing a film version of Hamlet. Branagh stated that when he first saw Hamlet performed, he did not understand much of the play's language, but he recalled that "[a]s Ophelia lost her reason, I was moved to tears" (xii). In their contrasting versions, these two directors depict Ophelia's character in quite different ways. Throughout Zeffirelli's <u>Hamlet</u> (1991), Helena Bonham Carter portrays Ophelia as almost childlike and dreamy, giddy around her brother Laertes and other characters, such as King Claudius and Queen Gertrude. In Branagh's <u>Hamlet</u> (1996), on the other hand, Kate Winslet's Ophelia seems more mature and strong-willed. These contrasting interpretations, reinforced through the films' different approaches to the staging of the action, to the acting, and to the cinematography, are particularly evident during the scene showing Ophelia's loss of sanity.

2   In Shakespeare's play, the "mad scene" comprises Act IV, scene 5. Prior to this scene, Hamlet has staged his "play within a play," the result of which convinces him that his uncle Claudius had indeed killed his own brother, Hamlet's father (just as the ghost of old King Hamlet had told his son). After the murder, Claudius became king and married Hamlet's mother, Gertrude. Following the play scene, Hamlet berates Gertrude and kills Polonius, Ophelia's father, mistaking the hidden counselor for Claudius. Claudius then sends Hamlet to England, intending to have him killed there. As Act IV, scene 5 begins, a "Gentleman" tells the queen and Horatio, Hamlet's faithful friend, of Ophelia's pitiful state. Gertrude agrees to see her, and Ophelia enters ("distracted"), and begins singing songs ("He is dead and gone, lady,/He is dead and gone"). The king enters and gently questions Ophelia but can get no sensible

reply from her. Claudius asks, "How long has she been thus?" Ophelia exits, and Claudius asks Horatio to keep watch over her. Soon afterwards a messenger arrives with word that Laertes, Ophelia's brother, has returned from France, angrily demanding to know what happened to Polonius, his father, and threatening to kill Claudius. The king eventually manages to calm Laertes, but then Ophelia re-enters, in her distracted state, to Laertes' amazement ("O heavens, is't possible a young maid's wits/Should be as mortal as an old man's life?"). Ophelia continues to sing songs, while distributing imaginary flowers to Laertes, Claudius, and Gertrude. She then exits for the last time. (We later hear from Gertrude that she has drowned herself.) As the scene ends, Claudius promises to give Laertes satisfaction for what has happened to his father and sister.

3   The "mad scene" is important dramatically because it sets up the final confrontation among the various antagonists and the catastrophic acts that leave the stage littered with corpses. The scene itself shows us the effect upon Ophelia of both her unaccountable rejection by Hamlet (who must give up his love to devote himself to avenging his father's death) and of the senseless death of her own father. Ophelia's condition further motivates Laertes to seek revenge upon Hamlet and gives Claudius the opportunity to plot Hamlet's death either through a poisoned sword wielded by Laertes or, if that plan fails, through a goblet of poisoned wine. As it turns out, Hamlet does indeed die, but so do Laertes, after Hamlet switches swords with him, Gertrude, who drinks the wine intended for Hamlet, and Claudius, who is killed by Hamlet after Laertes, in his dying moments, reveals the king's treachery.

4   Re-creating this scene, directors Zeffirelli and Branagh differ significantly in their staging of the action, in their direction of the actresses playing Ophelia, and in their use of cinematography. Consider first the differences in staging, or the way the director arranges the characters and the settings in front of the camera. Zeffirelli chooses to portray Ophelia as small, childlike, and helpless. At the outset of the scene, he invents a sequence in which we see Ophelia emerging from hiding, behind a wall. First the tips of her fingers, then her head pops up. She runs over to the castle battlements and, as Gertrude watches from the castle window, begins fondling the face and then mischievously tugging at the sash of an embarrassed sentry. The man awkwardly attempts to continue standing

at attention while ever so delicately fending off Ophelia's advances. Finally, another guard leads her away. We next see her running into the entryway of the castle demanding to see Gertrude ("Where is the beauteous majesty of Denmark?"). She is wearing a shapeless smock that makes her look like a little girl, especially when the camera views her from above. Running up the stone steps, she begins singing her songs to the startled assemblage. At this end of this part of the sequence, she again runs away, and ends up sobbing against the rough stone wall, sinking to her knees. Horatio must pick her up and carry her away, accompanied by three women attendants. She looks helpless and overwhelmed by the events that have befallen her.

5   Later we see a tiny Ophelia dwarfed by the tall back and sidepieces of the huge throne where she sits. She distributes her imaginary flowers (sticks and bones) to the dumbstruck Laertes, Gertrude, and Claudius. She leaves the room framed between two large guards in the foreground. Our final views of her show her running outside through a gully, then through a wooded area, to the stream where she will drown herself. As in the castle scenes, she seems small and insignificant and, again, is shot from above, helping reinforce our view of her as helpless.

6   Branagh stages this sequence very differently, in ways that downplay Ophelia's childlikeness and that rather emphasize her determination in the face of abuse by others. After a brief glimpse of Ophelia screaming in distress from behind a railing as her dead father is carried away, we next see her in a padded cell, garbed in a strait jacket, bouncing against the walls, trying to get out. When she makes her next appearance, with the line "Where is the beauteous majesty of Denmark?" she is not running into the room, like Zeffirelli's Ophelia, but lying prone on the floor, immobile in her strait jacket. As she sings her apparently nonsense songs, she writhes in sexual motion; Branagh intercuts a brief glimpse of Ophelia and Hamlet in happier times, in bed together. This Ophelia, we understand, is no child, but a mature woman, although one who has lost her sanity.

7   After the sequence in which she distributes imaginary flowers to Laertes, Claudius, and Gertrude, Ophelia is seen twice more in Branagh's film. First we view her being hosed down in her padded cell. (The shot reminds us of how civil rights demonstrators in the 1960s, fighting for their rights and their dignity, were attacked by police with water hoses.) After the guard

leaves, she changes her expression from one of distress
to determination and takes a key--the key to her cell--
out of her mouth. When we last see her, she is already
dead; shot from below, she is floating face down in the
stream. This is a woman who has been sorely abused, but
one who has, to some extent, taken her fate into her
own hands. Winslet's death is not accidental; Bonham
Carter's death might have been (she could have fallen
from her seat on the plank bridge over the stream).

8   These opposing visions of Ophelia are further
reinforced by the directors' and the actresses, approach
to the character. Zeffirelli likely cast Bonham Carter
as Ophelia because of her immature appearance: reviewer
Jeanne Cooper of The Washington Post noted that Bonham
Carter "looks childlike," as she did in one of her
previous films, Room with a View. Recall that when we
first see Bonham Carter's Ophelia in the "mad scene,"
she is behaving like a little girl who doesn't want to
get caught, hiding behind a wall getting ready to do
something bad. Before running to the sentry she darts a
quick look to one side to make sure that no one is
watching. Throughout the sequence, she suddenly, and
without any apparent motivation, changes expression and
mood, from happy to sad to whimsical to indignant. As
she talks she frequently opens her eyes wide. She makes
quick, often unexpected or repetitive movements, as if
she were not fully in control of her face or her body.
As she rocks back and forth, her messy hair hanging in
front of her eyes, she looks like a scared, lost child.
As web critic Ed Arnold noted, "[s]he was shy and
overpowered by the personalities around her. . . . [S]he
was bewildered by the conflicting messages and back-
biting." In Zeffirelli's film, as Ophelia descends into
madness, she reverts to an earlier stage of life.

9   Kate Winslet's Ophelia also becomes deranged, but
Winslet's insanity takes a different form. In general,
she seems angry at how she has been (and is being)
treated; and she appears to act with strong purpose.
Reviewer Janet Maslin of the New York Times noted
Winslet's "fervent performance." This Ophelia has not
reverted to an earlier, confused and more innocent stage
of life. She is in critic Roger Ebert's estimate,
"touchingly vulnerable . . . red-nosed and snuffling, her
world crumbling about her." But Branagh's Ophelia does
not come across as "shy and overpowered." On the
contrary, she strikes out--although illogically, even
insanely--at the injustice of what has happened to her
(and to Hamlet and to her father). She reacts no

differently to being confined in a strait jacket and to being hosed down in a padded cell than any sane person would. When she takes the key from her mouth after the guard has left, she appears, almost like Hamlet, to have been faking madness in order to throw others off the track about her true condition and intentions. During her song and speech directed to Laertes toward the end of the sequence, she barely moves. Her face is calm and composed and her voice is even; she displays none of the childlike mannerisms or facial tics of Bonham Carter's Ophelia. When she finishes talking, she quietly says "Goodbye, you" to her brother, looks meaningfully at him, then slowly gets up and walks away. At this moment, nearly our last view of her alive, she looks both sane and dignified.

10   The cinematography of each director reinforces these contrasting views of Ophelia. As mentioned earlier, many of Zeffirelli's shots of Ophelia are filmed from above; this high-angle point of view makes her look small or lost. Camera movement is also significant. In one segment, the camera follows Bonham Carter's Ophelia as she distributes flowers first to Laertes, then to Gertrude, then to Claudius. The movements of the camera, tracking Ophelia's apparently random movements, create a sense of confusion and haphazardness for the viewer. Where will she turn next? In contrast, Branagh's Ophelia, after her purposeful entrance, makes no such random movements; she sits down in front of the mirror and remains there. The stillness of the camera suggests that Ophelia at this point may have found a kind of peace as she prepares to end her life. Zeffirelli's and Branagh's cameras also differ in the way they show how the characters relate to one another. In Zeffirelli's film, the camera shows the individual reactions of Laertes, Gertrude, and Claudius to Ophelia's condition. They rarely appear in the same shot with her. Visually, they stand apart from Ophelia, as they react to her condition in amazement and sadness. In Branagh's film, in contrast, the camera frames these characters in pairs: Ophelia appears in the same shot as her brother; Claudius appears with Gertrude. By shooting this way, Branagh emphasizes the closeness of brother and sister; and he may be foreshadowing the coming break between Laertes and his co-conspirator Claudius.

11   While a play comes to us as a printed text, it doesn't live until it's performed--on stage or on film. Performance means interpretation: the director devises ways to stage the action for the audience and, working

with the actors, shapes intonation, facial expression, body movement, and more. An accomplished director will make such choices in line with a larger conception of the meaning of the play and its characters. Does the director see Ophelia as a dreamy child or as a strong-willed adult? Because either of these two Ophelias--as well as others--can be "read" into Shakespeare's Hamlet, we can expect to see as many Ophelias (and Hamlets and Gertrudes) as we have productions of the play. Zeffirelli's and Branagh's different renderings of the character demonstrate just how important a director's interpretations are to a production. Neither of their Ophelias can be called "definitive." Both make sense in the context of their productions and remind us that a play is always a creative partnership between writer and director.

Works Cited

Arnold, Ed. "Hamlet" (1990): Rev. of Hamlet, dir. Franco Zeffirelli. 1990. 14 June 2003, 2003 <http://reviews.imdb.com/Reviews/09/0941>.

Branagh, Kenneth. "Introduction." Hamlet by William Shakespeare: Screenplay and Introduction by Kenneth Branagh. New York: Norton, 1996.

Cooper, Jeanne. "Hamlet." Rev. of Hamlet, dir. Franco Zeffirelli. Washington Post 18 Jan. 1991. 18 June 2003 <http://www.washingtonpost.com/wp-srv/style/longterm/movies/videos/hamletpgcooper_a09ed5.htm>.

Ebert, Roger. "Hamlet." Rev. of Hamlet, dir. Kenneth Branagh. Chicago Sun-Times. 15 June 2003 <http://www.suntimes.com/ebert/ebert_reviews/1997/01/012401.html>.

Hamlet. Dir. Kenneth Branagh. Perf. Kenneth Branagh, Kate Winslet, Derek Jacobi, Julie Christie, Richard Briers, and Michael Maloney. Warner Brothers, 1996.

Hamlet. Dir. Franco Zeffirelli. Perf. Mel Gibson, Helena Bonham Carter, Alan Bates, Glenn Close, Ian Holm, and Nathaniel Parker. Warner Brothers, 1990.

Maslin, Janet. "Hamlet." Rev. of Hamlet dir. Kenneth Branagh. New York Times 25 Dec. 1996. 19 June 2003 <http://www.nytimes.com/library/film/hamlet.html>.

Shakespeare, William. The Tragedy of Hamlet Prince of Denmark. Ed. Edward Hubler. New York: Signet, 1963.

Discussion

The general strategy of this argument is an organization by criteria. The writer argues that the films differ in their approaches to presenting Ophelia primarily through (1) the staging of the dramatic action; (2) the acting; (3) the cinematography. The first of these criteria, the staging of the action, is given the greatest emphasis; the second two are presented in less detail.

In argument terms, the conclusion that the two films offer different conceptions of Ophelia is the *claim* that the writer is making. The *assumption* is that careful attention to staging, acting, and cinematography are important keys to the understanding of the differences between these two Ophelias. The *support* comes in the form not only of the obvious physical differences between the two actresses and the overall differences of setting and staging, but also in the form of specific details of the staging, acting, and cinematography, which serve as evidence proving the claim.

- **Paragraph 1:** The writer argues that Ophelia, who has often been overlooked because of the great interest in Hamlet's tragedy, is a complex character who deserves fuller attention. She will focus on how Ophelia's character has been presented in two very different ways in Zeffirelli's and Branagh's film versions of *Hamlet*, as revealed during the "mad scene." The criteria for comparison and contrast will be the staging of the action, the acting, and the cinematography.

- **Paragraph 2:** The writer summarizes the dramatic action of the scene in question, Act IV, Scene 5.

- **Paragraph 3:** The writer explains why this scene is dramatically significant for the play as a whole.

- **Paragraphs 4 and 5:** The writer begins the comparison-contrast proper. Focusing on the first of the three criteria, the staging of the action, the writer begins with Zeffirelli's treatment of this scene. She pays particular attention to how we first see Ophelia (Zeffirelli's invention of Ophelia's fondling of the guard), then describes the scenes in which Ophelia sings songs and distributes imaginary flowers, and finally the scene where she runs through the woods to the stream where she will drown herself.

- **Paragraphs 6 and 7:** The writer continues with the staging, contrasting Branagh's staging of these scenes with Zeffirelli's. She points out that Branagh's Ophelia is seen twice in a padded cell and also notes the sexual writhings of the mad Ophelia.

- **Paragraph 8:** The writer focuses on Helena Bonham Carter's acting, emphasizing how her facial expressions and bodily movements give Ophelia's madness a childlike quality.

- **Paragraph 9:** The writer contrasts Kate Winslet's acting of Ophelia with Bonham Carter's, emphasizing how much more assertive and, finally, how dignified (and un-childlike) Winslet appears when speaking to and taking leave of her brother.

- **Paragraph 10:** The writer contrasts the cinematography of the sequences in the two films, focusing on the use of high angle shots by Zeffirelli; a predominantly moving camera in one film, as opposed to a predominantly still camera in the other during one segment of the scene; and finally the choice to frame individual or paired characters as a means of providing dramatic contrast.

- **Paragraph 11:** The writer points out that the choices made by each director suggest a larger interpretation of the play as a whole. Neither director's choices are definitive, but each demonstrates the importance of the director in helping realize the writer's vision.

SUMMARY OF SYNTHESIS CHAPTERS

In this chapter and Chapter 4 preceding it, we've considered three main types of synthesis: the *explanatory synthesis*, the *argument synthesis*, and the *comparison-contrast synthesis*. Although for ease of comprehension we've placed them into separate categories, these types are not, of course, mutually exclusive. Both explanatory syntheses and argument syntheses often involve elements of one another, and comparison-contrast syntheses can fall into either of the previous categories. Which approach you choose will depend upon your *purpose* and the method that you decide is best suited to achieve this purpose.

If your main purpose is to help your audience understand a particular subject, and in particular to help them understand the essential elements or significance of this subject, then you will be composing an explanatory synthesis. If your main purpose, on the other hand, is to persuade your audience to agree with your viewpoint on a subject, or to change their minds, or to decide upon a particular course of action, then you will be composing an argument synthesis. If one effective technique of making your case is to establish similarities or differences between your subject and another one, then you will compose a comparison-contrast synthesis—which may well be just *part* of a larger synthesis.

In planning and drafting these syntheses, you can draw upon a variety of strategies: supporting your claims by summarizing, paraphrasing, and quoting from your sources; using appeal to *logos, pathos,* and *ethos;* and choosing from among strategies such as climactic or conventional order, counterargument, and concession, that will best help you to achieve your purpose.

The strategies of synthesis you've practiced in these last two chapters will be dealt with again in Chapter 7, on Research, where we'll consider a category of synthesis commonly known as the research paper. The research paper involves all of the skills in summary, critique, and synthesis that we've discussed so far, the main difference being, of course, that you won't find the sources you need in this particular text. We'll discuss approaches to locating and critically evaluating sources, selecting material from among them to provide support for your claims, and finally, documenting your sources in standard professional formats.

But first, we need to examine analysis, which is another important strategy for academic thinking and writing. Chapter 6, "Analysis," will introduce you to a strategy that, like synthesis, draws upon all the strategies you've been practicing as you move through *A Sequence for Academic Writing*.

6

Analysis

WHAT IS AN ANALYSIS?

An analysis is an argument in which you study the parts of something to understand how it works, what it means, or why it might be significant. The writer of an analysis uses an analytical tool: a *principle* or *definition* on the basis of which an object, an event, or a behavior can be divided into parts and examined. Here are excerpts from two analyses of L. Frank Baum's *The Wizard of Oz:*

> At the dawn of adolescence, the very time she should start to distance herself from Aunt Em and Uncle Henry, the surrogate parents who raised her on their Kansas farm, Dorothy Gale experiences a hurtful reawakening of her fear that these loved ones will be rudely ripped from her, especially her Aunt (Em—M for Mother!). [Harvey Greenberg, *The Movies on Your Mind* (New York: Dutton, 1975)]

> [*The Wizard of Oz*] was originally written as a political allegory about grassroots protest. It may seem harder to believe than Emerald City, but the Tin Woodsman is the industrial worker, the Scarecrow [is] the struggling farmer, and the Wizard is the president, who is powerful only as long as he succeeds in deceiving the people. [Peter Dreier, "Oz Was Almost Reality," *Cleveland Plain Dealer* 3 Sept. 1989.]

As these paragraphs suggest, what you discover through an analysis depends entirely on the principle or definition you use to make your insights. Is *The Wizard of Oz* the story of a girl's psychological development, or is it a story about politics? The answer is *both*. In the first example, psychiatrist Harvey Greenberg applies the

---

WHERE DO WE FIND WRITTEN ANALYSES?

Here are just a few types of writing that involve analysis:

Academic Writing

- **Experimental and lab reports.** Analyze the meaning or implications of study results in the Discussion section.
- **Research papers.** Analyze information in sources; apply theories to material being reported.
- **Process analysis.** Break down the steps or stages involved in completing a process.
- **Literary analysis.** Analyze characterization, plot, imagery, or other elements in works of literature.
- **Essay exams.** Demonstrate understanding of course material by analyzing data using course concepts.

Workplace Writing

- **Grant proposals.** Analyze the issues you seek funding for in order to address them.
- **Reviews of the arts.** Employ dramatic or literary analysis to assess artistic works.
- **Business plans.** Break down and analyze capital outlays, expenditures, profits, materials, and the like.
- **Medical charts.** Perform analytical thinking and writing in relation to patient symptoms and possible treatment options.
- **Legal briefs.** Break down and analyze facts of cases and elements of legal precedents; apply legal rulings and precedents to new situations.
- **Case studies.** Describe and analyze the particulars of a specific medical, social service, advertising, or business case.

---

principles of his profession and, not surprisingly, sees *The Wizard of Oz* in psychological terms. In the second example, a newspaper reporter applies the political theories of Karl Marx and, again not surprisingly, discovers a story about politics.

Different as they are, these analyses share an important quality: each is the result of a specific principle or definition used as a tool to divide an object into parts to see what it means and how it works. The writer's choice of analytical tool simultaneously creates and limits the possibilities for analysis. Thus, working with the principles of Freud, Harvey Greenberg sees *The Wizard of Oz* in psychological, not political, terms; working with the theories of Karl Marx, Peter Dreier understands the movie in terms of the economic relationships among characters. It's as if the writer of an analysis who adopts one analytical tool puts on a pair of glasses and sees an object in a specific way. Another writer, using a different tool (and a different pair of glasses), sees the object differently.

You might protest: Are there as many analyses of *The Wizard of Oz* as there are people to read it? Yes, or at least as many analyses as there are analytical tools. This does not mean that all analyses are equally valid or useful. The writer must convince the reader. In creating an essay of analysis, the writer must organize a series of related insights, using the analytical tool to examine first one part and then another of the object being studied. To read Harvey Greenberg's essay on *The Wizard of Oz* is to find paragraph after paragraph of related insights—first about Aunt Em, then the Wicked Witch, then Toto, and then the Wizard. All these insights point to Greenberg's single conclusion: that "Dorothy's 'trip' is a marvelous metaphor for the psychological journey every adolescent must make."* Without Greenberg's analysis, we probably would not have thought about the movie as a psychological journey. This is precisely the power of an analysis: its ability to reveal objects or events in ways we would not otherwise have considered.

The writer's challenge is to convince readers that (1) the analytical tool being applied is legitimate and well matched to the object being studied; and (2) the analytical tool is being used systematically to divide the object into parts and to make a coherent, meaningful statement about these parts and the object as a whole.

DEMONSTRATION OF ANALYSIS

Two examples of analyses follow. The first is written by a professional writer. The second is written by a student, in response to an assignment in his sociology class. Each analysis illustrates the two defining features of analysis just discussed: a statement of an analytical principle or definition, and the use of that principle or definition in closely examining an object, behavior, or event. As you read, try to identify these features. An exercise with questions for discussion follows each example.

The Plug-In Drug
Marie Winn

The following analysis of television viewing as an addictive behavior appeared originally in Marie Winn's 2002 book, The Plug-In Drug: Television, Computers, and Family Life. *A writer and media critic, Winn has been interested in the effect of television on both individuals and the larger culture. In this passage, she carefully defines the term* addiction *and then applies it systematically to the behavior under study.*

---

*See Harvey Greenberg, *Movies on Your Mind* (New York: Dutton, 1975).

1   The word "addiction" is often used loosely and wryly in conversation. People will refer to themselves as "mystery-book addicts" or "cookie addicts." E. B. White wrote of his annual surge of interest in gardening: "We are hooked and are making an attempt to kick the habit." Yet nobody really believes that reading mysteries or ordering seeds by catalogue is serious enough to be compared with addictions to heroin or alcohol. In these cases the word "addiction" is used jokingly to denote a tendency to overindulge in some pleasurable activity.

2   People often refer to being "hooked on TV." Does this, too, fall into the light-hearted category of cookie eating and other pleasures that people pursue with unusual intensity? Or is there a kind of television viewing that falls into the more serious category of destructive addiction?

3   Not unlike drugs or alcohol, the television experience allows the participant to blot out the real world and enter into a pleasurable and passive mental state. To be sure, other experiences, notably reading, also provide a temporary respite from reality. But it's much easier to stop reading and return to reality than to stop watching television. The entry into another world offered by reading includes an easily accessible return ticket. The entry via television does not. In this way television viewing, for those vulnerable to addiction, is more like drinking or taking drugs—once you start it's hard to stop.

4   Just as alcoholics are only vaguely aware of their addiction, feeling that they control their drinking more than they really do ("I can cut it out any time I want—I just like to have three or four drinks before dinner"), many people overestimate their control over television watching. Even as they put off other activities to spend hour after hour watching television, they feel they could easily resume living in a different, less passive style. But somehow or other while the television set is present in their homes, it just stays on. With television's easy gratifications available, those other activities seem to take too much effort.

5   A heavy viewer (a college instructor) observes:

> I find television almost irresistible. When the set is on, I cannot ignore it. I can't turn it off. I feel sapped, will-less, enervated. As I reach out to turn off the set, the strength goes out of my arms. So I sit there for hours and hours.

6   Self-confessed television addicts often feel they "ought" to do other things—but the fact that they don't read and don't plant their garden or sew or crochet or play games or have conversations means that those activities are no longer as desirable as television viewing. In a way, the lives of heavy viewers are as unbalanced by their television "habit" as drug addicts' or alcoholics' lives. They are living in a holding pattern, as it were, passing up the activities that lead to growth or development or a sense of accomplishment. This is one reason people talk about their television viewing so ruefully, so apologetically. They are aware that it is an unproductive experience, that by any human measure almost any other endeavor is more worthwhile.

7   It is the adverse effect of television viewing on the lives of so many people that makes it feel like a serious addiction. The television habit distorts the sense of time. It renders other experiences vague and curiously unreal while taking on

a greater reality for itself. It weakens relationships by reducing and sometimes eliminating normal opportunities for talking, for communicating.

8   And yet television does not satisfy, else why would the viewer continue to watch hour after hour, day after day? "The measure of health," wrote the psychiatrist Lawrence Kubie, "is flexibility . . . and especially the freedom to cease when sated." But heavy television viewers can never be sated with their television experiences. These do not provide the true nourishment that satiation requires, and thus they find that they cannot stop watching.

EXERCISE 6.1

Reading Critically: Winn

Typically in analyses, authors first present their analytical principle in full and then systematically apply parts of the principle to the object or phenomenon under study. In her brief analysis of television viewing, Marie Winn pursues an alternate, though equally effective, strategy by *distributing* parts of her analytical principle across the essay. Locate where Winn defines key elements of addiction. Locate where she uses each element as an analytical lens to examine television viewing as a form of addiction.

What function does paragraph 4 play in the analysis?

In the first two paragraphs, how does Winn create a funnel-like effect that draws readers into the heart of her analysis?

Recall a few television programs that genuinely moved you, educated you, humored you, or stirred you to worthwhile reflection or action. To what extent does Winn's analysis describe your positive experiences as a television viewer? (Consider how Winn might argue that from within an addicted state, a person may feel "humored, moved or educated" but is in fact—from a sober outsider's point of view—deluded.) If Winn's analysis of television viewing as an addiction does *not* account for your experience, does it follow that her analysis is flawed? Explain.

Edward Peselman wrote the following paper as a first-semester sophomore, in response to the following assignment from his sociology professor:

> Read chapter 3, "The Paradoxes of Power," in Randall Collins' *Sociological Insights: An Introduction to Non-Obvious Sociology* (2nd ed., 1992). Use any of Collins' observations to examine the sociology of power in a group with which you are familiar. Write for readers much like yourself: freshmen or sophomores who have taken one course in sociology. Your object in this paper is to use Collins as a way of learning something "nonobvious" about a group to which you belong or have belonged.

Note: The citations are in APA format. (See Chapter 7.)

            The Coming Apart of a Dorm Society
                     Edward Peselman
1   During my first year of college, I lived in a
    dormitory, like most freshmen on campus. We inhabitants

of the dorm came from different cultural and economic backgrounds. Not surprisingly, we brought with us many of the traits found in people outside of college. Like many on the outside, we in the dorm sought personal power at the expense of others. The gaining and maintaining of power can be an ugly business, and I saw people hurt and in turn hurt others all for the sake of securing a place in the dorm's prized social order. Not until one of us challenged that order did I realize how fragile it was.

2   Randall Collins, a sociologist at the University of California, Riverside, defines the exercise of power as the attempt "to make something happen in society" (1992, p. 61). A society can be understood as something as large and complex as "American society"; something more sharply defined--such as a corporate or organizational society; or something smaller still--a dorm society like my own, consisting of six 18-year-old men who lived at one end of dormitory floor in an all male dorm.

3   In my freshman year, my society was a tiny but distinctive social group in which people exercised power. I lived with two roommates, Dozer and Reggie. Dozer was an emotionally unstable, excitable individual who vented his energy through anger. His insecurity and moodiness contributed to his difficulty in making friends. Reggie was a friendly, happy-go-lucky sort who seldom displayed emotions other than contentedness. He was shy when encountering new people, but when placed in a socially comfortable situation he would talk for hours.

4   Eric and Marc lived across the hall from us and therefore spent a considerable amount of time in our room. Eric could be cynical and was often blunt: he seldom hesitated when sharing his frank and sometimes unflattering opinions. He commanded a grudging respect in the dorm. Marc could be very moody and, sometimes, was violent. His temper and stubborn streak made him particularly susceptible to conflict. The final member of our miniature society was Benjamin, cheerful yet insecure. Benjamin had certain characteristics which many considered effeminate, and he was often teased about his sexuality--which in turn made him insecure. He was naturally friendly but, because of the abuse he took, he largely kept to himself. He would join us occasionally for a pizza or late-night television.

5   Together, we formed an independent social structure. Going out to parties together, playing cards, watching television, playing ball: these were the activities through which we got to know each other and through which we established the basic pecking order of our community. Much like a colony of baboons, we established a hierarchy based on power relationships. According to Collins, what a powerful person wishes to happen must be achieved by

controlling others. Collins's observation can help to
define who had how much power in our social group. In the
dorm, Marc and Eric clearly had the most power. Everyone
feared them and agreed to do pretty much what they
wanted. Through violent words or threats of violence,
they got their way. I was next in line: I wouldn't dare
to manipulate Marc or Eric, but the others I could manage
through occasional quips. Reggie, then Dozer, and finally
Benjamin.

6   Up and down the pecking order, we exercised control
through macho taunts and challenges. Collins writes that
"individuals who manage to be powerful and get their own
way must do so by going along with the laws of social
organization, not by contradicting them" (p. 61). Until
mid year, our dorm motto could have read: "You win
through rudeness and intimidation." Eric gained power
with his frequent and brutal assessments of everyone's
behavior. Marc gained power with his temper--which, when
lost, made everyone run for cover. Those who were not
rude and intimidating drifted to the bottom of our social
world. Reggie was quiet and unemotional, which allowed us
to take advantage of him because we knew he would back
down if pressed in an argument. Yet Reggie understood
that on a "power scale" he stood above Dozer and often
shared in the group's tactics to get Dozer's food (his
parents were forever sending him care packages). Dozer,
in turn, seldom missed opportunities to take swipes at
Benjamin, with references to his sexuality. From the very
first week of school, Benjamin could never--and never
wanted to--compete against Erik's bluntness or Marc's
temper. Still, Benjamin hung out with us. He lived in our
corner of the dorm, and he wanted to be friendly. But
everyone, including Benjamin, understood that he occupied
the lowest spot in the order.

7   That is, until he left mid-semester. According to
Collins, "any social arrangement works because people
avoid questioning it most of the time" (p. 74). The
inverse of this principle is as follows: when a social
arrangement is questioned, that arrangement can fall
apart. The more fragile the arrangement (the flimsier the
values on which it is based), the more quickly it will
crumble. For the entire first semester, no one questioned
our rude, macho rules and because of them we pigeon-holed
Benjamin as a wimp. In our dorm society, gentle men had
no power. To say the least, ours was not a compassionate
community. From a distance of one year, I am shocked to
have been a member of it. Nonetheless, we had created a
mini-society that somehow served our needs.

8   At the beginning of the second semester, we found
Benjamin packing up his room. Marc, who was walking down
the hall, stopped by and said something like: "Hey

buddy, the kitchen get too hot for you?" I was there, and I saw Benjamin turn around and say: "Do you practice at being such a _____, or does it come naturally? I've never met anybody who felt so good about making other people feel lousy. You'd better get yourself a job in the army or in the prison system, because no one else is going to put up with your _____." Marc said something in a raised voice. I stepped between them, and Benjamin said: "Get out." I was cheering.

9   Benjamin moved into an off-campus apartment with his girlfriend. This astonished us, first because of his effeminate manner (we didn't know he had a girlfriend) and second because none of the rest of us had been seeing girls much (though we talked about it constantly). Here was Benjamin, the gentlest among us, and he blew a hole in our macho society. Our social order never really recovered, which suggests its flimsy values. People in the dorm mostly went their own ways during the second semester. I'm not surprised, and I was more than a little grateful. Like most people in the dorm, save for Eric and Marc, I both got my lumps and I gave them, and I never felt good about either. Like Benjamin, I wanted to fit in with my new social surroundings. Unlike him, I didn't have the courage to challenge the unfairness of what I saw.

10   By chance, six of us were thrown together into a dorm and were expected, on the basis of proximity alone, to develop a friendship. What we did was sink to the lowest possible denominator. Lacking any real basis for friendship, we allowed the forceful, macho personalities of Marc and Eric to set the rules, which for one semester we all subscribed to--even those who suffered.

11   The macho rudeness couldn't last, and I'm glad it was Benjamin who brought us down. By leaving, he showed a different and a superior kind of power. I doubt he was reading Randall Collins at the time, but he somehow had come to Collins' same insight: as long as he played by the rules of our group, he suffered because those rules placed him far down in the dorm's pecking order. Even by participating in pleasant activities, like going out for pizza, Benjamin supported a social system that ridiculed him. Some systems are so oppressive and small minded that they can't be changed from the inside. They've got to be torn down. Benjamin had to move, and in moving he made me (at least) question the basis of my dorm friendships.

Reference

Collins, R. 1992 *Sociological insight: An introduction to non-obvious sociology.* 2nd ed. New York: Oxford University Press.

Reading Critically: Peselman

What is the function of ¶1? Though Peselman does not use the word *sociology*, what signals does he give that this will be a paper that examines the social interactions of a group? Peselman introduces Collins in ¶2. Why? What does Peselman accomplish in ¶s3–4? How does his use of Collins in ¶5 logically follow the presentation in ¶3–4? The actual analysis in this paper takes place in ¶s5–11. Point to where Peselman draws on the work of Randall Collins, and explain how he uses Collins to gain insight into dorm life.

HOW TO WRITE AN ANALYSIS

Consider Your Purpose

Whether you are assigned a topic to write on or are left to your own devices, you inevitably face this question: What is my idea? Like every paper, an analysis has at its heart an idea you want to convey. For Edward Peselman, it was the idea that a social order based on flimsy values is not strong enough to sustain a direct challenge to its power, and thus will fall apart eventually. From beginning to end, Peselman advances this one idea: first, by introducing readers to the dorm society he will analyze; next, by introducing principles of analysis (from Randall Collins); and finally, by examining his dorm relationships in light of these principles. The entire set of analytical insights coheres as a paper because the insights are *related* and point to Peselman's single idea.

Peselman's paper offers a good example of the personal uses to which analysis can be put. Notice that he gravitated toward events in his life that confused him and about which he wanted some clarity. Such topics can be especially fruitful for analysis because you know the particulars well and can provide readers with details; you view the topic with some puzzlement; and, through the application of your analytical tool, you may come to understand it. When you select topics to analyze from your experience, you provide yourself with a motivation to write and learn. When you are motivated in this way, you spark the interest of readers.

Using Randall Collins as a guide, Edward Peselman returns again and again to the events of his freshman year in the dormitory. We sense that Peselman himself wants to know what happened in that dorm. He writes, "I saw people hurt and in turn hurt others all for the sake of securing a place in the dorm's prized social order." Peselman does not approve of what happened, and the analysis he launches is meant to help him understand.

Locate an Analytical Principle

When you are given an assignment that asks for analysis, use two specific reading strategies to identify principles and definitions in source materials.

- **Look for a sentence that makes a general statement about the way something works.** The statement may strike you as a rule or a law. The line that Edward Peselman quotes from Randall Collins has this quality: "[A]ny social arrangement works because people avoid questioning it most of the time." Such statements are generalizations, conclusions to sometimes complicated and extensive arguments. You can use these conclusions to guide your own analyses as long as you are aware that for some audiences, you will need to re-create and defend the arguments that resulted in these conclusions.

- **Look for statements that take this form: "X" can be defined as (or "X" consists of) the following: A, B, and C.** The specific elements of the definition—A, B, and C—are what you use to identify and analyze parts of the object being studied. You've seen an example of this approach in Marie Winn's multipart definition of addiction, which she uses to analyze television viewing. As a reader looking for definitions suitable for conducting an analysis, you might come across Winn's definition of addiction and then use it for your own purposes, perhaps to analyze the playing of video games as an addiction.

Essential to any analysis is the validity of the principle or definition being applied, the analytical tool. Make yourself aware, both as writer and reader, of a tool's strengths and limitations. Pose these questions of the analytical principles and definitions you use: Are they accurate? Are they well accepted? Do *you* accept them? What are the arguments against them? What are their limitations? Since every principle or definition used in an analysis is the end product of an argument, you are entitled—even obligated—to challenge it. If the analytical tool is flawed, then the analysis that follows from it will be flawed also.

Following is a page from *Sociological Insight* by Randall Collins; Edward Peselman uses a key sentence from this extract as an analytical tool in his essay on power relations in his dorm (see p. 249). Notice that Peselman underlines the sentence he will use in his essay:

> Try this experiment some time. When you are talking to someone, make them explain everything they say that isn't completely clear. The result, you will discover, is a series of uninterrupted interruptions:
>
> A: Hi, how are you doing?
> B: What do you mean when you say "how"?
> A: You know. What's happening with you?
> B: What do you mean, "happening"?

A: Happening, you know, what's going on.

B: I'm sorry. Could you explain what you mean by "what"?

A: What do you mean, what do I mean? Do you want to talk to me or not?

It is obvious that this sort of questioning could go on endlessly, at any rate if the listener doesn't get very angry and punch you in the mouth. But it illustrates two important points. First, virtually everything can be called into question. We are able to get along with other people not because everything is clearly spelled out, but because we are willing to take most things people say without explanation. Harold Garfinkel, who actually performed this sort of experiment, points out that there is an infinite regress of assumptions that go into any act of social communication. Moreover, some expressions are simply not explainable in words at all. A word like "you," or "here," or "now" is what Garfinkel calls "indexical." You have to know what it means already; it can't be explained.

"What do you mean by 'you'?"

"I mean *you, you*!" About all that can be done here is point your finger.

The second point is that people get mad when they are pressed to explain things that they ordinarily take for granted. This is because they very quickly see that explanations could go on forever and the questions will never be answered. If you really demanded a full explanation of everything you hear, you could stop the conversation from ever getting past its first sentence. The real significance of this for a sociological understanding of the way the world is put together is not the anger, however. It is the fact that people try to avoid these sorts of situations. They tacitly recognize that we have to avoid these endless lines of questioning. Sometimes small children will start asking an endless series of "whys," but adults discourage this.

<u>In sum, any social arrangement works because people avoid questioning it most of the time.</u> That does not mean that people do not get into arguments or dispute about just what ought to be done from time to time. But to have a dispute already implies there is a considerable area of agreement. An office manager may dispute with a clerk over just how to take care of some business letter, but they at any rate know more or less what they are disputing about. They do not get off into a . . . series of questions over just what is meant by everything that is said. You could very quickly dissolve the organization into nothingness if you followed that route: there would be no communication at all, even about what the disagreement is over.

Social organization is possible because people maintain a certain level of focus. If they focus on one thing, even if only to disagree about it, they are taking many other things for granted, thereby reinforcing their social reality.

The statement that Peselman has underlined—"any social arrangement works because people avoid questioning it most of the time"—is the end result of an argument that takes Collins several paragraphs to develop.

Peselman agrees with the conclusion and uses it in ¶7 of his essay. Observe that for his own purposes Peselman does *not* reconstruct Collins's argument. He selects *only* Collins's conclusion and then imports that into his essay. Once he identifies in Collins a principle he can use in his analysis, he converts the principle into questions that he then directs to his topic: life in his freshman dorm. Two questions follow directly from Collins's insight:

1. What was the social arrangement in the dorm?
2. How was this social arrangement questioned?

Peselman clearly defines his dormitory's social arrangement in ¶s3–6 (with the help of another principle borrowed from Collins). Beginning with ¶7, he explores how one member of his dorm questioned that arrangement:

```
          That is, until he left mid-semester.
According to Collins, "any social arrangement
works because people avoid questioning it most of
the time" (p. 74). The inverse of this principle
is as follows: when a social arrangement is
questioned, that arrangement can fall apart. The
more fragile the arrangement (the flimsier the
values on which it is based), the more quickly it
will crumble. For the entire first semester, no
one questioned our rude, macho rules and because
of them we pigeon-holed Benjamin as a wimp. In
our dorm society, gentle men had no power. To say
the least, ours was not a compassionate
community. From a distance of one year, I am
shocked to have been a member of it. Nonetheless,
we had created a mini-society that somehow served
our needs.
```

Formulate a Thesis

An analysis is a two-part argument. The first part states and establishes the writer's agreement with a certain principle or definition.

PART ONE OF THE ARGUMENT

This first argument essentially takes this form:

Claim #1: Principle "X" (or definition "X") is valuable.

Principle "X" can be a theory as encompassing and abstract as the statement that *myths are the enemy of truth*. Principle "X" can be as modest as the definition of a term—for instance, "addiction" or "comfort." As you move from one subject area to another, the principles and definitions you use for analysis will change, as these assignments illustrate:

Sociology: Write a paper in which you place yourself in American society by locating both your absolute position and relative rank on each single criterion of social stratification used by Lenski & Lenski. For each criterion, state whether you have attained your social position by yourself or if you have "inherited" that status from your parents.

Literature: Apply principles of Jungian psychology to Hawthorne's "Young Goodman Brown." In your reading of the story, apply Jung's principles of the *shadow, persona,* and *anima.*

Physics: Use Newton's second law ($F = ma$) to analyze the acceleration of a fixed pulley, from which two weights hang: m_1 (.45 kg) and m_2 (.90 kg). Explain in a paragraph the principle of Newton's law and your method of applying it to solve the problem. Assume your reader is not comfortable with mathematical explanations: do not use equations in your paragraph.

Finance: Using Guidford C. Babcock's "Concept of Sustainable Growth" [*Financial Analysis* 26 (May–June 1970): 108–14], analyze the stock price appreciation of the XYZ Corporation, figures for which are attached.

The analytical tools to be applied in these assignments change from discipline to discipline. Writing in response to the sociology assignment, you would use sociological principles developed by Lenski and Lenski. In your literature class, you would use principles of Jungian psychology; in physics, Newton's second law; and in finance, a particular writer's concept of "sustainable growth." But whatever discipline you are working in, the first part of your analysis will clearly state which (and whose) principles and definitions you are applying. For audiences unfamiliar with these principles, you will need to explain them; if you anticipate objections, you will need to argue that they are legitimate principles capable of helping you as you conduct an analysis.

PART TWO OF THE ARGUMENT

In the second part of an analysis, you *apply* specific parts of your principle or definition to the topic at hand. Regardless of how it is worded, this second argument in an analysis can be rephrased to take this form:

> **Claim #2:** By applying Principle (or definition) "X," we can understand ___*(topic)*___ as ___*(conclusion based on analysis).*___

This is your thesis, the main idea of your analytical essay. Fill in the first blank with the specific object, event, or behavior you are examining. Fill in the second blank with your conclusion about the meaning or significance of this object, based on the insights made during your analysis. Marie Winn completes the second claim of her analysis this way:

GUIDELINES FOR WRITING ANALYSES

Unless you are asked to follow a specialized format, especially in the sciences or the social sciences, you can present your analysis as a paper by following the guidelines below. As you move from one class to another, from discipline to discipline, the principles and definitions you use as the basis for your analyses will change, but the following basic components of analysis will remain the same:

- Create a context for your analysis. Introduce and summarize for readers the object, event, or behavior to be analyzed. Present a strong case about why an analysis is needed: Give yourself a motivation to write, and give readers a motivation to read. Consider setting out a problem, puzzle, or question to be investigated.
- Introduce and summarize the key definition or principle that will form the basis of your analysis. Plan to devote the first part of your analysis to arguing for the validity of this principle or definition *if* your audience is not likely to understand it or if they are likely to think that the principle or definition is *not* valuable.
- Analyze your topic. Systematically apply elements of this definition or principle to parts of the activity or object under study. You can do this by posing specific questions, based on your analytic principle or definition, about the object. Discuss what you find part by part (organized, perhaps, by question), in clearly defined sections of the essay.
- Conclude by stating clearly what is significant about your analysis. When considering your essay as a whole, what new or interesting insights have you made concerning the object under study? To what extent has your application of the definition or principle helped you to explain how the object works, what it might mean, or why it is significant?

By applying my multipart definition, *television viewing* can be understood as *an addiction*.

Develop an Organizational Plan

You will benefit enormously in the writing of a first draft if you plan out the logic of your analysis. You will want to turn key elements of your analytical principle or definition into questions and then develop the paragraph-by-paragraph logic of the paper.

TURNING KEY ELEMENTS OF A PRINCIPLE OR DEFINITION INTO QUESTIONS

Prepare for an analysis by developing questions based on the definition or principle you are going to apply, and then by directing these questions to the activity or object to be studied. The method is straightforward: State as clearly as possible the principle or definition to be applied. Divide the principle or definition into its parts and, using each part, develop a question. For example, Marie Winn develops a multipart definition of addiction, each part of which is readily turned into a question that she directs at a specific behavior: television viewing. Her analysis of television viewing can be understood as *responses* to each of her analytical questions. Note that in her brief analysis, Winn does not first define addiction and then analyze television viewing. Rather, *as* she defines aspects of addiction, she analyzes television viewing.

DEVELOPING THE PARAGRAPH-BY-PARAGRAPH LOGIC OF YOUR PAPER

The following paragraph from Edward Peselman's essay illustrates the typical logic of a paragraph in an analytical essay:

> Up and down the pecking order, we exercised
> control through macho taunts and challenges.
> Collins writes that "individuals who manage to be
> powerful and get their own way must do so by
> going along with the laws of social organization,
> not by contradicting them" (p. 61). Until mid
> year, our dorm motto could have read: "You win
> through rudeness and intimidation." Eric gained
> power with his frequent and brutal assessments of
> everyone's behavior. Marc gained power with his
> temper—which, when lost, made everyone run for
> cover. Those who were not rude and intimidating
> drifted to the bottom of our social world. Reggie
> was quiet and unemotional, which allowed us to
> take advantage of him because we knew he would
> back down if pressed in an argument. Yet Reggie
> understood that on a "power scale" he stood above
> Dozer and often shared in the group's tactics to
> get Dozer's food (his parents were forever
> sending him care packages). Dozer, in turn,
> seldom missed opportunities to take swipes at
> Benjamin, with references to his sexuality. From
> the very first week of school, Benjamin could
> never—and never wanted to—compete against Eric's
> bluntness or Marc's temper. Still, Benjamin hung
> out with us. He lived in our corner of the dorm,
> and he wanted to be friendly. But everyone,
> including Benjamin, understood that he occupied
> the lowest spot in the order.

We see in this example paragraph the typical logic of analysis.

The writer introduces a specific analytical tool.   Peselman quotes a line from Randall Collins:

"[I]ndividuals who manage to be powerful and get their own way must do so by going along with the laws of social organization, not by contradicting them."

The writer applies this analytical tool to the object being examined. Peselman states *his* dorm's law of social organization:

Until mid year, our dorm motto could have read: "You win through rudeness and intimidation."

The writer uses the tool to identify and then examine the meaning of parts of the object.   Peselman shows how each member (the "parts") of his dorm society conforms to the laws of "social organization":

Eric gained power with his frequent and brutal assessments of everyone's behavior. Marc gained power with his temper—which, when lost, made everyone run for cover. Those who were not rude and intimidating drifted to the bottom of our social world. . . .

An analytical paper takes shape when a writer creates a series of such paragraphs and then links them with an overall logic. Here is the logical organization of Edward Peselman's paper:

¶1:   Introduction states a problem—provides a motivation to write and to read.

¶2:   Randall Collins is introduced—the author whose work will provide principles for analysis.

¶s3–4:   Background information is provided—the cast of characters in the dorm.

¶s5–9:   The analysis proceeds—specific parts of dorm life are identified and found significant, using principles from Collins.

¶s10–11:   Summary and conclusion are provided—the freshman dorm society disintegrated for reasons set out in the analysis. A larger point is made: Some oppressive systems must be torn down.

Draft and Revise Your Analysis

You will usually need at least two drafts to produce a paper that presents your idea clearly. The biggest changes in your paper will typically come between your first and second drafts. No paper that you write, including an analysis, will be complete until you revise and refine your single compelling idea: your analytical conclusion about what the object, event, or behavior being examined means or how it is significant. You revise and refine by evaluating your first draft, bringing to it many of the same questions you pose when evaluating any piece of writing, including these:

- Are the facts accurate?
- Are my opinions supported by evidence?
- Are the opinions of others authoritative?
- Are my assumptions clearly stated?
- Are key terms clearly defined?
- Is the presentation logical?
- Are all parts of the presentation well developed?
- Are dissenting points of view presented?

Address these same questions to the first draft of your analysis, and you will have solid information to guide your revision.

WRITE AN ANALYSIS, NOT A SUMMARY

The most common error made in writing analyses—which is *fatal* to the form—is to present readers with a summary only. For analyses to succeed, you must *apply* a principle or definition and reach a conclusion about the object, event, or behavior you are examining. By definition, a summary (see Chapter 1) includes none of your own conclusions. Summary is naturally a part of analysis; you will need to summarize the object or activity being examined and, depending on the audience's needs, summarize the principle or definition being applied. But in an analysis, you must take the next step and share insights that suggest the meaning or significance of some object, event, or behavior.

MAKE YOUR ANALYSIS SYSTEMATIC

Analyses should give the reader the sense of a systematic, purposeful examination. Marie Winn's analysis illustrates the point: She sets out specific elements of addictive behavior in separate paragraphs and then uses each, within its paragraph, to analyze television viewing. Winn is systematic in her method, and we are never in doubt about her purpose.

Imagine another analysis in which a writer lays out four elements of a definition but then applies only two, without explaining the logic for omitting the others. Or imagine an analysis in which the writer offers a principle for analysis but directs it to only a half or a third of the object being discussed, without providing a rationale for doing so. In both cases, the writer would be failing to deliver on a promise basic to analyses: Once a principle or definition is presented, it should be thoroughly and systematically applied.

ANSWER THE "SO WHAT" QUESTION

An analysis should make readers *want* to read. It should give readers a sense of getting to the heart of the matter, that what is important in the object or activity under analysis is being laid bare and discussed in revealing ways. If when rereading the first draft of your essay, you cannot imagine readers saying, "I never thought of ____ this way," then something may be seriously wrong. Reread closely to determine why the paper might leave readers flat and exhausted, as opposed to feeling that they have gained new and important insights. Closely reexamine your own motivations for writing. Have *you* learned anything significant through the analysis? If not, neither will readers, and they will turn away. If you have gained important insights through your analysis, communicate them clearly. At some point, pull together your related insights and say, in effect: "Here's how it all adds up."

ATTRIBUTE SOURCES APPROPRIATELY

By nature of the form, in an analysis you work with one or two sources and apply insights from those to some object or phenomenon you want to understand more thoroughly. Because you are not synthesizing a great many sources, and because the strength of an analysis derives mostly from *your* application of a principle or definition, the opportunities for not appropriately citing sources are diminished. Take special care to cite and quote, as necessary, the one or two sources you use throughout the analysis.

CRITICAL READING FOR ANALYSIS

- **Read to get a sense of the whole in relation to its parts.** Whether you are clarifying for yourself a principle or definition to be used in an analysis, or are reading a text that you will analyze, understand how parts function to create the whole. If a definition or principle consists of parts, use these to organize sections of your analysis. If your goal is to analyze a text, be aware of its structure: note the title and subtitle; identify the main point and subordinate points and where they are located; break the material into sections.
- **Read to discover relationships within the object being analyzed.** Watch for patterns. When you find them, be alert—for you create an occasion to analyze, to use a principle or definition as a guide in discussing what the pattern may mean.

In fiction, a pattern might involve responses of characters to events or to each other, recurrence of certain words or phrasings, images, themes, or turns of plot, to name a few.

In poetry, a pattern might involve rhyme schemes, rhythm, imagery, figurative or literal language, and more.

Your challenge as a reader is first to see a pattern (perhaps using a guiding principle or definition to do so) and then to locate other instances of that pattern. By reading carefully in this way, you prepare yourself to conduct an analysis.

Writing Assignment: Analysis

Read the following passage, "A Theory of Human Motivation" by Abraham Maslow. Then write a paper using Maslow's theory as an analytical tool, applying what he says about human motivation to some element of your own reading, knowledge, or personal experience. You may wish to use Edward Peselman's analysis of Randall Collins's theories as a model for your own paper. (More specific suggestions follow the passage.)

Abraham Maslow (1908–1970) was one of the most influential humanistic psychologists of the twentieth century. He earned his PhD at the University of Wisconsin and spent most of his academic career at Brandeis University in Waltham, Massachusetts. Maslow's theories have been widely applied in business, the military, and academia. His books include *Motivation and Psychology* (1954) and *Toward a Psychology of Being* (1962). This selection is excerpted from an article that first appeared in *Psychological Review* 50 (1943): 371–96.

A Theory of Human Motivation
Abraham H. Maslow

The Basic Needs

1   *The "physiological" needs*   The needs that are usually taken as the starting point for motivation theory are the so-called physiological drives. . . .

2   [A]ny of the physiological needs . . . serve as channels for all sorts of other needs as well. That is to say, the person who thinks he is hungry may actually be seeking more for comfort, or dependence, than for vitamins or proteins. Conversely, it is possible to satisfy the hunger need in part by other activities such as drinking water or smoking cigarettes. . . .

3   Undoubtedly these physiological needs . . . exceed all others in power. What this means specifically is, that in the human being who is missing everything in life in an extreme fashion, it is most likely that the major motivation would be the physiological needs rather than any others. A person who is lacking food, safety, love, and esteem would most probably hunger for food more strongly than for anything else.

4   Obviously a good way to obscure the "higher" motivations, and to get a lopsided view of human capacities and human nature, is to make the organism extremely and chronically hungry or thirsty. Anyone who attempts to make an emergency picture into a typical one, and who will measure all of man's goals and desires by his behavior during extreme physiological deprivation is certainly being blind to many things. It is quite true that man lives by bread alone—when there is no bread. But what happens to man's desires when there is plenty of bread and when his belly is chronically filled?

5   At once other (and "higher") needs emerge and these, rather than physiological hungers, dominate the organism. And when these in turn are satisfied, again new (and still "higher") needs emerge and so on. This is what we mean by saying that the basic human needs are organized into a hierarchy of relative prepotency.

6   One main implication of this phrasing is that gratification becomes as important a concept as deprivation in motivation theory, for it releases the organism from the domination of a relatively more physiological need, permitting thereby the emergence of other more social goals. The physiological needs, along with their partial goals, when chronically gratified cease to exist as active determinants or organizers of behavior. They now exist only in a potential fashion in the sense that they may emerge again to dominate the organism if they are thwarted. But a want that is satisfied is no longer a want. The organism is dominated and its behavior organized only by unsatisfied needs. If hunger is satisfied, it becomes unimportant in the current dynamics of the individual.

7   *The safety needs*   If the physiological needs are relatively well gratified, there then emerges a new set of needs, which we may categorize roughly as the safety needs. All that has been said of the physiological needs is equally true, although in lesser degree, of these desires. The organism may equally well be wholly dominated by them. They may serve as the almost exclusive organizers of behavior, recruiting all the capacities of the organism in their service, and we may then fairly

describe the whole organism as a safety-seeking mechanism. Again we may say of the receptors, the effectors, of the intellect and the other capacities that they are primarily safety-seeking tools. Again, as in the hungry man, we find that the dominating goal [strongly determines] not only of his current world-outlook and philosophy but also of his philosophy of the future. Practically everything looks less important than safety (even sometimes the physiological needs which being satisfied, are now underestimated). A man, in this state, if it is extreme enough and chronic enough, may be characterized as living almost for safety alone. . . .

8   The healthy, normal, fortunate adult in our culture is largely satisfied in his safety needs. The peaceful, smoothly running, 'good' society ordinarily makes its members feel safe enough from wild animals, extremes of temperature, criminals, assault and murder, tyranny, etc. Therefore, in a very real sense, he no longer has any safety needs as active motivators. Just as a sated man no longer feels hungry a safe man no longer feels endangered. If we wish to see these needs directly and clearly we must turn to neurotic or near-neurotic individuals, and to the economic and social underdogs. In between these extremes, we can perceive the expressions of safety needs only in such phenomena as, for instance, the common preference for a job with tenure and protection, the desire for a savings account, and for insurance of various kinds (medical, dental, unemployment, disability, old age).

8   Other broader aspects of the attempt to seek safety and stability in the world are seen in the very common preference for familiar rather than unfamiliar things, or for the known rather than the unknown. The tendency to have some religion or world-philosophy that organizes the universe and the men in it into some sort of satisfactorily coherent, meaningful whole is also in part motivated by safety-seeking. Here too we may list science and philosophy in general as partially motivated by the safety needs.

10   ***The love needs***   If both the physiological and the safety needs are fairly well gratified, then there will emerge the love and affection and belongingness needs, and the whole cycle already described will repeat itself with this new center. Now the person will feel keenly, as never before, the absence of friends, or a sweetheart, or a wife, or children. He will hunger for affectionate relations with people in general, namely, for a place in his group, and he will strive with great intensity to achieve this goal. He will want to attain such a place more than anything else in the world and may even forget that once, when he was hungry he sneered at love. . . .

11   One thing that must be stressed at this point is that love is not synonymous with sex. Sex may be studied as a purely physiological need. Ordinarily sexual behavior is multi-determined, that is to say, determined not only by sexual but also by other needs, chief among which are the love and affection needs. Also not to be overlooked is the fact that the love needs involve both giving and receiving love.

12   ***The esteem needs***   All people in our society (with a few pathological exceptions) have a need or desire for a stable, firmly based, (usually) high evaluation of themselves, for self-respect, or self-esteem, and for the esteem of others. By firmly based self-esteem, we mean that which is soundly based upon . . . achievement and respect from others. These needs may be classified into two subsidiary sets. These are, first, the desire for strength, for achievement, for

adequacy, for confidence in the face of the world, and for independence and freedom. Secondly, we have what we may call the desire for reputation or prestige (defining it as respect or esteem from other people), recognition, attention, importance or appreciation. . . .

13   Satisfaction of the self-esteem need leads to feelings of self-confidence, worth, strength, capability and adequacy of being useful and necessary in the world. But thwarting of these needs produces feelings of inferiority, of weakness and of helplessness. These feelings in turn give rise to either basic discouragement or else compensatory or neurotic trends. An appreciation of the necessity of basic self-confidence and an understanding of how helpless people are without it, can be easily gained from a study of severe traumatic neurosis.

14   *The need for self-actualization*   Even if all these needs are satisfied, we may still often (if not always) expect that a new discontent and restlessness will soon develop, unless the individual is doing what he is fitted for. A musician must make music, an artist must paint, a poet must write, if he is to be ultimately happy. What a man can be, he must be. This need we may call self-actualization.

15   This term . . . refers to the desire for self-fulfillment, namely, to the tendency for him to become actualized in what he is potentially. This tendency might be phrased as the desire to become more and more what one is, to become everything that one is capable of becoming.

16   The specific form that these needs will take will of course vary greatly from person to person. In one individual it may take the form of the desire to be an ideal mother, in another it may be expressed athletically, and in still another it may be expressed in painting pictures or in inventions. It is not necessarily a creative urge although in people who have any capacities for creation it will take this form.*

17   The clear emergence of these needs rests upon prior satisfaction of the physiological, safety, love and esteem needs. We shall call people who are satisfied in these needs, basically satisfied people, and it is from these that we may expect the fullest (and healthiest) creativeness. Since, in our society, basically satisfied people are the exception, we do not know much about self-actualization, either experimentally or clinically. It remains a challenging problem for research. . . .

Further Characteristics of the Basic Needs

The degree of fixity of the hierarchy of basic needs   We have spoken so far
18 as if this hierarchy were a fixed order but actually it is not nearly as rigid as we may have implied. It is true that most of the people with whom we have worked have seemed to have these basic needs in about the order that has been indicated. However, there have been a number of exceptions.

Degrees of relative satisfaction   So far, our theoretical discussion may have given the impression that these five sets of needs are somehow in a step-wise,

---

* In another section of his article Maslow considers the human "desires to know and to understand" as "in part, techniques for the achievement of basic safety in the world," and in part, "expressions of self-actualization." Maslow also indicates that "freedom of inquiry and expression" are "preconditions of satisfactions of the basic needs." [Eds.]

19 all-or-none relationships to each other. We have spoken in such terms as the following: "If one need is satisfied, then another emerges." This statement might give the false impression that a need must be satisfied 100 percent before the next need emerges. In actual fact, most members of our society who are normal, are partially satisfied in all their basic needs and partially unsatisfied in all their basic needs at the same time. A more realistic description of the hierarchy would be in terms of decreasing percentages of satisfaction as we go up the hierarchy of prepotency. For instance, if I may assign arbitrary figures for the sake of illustration, it is as if the average citizen is satisfied perhaps 85 percent in his physiological needs, 70 percent in his safety needs, 50 percent in his love needs, 40 percent in his self-esteem needs, and 10 percent in his self-actualization needs.

20 As for the concept of emergence of a new need after satisfaction of the prepotent need, this emergence is not a sudden salutatory phenomenon but rather a gradual emergence by slow degrees from nothingness. For instance, if . . . need A is satisfied only 10 percent then need B may not be visible at all. However, as this need A becomes satisfied 25 percent, need B may emerge 5 percent, as need A becomes satisfied 75 percent need B may emerge 90 percent, and so on.

21 ***Unconscious character of needs***   These needs are neither necessarily conscious nor unconscious. On the whole, however, in the average person, they are more often unconscious rather than conscious. It is not necessary at this point to overhaul the tremendous mass of evidence which indicates the crucial importance of unconscious motivation. It would by now be expected . . . that unconscious motivations would on the whole be rather more important than the conscious motivations. What we have called the basic needs are very often largely unconscious although they may, with suitable techniques, and with sophisticated people, become conscious. . . .

22 ***Multiple motivations of behavior***   These needs must be understood not to be exclusive or single determiners of certain kinds of behavior. An example may be found in any behavior that seems to be physiologically motivated, such as eating, or sexual play or the like. The clinical psychologists have long since found that any behavior may be a channel through which flow various determinants. Or to say it in another way, most behavior is multi-motivated. Within the sphere of motivational determinants any behavior tends to be determined by several or all of the basic needs simultaneously rather than by only one of them. The latter would be more an exception than the former. Eating may be partially for the sake of filling the stomach, and partially for the sake' of comfort and amelioration of other needs. One may make love not only for pure sexual release, but also to convince one's self of one's masculinity: or to make a conquest, to feel powerful, or to win more basic affection. As an illustration, I may point out that it would be possible (theoretically if not practically) to analyze a single act of an individual and see in it the expression of his physiological needs, his safety needs, his love needs, his esteem needs and self-actualization.

References

Cannon, W. B. (1932). *Wisdom of the body*. New York: Norton.
Kardiner. A. (1941). *The traumatic neuroses of war*. New York: Hoeber.

Young, P. (1936). *Motivation of behavior.* New York: Wiley.
———. (1941). The experimental analysis of appetite. *Psychology Bulletin,* 38, 129–164.

In his final sentence, Maslow himself points the way to a potentially productive analysis using his hierarchy of needs: "I may point out that it would be possible (theoretically if not practically) to analyze a single act of an individual and see in it the expression of his physiological needs, his safety needs, his love needs, his esteem needs and self-actualization." One way, then, of conceiving your analysis is as follows: Choose a single act—yours or anyone's—and analyze it according to Maslow's system. You might begin by introducing the person and setting a context for the act; introducing Maslow's hierarchy, and then proceeding with the analysis itself as you apply one element of the hierarchy at a time. Use each element as a lens through which you look and see the act in a new or revealing way. As you conduct your analysis, recall Maslow's caution: that single acts will typically have "multiple motivations."

ANALYZING VISUAL MEDIA

Some people believe that visual literacy—that is, the ability to read and understand visual artifacts, such as painting, architecture, film, and graphic arts (including Web design)—will be as important in the twenty-first century as textual literacy was in earlier times. While this may be an extreme view, there's no denying that in this multimedia age, interpreting visual media is a vital skill. And of the various forms of visual media, advertising is perhaps the most omnipresent.

Scholars in the humanities and social sciences study advertising from a number of angles: In the fields of cultural studies, literary studies, and American studies, scholars interpret the messages of advertisements much as they do the messages and meanings of artifacts from "high culture," such as literature and art. In opposition to high culture, advertisements (along with television shows, films, and the like) are considered examples of "popular culture" (or "pop culture"), and in the past 20 years or so, the study of these highly pervasive and influential works has attracted academic attention. Scholars in the fields of sociology, communications, and anthropology are also interested in studying pop cultural artifacts, since they exert such powerful influences on our lives.

Analysis of advertisements has therefore become a fairly common practice in academia. Let's now take the analytical thinking skills we used in analysis of a social situation (the subject of the Peselman paper), and apply them to print advertisements. In this case, rather than lead you through the analytical process, we will show you several advertisements, along with two critical approaches to analyzing advertisements, and then ask you to perform your own analysis of the ads' features, thereby arriving at a sense of their overall meaning or significance.

Writing Assignment: Analyzing Visual Media

Following are three advertisements. The first was created to promote Fancy Feast cat food; the second was created to promote Bernstein's Italian Salad Dressing and Marinade and Deming's Red Sockeye Salmon; and the third advertises G.E. Monogram kitchen appliances. Study the illustrations and the text in the ads. Then read the two selections following. The first, Roland Marchand's "The Appeal of the Democracy of Goods," from his 1985 book *Advertising the American Dream,* describes a common theme underlying many advertisements. The second, Dorothy Cohen's "Elements of an Effective Layout," offers a number of guiding principles for assessing the layout of visual elements in print advertising.

In addition to Cohen's principles, consider some of the following questions concerning the particular ad on which you focus.

- What is depicted in the ad's images?
- What is the ad's text?
- How do text and images relate to each other in creating the ad's meaning?
- How are shading/font styles used?
- How are words and various images in the ad placed in relation to one another, and how do these spatial relationships create meaning?
- What is the mood—i.e., the emotional output—of the ad? How does this mood help create the ad's meaning?
- How does the ad allude to images/ideas/events/trends from our knowledge of the contemporary world?

Choose one or more of these advertisements and the passage by *either* Cohen *or* Marchand. Use the principles presented in the passage you have selected to analyze the ad or ads of your choice. Apply the principles of analytical reasoning demonstrated in the analysis by Edward Peselman in the first part of this chapter. That is, apply one or more of the principles explained in the article to the subject of study—in this case, one or more advertisements. Develop your analysis in a well-organized, well-developed paper. (*Note:* Before attempting this assignment, you may want to "limber up" by completing Exercise 6.3 on page 273.)

For a more ambitious version of this paper, you might consider using *two* or even *three* ads as the subject of your paper. (Review the principles of comparison and contrast in Chapter 5 (pp. 232–44). And for an even more ambitious assignment, you could perform a complex analysis, applying both Marchand's *and* Cohen's principles to one or more ads. That is, show how (a) the graphic elements of the ad and (b) its underlying message work to create a unified effect on readers, influencing them to want to buy the product(s) being advertised.

Get away from mundane meals. Enjoy a light picnic dinner with a classic Salmon Waldorf Salad and pocket bread sandwiches featuring Deming's Red Sockeye Salmon and Bernstein's Italian Dressing & Marinade.

With Bernstein's and Deming's, you can economize with impeccable taste. Both Bernstein's Italian Dressing & Marinade and Deming's Red Sockeye Salmon are 100% natural and nutritious.

Bernstein's is made with the purest oils and vinegars, the freshest garlic and a touch of real vino. Deming's premiere quality Red Sockeye salmon is caught in the icy waters of Alaska and packed fresh. Together they're marvelous.

Look for the Bernstein's & Deming's display at your favorite food store and take home a copy of these other fine recipes: Salmon Potato Casserole, Salmon Pasta Salad, Salmonburger Supreme, and Salmon Antipasto.

Economize
without compromise.

90th FL 10 RMS W VU.   NEW YORK AT YOUR FEET.
$17 MILLION.

SO WHAT'S COOKING IN THE KITCHEN ?

In this unoccupied 90th floor penthouse, there's a
GE Monogram kitchen.
Every other apartment in this, the tallest residential
building in the world, has a GE Monogram kitchen, too.
Interested parties, please contact Mr. Trump personally.

GE Monogram
Visit monogram.com

imagination at work

Analyzing an Advertisement

As a preliminary exercise prior to writing the paper, work through the questions listed above (p. 269), answering them in as much detail as you can. Then use your answers, along with some of the analytical principles described by Cohen or Marchand, to write a paragraph proposing an overall interpretation of the ad's message.

An alternate exercise: Look through a popular magazine and find an ad that interests you—for whatever reason—and analyze the ad's features, using the questions above and some of the principles discussed by Cohen. Remember to be critical and detailed as you take apart the ad's elements and ultimately put them back together to arrive at an interpretation of the ad's message. Describe both its explicit message (usually just "buy this product") as well as any implicit or covert messages about what kind of person the product might help you become, or what kinds of values the ad is portraying as desirable.

The Appeal of the Democracy of Goods
Roland Marchand

Roland Marchand is a professor of history at the University of California, Davis. The following selection originally appeared in Marchand's 1985 book Advertising the American Dream: Making Way for Modernity 1920–1940.

1   As they opened their September 1929 issue, readers of the *Ladies Home Journal* were treated to an account of the care and feeding of young Livingston Ludlow Biddle III, son and heir of the wealthy Biddles of Philadelphia, whose family coat-of-arms graced the upper right-hand corner of the page. Young Master Biddle, mounted on his tricycle, fixed a serious, slightly pouting gaze upon the reader, while the Cream of Wheat Corporation rapturously explained his constant care, his carefully regulated play and exercise, and the diet prescribed for him by "famous specialists." As master of Sunny Ridge Farm, the Biddle's winter estate in North Carolina, young Livingston III had "enjoyed every luxury of social position and wealth, since the day he was born." Yet, by the grace of a . . . modern providence, it happened that Livingston's health was protected by "a simple plan every mother can use." Mrs. Biddle gave Cream of Wheat to the young heir for both breakfast and supper. The world's foremost child experts knew of no better diet; great wealth could procure no finer nourishment. Cream of Wheat summarized the central point of the advertisement by claiming that "every mother can give her youngsters the fun and benefits of a Cream of Wheat

breakfast just as do the parents of these boys and girls who have the best that wealth can command."

2   While enjoying this glimpse of childrearing among the socially distinguished, *Ladies Home Journal* readers found themselves drawn in by one of the most pervasive of all advertising strategies of the 1920's—the concept of the Democracy of Goods. According to this idea, the wonders of modern mass production and distribution enabled everyone to enjoy society's most desirable pleasures, conveniences, or benefits. The particular pleasure, benefit, or convenience varied, of course, with each advertiser who used the formula. But the cumulative effect of the constant reminders that "any woman can . . ." and "every home can afford . . ." was to publicize an image of American society in which concentrated wealth at the top of a hierarchy of social classes restricted no family's opportunity to acquire the most desirable products. By implicitly defining "democracy" in terms of equal access to consumer products, these advertisements offered Americans an inviting vision of their society as one of incontestable equality.

3   In its most common advertising formula, the concept of the Democracy of Goods asserted that although the rich enjoyed a great variety of luxuries, the acquisition of their *one* most precious luxury would provide anyone with the ultimate in satisfaction. For instance, a Chase and Sanborn's Coffee advertisement, with an elegant butler serving a family in a dining room with a sixteen-foot ceiling, reminded Chicago families that although "compared with the riches of the more fortunate, your way of life may seem modest indeed," yet no one—"king, prince, statesman, or capitalist"—could enjoy better coffee. The Association of Soap and Glycerine Producers proclaimed that the charm of cleanliness was as readily available to the poor as to the rich, and Ivory Soap reassuringly related how one young housewife, who couldn't afford a $780-a-year maid like her neighbor, still maintained "nice hands" by using Ivory. The C. F. Church Manufacturing Company epitomized this feature of the Democracy of Goods technique in an ad entitled "a bathroom luxury everyone can afford": "If you lived in one of those palatial apartments on Park Avenue, in New York City, where you have to pay $2,000 to $7,000 a year rent, you still couldn't have a better toilet seat in your bathroom than they have—the Church Sani-white Toilet Seat, which you can afford to have right now."

4   Thus, according to the concept of the Democracy of Goods, no differences in wealth could prevent the humblest citizens, provided they chose their purchases wisely, from coming home to a setting in which they could contemplate their essential equality, through possession of a particular product, with the nation's millionaires. In 1929, Howard Dickinson, a contributor to *Printers' Ink,* concisely expressed the social psychology behind Democracy of Goods advertisements: "With whom do the mass of people think they want to foregather?' asks the psychologist in advertising. 'Why, with the wealthy and socially distinguished, of course!' If we can't get an invitation to tea for our millions of customers, we can at least present the fellowship of using the same brand of merchandise. And it works."

Elements of an Effective Layout
Dorothy Cohen

This passage orignally appeared in Dorothy Cohen's Advertising *(1988).*

1 Fundamentally a good layout should attract attention and interest and should provide some control over the manner in which the advertisement is read. The message to be communicated may be sincere, relevant, and important to the consumer, but because of the competitive "noise" in the communication channel, the opportunity to be heard may depend on the effectiveness of the layout. In addition to attracting attention, the most important requisites for an effective layout are balance, proportion, movement, utility, clarity, and emphasis.

Balance

2 Balance is a fundamental law in nature and its application to layout design formulates one of the basic principles of this process. Balance is a matter of weight distribution; in layout it is keyed to the *optical center* of an advertisement, the point which the reader's eye designates as the center of an area. In an advertisement a vertical line which divides the area into right and left halves contains the center; however the optical center is between one-tenth and one-third the distance above the mathematical horizontal center line. . . .

3   In order to provide good artistic composition, the elements in the layout must be in equilibrium. Equilibrium can be achieved through balance, and this process may be likened to the balancing of a seesaw. The optical center of the advertisement serves as the fulcrum or balancing point, and the elements may be balanced on both sides of this fulcrum through considerations of their size and tonal quality.

4   The simplest way to ensure formal balance between the elements to the right and left of the vertical line is to have all masses in the left duplicated on the right in size, weight, and distance from the center. . . . Formal balance imparts feelings of dignity, solidity, refinement, and reserve. It has been used for institutional advertising and suggests conservatism on the part of the advertiser. Its major deficiency is that it may present a static and somewhat unexciting appearance; however, formal balance presents material in an easy-to-follow order and works well for many ads.

5   To understand informal balance, think of children of unequal weight balanced on a seesaw; to ensure equilibrium it is necessary to place the smaller child far from the center and the larger child closer to the fulcrum. In informal balance the elements are balanced, but not evenly, because of different sizes and color contrast. This type of a symmetric balance requires care so that the various elements do not create a lopsided or top-heavy appearance. A knowledge or a sense of the composition can help create the feeling of symmetry in what is essentially asymmetric balance.

6   Informal balance presents a fresh, untraditional approach. It creates excitement, a sense of originality, forcefulness, and, to some extent, the element of surprise. Whereas formal balance may depend on the high interest value of the illustration to attract the reader, informal balance may attract attention through the design of the layout. . . .

Proportion

7   Proportion helps develop order and creates a pleasing impression. It is related to balance but is concerned primarily with the division of the space and the emphasis to be accorded each element. Proportion, to the advertising designer, is the relationship between the size of one element in the ad to another, the amount of space between elements, as well as the width of the total ad to its depth. Proportion also involves the tone of the ad: the amount of light area in relation to dark area and the amount of color and noncolor.[*]

8   As a general rule unequal dimensions and distances make the most lively design in advertising. The designer also places the elements on the page so that each element is given space and position in proportion to its importance in the total advertisement and does not look like it stands alone.

Movement

9   If an advertisement is to appear dynamic rather than static, it must contain some movement. *Movement* (also called *sequence)* provides the directional flow for the advertisement, gives it its follow-through, and provides coherence. It guides the reader's eye from one element to another and makes sure he or she does not miss anything.

10   Motion in layout is generally from left to right and from top to bottom—the direction established through the reading habits of speakers of Western language. The directional impetus should not disturb the natural visual flow but should favor the elements to be stressed, while care should be taken not to direct the reader's eye out of the advertisement. This can be done by the following:

- *Gaze motion* directs the reader's attention by directing the looks of the people or animals in an ad. If a subject is gazing at a unit in the layout, the natural tendency is for the reader to follow the direction of that gaze; if someone is looking directly out of the advertisement, the reader may stop to see who's staring.

- *Structural motion* incorporates the lines of direction and patterns of movement by mechanical means. An obvious way is to use an arrow or a pointed finger. . . .

Unity

11   Another important design principle is the unification of the layout. Although an advertisement is made up of many elements, all of these should be welded into a compact composition. Unity is achieved when the elements tie into one another by using the same basic shapes, sizes, textures, colors, and mood. In addition, the type should have the same character as the art.

12   A *border* surrounding an ad provides a method of achieving unity. Sets of borders may occur within an ad, and, when they are similar in thickness and tone, they provide a sense of unity.

13   Effective use of white space can help to establish unity. . . . *White space* is defined as that part of the advertising space which is not occupied by any other elements; in this definition, white space is not always white in color. White space may be used to feature an important element by setting it off, or to imply luxury and prestige by preventing a crowded appearance. It may be used to direct and control the reader's attention by tying elements together. If white space is used incorrectly, it may cause separation of the elements and create difficulty in viewing the advertisement as a whole.

Clarity and Simplicity

14 The good art director does not permit a layout to become too complicated or tricky. An advertisement should retain its clarity and be easy to read and easy to understand. The reader tends to see the total image of an advertisement; thus it should not appear fussy, contrived, or confusing. Color contrasts, including tones of gray, should be strong enough to be easily deciphered, and the various units should be clear and easy to understand. Type size and design should be selected for ease of reading, and lines of type should be a comfortable reading length. Too many units in an advertisement are distracting; therefore, any elements that can be eliminated without destroying the message should be. One way in which clarity can be achieved is by combining the logo, trademark, tag line, and company name into one compact group.

Emphasis

15 Although varying degrees of emphasis may be given to different elements, one unit should dominate. It is the designer's responsibility to determine how much emphasis is necessary, as well as how it is to be achieved. The important element may be placed in the optical center or removed from the clutter of other elements. Emphasis may also be achieved by contrasts in size, shape, and color, or the use of white space.

---

* Roy Paul Nelson, *The Design of Advertising*, 4th ed. (Dubuque, IA: Wm. C. Brown Co., 1981), 18.

ANALYSIS: A TOOL FOR UNDERSTANDING

As this chapter has demonstrated, analysis involves applying principles as a way to probe and understand. With incisive principles guiding your analysis, you will be able to pose questions, observe patterns and relationships, and derive meaning. Do not forget that this meaning will be one of several possible meanings. Someone else, possibly you, using different analytical tools could observe the same phenomena and arrive at very different conclusions regarding meaning or significance. We end the chapter, therefore, as we began it: with the two brief analyses of *The Wizard of Oz*. The conclusions expressed in one look nothing like the conclusions expressed in the other, save for the fact that both seek to interpret the same movie. And yet we can say that both are useful. Both reveal meaning:

> At the dawn of adolescence, the very time she should start to distance herself from Aunt Em and Uncle Henry, the surrogate parents who raised her on their Kansas farm, Dorothy Gale experiences a hurtful reawakening of her fear that these loved ones will be rudely ripped from her, especially her Aunt (Em—M for Mother!). [Harvey Greenberg, *The Movies on Your Mind* (New York: Dutton, 1975]

> [*The Wizard of Oz*] was originally written as a political allegory about grass-roots protest. It may seem harder to believe than Emerald City, but the Tin Woodsman is the industrial worker, the Scarecrow [is] the struggling farmer, and the Wizard is the president, who is powerful only as long as he succeeds in deceiving the people. [Peter Dreier, "Oz Was Almost Reality," *Cleveland Plain Dealer* 3 Sept. 1989]

You have seen in this chapter how it is possible for two writers, analyzing the same object or phenomenon but applying different analytical principles, to reach vastly different conclusions about what the object or phenomenon may mean or why it is significant. *The Wizard of Oz* is both an inquiry into the psychology of adolescence and a political allegory. What else the classic film may be awaits revealing with the systematic application of other analytical tools. The insights you gain as a writer of analyses depend entirely on your choice of tool and the subtlety with which you apply it.

7

Locating, Mining, and Citing Sources

SOURCE-BASED PAPERS

Summaries, critiques, and analyses are generally based on only one or two sources. Syntheses, by contrast (and by definition), are based on multiple sources. But whatever you call the final product, the quality of your paper will be directly related to your success in locating and using a sufficient quantity of relevant, significant, reliable, and up-to-date sources.

Research involves many of the skills we have been discussing in this book. It requires you to (1) locate and take notes on relevant sources; (2) organize your findings; (3) summarize, paraphrase, or quote these sources accurately and ethically; (4) critically evaluate them for their value and relevance to your subject; (5) synthesize information and ideas from several sources that best support your own critical viewpoint; and (6) analyze subjects for meaning and significance.

The model argument synthesis in Chapter 5, "Keeping Volunteering Voluntary" (pp. 217–24) is an example of a research paper that fulfills these requirements.

THE RESEARCH QUESTION

Research handbooks generally advise students to narrow their subjects as much as possible, as we discussed in Chapter 3. A ten-page paper on the modern feminist movement would be unmanageable. You would have to do an enormous quantity of research (a preliminary computer search of this subject would yield several thousand items), and you couldn't hope to produce anything other than a superficial treatment of such a broad subject. You could, however, write a paper on the

---

> ## WHERE DO WE FIND WRITTEN RESEARCH?
>
> *Here are just a few types of writing that involve research:*
>
> ### Academic Writing
>
> - **Research papers.** Research an issue and write a paper incorporating the results of that research.
> - **Literature reviews.** Research and review relevant studies and approaches to a particular science or social-science topic.
> - **Experimental reports.** Research previous studies in order to refine—or show need for—your current approach; conduct primary research.
> - **Case studies.** Conduct both primary and secondary research.
> - **Position papers.** Research approaches to an issue in order to formulate your own approach.
>
> ### Workplace Writing
>
> - Reports in business, science, engineering, social services, medicine
> - Market analyses
> - Business plans
> - Environmental impact reports
> - Legal research: memorandum of points and authorities

contemporary feminist response to a particular social issue, or the relative power of current feminist political organizations. It's difficult to say, however, how narrow is narrow enough. (A literary critic once produced a 20-page article analyzing the first paragraph of Henry James's *The Ambassadors*.)

Perhaps more helpful as a guideline on focusing your research is to seek to answer a particular question, a *research question*. For example, how did the Clinton administration respond to criticisms of bilingual education? To what extent is America perceived by social critics to be in decline? What factors led to the WorldCom collapse? How has the debate over genetic engineering evolved during the past decade? To what extent do contemporary cigarette ads perpetuate sexist attitudes? Or how do contemporary cigarette ads differ in message and tone from cigarette ads in the 1950s? Focusing on questions such as these and approaching your research as a way of answering such questions is probably the best way to narrow your subject and ensure focus in your paper. The essential answer to this research question eventually becomes your *thesis,* which we discussed in Chapter 3; in the paper, you present evidence that systematically supports your thesis.

Constructing Research Questions

Moving from a broad topic or idea to formulation of precise research questions can be challenging. Practice this skill by working with small groups of your classmates to construct research questions about the following topics (or come up with some topics of your own). Write at least one research question for each topic listed, then discuss these topics and questions with the other groups in class.

Racial or gender stereotypes in television shows
Drug addiction in the U.S. adult population
Global environmental policies
Employment trends in high-technology industries
U.S. energy policy

LOCATING SOURCES

Once you have a research question, you want to see what references are available. You'll begin with what we call "preliminary research," in which you familiarize yourself quickly with the basic issues and generate a preliminary list of sources. This effort will help you refine your research question and conduct efficient research once you move into the stage that we call "focused research."

TYPES OF RESEARCH DATA
(SEE ALSO CHAPTER 3, PP. 93–95)

Primary Sources

- Data gathered directly by a researcher using research methods appropriate to a particular field

  sciences: experiments, observations
  social sciences: experiments, surveys, interviews
  humanities: close reading/observation and interpretation

Secondary Sources

- Information and ideas collected or generated by others who have performed their own primary and/or secondary research

  library research: books, periodicals, etc.
  online research

WRITING THE RESEARCH PAPER

Here is an overview of the main steps involved in writing research papers. Keep in mind that, as with other writing projects, writing such papers is a recursive process. For instance, you will gather data at various stages of your writing, as the list below illustrates.

Developing the Research Question

- **Find a subject.** Decide what subject you are going to research and write about.
- **Develop a research question.** Formulate an important question that you would like to answer through your research.

Locating Sources

- **Conduct preliminary research.** Consult knowledgeable people, general and specialized encyclopedias, overviews and bibliographies in recent books, the *Bibliographic Index*, and subject heading guides.
- **Refine your research question.** Based on your preliminary research, brainstorm about your topic and ways to answer your research question. Sharpen your focus, refining your question and planning the sources you'll need to consult.
- **Conduct focused research.** Consult books, electronic databases, general and specialized periodicals, biographical indexes, general and specialized dictionaries, government publications, and other appropriate sources. Conduct interviews and surveys, as necessary.

Mining Sources

- **Develop a working thesis.** Based on your initial research, formulate a working thesis that attempts to respond to your research question.
- **Develop a working bibliography.** Keep track of your sources, either on paper or electronically, including both bibliographic information and key points about each source. Make this bibliography easy to sort and rearrange.
- **Evaluate sources.** Attempt to determine the veracity and reliability of your sources; use your critical reading skills; check *Book Review Digest*; look up biographies of authors.
- **Take notes from sources.** Paraphrase and summarize important information and ideas from your sources. Copy down important quo-

tations. Note page numbers from sources of this quoted and summarized material.

- **Develop a working outline and arrange your notes according to your outline.**

Drafting; Citing Sources

- **Write your draft.** Write the preliminary draft of your paper, working from your notes, according to your outline.
- **Avoid plagiarism.** Take care to cite all quoted, paraphrased, and summarized source material, making sure that your own wording and sentence structure differ from those of your sources.
- **Cite sources.** Use in-text citations and a Works Cited or References list, according to the conventions of the discipline (e.g., MLA, APA, CSE).

Revising (global and local changes)

- **Revise your draft.** Consider global, local, surface revisions. Check that your thesis still fits with your paper's focus. Review topic sentences and paragraph development and logic. Use transitional words and phrases to ensure coherence. Make sure that the research paper reads smoothly and clearly from beginning to end.

Editing (surface changes)

- **Edit your draft.** Check for style, combining short, choppy sentences and ensuring variety in your sentence structures. Check for grammatical correctness, punctuation, and spelling.

PRELIMINARY RESEARCH

You can go about finding preliminary sources in many ways; some of the more effective ones are listed in the box on the next page. We'll consider a few of these suggestions in more detail.

Consulting Knowledgeable People

When you think of research, you may immediately think of libraries and print material. But don't neglect a key reference—other people. Your *instructor* probably can suggest fruitful areas of research and some useful sources. Try to see your instructor during office hours, however, rather than immediately before or after class, so that you'll have enough time for a productive discussion.

LOCATING PRELIMINARY SOURCES

- Ask your instructor to recommend sources on the subject.
- Scan the "Suggestions for Further Reading" sections of your textbooks. Ask your college librarian for useful reference tools in your subject area.
- Read an encyclopedia article on the subject and use the bibliography following the article to identify other sources.
- Read the introduction to a recent book on the subject and review that book's bibliography to identify more sources.
- Consult the annual *Bibliographic Index* (see page 287 for details).
- Use an Internet search engine to explore your topic. Type in different keyword or search term combinations and browse the sites you find for ideas and references to sources you can look up later (see the box on pages 292–93 for details).

NARROWING THE SUBJECT VIA RESEARCH

If you need help narrowing a broad subject, try one or more of the following:

- Search by subject in an electronic database to see how the subject breaks down into components
- Search the subject heading in an electronic periodical catalog, such as *InfoTrac,* or in a print catalog such as the *Readers' Guide to Periodical Literature*
- Search the *Library of Congress Subject Headings* catalog (see Subject-Heading Guides, page 287 for details)

Once you get to the library, ask a *reference librarian* which reference sources (e.g., bibliographies, specialized encyclopedias, periodical indexes, statistical almanacs) you need for your particular area of research. Librarians won't do your research for you, but they'll be glad to show you how to research efficiently and systematically.

You can also obtain vital primary information from people when you interview them, ask them to fill out questionnaires or surveys, or have them participate in experiments. We'll cover this aspect of research in more detail below.

Encyclopedias

Reading an encyclopedia entry about your subject will give you a basic understanding of the most significant facts and issues. Whether the subject is American politics or the mechanics of genetic engineering, the encyclopedia article—written by a specialist in the field—offers a broad overview that may serve as a launching point to more specialized research in a particular area. The article may illuminate areas or raise questions that you feel motivated to pursue further. Equally important, the encyclopedia article frequently concludes with an *annotated bibliography* describing important books and articles on the subject.

Encyclopedias have certain limitations, however. First, most professors don't accept encyclopedia articles as legitimate sources for academic papers. You should use encyclopedias primarily to familiarize yourself with (and to select a particular aspect of) the subject area and as a springboard for further research. Also, because new editions of encyclopedias appear only once every five or ten years, the information they contain—including bibliographies—may not be current. Current editions of the *Encyclopaedia Britannica* and the *Encyclopedia Americana*, for instance, may not include information about the most recent developments in biotechnology. Some encyclopedias are now also available online—Britannica Online, for example—and this may mean, but not guarantee, that information is up to date.

Some of the most useful general encyclopedias include the following:

Academic American Encyclopedia

Encyclopedia Americana

New Encyclopaedia Britannica (or Britannica Online)

Keep in mind that the library also contains a variety of more *specialized encyclopedias*. These encyclopedias restrict themselves to a particular disciplinary area, such as chemistry, law, or film, and are considerably more detailed in their treatment of a subject than are general encyclopedias. Here are examples of specialized encyclopedias:

Social Sciences

Encyclopedia of Education

Encyclopedia of Psychology

West's Encyclopedia of American Law

International Encyclopedia of the Social & Behavioral Sciences

Humanities

Encyclopedia of American History

Dictionary of Art

Encyclopedia of Religion and Ethics

Film Encyclopedia

The New Grove Encyclopedia of Music

Science and Technology

Encyclopedia of Life Sciences

Encyclopedia of Electronics

Encyclopedia of Artificial Intelligence

Encyclopedia of Physics

McGraw-Hill Encyclopedia of Environmental Science

Van Nostrand's Scientific Encyclopedia

Business

Encyclopedia of Banking and Finance

International Encyclopedia of Economics

EXERCISE 7.2

Exploring Specialized Encyclopedias

Go to the Reference section of your campus library and locate several specialized encyclopedias within your major or area of interest. Look through the encyclopedias, noting their organization, and read entries on topics that interest you. Jot down some notes describing the kinds of information you find. You might also use this opportunity to look around at the other materials available in the Reference section of the library, including the *Bibliographic Index,* and the *Book Review Digest.*

Overviews and Bibliographies in Recent Books

If your professor or a bibliographic source directs you to an important recent book on your subject, skim the introductory (and possibly the concluding) material to the book, along with the table of contents, for an overview of key issues. Look also for a bibliography, works cited, and/or references list. These lists are extremely valuable resources for locating material for research. For example, Robert Dallek's 2003 book *An Unfinished Life: John Fitzgerald Kennedy, 1917–1963* includes a seven-page bibliography of reference sources on President Kennedy's life and times.

Keep in mind that authors are not necessarily objective about their subjects, and some have particularly biased viewpoints that you may unwittingly carry over to your paper, treating them as objective truth.* However, you may still be able to get some useful information out of such sources. Alert yourself to authorial biases by looking up the reviews of your book in the *Book Review Digest* (described on the next page). Additionally, look up biographical information on the author (see Biographical Indexes, p. 300), whose previous writings or professional associations may suggest a predictable set of attitudes on the subject of your book.

BIBLIOGRAPHIC INDEX

The *Bibliographic Index* is a series of annual volumes that enables you to locate bibliographies on a particular subject. The bibliographies referred to in the Index generally appear at the end of book chapters or periodical articles, or they may themselves be book or pamphlet length. Browsing through the *Bibliographic Index* in a general subject area may give you ideas for further research in particular aspects of the subject, along with particular references.

SUBJECT-HEADING GUIDES

Seeing how a general subject (e.g., education) is broken down in other sources also could stimulate research in a particular area (e.g., bilingual primary education in California). In the subsequent sources, general subjects are analyzed into secondary subject headings, as chapter titles in a book's table of contents represent subcomponents of a general subject (indicated in the book title). To locate such sets of secondary subject headings, consult:

An electronic database

An electronic or print periodical catalog (e.g., *InfoTrac, Readers' Guide, Social Science Index*)

The Library of Congress Subject Headings catalog

The *Propaedia* volume of the *New Encyclopaedia Britannica* (1998)

---

*Bias is not necessarily bad. Authors, like all other people, have certain preferences and predilections that influence the way they view the world and the kinds of arguments they make. As long as they inform you of their biases, or as long as you are aware of them and take them into account, you can still use these sources judiciously. (You might gather valuable information from a book about the Watergate scandal, even if it were written by former president Richard Nixon or one of his top aides, as long as you make proper allowance for their understandable biases.) Bias becomes a potential problem only when it masquerades as objective truth or is accepted as such by the reader. For suggestions on identifying and assessing authorial bias, see the material in Chapter 2 on persuasive writing (pp. 64–74) and evaluating assumptions (pp. 76–77).

Once you've used these kinds of tools to narrow your scope to a particular subject and research question (or set of research questions), you're ready to undertake more focused research.

FOCUSED RESEARCH

Your objective now is to learn as much as you can about your particular subject. Only in this way will you be qualified to make an informed response to your research question. This means you'll have to become something of an expert on the subject—or, if that's not possible, given time constraints, you can at least become someone whose critical viewpoint is based solidly on the available evidence. In the following pages we'll suggest how to find sources for this kind of focused research. In most cases, your research will be *secondary* in nature, based on (1) books; (2) electronic databases; (3) articles; and (4) specialized reference sources. In certain cases, you may gather your own *primary* research, using (5) interviews, surveys, structured observation, or content/textual analysis.

Books

Books are useful in providing both breadth and depth of coverage of a subject. Because they generally are published at least a year or two after the events treated, they also tend to provide the critical distance that is sometimes missing from articles. Conversely, this delay in coverage also means that the information you find in books will not be as current as information you find in journals. And, of course, books also may be shallow, inaccurate, outdated, or hopelessly biased; for help in making such determinations, see *Book Review Digest*, discussed below. You can locate relevant books through the electronic or card catalog. When using this catalog, you may search in four ways: (1) by *author*, (2) by *title*, (3) by *subject*, and (4) by *keyword*. Entries include the call number, publication information, and frequently, a summary of the book's contents. Larger libraries use the Library of Congress cataloging system for call numbers (e.g., E111/C6); smaller ones use the Dewey Decimal System (e.g., 970.015/C726).

BOOK REVIEW DIGEST

Perhaps the best way to determine the reliability and credibility of a book you may want to use is to look it up in the *Book Review Digest* (also available online and issued monthly and cumulated annually). These volumes list (alphabetically by author) the most significant books published during the year, supply a brief description of each, and most important, provide excerpts from (and references to) reviews. If a book receives bad reviews, you don't necessarily have to avoid it (the book still may have something useful to offer, and the review itself may be unreliable). But you should take any negative reaction into account when using that book as a source.

Electronic Databases

Much of the information that is available in print—and a good deal that is not—is also available in electronic form. Almost certainly, your library card catalog has been computerized, allowing you to conduct searches much faster and more easily than in the past. Increasingly, researchers access magazine, newspaper, and journal articles and reports, abstracts, and other forms of information through *online databases* (many of them on the Internet) and through databases on *CD-ROMs*. One great advantage of using databases (as opposed to print indexes) is that you can search several years' worth of different periodicals at the same time.

Online databases—that is, those that originate outside your computer—are available through international, national, or local (e.g., campus) networks. The largest such database is DIALOG, which provides access to more than 300 million records in more than 400 databases, ranging from sociology to business to chemical engineering. Another large database is LEXIS-NEXIS (like DIALOG, available only through online subscription). *LEXIS-NEXIS Academic* provides access to numerous legal, medical, business, and news sources. In addition to being efficient and comprehensive, online databases are generally far more up-to-date than print sources. If you have an Internet connection from your own computer, you can access many of these databases—including those available through commercial online services such as CompuServe and America Online—without leaving your room.

Access to online databases often requires an account and a password, which you may be able to obtain by virtue of your student status. In some cases, you will have to pay a fee to the local provider of the database, based on how long you are online. But many databases will be available to you free of charge. For example, your library's computers may offer access to magazine and newspaper databases, such as Expanded Academic ASAP, InfoTrac, EbscoHost, and National Newspaper Index, as well as to the Internet itself.

The *World Wide Web* offers graphics, multimedia, and hyperlinks to related material in numerous sources. To access these sources, you can either browse (i.e., follow your choice of paths or links wherever they lead) or type in a site's address.

To search for Web information on a particular topic, try using one of the more popular search engines:

Google: http://www.google.com
Yahoo: http://www.yahoo.com
Alta Vista: http://altavista.com
WebCrawler: http://webcrawler.com
SearchCom: http://www.search.com
Lycos: http://www.lycos.com

Review the "Help" and "Advanced Search" sections of search engines to achieve the best results. See the box on pages 292–93 for some general tips on searching online.

Many databases and periodical indexes are available online. Among them: the *Readers' Guide to Periodical Literature* [index only], *The New York Times* [available full-text online], *Film Index International* [index only], *PAIS International* [index only], and *America: History and Life* [index only], as are other standard reference sources, such as *Statistical Abstract of the U.S* [full text], *The Encyclopaedia Britannica* [full text—called *Britannica Online*], *Bibliography of Native North Americans* [*index only*], *Environment Reporter* [full text], and *National Criminal Justice Reference Service* [index with some links to full text]. Of particular interest is *InfoTrac*, which (if you are in a participating library or have a password) provides access to more than 1,000 general interest, business, government, and technological periodicals. In recent years, CD-ROM (compact disk-read only memory) indexes and databases have given way to online versions.

Keep in mind, however, that while electronic sources make it far easier to access information than do their print counterparts, they often do not go back more than 15 years. For earlier information, therefore (e.g., the original reactions to the Milgram experiments of the 1960s), you would have to rely on print indexes.

EXERCISE **7.3**

Exploring Electronic Sources

Use your library's Internet connection (or your home computer if you have Internet access) to access a search engine or academic/professional database. Select a topic/research question of interest to you, review the box on "Using Keywords and Boolean Logic to Refine Online Searches" (pp. 292–93) and try different combinations of keywords and Boolean operators to see what sources you can find for your topic. Jot down notes describing the kinds of sources you find and which terms seem to yield the best results. Effective searching on the Internet takes practice; you'll save time when conducting research if you have a good sense of how to use these search strategies.

The Benefits and Pitfalls of the World Wide Web

In the past few years, the Web has become not just a research tool, but a cultural phenomenon. The pop artist Andy Warhol once said that in the future everyone would be famous for 15 minutes. He might have added that everyone would also have a personal Web site. People use the Web not just to look up information, but also to shop, to make contact with long-lost friends and relatives, to grind their personal or corporate axes, and to advertise themselves and their accomplishments.

The Web makes it possible for people sitting at home, work, or school to gain access to the resources of large libraries and explore corporate and government databases. In her informative book *The Research Paper and the World Wide Web*, Dawn Rodrigues quotes Bruce Dobler and Harry Bloomberg on the essential role of the Web in modern research:

> It isn't a matter anymore of using computer searches to locate existing documents buried in some far-off library or archive. The Web is providing documents and resources that simply would be too expensive to publish on paper or CD-ROM.
>
> Right now—and not in some distant future—doing research without looking for resources on the Internet is, in most cases, not really looking hard enough. . . . A thorough researcher cannot totally avoid the Internet and the Web.*

And indeed, Web sites are increasingly showing up as sources in both student and professional papers. But like any other rapidly growing and highly visible cultural phenomenon, the Web has created its own backlash. First, as anyone who has tried it knows, for many subjects, systematic research on the Web is rarely possible. For all the information that is on the Internet, a great deal more is not and never will be converted to digital format. One library director has estimated that only about 4,000 of 150,000 published scholarly journals are available online, and many of these provide only partial texts of relatively recent articles in the paper editions. *The New York Times* is available on the Web, but the online edition includes only a fraction of the content of the print edition, and online versions of the articles generally are abridged and often must be paid for. If you are researching the rise of McCarthyism in America during the early 1950s or trying to determine who else, since Stanley Milgram, has conducted psychological experiments on obedience, you are unlikely to find much useful information for your purpose on the Web.

Moreover, locating what *is* available is not always easy, since there's no standardized method—like the Library of Congress subheading and call number system—of cataloging and cross-referencing online information. The tens of thousands of Web sites and millions of Web pages, together with the relative crudity of search engines such as Yahoo, Google, AltaVista, and WebCrawler, have made navigating an ever-expanding cyberspace an often daunting and frustrating procedure.

Second, it is not a given that people who do research on the Web will produce better papers as a result. David Rothenberg, a professor of philosophy at New Jersey Institute of Technology, believes that "his students' papers had declined in quality since they began using the Web for research."[†] Neil Gabler, a cultural critic, writes:

---

*Dawn Rodrigues, *The Research Paper and the World Wide Web* (Upper Saddle River, N.J.: Prentice-Hall, 1997).

†Steven R. Knowlton, "Students Lost in Cyberspace," *Chronicle of Higher Education* 2 Nov. 1997: 21.

The Internet is such a huge receptacle of rumor, half-truth, misinformation and disinformation that the very idea of objective truth perishes in the avalanche. All you need to create a "fact" in the web world is a bulletin board or chat room. Gullible cybernauts do the rest.*

Another critic is even blunter: "Much of what purports to be serious information is simply junk—neither current, objective, nor trustworthy. It

---

USING KEYWORDS AND BOOLEAN LOGIC TO REFINE ONLINE SEARCHES

You will find more—and more relevant—sources on Internet search engines and library databases if you carefully plan your search strategies. *Note: Some search engines and online databases have their own systems for searching, so review the "Help" section of each search engine, and use "Advanced Search" options where available. The following tips are general guidelines, and their applicability in different search engines may vary somewhat.*

1. **Identify multiple keywords:**

    Write down your topic and/or your research question, then brainstorm synonyms and related terms for the words in that topic/question.

    Sample topic: Political activism on college campuses.

    Sample research question: What kinds of political activism are college students involved in today?

    Keywords: Political activism; college students

    Synonyms and related terms: politics; voting; political organizations; protests; political issues; universities; colleges; campus politics.

2. **Conduct searches using different combinations of synonyms and related terms.**

3. **Find new terms in the sources you locate and search with these.**

4. **Use quotation marks around terms you want linked: "political activism"**

5. **Use "Boolean operators" to link keywords:**

    (continued, next page)

---

*Neil Gabler, "Why Let Truth Get in the Way of a Good Story?" *Los Angeles Times* "Opinion," 26 Oct. 1997: 1.

may be impressive to the uninitiated, but it is clearly not of great use to scholars."*

Of course, print sources are not necessarily objective or reliable either, and in Chapter 2, Critical Reading and Critique, we discussed some criteria by which readers may evaluate the quality and reliability of information and ideas in *any* source (pages 63–74). Web sources, however—particularly self-published Web pages—present a special problem. In most cases, material destined for print has to go through one or more editors and fact checkers

The words AND, OR, and NOT are used in "Boolean logic" to combine search terms and get more precise results than using keywords alone.

AND: Connecting keywords with AND narrows a search by retrieving only sources that contain *both* keywords:

political activism AND college students

OR: Connecting keywords with OR broadens a search by retrieving all sources that contain at least one of the search terms. This operator is useful when you have a topic/keyword for which there are a number of synonyms. Linking synonyms with OR will lead you to the widest array of sources:

political activism OR protests OR political organizing OR voting OR campus politics

college OR university OR campus OR students

AND and OR: You can use these terms in combination, by putting the OR phrase in parentheses:

(political activism OR protests) AND (college OR university)

NOT: Connecting keywords with NOT (or, in some cases, AND NOT) narrows a search by excluding certain terms. If you want to focus upon a very specific topic, NOT can be used to limit what the search engine retrieves; however, this operator should be used carefully as it can cause you to miss sources that may actually be relevant:

college students NOT high school

political activism NOT voting

*William Miller, "Troubling Myths About On-Line Information," *Chronicle of Higher Education* 1 Aug. 1997: A44.

before being published, since most authors don't have the resources to publish and distribute their own writing. But anyone with a computer and a modem can "publish" on the Web; furthermore, those with a good Web authoring program and graphics software can create sites that, outwardly at least, look just as professional and authoritative as those of the top academic, government, and business sites. These personal sites will appear in search-engine listings—generated through keyword matches rather than through independent assessments of quality or relevance—and uncritical researchers who use their information as a factual basis for the claims they make in their papers do so at their peril.

The Internet has also led to increased problems with plagiarism. Many college professors complain these days about receiving work copied directly off of Web sites. Such copying runs the gamut from inadvertent plagiarism of passages copied and pasted off the Web into notes and then transferred verbatim to papers, to intentional theft of others' work, pasted together into a document and claimed as the student's own. In one recent case, an instructor reports that she received a student paper characterized by a more professional writing style than usual for that student. The instructor typed a few keywords from the paper into an Internet search engine, and one of the first sources retrieved turned out to be a professional journal article from which the student had copied whole passages and pasted them together to create a "report." This student received an "F" in the course and was referred to a university disciplinary committee for further action.

The Internet sometimes proves a very tempting source from which to lift materials. But not only is such activity ethically wrong, it is also likely to result in serious punishment, such as permanent notations on your academic transcript or expulsion from school. One thing all students should know is that while cheating is now made easier by the Internet, the converse is also true: Instructors can often track down the sources for material plagiarized from the Internet just as easily as the student found them in the first place. (Easier, in fact, because now instructors can scan papers into software or Internet programs that will search the Web for matching text.) For more on plagiarism, see the section devoted to this subject in Chapter 1, pages 53 to 55.

We certainly don't mean to discourage Web research. Thousands of excellent sites exist in cyberspace. The reference department of most college and university libraries will provide lists of such sites, arranged by discipline, and the most useful sites also are listed in the research sections of many handbooks. Most people locate Web sites, however, by using search engines and by "surfing" the hyperlinks. And for Web sources, more than print sources, the warning *caveat emptor*—let the buyer beware—applies.

Evaluating Web Sources

In their extremely useful site "Evaluating Web Resources" (http://www2.widener.edu/Wolfgram-Memorial-Library/webevaluation/webeval.htm), reference librarians Jan Alexander and Marsha Tate offer important guidelines for assessing Web sources. First, they point out, it's important to determine what *type* of Web page you are dealing with. Web pages generally fall into one of six types, each with a different purpose: (1) entertainment, (2) business/marketing, (3) reference/information, (4) news, (5) advocacy of a particular point of view or program, (6) personal page. The purpose of the page—informing, selling, persuading, entertaining—has a direct bearing on the objectivity and reliability of the information presented.

Second, when evaluating a Web page, one should apply the same general criteria as are applied to print sources: (1) accuracy, (2) authority, (3) objectivity, (4) currency, (5) coverage. As we've noted, when assessing the *accuracy* of a Web page, it's important to consider the likelihood that its information has been checked by anyone other than the author. When assessing the *authority* of the page, one considers the author's qualifications to write on the subject and the reputability of the publisher. In many cases on the Web, it's difficult to determine not just the qualifications, but the very identity of the author. When assessing the *objectivity* of a Web page, one considers the bias on the part of the author or authors and the extent to which they are trying to sway their reader's opinion. Many Web pages passing themselves off as informational are in fact little more than "infomercials." When assessing the *currency* of a Web page, one asks whether the content is up-to-date and whether the publication date is clearly labeled. Many Web pages lack clearly indicated dates. And even if a date is provided, it may be difficult to tell whether the date indicates when the page was written, when it was placed on the Web, or when it was last revised. Finally, when assessing the *coverage* of a Web page, one considers which topics are included (and not included) in the work and whether the topics are covered in depth. Depth of coverage has generally not been a hallmark of Web information.

Other pitfalls of Web sites: Reliable sites may include links to other sites that are inaccurate or outdated, so users cannot rely on the link as a substitute for evaluating the five criteria just outlined. Also, Web pages also are notoriously unstable, frequently changing or even disappearing without notice.

Perhaps most serious, the ease with which it's possible to surf the Net can encourage intellectual laziness and make researchers too dependent on Web resources. Professors are increasingly seeing papers largely or even entirely based on information in Web sites. While Web sources are indeed an important new source of otherwise unavailable information, there's usually no substitute for library or primary research, such as interviews or field study. The vast majority of printed material in even a small college library—much of it essential to informed research—does not appear on the Web, nor is it likely to in the immediate future. Much of the material you will research in the next few years remains bound within covers. You may well learn of its existence in electronic databases, but at some point you'll have to walk over to a library shelf, pull out a book, and turn printed pages.

Above all, remember that you must apply the critical reading skills you've been practicing throughout this textbook to all your sources—no matter what types they are or where you found them (see Chapter 2 for coverage of critical reading).

EXERCISE 7.4

Practice Evaluating Web Sources

To practice applying the evaluation criteria discussed in the section above on Web sources, go to an Internet search engine and look for sources addressing a topic of interest to you (perhaps following completion of Exercise 7.3, page 290). Try to locate one source representing each of the six types of Web pages (i.e., entertainment, business/marketing, reference/information, news, advocacy, and personal). Print out the main page of each of these sources and bring the copies to class. In small groups of your classmates look over the sites each student found and make notes on each example's (1) accuracy; (2) authority; (3) objectivity; (4) currency; (5) coverage.

Periodicals: General

Because many more periodical articles than books are published every year, you are likely (depending on the subject) to find more information in periodicals than in books. By general periodicals, we mean the magazines and newspapers that are generally found on newsstands, such as *The New York Times, Newsweek,* or *The New Republic.* By their nature, general periodical articles tend to be more current than books. The best way, for example, to find out about the federal government's current policy on Social Security reform is to look for articles in periodicals and newspapers. However, periodical articles may have less critical distance than books, and like books, they may become dated, to be superseded by more recent articles. Let's first look at the use of magazines from a research perspective.

MAGAZINES

General periodicals (such as *Time, The New Republic,* and *The Nation*) are intended for nonspecialists. Their articles, which tend to be highly readable, may be written by staff writers, freelancers, or specialists. But usually they do not provide citations or other indications of sources, and so are of limited usefulness for scholarly research.

The most well-known general index to this kind of material is the *Readers' Guide to Periodical Literature,* an index of articles that have appeared in several hundred general-interest magazines and a few more specialized magazines such as *Business Week* and *Science Digest.* Articles in the *Readers' Guide* are indexed by author, title, and subject.

Another general reference for articles is the *Essay and General Literature Index,* which indexes essays (sometimes called book articles) contained in anthologies.

Increasingly, texts and abstracts of articles are available on online databases. These texts may be downloaded to your computer or e-mailed to you.

NEWSPAPERS

News stories, feature stories, and editorials (even letters to the editor) may be important sources of information. Your library certainly will have the *New York Times* index, and it may have indexes to other important newspapers, such as the *Washington Post*, the *Los Angeles Times*, the *Chicago Tribune*, the *Wall Street Journal*, and the *Christian Science Monitor*. Newspaper holdings will be on microfilm, CD-ROM, or online. You will need a micro-printer/viewer to get hard copies if you are using microfilm.

Note: Because of its method of cross-referencing, the *New York Times* index may at first be confusing. Suppose that you want to find stories on bilingual education during a given year. When you locate the "Bilingual education" entry, you won't find citations but rather a *"See also* Education" reference that directs you to seven dates (August 14, 15, and 17; September 11; October 20, 29, and 30) under the heading of "Education." Under this major heading, references to stories on education are arranged in chronological order from January to December. When you look up the dates you were directed to, you'll see brief descriptions of these stories on bilingual education.

Periodicals: Specialized

Many professors will expect at least some of your research to be based on articles in specialized periodicals or "scholarly journals." So instead of (or in addition to) relying on an article from *Psychology Today* (which would be considered a general periodical even though its subject is somewhat specialized) for an account of the effects of crack cocaine on mental functioning, you might also rely on an article from the *Journal of Abnormal Psychology*. If you are writing a paper on the satirist Jonathan Swift, in addition to a recent reference that may have appeared in the *New Yorker*, you may need to locate a relevant article in *Eighteenth-Century Studies*. Articles in such journals normally are written by specialists and professionals in the field, rather than by staff writers or freelancers, and the authors will assume that their readers already understand the basic facts and issues concerning the subject. Other characteristics of scholarly journals: they tend to be heavily researched, as indicated by numerous footnotes/endnotes and references; they are generally published by university presses; most of the authors represented are university professors; the articles, which have a serious, formal, and scholarly tone, are generally peer reviewed by other scholars in the field.

To find articles in specialized periodicals, you'll use specialized indexes—that is, indexes for particular disciplines. You also may find it helpful to refer to *abstracts*. Like specialized indexes, abstracts list articles published in a particular discipline over a given period, but they also provide summaries of the articles listed. Abstracts tend to be more selective than indexes, since they consume more space (and involve considerably more work to compile); but, because they also describe the contents of the articles covered, they can save you a lot of time in determining which articles you should read and which ones you can safely skip. Don't treat abstracts alone as sources for research; if you find useful material in an abstract, you need to locate the article to which it applies and use that as your source of information.

Here are some of the more commonly used specialized periodical indexes and abstracts in the various disciplines.

Note: The format (print, online, or CD-ROM) of these databases will vary by library. Online databases (as opposed to their print counterparts) are enhanced by more flexible search capability and, in some cases, by links to the full text.

Social Science

Anthropological Index

Education Index

Index to Legal Periodicals

Psychological Abstracts (online as *PsycInfo)*

Public Affairs Information Service (PAIS)

Social Science Index

Sociological Abstracts

Women's Studies Abstracts

ERIC (Educational Resources Information Center)

Social SciSearch

Worldwide Political Science Abstracts

Humanities

America: History and Life

Art Index

Essay and General Literature Index

Film/Literature Index

Historical Abstracts

Humanities Index

International Index of Film Periodicals

MLA International Bibliography of Books and Articles on Modern Languages and Literature

Music Index

Religion Index

Year's Work in English Studies

Arts and Humanities Citation Index

MLA Bibliography

Philosophers' Index

Historical Abstracts

Science and Technology Indexes

Applied Science and Technology Index

Biological Abstracts

Chemical Abstracts

Engineering Index

General Science Index

Index to Scientific and Technical Proceedings (ceased publication in 1999)

Science and Technology

Aerospace & High Technology Database

Agricola (agriculture)

Biosis Previews (biology, botany)

Chemical Abstracts (chemistry)

Compendex (engineering)

Environment Abstracts

INSPEC (engineering)

MathSciNetPubMed (medical)

ScienceCitation Index

SciSearch

Business Indexes

Business Index

Business Periodicals Index

Economic Titles/Abstracts

Wall Street Journal *Index*

Business Databases

ABI/INFORM (index with access to some full text)

EconLit (index only)

STAT-USA (full text)

Standard & Poor's News (full text)

Law Databases

LEXIS-NEXIS (full text)

Westlaw (full text)

Exploring Specialized Periodicals

Visit your campus library and locate the specialized periodical indexes for your major or area of interest (ask a Reference librarian to help you). Note the call numbers for specialized periodicals (also called academic journals) in your field, and visit the periodical room or section of the library, where recent editions of academic journals are usually housed. Locate the call numbers you've noted, and spend some time looking through the specialized periodicals in your field. The articles you find in these journals represent some of the most recent scholarship in your field—the kind of scholarship many of your professors are busy conducting. Write half a page or so describing some of the articles you find interesting, and why.

Biographical Indexes

To look up information on particular people, you can use not only encyclopedias but an array of biographical sources. You can also use these biographical sources to alert yourself to potential biases on the part of your source authors, as such biases may be revealed by other work these authors have done and details of their backgrounds. A brief selection of biographical indexes follows.

Living Persons

Contemporary Authors: A Biographical Guide to Current Authors and Their Works

Current Biography

International Who's Who

Who's Who in America

Persons No Longer Living

Dictionary of American Biography

Dictionary of National Biography (Great Britain)

Dictionary of Scientific Biography

Who Was Who

Persons Living or Dead

Biography Almanac

McGraw-Hill Encyclopedia of World Biography

Webster's Biographical Dictionary

Dictionaries

Use dictionaries to look up the meaning of general or specialized terms. Here are some of the most useful dictionaries:

General

Oxford English Dictionary
Webster's New Collegiate Dictionary
Webster's Third New International Dictionary of the English Language

Social Sciences

Black's Law Dictionary
Dictionary of the Social Sciences
McGraw-Hill Dictionary of Modern Economics

Humanities

Dictionary of American History
Dictionary of Films
Dictionary of Philosophy
Harvard Dictionary of Music
McGraw-Hill Dictionary of Art

Science and Technology

Computer Dictionary and Handbook
Condensed Chemical Dictionary
Dictionary of Biology
Dorland's Medical Dictionary

Business

Dictionary of Advertising Terms
Dictionary of Business and Economics
Mathematical Dictionary for Economics and Business Administration
McGraw-Hill Dictionary of Modern Economics: A Handbook of Terms and Organizations

Other Sources/Government Publications

Besides those already listed, you have many other options and potential sources for research. Here are only some of your options: For statistical and other basic reference information on a subject, consult a *handbook* (such as *Statistical Abstracts of the United States*). For current information on a subject as of a given year, consult an *almanac* (such as *World Almanac*). For annual updates of information, consult a *yearbook* (such as *The Statesman's Yearbook*). For maps and other geographic information, consult an *atlas* (such as *New York Times Atlas of the World*). Often, simply browsing through the reference shelves for data on your general subject—such as biography, public affairs, psychology—will reveal valuable sources of information. And of course,

---

CRITICAL READING FOR RESEARCH

- **Use all the critical reading tips we've suggested thus far.** The tips contained in the boxes on Critical Reading for Summary on page 6, Critical Reading for Critique on page 84, Critical Reading for Synthesis on page 159, and Critical Reading for Analysis on page 263 are all useful for the kinds of reading used in conducting research.
- **Read for relationships to your research question.** How does the source help you formulate and clarify your research question?
- **Read for relationships between sources.** How does each source illustrate, support, expand upon, contradict, or offer an alternative perspective to those of your other sources?
- **Consider the relationship between your source's form and content.** How does the form of the source—specialized encyclopedia, book, article in a popular magazine, article in a professional journal—affect its content, the manner in which that content is presented, and its relationship to other sources?
- **Pay special attention to the legitimacy of Internet sources.** Consider how the content and validity of the information on the Web page may be affected by the purpose of the site. Assess Web-based information for its (1) accuracy; (2) authority; (3) objectivity; (4) currency; and (5) coverage (Alexander and Tate; see pages 294–95).

---

much reference information is available on government sites on the Web.

In addition to all their other holdings, many libraries keep pamphlets in a *vertical file* (i.e., a file cabinet). For example, a pamphlet on global warming might be found in the vertical file rather than in the library stacks. Such material is accessible through the *Vertical File Index* (a monthly subject-and-title index to pamphlet material).

Finally, note that the U.S. government regularly publishes large quantities of useful information. Some indexes to government publications include the following:

American Statistics Index
Congressional Information Service

Interviews and Surveys

Depending on the subject of your paper, some or all of your research may be conducted outside the library. In conducting such primary research, you may perform experiments in science labs or make observations or gather data in courthouses, city government files, shopping malls (if you are observing, say,

GUIDELINES FOR CONDUCTING INTERVIEWS

- Become knowledgeable about the subject before the interview so that you can ask intelligent questions. Prepare most of your questions beforehand.
- Ask "open-ended" questions designed to elicit meaningful responses, rather than "forced choice" questions that can be answered with a word or two, or "leading questions" that presume a particular answer. For example, instead of asking "Do you think that male managers should be more sensitive to women's concerns for equal pay in the workplace?" ask, "To what extent do you see evidence that male managers are insufficiently sensitive to women's concerns for equal pay in the workplace?"
- Ask follow-up questions to elicit additional insights or details.
- If you record the interview (in addition to or instead of taking notes), get your subject's permission, preferably in writing.

GUIDELINES FOR CONDUCTING SURVEYS AND DESIGNING QUESTIONNAIRES

- Determine your *purpose* in conducting the survey: what kind of *information* you seek, and *whom* (i.e., what subgroup of the population) you intend to survey.
- Decide whether you want to collect information on the spot or have people send their responses back to you. (You will get fewer responses if they are sent back to you, but those you do get will likely be more complete than surveys conducted on the spot.)
- Devise and word questions carefully so that they (1) are understandable and (2) don't reflect your own biases. For example, if, for a survey on attitudes toward capital punishment, you ask, "Do you believe that the state should endorse legalized murder?" you've loaded the question to influence people to answer in the negative.
- Devise short answer or multiple-choice questions; open-ended questions encourage responses that are difficult to quantify. (You may want to leave space, however, for "additional comments.") Conversely, "yes" or "no" responses or rankings on a 5-point scale are easy to quantify.
- It may be useful to break out the responses by as many meaningful categories as possible—for example, gender, age, ethnicity, religion, education, geographic locality, profession, and income.

patterns of consumer behavior), the quad in front of the humanities building, or in front of TV screens (if you are analyzing, say, situation comedies or commercials, or if you are drawing on documentaries or interviews—in which cases you should try to obtain transcripts or tape the programs).

You may also want to *interview* your professors, your fellow students, or other individuals knowledgeable about your subject. Additionally, or alternatively, you may wish to conduct *surveys* via *questionnaires*. When well prepared and insightfully interpreted, such tools can produce valuable information about the ideas or preferences of a group of people.

MINING SOURCES

Having located your sources (or at least having begun the process), you'll proceed to "mining" them—that is, extracting from them information and ideas that you can use in your paper. To keep track of these sources, you'll need to compile a working bibliography so that you know what information you have and how it relates to your research question. Of course, you'll need to take notes on your sources and evaluate them for reliability and relevance. And you should develop some kind of outline—formal or informal—that allows you to see how you are going to subdivide and organize your discussion and, thus, at what points you'll be drawing on relevant sources. In doing this you are engaging in a process that has identifiable stages. For an extended discussion of this writing process, see Chapter 3.

THE WORKING BIBLIOGRAPHY

As you conduct your research, keep a *working bibliography*—that is, a compilation of bibliographic information on all the sources you're likely to use in preparing the paper. Note full bibliographic information on each source you consider. If you're meticulous about this during the research process, you'll be spared the frustration of having to go back to retrieve information—such as the publisher or the date—just as you're typing your final draft.

Now that library catalogs and databases are available online, it's easy to copy and paste your sources' (or potential sources') bibliographic information into a document, or to e-mail citations to yourself for cutting and pasting later. A more traditional but still very efficient way to compile bibliographic information is on 3" × 5" cards. (Note, also, that certain software programs allow you to create sortable electronic records.) Using any of these methods, you can easily add, delete, and rearrange individual bibliographic records as your research progresses. Whether you keep bibliographic information on 3" × 5" cards or in a document, be sure to record the following:

• The author or editor (last name first) and, if relevant, the translator

- The title (and subtitle) of the book or article
- The publisher and place of publication (if a book) or the title of the periodical
- The date and/or year of publication; if periodical, volume and issue number
- The edition number (if a book beyond its first edition)
- The inclusive page numbers (if article)
- The specific page number of a quote or other special material you might paraphrase

You also may want to include:

- A brief description of the source (to help you recall it later in the research process)
- The library call number (to help you relocate the source if you haven't checked it out)
- A code number, which you can use as a shorthand reference to the source in your notes

Your final bibliography, known as "Works Cited" in Modern Language Association (MLA) format and "References" in American Psychological Association (APA) format, consists of the sources you have actually summarized, paraphrased, or quoted in your paper. When you compile the bibliography, arrange your sources alphabetically by authors' last names.

Here is an example of a working bibliography notation or record for a book:

> Gorham, Eric B. *National Service, Political Socialization, and Political Education.* Albany: SUNY P, 1992.
>
> Argues that the language government uses to promote national service programs betrays an effort to "reproduce a postindustrial, capitalist economy in the name of good citizenship." Chap. 1 provides a historical survey of national service.

Here is an example of a working bibliography record for an article:

> Gergen, David. "A Time to Heed the Call." *U.S. News & World Report* 24 Dec. 2001: 60-61.
>
> Argues that in the wake of the surge of patriotism that followed the September 11 terrorist attacks, the government should encourage citizens to participate in community and national service. Supports the McCain-Bayh bill.

Here is an example of a working bibliography record for an online source:

> Bureau of Labor Statistics. "Table 1: Volunteers by Selected Characteristics, September 2002 and 2003." 18 Dec. 2003. Accessed 17 Jan. 2004. <http://www.bls.gov/newsrelease/volunt01.htm>. Provides statistical data on volunteerism in the U.S.

Some instructors may ask you to prepare—either in addition to or instead of a research paper—an *annotated bibliography*. This is a list of relevant works on a subject, with the contents of each briefly described or assessed. The sample bibliography records shown could become the basis for two entries in an annotated bibliography on national service. Annotations differ from *abstracts* in that annotations do not claim to be comprehensive summaries; they indicate, rather, how the items may be useful to the researcher.

Note-Taking

People have their favorite ways of note-taking. Some use use legal pads or spiral notebooks; yet others type notes into a laptop computer, perhaps using a database program. Some prefer 4" × 6" cards for note-taking. Such cards have some of the same advantages as 3" × 5" cards for working bibliographies: They can easily be added to, subtracted from, and rearranged to accommodate changing organizational plans. Also, discrete pieces of information from the same source can easily be arranged (and rearranged) into subtopics—a difficult task if you have taken three pages of notes on an article without breaking the notes down into subtopics.

Whatever your preferred approach, we recommend including, along with the note itself,

- A topic or subtopic label, corresponding to your outline (see below)
- A code number, corresponding to the number assigned the source in the working bibliography
- A page reference at end of note

Here is a sample note record for the table "Volunteers by Selected Characteristics, September 2002 and 2003" by the Bureau of Labor Statistics (bibliographic record above):

> Pervasiveness of Volunteerism (A)   7
>
> Shows that 28.8 percent of Americans age 16 and older, 63.8 million in all, devote time to community service.

Here is a notecard for the periodical article by Gergen (see bibliography note on page 305):

> *Beneficial paid volunteer programs* (D3 C(1))   12
>
> Both the community and the individual benefit from voluntary service programs. Cites Teach for America, Alumni of City Year, Peace Corps as programs in which participants receive small stipends and important benefits. (60) "Voluntary service when young often changes people for life. They learn to give their fair share." (60).

Both note records are headed by a topic label followed by the tentative location in the paper outline where the information may be used. The number in the upper right corner corresponds to the bibliography note. The note itself in the first record uses *summary*. The note in the second record uses *summary* (sentence 1), *paraphrase* (sentence 2), and *quotation* (sentence 3). Summary is used to condense important ideas treated in several paragraphs in the sources; paraphrase (with relevant page number), for the important detail on specific programs; quotation (again with relevant page number), for particularly incisive language by the source authors. For general hints on when to use each of these three forms, see Chapter 1, page 53.

At this point we must stress the importance of using quotation marks around quoted language *in your notes.* Making sure to note the difference between your own and quoted language will help you avoid unintentionally using someone else's words or ideas without crediting them properly. Such use, whether intentional or unintentional, constitutes plagiarism—a serious academic offense—something that professors don't take lightly; you don't want to invite suspicion of your work, even unintentionally. See the discussion of plagiarism on pages 53–55 for more details.

Evaluating Sources

Sifting through what seems a formidable mountain of material, you'll need to work quickly and efficiently; you'll also need to do some selecting. This means, primarily, distinguishing the more important from the less important (and the unimportant) material. Draw on your critical reading skills to help you determine the reliability and relevance of a source. See the box on Critical Reading for Research on page 302, and review Chapter 2 on Critical Reading and Critique, particularly the sections of "Evaluating Informative Writing" (pp. 63–64) and "Evaluating Persuasive Writing" (pp. 65–74). The hints in the box on the next page may also simplify the task.

ARRANGING YOUR NOTES: THE OUTLINE

Using your original working thesis (see Chapter 3 on theses)—or a new thesis that you have developed during the course of data-gathering and invention—you can begin constructing a *preliminary outline.* This outline indicates the order in which you plan to support your thesis.

Some people prefer not to develop an outline until they have more or less completed their research. At that point they will look over their note records,

---

GUIDELINES FOR EVALUATING SOURCES

- **Skim** the source. With a book, look over the table of contents, the introduction and conclusion, and the index; zero in on passages that your initial survey suggests are important. With an article, skim the introduction and the headings.
- Be alert for **references** in your sources to other important sources, particularly to sources that several authors treat as important.
- Other things being equal, the more **recent** the source, the better. Recent work usually incorporates or refers to important earlier work.
- If you're considering making multiple references to a book, look up the **reviews** in the *Book Review Digest* or the *Book Review Index*. Also, check the author's credentials in a source such as *Contemporary Authors* or *Current Biography*.

---

consider the relationships among the various pieces of evidence, possibly arrange notes or cards into separate piles, then develop an outline based on their perceptions and insights about the material. Subsequently, they rearrange and code the note records to conform to their outline—an informal outline indicating just the main sections of the paper and possibly one level below that. Thus, the model paper on national service (see Chapter 5) could be informally outlined as follows:

```
Intro: Pervasiveness of volunteerism in America;
       -Thesis: We should not turn the success of
       volunteerism in America into an argument
       for compulsory national service.
Intellectual history of public service: James,
       Plato
Can government compel citizens to public service?
       Military service: yes, in time of war
       Civilian service: no--logical, legal,
          moral  reasons
Conclusion: Government should expand
       opportunities for public service, but
       should not compel such service.
```

Such an outline will help you organize your research and should not be unduly restrictive as a guide to writing.

The *formal outline* (a multileveled plan with Roman and Arabic numerals, capital and small lettered subheadings) may still be useful, not so much as an exact blueprint for composition—although some writers do find it useful for this purpose—but rather as a guide to revision. That is, after you have written your draft, outlining it may help you discern structural problems: illogical sequences of material; confusing relationships between ideas; poor unity or coherence; sections that are too abstract or underdeveloped. (See the discussion of *reverse outlines* in Chapter 3, page 114.) Many instructors also require that formal outlines accompany the finished research paper.

The formal outline should indicate the logical relationships in the evidence you present. But it also may reflect the general conventions of a particular academic field. Thus, after an *introduction,* papers in the social sciences often proceed with a description of the *methods* of collecting information, continue with a description of the *results* of the investigation, and end with a *conclusion.* Papers in the sciences often follow a similar pattern. Papers in the humanities generally are less standardized in form. In devising a logical organization for your paper, ask yourself how your reader might best be introduced to the subject, be guided through a discussion of the main issues, and be persuaded that your viewpoint is a sound one.

Formal outlines are generally of two types: *topic* and *sentence outlines.* In the topic outline, headings and subheadings are indicated by words or phrases—as in the informal outline above. In the sentence outline, each heading and subheading is indicated in a complete sentence. Both topic and sentence outlines generally are preceded by the thesis.

You'll find a formal topic outline of the national service paper in Chapter 5, pp. 215–16.

Citing Sources

When you refer to or quote the work of another, you are obligated to credit or cite your source properly. There are two types of citations—in-text citations and full citations at the end of a paper—and they work in tandem.

If you are writing a paper in the humanities, you probably will be expected to use the Modern Language Association (MLA) format for citation. This format is fully described in the *MLA Handbook for Writers of Research Papers,* 6th ed. (New York: Modern Language Association of America, 2003). A paper in the social sciences will probably use the American Psychological Association (APA) format. This format is fully described in the *Publication Manual of the American Psychological Association,* 5th ed. (Washington, D.C.: American Psychological Association, 2001).

In the following section, we will focus on MLA and APA styles, the ones you are most likely to use in your academic work. Keep in mind, however, that instructors often have their own preferences. Some require the documentation style specified in the *Chicago Manual of Style,* 15th ed. (Chicago: University of Chicago Press, 2003). This style is similar to the American Psychological Association style, except that publication dates are not placed within parentheses. Instructors in the sciences often follow the Council of Science Editors (CSE) format (formerly Council of Biology Editors). Or they may prefer a number format: Each source listed on the bibliography page is assigned a number, and all text references to the source are followed by the appropriate number within parentheses. Some instructors like the old MLA style, which calls for footnotes and endnotes. Check with your instructor for the preferred documentation format if this is not specified in the assignment.

IN-TEXT CITATION

The general rule for in-text citation is to include only enough information to alert the reader to the source of the reference and to the location within that source. Normally, this information includes the author's last name and the page number (plus the year of publication, if using APA guidelines). But if you have already named the author in the preceding text, just the page number is sufficient.

TYPES OF CITATIONS

- Citations that indicate the source of quotations, paraphrases, and summarized information and ideas. These citations, generally limited to author's last name, relevant page number, and publication date of source, appear *in text*, within parentheses.
- Citations that appear in an alphabetical list of "Works Cited" or "References" *following the paper*. These citations provide full bibliographical information on the source.

Content Notes

Occasionally, you may want to provide a footnote or an endnote as a *content note*—one that provides additional information bearing on or illuminating, but not directly related to, the discussion at hand. For example

> ¹ Equally well-known is Forster's distinction between story and plot: In the former, the emphasis is on sequence ("the king died and then the queen died"); in the latter, the emphasis is on causality ("the king died and then the queen died of grief").

Notice the format: The first line is indented five spaces or one-half inch and the note number is raised one-half line. A single space from there, the note begins. Subsequent lines of the note are flush with the left margin. If the note is at the bottom of the page (a footnote), it is placed four lines below the text of the page, and the note itself is single-spaced. Double spaces are used between notes. Content notes are numbered consecutively throughout the paper; do not begin renumbering on each page. Most word-processing programs have functions for inserting consecutive footnotes, formatting them, and placing them in the appropriate position on your pages.

FULL CITATIONS

In MLA format, your complete list of sources, with all information necessary for a reader to locate a source, is called "Works Cited (which should begin on a new page)." In APA format, the list of sources is called "References." Entries in such listings should be double-spaced, with second and subsequent lines of each entry indented (a "hanging indent")—five spaces or one-half inch. In both styles, a single space follows the period. For comparison of MLA and APA citation styles, here are two samples of journal citations. Citation of books and other sources follow slightly different guidelines:

Sample MLA Full Citation (for a journal article)

Haan, Sarah C. "The 'Persuasion Route' of the Law: Advertising and Legal Persuasion." <u>Columbia Law Review</u> 100 (2000): 1281-1326.

Sample APA Full Citation (for a journal article)

Haan, S. C. (2000). The "persuasion route" of the law: Advertising and legal persuasion. *Columbia Law Review, 100,* 1281-1326.

The main differences between MLA and APA styles are these: (1) In MLA style, the date of the publication follows the name of the publisher; in APA style, the date is placed within parentheses following the author's name. (2) In APA style, only the initial of the author's first name is given, and only the first word (and any proper noun) of the book or article title is capitalized. The first letter of the subtitle (after a colon in a title) is also capitalized. In MLA style, the author's full name is given, and all words following the first word of the title (except articles and prepositions) are capitalized. (3) In APA style (unlike MLA style), quotation marks are not used around journal/magazine article titles. (4) APA style (unlike MLA style) requires the use of "p." and "pp." in in-text citations to indicate page numbers of periodical articles. (5) In APA format, titles of books and journals are italicized, as are the punctuation that follows and the volume (but not issue) numbers; MLA requires underlining for book and journal titles. (6) When citing books, both MLA and APA rules dictate that publishers' names should be shortened; thus, "Random House" becomes "Random"; "William Morrow" becomes "Morrow." However, MLA style uses a more extensive system of abbreviations for publishers' names.

Note: The hanging indent (second and subsequent lines indented) is the recommended format for both MLA and APA style references.

Provided below are some of the most commonly used citations in MLA and APA formats. For a more complete listing, consult the MLA *Handbook,* the APA's *Publication Manual,* or whichever style guide your instructor has specified. Please note that achieving conformance to either citation systems requires precision and attention to detail, down to every keystroke and punctuation mark.

MLA STYLE

In-Text Citation

Here are sample in-text citations using the MLA system:

> From the beginning, the AIDS antibody test has been "mired in controversy" (Bayer 101).

Notice that in the MLA system no date and no punctuation come between the author's name and the page number within the parentheses. Notice also that the parenthetical reference is placed *before* the final punctuation of the sentence, because it is considered part of the sentence.

If you have already mentioned the author's name in the text—in a *signal phrase*—it is not necessary to repeat it in the citation:

> According to Bayer, from the beginning, the AIDS antibody test has been "mired in controversy" (101).

In MLA format, you must supply page numbers for summaries and paraphrases, as well as for quotations:

> According to Bayer, the AIDS antibody test has been controversial from the outset (101).

Use a block, or indented form, for quotations of five lines or more. Introduce the block quotation with a full sentence followed by a colon. Indent one inch or ten spaces (that is, double the normal paragraph indentation). Place the parenthetical citation *after* the final period:

> Robert Flaherty's refusal to portray primitive people's contact with civilization arose from an inner conflict:
>
> > He had originally plunged with all his heart into the role of explorer and prospector; before Nanook, his own father was his hero. Yet as he entered the Eskimo world, he knew he did so as the advance guard of industrial civilization, the world of United

```
States Steel and Sir William Mackenzie
and railroad and mining empires. The
mixed feeling this gave him left his
mark on all his films. (Barnouw 45)
```

Again, were Barnouw's name mentioned in the sentence leading into the quotation, the parenthetical reference would be simply (45).

Usually parenthetical citations appear at the end of your sentences; however, if the reference applies only to the first part of the sentence, the parenthetical information is inserted at the appropriate points *within* the sentence:

```
While Baumrind argues that "the laboratory is not
the place to study degree of obedience" (421),
Milgram asserts that such arguments are groundless.
```

At times, you must modify the basic author/page number reference. Depending on the nature of your source(s), you may need to use one of the following citation formats:

Quoted Material Appearing in Another Source

```
(qtd. in Garber 211)
```

An Anonymous Work

```
("Obedience" 32)
```

Two Authors

```
(Bernstein and Politi 208)
```

A Particular Work by an Author, When You List Two or More Works by That Author in the List of Works Cited

```
(Toffler, Wave 96-97)
```

Two or More Sources as the Basis of Your Statement

```
(Butler 109; Carey 57)
```

The Location of a Passage in a Literary Text

```
for example, Hardy's The Return of the Native
(224; ch. 7)
```

[Page 224 in the edition used by the writer; the chapter number, 7, is provided for the convenience of those referring to another edition.]

A Multivolume Work

```
(3: 7-12) [volume number: page numbers; note the space
between the colon and the page numbers]
```

The Location of a Passage in a Play

> (1.2.308-22) [act.scene.line number(s)]

The Bible

> (John 3.16)
> (Col. 3.14) [book. chapter.verse]

IN-TEXT CITATION OF ELECTRONIC SOURCES (MLA)

Web sites, CD-ROM data, and e-mail generally do not have numbered pages. Different browsers may display and printers may produce differing numbers of pages for any particular site. You should therefore omit both page numbers and paragraph numbers from in-text citations to electronic sources, unless these page or paragraph numbers are provided within the source itself. For in-text citations of electronic sources, MLA prefers that you cite the author's name in the sentence rather than in a parenthetical, where possible. In APA style, use parentheses for citation of author's name and the year of publication as you would when citing print material.

Examples of MLA Citations in Works Cited List

BOOKS (MLA)
One Author

> Fahs, Alice. The Imagined Civil War: Popular Literature of the
>
> North and South, 1861-1865. Chapel Hill: U of North
>
> Carolina P, 2003.

Note: MLA convention dictates abbreviating the names of university presses (e.g., Oxford UP for Oxford University Press or the above for University of North Carolina Press). Commercial publishing companies are also shortened by dropping such endings as "Co.," or "Inc." The *MLA Handbook* includes a list of abbreviations for publishers' names.

Two or More Books by the Same Author

> Gubar, Susan. Critical Condition: Feminism at the Turn of the
>
> Century. New York: Columbia UP, 2000.
>
> ---. Racechanges: White Skin, Black Face in American Culture.
>
> New York: Oxford UP, 1997.

Note: For MLA style, references to works by the same author are listed in alphabetical order of title.

Two Authors

Gerson, Allan, and Jerry Adler. The Price of Terror. New York:

Harper, 2003.

Three Authors

Booth, Wayne C., Gregory G. Colomb, and Joseph M. Williams. The

Craft of Research. 2nd ed. Chicago: U of Chicago P, 2003.

More than Three Authors

Burawoy, Michael, et al. Global Ethnography: Forces, Connec-

tions, and Imaginations in a Postmodern World. Berkeley: U

of California P, 2000.

Book with an Editor and No Author

Dean, Bartholomew, and Jerome M. Levi, eds. At the Risk of Being

Heard: Identity, Indigenous Rights, and Postcolonial

States. Ann Arbor: U of Michigan P, 2003.

Later Edition

Whitten, Phillip. Anthropology: Contemporary Perspectives. 8th

ed. Boston: Allyn, 2001.

Republished Book

Dreiser, Theodore. An American Tragedy. 1925. Cambridge, UK:

Bentley, 1978.

A Multivolume Work

Slovenko, Ralph. Psychiatry in Law/Law in Psychiatry. 2 vols.

New York: Brunner-Routledge, 2002.

Translation

Saramago, Jose. All the Names. Trans. Margaret Jull Kosta. New

York: Harcourt, 1999.

Selection from an Anthology

Hardy, Melissa. "The Heifer." The Best American Short Stories.

    Ed. Sue Miller. Boston: Houghton, 2002. 97–115.

Government Publication

National Institute of Child Health and Human Development.

    Closing the Gap: A National Blueprint to Improve the

    Health of Persons with Mental Retardation. Washington: GPO,

    2002.

United States. Cong. House. Committee on Government Reform.

    Interim Report of the Activities of the House Committee on

    Government Reform. 107th Cong. 1st sess. Washington: GPO,

    2001.

The Bible

The New English Bible. New York: Oxford UP, 1972.

Signed Encyclopedia Article

Kunzle, David M. "Caricature, Cartoon, and Comic Strip." The New

    Encyclopaedia Britannica: Macropaedia. 15th ed. 2002.

Unsigned Encyclopedia Article

"Tidal Wave." Encyclopedia Americana. 2nd ed. 2001.

Periodicals (MLA)

Continuous Pagination throughout Annual Cycle

Binder, Sarah. "The Dynamics of Legislative Gridlock, 1947–

    1996." American Political Science Review 93 (1999): 519–31.

Separate Pagination Each Issue

O'Mealy, Joseph H. "Royal Family Values: The Americanization of

    Alan Bennett's The Madness of King George III."

    Literature/Film Quarterly 27.2 (1999): 90–97.

Monthly Periodical

Davison, Peter. "Girl, Seeming to Disappear." Atlantic Monthly

May 2000: 108-11.

Signed Article in Weekly Periodical

Gladwell, Malcolm. "The New-Boy Network." New Yorker 29 May

2000: 68-86.

Unsigned Article in Weekly Periodical

"GOP Speaker Admits 'Exaggerations.'" New Republic 14 Aug. 2000:

10-11.

Signed Article in Daily Newspaper

Vise, David A. "FBI Report Gauges School Violence Indicators."

Washington Post 6 Sept. 2000: B1+.

Unsigned Article in Daily Newspaper

"The World's Meeting Place." New York Times 6 Sept. 2000: A11.

Review

Barber, Benjamin R. "The Crack in the Picture Window." Rev. of

Bowling Alone: The Collapse and Revival of American

Community, by Robert D. Putnam. Nation 7 Aug. 2000: 29-34.

OTHER SOURCES (MLA)

Interview Conducted by the Researcher

Emerson, Robert. Personal interview. 10 Oct. 2002.

Dissertation (Abstracted in Dissertation Abstracts International)

Sheahan, Mary Theresa. "Living on the Edge: Ecology and Economy

in Willa Cather's 'Wild Land': Webster County Nebraska,

1870-1900." Diss. Northern Illinois U, 1999. DAI 60 (1999):

1298A.

Note: If the dissertation is published on microfilm by University Microfilms, give the order number at the conclusion of the reference. Example, in MLA format: Ann Arbor: UMI, 1999. AAT 9316566.

Lecture

Osborne, Michael. "The Great Man Theory: Caesar." Lecture.

History 401. University of California, Santa Barbara, 5

Nov. 2003.

Paper Delivered at a Professional Conference

Brodkey, Linda. "The Rhetoric of Race in Practice." Conf. on

Coll. Composition and Communication. Palmer House, Chicago.

20 Mar. 2003.

Film

The Pianist. Dir. Roman Polanski. Perf. Adrien Brody. Focus

Features and Universal, 2002.

Recording of a TV Program or Film

Legacy of the Hollywood Blacklist. Dir. Judy Chaikin.

Videocassette. One Step Productions and Public Affairs TV,

1987.

Audio Recording

Raman, Susheela. "Song to the Siren." Salt Rain. Narada, 2001.

Schumann, Robert. Symphonies no. 1 and 4. Cond. George Szell.

Cleveland Orchestra. Columbia, 1978.

Or, to emphasize the conductor rather than the composer:

Szell, George, cond. Symphonies no. 1 and 4. By Robert Schumann.

Cleveland Orchestra. Columbia, 1978.

ELECTRONIC SOURCES (MLA)

According to guidelines in the 2003 *MLA Handbook for Writers of Research Papers*, the following information should be included when crediting electronic sources:

1. *Name of the author, editor, compiler, or translator* (if given)
2. *Title* of the work, with quotation marks if something other than a book; underlined if it is a book
3. Information, if any, about *print publication*
4. Information about electronic publication, including title of the Internet site or name of any organization or institution sponsoring the site
5. *Access information*, including
   a. the date of electronic publication or latest update, if available
   b. the researcher's date of access
   c. the URL

If the URL of the exact document is extremely long and complex, making transcription errors possible, instead give the URL of the relevant search page or home page. From there, using other publication facts given in the citation, readers should be able to locate the cited document. URLs should include the access-mode identifier—*http, ftp, gopher,* or *telnet*. Enclose URLs in angle brackets (< >). When a URL continues from one line to the next, break it only after a slash. Do not add a hyphen.

Because few standards currently exist for those who post publications on the Internet, you may not necessarily be able to find or supply all the desired information. Thus, you may simply settle for what is available while aiming for comprehensiveness. Formatting conventions are illustrated by the following models:

An Entire Internet Site for an Online Scholarly Project or Database

```
The Piers Plowman Electronic Archive. Ed. Robert Adams et al.

    2003. Society for Early English and Norse Electronic Texts,

    University of Virginia Institute for Advanced Technology in

    the Humanities. 15 July 2003 <http://www.iath.virginia.edu/

    seenet/piers/piersmain.html>.
```

Note: information presented is (1) title of site, project, or database; (2) name of the editor of project or site; (3) electronic publication information, including date of electronic publication or latest update and name of sponsoring institution; and (4) date of access and URL.

A Short Work within a Scholarly Project

Dugan, Hoyt N. "The Nature of the Problem." <u>The Piers Plowman</u>

<u>Electronic Archive</u>. Ed. Robert Adams et al. 2003. Society

for Early English and Norse Electronic Texts, University of

Virginia Institute for Advanced Technology in the

Humanities. 15 July 2003 <http://www.iath.virginia.edu/

seenet/piers/pagearchivegoals1994body.html#natureofproblem>.

A Personal Home Page or Professional Site

Winter, Mick. <u>How to Talk New Age</u>. 28 July 2003

<http://www.well.com/user/mick/newagept.html>.

Note: In addition to date of access (shown here), the citation should include the date of last update, if given.

An Online Book

Smith, Adam. <u>The Wealth of Nations</u>. Oxford: Oxford UP, 1985. <u>The</u>

<u>Adam Smith Institute</u>. 2001. 15 July 2003 <http://

www.adamsmith.org/smith/won-intro.htm>.

A Part of an Online Book

Smith, Adam. "Of the Division of Labour." <u>The Wealth of Nations</u>.

Oxford: Oxford UP, 1985. <u>The Adam Smith Institute</u>. 2001. 15

July 2003 <http://www.adamsmith.org/smith/won-b1-c1.htm>.

An Article in a Scholarly Journal

Epstein, Paul. "The Imitation of Athena in the <u>Lysistrata</u> of

Aristophanes." <u>Animus</u> 7 (2002). 16 July 2003 <http://

www.swgc.mun.ca/animus/current/epstein7.htm>.

An Unsigned Article in a Newspaper or on a Newswire

"Verizon to Rehire 1,100 Laid-off Workers." <u>AP Online</u> 16 July

2003. 18 July 2003 <http://www.nytimes.com/aponline/

technology/AP-Verizon-Jobs.html>.

A Signed Article in a Newspaper or on a Newswire

> Vartabedian, Ralph. "Columbia's Crew Lived after Radio Calls
>
> Ended." <u>Chicago Tribune</u> 16 July 2003. 20 July 2003
>
> <http://www.chicagotribune.com/technology/
>
> la-na-shuttle16jul16,1,1997210.story?coll=chi-news-hed>.

An Article in a Magazine

> Kim, Jimin. "When Cell Phones Meet Camcorders." <u>Forbes</u> 16 July
>
> 2003. 12 Aug. 2003 <http://www.forbes.com/home/2003/07/16/
>
> cx_jk_0716tentech.html>.

A Review

> Vaneechoutte, Mario. Rev. of <u>The Theory and Practice of Institu-</u>
>
> <u>tional Transplantation</u>, ed. M. De Jong et al. <u>Journal of</u>
>
> <u>Mimetics</u> 7.2(2003). 13 Jan. 2004 <http://jom-emit.cfpm.org/
>
> 2003/vol7/vaneechoutte_m.html>.

An Editorial or Letter to the Editor

> Park, Charlie. "The Matrix Is Everywhere." Letter. <u>Wired</u> 11.7
>
> (July 2003). 13 Jan. 2004 <http://www.wired.com/wired/
>
> archive/11.07/rants.html>.

An Abstract

> Arden, Heather. "The Harry Potter Stories and French Arthurian
>
> Romance." <u>Arthuriana</u> 13.2 (2003): 54-68. Abstract. 16 July
>
> 2003 <http://www.smu.edu/arthuriana/>. Path: Abstracts;
>
> A-F.

Material from a Periodically Published Database on CD-ROM

> Ellis, Richard. "Whale Killing Begins Anew." <u>Audubon</u> 94.6
>
> (1992): 20-22. <u>General Periodicals Ondisc-Magazine Express</u>.
>
> CD-ROM UMI-Proquest. 1992.

A Nonperiodical Source on CD-ROM, Diskette, or Magnetic Tape

Clements, John. "War of 1812." <u>Chronology of the United States</u>.

CD-ROM. Dallas: Political Research, 1997.

An E-Mail Communication

Mendez, Michael R. "Re: Solar power." E-mail to Edgar V.

Atamian. 11 Sept. 2003.

Armstrong, David J. E-mail to the author. 30 Aug. 2003.

An Online Posting   For online postings, discussion groups, or synchronous communications, cite a version stored as a Web file, if one exists, so that your readers can more easily find your sources. Label sources as needed (e.g., Online posting, Online defense of dissertation, etc., with neither underlining nor quotation marks). Several models follow.

An Online Posting

Flanders, Julia. "Mentoring in Humanities Computing." Online

posting. 8 May 2003. Humanist Discussion Group. 16 July

2003 <http://lists.village.virginia.edu/lists_archive/

Humanist/v17/0001.html>.

Synchronous Communication

Mendez, Michael R. Online debate. "Solar Power Versus Fossil

Fuel Power." 3 Apr. 2000. CollegeTownMOO. 3 Apr. 2000

<telnet://next.cs.bvc.edu.7777>.

Downloaded Computer Software

Quicktime. Vers. 6.3. 16 July 2003 <http://www.apple.com/

quicktime/download/>.

APA STYLE

In-Text Citation

Here are sample in-text citations using the APA system:

Much research shows that rather than inducing any

lasting changes in a child's behavior, punishment

```
"promotes only momentary compliance"(Berk, 2002,
p. 383).
```

Notice that in the APA system, there is a comma between the author's name, the date, and the page number, and the number itself is preceded by "p." or "pp." Notice also that the parenthetical reference is placed *before* the final punctuation of the sentence.

If you have already mentioned the author's name in the text, it is not necessary to repeat it in the citation:

```
According to Berk (2002), much research shows
that rather than inducing any lasting changes in
a child's behavior, punishment "promotes only
momentary compliance"(p. 383).
```

or:

```
According to Berk, much research shows that
rather than inducing any lasting changes in a
child's behavior, punishment "promotes only
momentary compliance"(2002, p. 383).
```

When using the APA system, provide page numbers only for direct quotations, not for summaries or paraphrases. If you do not refer to a specific page, simply indicate the date:

```
Berk (2002) asserted that many research findings
view punishment as a quick fix rather than a
long-term solution to behavior problems in
children.
```

For quotations of 40 words or more, use block (indented) quotations. In these cases, place the parenthetical citation *after* the period:

```
Various strategies exist for reducing children's
tendency to view the world in a gender-biased
fashion:
              Once children notice the vast array of
              gender stereotypes in their society,
              parents and teachers can point out
              exceptions. For example, they can
              arrange for children to see men and
              women pursuing nontraditional careers.
              And they can reason with children,
              explaining that interests and skills,
              not sex, should determine a person's
```

> occupation and activities. (Berk, 2002, p. 395)

Again, were Berk's name mentioned in the sentence leading into the quotation, the parenthetical reference would be simply (2002, p. 395) for APA style.

If the reference applies only to the first part of a sentence, the parenthetical reference is inserted at the appropriate points *within* the sentence:

> Shapiro (2002) emphasizes the idea that law firms are "continually in flux" (p. 32), while Sikes focuses on their stability as institutions.

At times you must modify the basic author/page number reference. Depending on the nature of your source(s), you may need to use one of the following citation formats:

Quoted Material Appearing in Another Source

> (as cited in Garber, 2000, p. 211)

An Anonymous Work

> ("Obedience," 2003, p. 32)

Two Authors

> (Striano & Rochat, 2000, p. 257)

Two or More Sources as the Basis of Your Statement (Arrange Entries in Alphabetic Order of Surname)

> (Ehrenreich 2001, p. 68; Hitchens, 2001, p. 140)

A Multivolume Work

> (Brown, 2003, vol. 2, p. 88)

IN-TEXT CITATION OF ELECTRONIC SOURCES (APA)

As noted earlier, Web sites, CD-ROM data, and e-mail generally do not have numbered pages (unless they are PDF reproductions of print material). If paragraph numbers are visible in the source, you can use them instead of page numbers for in-text citations. If the document has headings but no page or paragraph numbers, cite the heading and the number of the paragraph following it.

Citation to an Electronic Source with Headings

> (Kishlansky, 2002, Conclusion section, ¶2)

Examples of APA Citations in References List

BOOKS
One Author

> Fahs, Alice. (2003). *The imagined civil war: Popular literature*
>
> *of the north and south, 1861-1865.* Chapel Hill: University
>
> of North Carolina Press.

Two or More Books by the Same Author

> Gubar, S. (1997). *Racechanges: White skin, black face in Ameri-*
>
> *can culture.* New York: Oxford University Press.
>
> Gubar, S. (2000). *Critical condition: Feminism at the turn of*
>
> *the century.* New York: Columbia University Press.

Note: For APA style, references to works by the same author are listed in chronological order of publication, earliest first. Use the author's name in all entries.

Two Authors

> Gerson, A., & Adler, J. (2003). *The price of terror.* New York:
>
> Harper.

Three Authors

> Booth, W. C., Colomb, G. C., & Williams, J. M. (2003). *The craft*
>
> *of research* (2nd ed.). Chicago: University of Chicago
>
> Press.

More than Three Authors

> Burawoy, M., Blum, J. A., George, S., Gille, Z., Gowan, T.,
>
> Haney, L., et al. (2000). *Global ethnography: Forces,*
>
> *connections, and imaginations in a postmodern world.* Berke-
>
> ley: University of California Press.

Note: If more than six, list only the first six, followed by *et al.*

Book with an Editor and No Author

Dean, B., & Levi, J. M. (Eds.). (2003). *At the risk of being heard: Identity, indigenous rights, and postcolonial states.* Ann Arbor: University of Michigan Press.

Later Edition

Whitten, P. (2001). *Anthropology: Contemporary perspectives* (8th ed.). Boston: Allyn & Bacon.

Republished Book

Dreiser, T. (1978). *An American tragedy.* Cambridge, Mass.: R. Bentley. (Original work published 1925).

A Multivolume Work

Slovenko, R. (2002). *Psychiatry in law/law in psychiatry.* (Vols. 1–2). New York: Brunner-Routledge.

Translation

Saramago, J. (1999). *All the names.* (M. J. Kosta, Trans.). New York: Harcourt.

Selection from an Anthology

Halberstam, D. (2002). Who we are. In S. J. Gould (Ed.), *The best American essays 2002* (pp. 124–136). New York: Houghton Mifflin.

Government Publication

National Institute of Child Health and Human Development. (2002). *Closing the gap: A national blueprint to improve the health of persons with mental retardation.* Washington, DC: U.S. Government Printing Office.

Caring for children act of 2003: Report of the Senate Committee on Health, Education, Labor, and Pensions, S. Rep. No. 108-37 (2003).

Signed Encyclopedia Article

Kunzle, D. M. (2002). Caricature, cartoon, and comic strip. In *The new encyclopaedia Britannica.* (Vol. 15, pp. 539–552). Chicago: Encyclopaedia Britannica.

Unsigned Encyclopedia Article

Tidal wave. (2001). In *The encyclopedia Americana.* (Vol. 26, p. 730). Danbury, CT: Grolier.

PERIODICALS (APA)

Continuous Pagination throughout Annual Cycle

Tomlins, C. L. (2003). In a wilderness of tigers: Violence, the discourse of English colonizing, and the refusals of American history. *Theoretical Inquiries in Law, 4,* 505–543.

Separate Pagination Each Issue

O'Mealy, J. H. (1999). Royal family values: The Americanization of Alan Bennett's *The Madness of King George III. Literature/Film Quarterly, 27*(2), 90–97.

Monthly Periodical

Davison, P. (2000, May). Girl, seeming to disappear. *Atlantic Monthly, 285,* 108–111.

Signed Article in Weekly Periodical

Gladwell, M. (2000, May 29). The new-boy network. *The New Yorker,* 68–86.

Unsigned Article in Weekly Periodical

Spain and the Basques: Dangerous stalemate. (2003, July 5). *The*

Economist, 368, 44–45.

Signed Article in Daily Newspaper, Discontinuous Pages

Vise, D. A. (2000, September 6). FBI report gauges school vio-

lence indicators. *The Washington Post,* pp. B1, B6.

Unsigned Article in Daily Newspaper

The world's meeting place. (2000, September 6). *The New York*

Times, p. A11.

Review

Barber, B. R. (2000, August 7). The crack in the picture window.

[Review of the book *Bowling alone: The collapse and revival*

of American community]. *The Nation,* 29–34.

Note: Some weekly magazines do not have volume numbers, in which case, include only the date and page numbers in your reference.

OTHER SOURCES (APA)

Dissertation (Abstracted in Dissertation Abstracts International)

Sheahan, M. T. (1999). Living on the edge: Ecology and economy

in Willa Cather's "Wild Land": Webster County, Nebraska,

1870–1900 (Doctoral dissertation, Northern Illinois Univer-

sity, 1999). *Dissertation Abstracts International, 60,*

1298A.

Note: If the dissertation is obtained from University Microfilms, give the UMI number in parentheses at the conclusion of the reference, after the DAI number: (UMI No. AAD9315947).

Lecture

Baldwin, J. (1999, January 11). *The self in social interactions.*

Sociology 2 lecture, University of California, Santa Barbara.

Paper Delivered at a Professional Conference

> Hollon, S. D. (2003, August). Treatment and prevention of de-
>
> pression with drugs and psychotherapy. Paper presented at
>
> the annual convention of the American Psychological Associ-
>
> ation, Toronto, Ontario.

Film

> Polanski, R. (Director). (2002). *The pianist* [Motion picture].
>
> United States: Focus Features and Universal.

TV Series

> Chase, D. (Producer). (2001). *The Sopranos* [Television series].
>
> New York: HBO.

Music Recording

> Raman, S. (2001). Song to the siren. On *Salt Rain* [CD]. Milwau-
>
> kee, WI: Narada.

ELECTRONIC SOURCES (APA)

The basic information needed to cite electronic sources using APA documentation style includes

1. *Name of the author* (if given)
2. *Date* of publication, update, or retrieval
3. *Document title, description, and/or source*
4. The *URL,* or Internet address (the most crucial element)

The *APA Publications Manual* recommends that writers check the URLs regularly, while drafting a paper and before submission, as the location of documents sometimes changes. As with MLA citations, include as much pertinent information as is available to help your reader find the source, such as volume and issue numbers if available.

The general APA format for online periodical sources is as follows:

> Author, I. (date). Title of article. *Name of Periodical. Volume*
>
> and issue number (if available). Retrieved month, day,
>
> year, from source

For online sources, do not add periods or other punctuation immediately following URLs. Also, if you need to continue a URL across lines, break the URL after a slash or before a period. Do not use a hyphen. An extra hyphen or period may prevent a reader from accessing the source.

An Article in an Internet-Only Scholarly Journal

> Sheehan, K. B., & Hoy, M. G. (1999). Using e-mail to survey
>
>   Internet users in the United States: Methodology and
>
>   assessment. *Journal of Computer-Mediated Communication,*
>
>   *4*(3). Retrieved August 14, 2001, from
>
>   http://www.ascusc.org/jcmc/vol4/issue3/sheehan.html

Note: The APA guidelines distinguish between Internet articles that are based on a print source, and those that appear in Internet-only journals. When an Internet article is reproduced from a print source, simply follow the usual journal article reference format, and include the phrase "Electronic version" in brackets following the title of the article. In such a case, you don't need to include the URL or date retrieved from the Internet.

Stand-alone document with author and date

> Winter, M. (2003) *How to talk new age.* Retrieved July 25, 2003,
>
>   from http://www.well.com/user/mick/newagept.html

Note: When no date of publication is given, indicate this with n.d. for "no date" in parentheses where the date usually would appear. If no author is identified, begin the reference with the document title.

An Unsigned Article in a Newspaper or on a Newswire

> Verizon to rehire 1,100 laid-off workers. (2003, 16 July).
>
>   *AP Online.* Retrieved July 18, 2003, from http://
>
>   www.nytimes.com/aponline/technology/AP-Verizon-Jobs.html

A Signed Article in a Newspaper or on a Newswire

> Vartabedian, R. (2003, 16 July). Columbia's crew lived after ra-
>
>   dio calls ended. *Chicago Tribune.* Retrieved July 20, 2003,
>
>   from http://www.chicagotribune.com/technology/
>
>   la-na-shuttle16jul16,1,1997210.story?coll=chi-news-hed

An Article in a Magazine

Kim, J. (2003, July 16). When cell phones meet camcorders.

Forbes. Retrieved August 12, 2003, from http://

www.forbes .com/home/2003/07/16/cx_jk_0716tentech.html

An Abstract

Eliaphson, N., & Lichterman, P. (2003). Culture in interaction.

American Journal of Sociology. Abstract retrieved

October 25, 2003, from http://www.journals.uchicago.edu/

AJS/journal/issues/v108n4/040241/brief/

040241.abstract.html

Electronic Copy of a Periodical Article Retrieved from a Database

Bergeron, L. R. (2002). Family preservation: An unidentified ap-

proach in elder abuse protection. *Families in Society, 83,*

547–556. Retrieved July 28, 2003, from XanEdu Research En-

gine, ProQuest.

For online postings or synchronous communications, the APA recommends referencing only those sources that are maintained in archived form. However, archived discussions or postings are rarely peer reviewed, are not generally regarded as having scholarly content, and are not archived for very long, so APA advises that you cite them with care in formal works. APA also advises against using nonarchived postings, as they are not retrievable by your readers. If you do choose to include sources that are not archived—and this includes e-mail communications between individuals—the APA suggests citing them as personal communications in the text of your work, but leaving them out of the References list. For archived sources, follow these models as appropriate.

Message Posted to an Electronic Mailing List

Hammond, T. (2002, July 19). A bootstrapping mechanism for DOI.

Message posted to General DOI Discussion Forum, archived

at http://www.doi.org/mail-archive/discuss-doi/

msg00440.html

Message Posted to an Online Forum or Discussion Group

```
Pagdin, F. (2001, July 3). New medium for therapy [Msg 498].

    Message posted to http://www.groups.yahoo.com/group/

    cybersociology/message/498
```

Computer Software

```
Gamma UniType for Windows 1.5 (Version 1.1) [Computer software].

    (1997). San Diego, CA: Gamma Productions.
```

Note: Reference entries are needed for specialized or limited-distribution software only. If an individual has proprietary rights to the software, name that person as the author.

 ## Writing Assignment: Source-Based Paper

Using the methods we have outlined in this chapter—and incorporating the skills covered in this textbook as a whole—conduct your own research on a topic and research question that falls within your major or your area of interest. Your research process should culminate in a 1500- to 1700-word paper in which you use your sources to present an answer to your research question.

Appendix:
More on Introductions
and Conclusions

Introductions

Following are six strategies for beginning your papers. See pages 108-09 (in Chapter 3) for an overview of introductions and for a seventh strategy.

HISTORICAL REVIEW

In many cases, the reader will be unprepared to follow the issue you discuss unless you provide some historical background. Consider the following introduction to a paper on the film-rating system:

> Sex and violence on the screen are not new issues. In the Roaring Twenties there was increasing pressure from civic and religious groups to ban depictions of "immorality" from the screen. Faced with the threat of federal censorship, the film producers decided to clean their own house. In 1930, the Motion Picture Producers and Distributors of America established the Production Code. At first, adherence to the Code was voluntary; but in 1934 Joseph Breen, newly appointed head of the MPPDA, gave the Code teeth. Henceforth all newly produced films had to be submitted for approval to the Production Code Administration, which had the power to award or withhold the Code seal. Without a Code seal, it was virtually impossible for a film to be shown anywhere in the United States, since exhibitors would not accept it. At about the same time, the Catholic Legion of Decency was formed to advise the faithful which films were and were not objectionable. For several decades the Production Code Administration exercised powerful control over what was portrayed in American theatrical films. By the 1960s, however, changing standards of morality had considerably weakened the Code's grip. In 1968, the Production Code was replaced with a rating system designed to keep

younger audiences away from films with high levels of sex or violence. Despite its imperfections, this rating system has proved more beneficial to American films than did the old censorship system.

The paper following the introduction above concerns the relative benefits of the rating system. By providing some historical background on the rating system, the writer helps readers understand his arguments. Notice the chronological development of details.

REVIEW OF A CONTROVERSY

A particular type of historical review provides the background on a controversy or debate. Consider the following introduction:

> The *American Heritage Dictionary*'s definition of civil disobedience is rather simple: "the refusal to obey civil laws that are regarded as unjust, usually by employing methods of passive resistance." However, despite such famous (and beloved) examples of civil disobedience as the movements of Mahatma Gandhi in India and the Reverend Martin Luther King, Jr., in the United States, the question of whether or not civil disobedience should be considered an asset to society is hardly clear cut. For instance, Hannah Arendt, in her article "Civil Disobedience," holds that "to think of disobedient minorities as rebels and truants is against the letter and spirit of a constitution whose framers were especially sensitive to the dangers of unbridled majority rule." On the other hand, a noted lawyer, Lewis Van Dusen, Jr., in his article "Civil Disobedience: Destroyer of Democracy," states that "civil disobedience, whatever the ethical rationalization, is still an assault on our democratic society, an affront to our legal order and an attack on our constitutional government." These two views are clearly incompatible. I believe, though, that Van Dusen's is the more convincing. On balance, civil disobedience is dangerous to society.*

The negative aspects of civil disobedience, rather than Van Dusen's essay, are the topic of this paper. But to introduce this topic, the writer has provided quotations that represent opposing sides of the controversy over civil disobedience, as well as brief references to two controversial practitioners. By focusing at the outset on the particular rather than on the abstract qualities of the topic, the writer hoped to secure the attention of her readers and involve them in the controversy that forms the subject of her paper.

FROM THE GENERAL TO THE SPECIFIC

Another way of providing a transition from the reader's world to the less familiar world of the paper is to work from a general subject to a specific one.

---

*Michele Jacques, "Civil Disobedience: Van Dusen vs. Arendt," unpublished paper, 1993, 1. Used by permission.

The following introduction begins a paper on improving our air quality by inducing people to trade the use of their cars for public transportation.

> While generalizations are risky, it seems pretty safe to say that most human beings are selfish. Self-interest may be part of our nature, and probably aids the survival of our species, since self-interested pursuits increase the likelihood of individual survival and genetic reproduction. Ironically, however, our selfishness has caused us to abuse the natural environment upon which we depend. We have polluted, deforested, depleted, deformed, and endangered our earth, water, and air to such an extent that now our species' survival is gravely threatened. In America, air pollution is one of our most pressing environmental problems, and it is our selfish use of the automobile that poses the greatest threat to clean air, as well as the greatest challenge to efforts to stop air pollution. Very few of us seem willing to give up our cars, let alone use them less. We are spoiled by the individual freedom afforded us when we can hop into our gas-guzzling vehicles and go where we want, when we want. Somehow, we as a nation will have to wean ourselves from this addiction to the automobile, and we can do this by designing alternative forms of transportation that serve our selfish interests.[*]

FROM THE SPECIFIC TO THE GENERAL: ANECDOTE, ILLUSTRATION

The following paragraph quotes an anecdote in order to move from the specific to a general subject:

> In an article on the changing American family, Ron French tells the following story:
>
>> Six-year-old Sydney Papenheim has her future planned. "First I'm going to marry Jared," she told her mother. "Then I'm going to get divorced and marry Gabby." "No, honey," Lisa Boettcher says, "you don't plan it like that." That's news to Sydney. Her mother is divorced and remarried, as is her stepdad. Her grandparents are divorced and remarried, as are enough aunts and uncles to field a team for "Family Feud." She gets presents from her stepfather's ex-wife. Her stepfather's children sometimes play at the house of her father. "You never know what is going to happen from day to day," says Sydney's stepdad, Brian Boettcher. "It's an evolution." It's more like a revolution, from Norman Rockwell to Norman Lear.[**][†]

---

[*]Travis Knight, "Reducing Air Pollution with Alternative Transportation," unpublished paper, 1998, 1. Used by permission.

[**]Ron French, "Family: The D-Word Loses Its Sting as Households Blend," *Detroit News* 1 Jan. 2000, 17 Aug. 2000 <http://detnews.com/specialreports/2000/journey/family/family.htm>.

[†] Norman Lear (b. 1922): American television writer and producer noted for developing groundbreaking depictions of the American family in the 1970s, such as "All in the Family," "Sanford and Son," and "Maude."

> French continues on to report that by the year 2007, blended families such as the Boettcher's will outnumber traditional nuclear families. Yet most people continue to lament this change. We as a nation need to accept this new reality: the "till death do us part" version of marriage no longer works.*

The previous introduction went from the general (the statement that human beings are selfish) to the specific (how to decrease air pollution); this one goes from the specific (one little girl's understanding of marriage and divorce) to the general (the changing American family). The anecdote is one of the most effective means at your disposal for capturing and holding your reader's attention. For decades, speakers have begun their remarks with a funny, touching, or otherwise appropriate story; in fact, plenty of books are nothing but collections of such stories, arranged by subject.

QUESTION

Frequently, you can provoke the reader's attention by posing a question or a series of questions:

> Are gender roles learned or inherited? Scientific research has established the existence of biological differences between the sexes, but the effect of biology's influence on gender roles cannot be distinguished from society's influence. According to Michael Lewis of the Institute for the Study of Exceptional Children, "As early as you can show me a sex difference, I can show you the culture at work." Social processes, as well as biological differences, are responsible for the separate roles of men and women.†

Opening your paper with a question can be provocative, since it places the reader in an active role: He or she begins by considering answers. *Are* gender roles learned? *Are* they inherited? In this active role, the reader is likely to continue reading with interest.

STATEMENT OF THESIS

Perhaps the most direct method of introduction is to begin immediately with the thesis:

> Every college generation is defined by the social events of its age. The momentous occurrences of an era—from war and economics to politics and inventions—give meaning to lives of the individuals who live through them. They also serve to knit those individuals together by creating a collective memory and a common historic or generational identity. In 1979, I went to 26 college and university campuses, selected to represent the diversity of American higher education, and asked

---

*Veronica Gonzalez, "New Family Formations," unpublished paper, 1999, 1. Used by permission.

†Tammy Smith, "Are Sex Roles Learned or Inherited?" unpublished paper, 1994, 1. Used by permission.

students what social or political events most influenced their generation. I told them that the children who came of age in the decade after
World War I might have answered the Great Depression. The bombing
of Pearl Harbor, World War II, or perhaps the death of Franklin
Roosevelt might have stood out for those born a few years later. For my
generation, born after World War II, the key event was the assassina-
tion of John F. Kennedy. We remember where we were when we heard
the news. The whole world seemingly changed in its aftermath.*

This paper begins with a general assertion—that large-scale social events
shape generations of college students. Beginning like this immediately establishes the broader context. Stating your thesis in the first sentence of an
introduction also works when you make a controversial argument. Stating a
provocative point right away, such as "American democracy is dead," for a
paper examining the problems plaguing representative government in current society, forces the reader to sit up and take notice—perhaps even to begin protesting. This "hooks" a reader, who is likely to want to find out how
your paper will support its strong thesis. In the example paragraph above,
the thesis is followed by specific examples of social events, which prepares
the reader to consider the experiences of students who were in college in
1979 and compare them to those of earlier generations.

One final note about our model introductions: They may be longer than
introductions you have been accustomed to writing. Many writers (and
readers) prefer a shorter, snappier introduction. The length of an introduction can depend on the length of the paper it introduces, and it is also largely
a matter of personal or corporate style. There is no rule concerning the correct length of an introduction. If you feel that a short introduction is appropriate, use one. Or you may wish to break up what seems like a long introduction into two paragraphs.

Conclusions

Following are six strategies for concluding your papers. See pages 110-11 (in
Chapter 3) for an overview of conclusions and for a seventh strategy.

CALL FOR FURTHER RESEARCH

In the scientific and social scientific communities, papers often end with a review of what has been presented (as, for instance, in an experiment) and the
ways in which the subject under consideration needs to be further explored.
A word of caution: If you raise questions that you call on others to answer,
make sure you know that the research you are calling for hasn't already been
conducted.

The following conclusion comes from a sociological report on the placement of elderly men and women in nursing homes.

---

*Arthur Levine, "The Making of a Generation," *Change* Sept.–Oct. 1993, 8.

Thus, our study shows a correlation between the placement of elderly citizens in nursing facilities and the significant decline of their motor and intellectual skills over the ten months following placement. What the research has not made clear is the extent to which this marked decline is due to physical as opposed to emotional causes. The elderly are referred to homes at that point in their lives when they grow less able to care for themselves—which suggests that the drop-off in skills may be due to physical causes. But the emotional stress of being placed in a home, away from family and in an environment that confirms the patient's view of himself as decrepit, may exacerbate—if not itself be a primary cause of—the patient's rapid loss of abilities. Further research is needed to clarify the relationship between depression and particular physical ailments as these affect the skills of the elderly in nursing facilities. There is little doubt that information yielded by such studies can enable health care professionals to deliver more effective services.

Notice how this call for further study locates the author in a larger community of researchers on whom she depends for assistance in answering the questions that have come out of her own work. The author summarizes her findings (in the first sentence of the paragraph), states what her work has not shown, and then extends her invitation.

SOLUTION/RECOMMENDATION

The purpose of your paper might be to review a problem or controversy and to discuss contributing factors. In such a case, it would be appropriate, after summarizing your discussion, to offer a solution based on the knowledge you've gained while conducting research, as the writer of the following conclusion does. If your solution is to be taken seriously, however, your knowledge must be amply demonstrated in the body of the paper.

. . . The major problem in college sports today is not commercialism— it is the exploitation of athletes and the proliferation of illicit practices which dilute educational standards.

Many universities are currently deriving substantial benefits from sports programs that depend on the labor of athletes drawn from the poorest sections of America's population. It is the responsibility of educators, civil rights leaders, and concerned citizens to see that these young people get a fair return for their labor both in terms of direct remuneration and in terms of career preparation for a life outside sports.

Minimally, scholarships in revenue-producing sports should be designed to extend until graduation, rather than covering only four years of athletic eligibility, and should include guarantees of tutoring, counseling, and proper medical care. At institutions where the profits are particularly large (such as Texas A & M, which can afford to pay its football coach $280,000 a year), scholarships should also provide salaries that extend beyond room, board, and tuition. The important thing is that the athlete be remunerated fairly and have the opportunity to gain skills from a university environment without undue competition from a physically and psychologically demanding full-time job. This may well require that scholarships be extended over five or six years, including summers.

Such a proposal, I suspect, will not be easy to implement. The current amateur system, despite its moral and educational flaws, enables universities to hire their athletic labor at minimal cost. But solving the fiscal crisis of the universities on the backs of America's poor and minorities is not, in the long run, a tenable solution. With the support of concerned educators, parents, and civil rights leaders, and with the help from organized labor, the college athlete, truly a sleeping giant, will someday speak out and demand what is rightly his—and hers—a fair share of the revenue created by their hard work.*

In this conclusion, the author summarizes his article in one sentence: "The major problem in college sports today is not commercialism—it is the exploitation of athletes and the proliferation of illicit practices which dilute educational standards." In paragraph 2, he continues with an analysis of the problem just stated and follows with a general recommendation—that "educators, civil rights leaders, and concerned citizens" be responsible for the welfare of college athletes. In paragraph 3, he makes a specific proposal, and in the final paragraph, he anticipates resistance to the proposal. He concludes by discounting this resistance and returning to the general point, that college athletes should receive a fair deal.

ANECDOTE

As you learned in the context of introductions, an anecdote is a briefly told story or joke, the point of which in a conclusion is to shed light on your subject. The anecdote is more direct than an allusion. With an allusion, you merely refer to a story ("Too many people today live in Plato's cave . . ."); with the anecdote, you actually retell the story. The anecdote allows readers to discover for themselves the significance of a reference to another source—an effort most readers enjoy because they get to exercise their creativity.

The following anecdote concludes a political-philosophical essay. First, the author includes a paragraph summing up her argument, and she follows that with a brief story.

> Ironically, our economy is fueled by the very thing that degrades our value system. But when politicians call for a return to "traditional family values," they seldom criticize the business interests that promote and benefit from our coarsened values. Consumer capitalism values things over people; it thrives on discontent and unhappiness since discontented people make excellent consumers, buying vast numbers of things that may somehow "fix" their inadequacies. We

---

*Mark Naison, "Scenario for Scandal," *Commonweal* 109.16 (1982).

buy more than we need, the economy chugs along, but such material- ism is the real culprit behind our warped value systems. Anthony de Mello tells the following story:

> Socrates believed that the wise person would instinctively lead a fru- gal life, and he even went so far as to refuse to wear shoes. Yet he con- stantly fell under the spell of the marketplace and would go there of- ten to look at the great variety and magnificence of the wares on display.
>
> A friend once asked him why he was so intrigued with the allures of the market. "I love to go there," Socrates replied, "to discover how many things I am perfectly happy without." (27)*

The writer chose to conclude the article with this anecdote. She could have developed an interpretation, but this would have spoiled the dramatic value for the reader. The purpose of using an anecdote is to make your point with subtlety, so resist the temptation to interpret. When selecting an anecdote, keep in mind four guidelines: the anecdote should fit your content; it should be prepared for (readers should have all the information they need to under- stand it), it should provoke the reader's interest, and it should not be so ob- scure as to be unintelligible.

QUOTATION

A favorite concluding device is the quotation—the words of a famous person or an authority in the field on which you are writing. The purpose of quoting another is to link your work to theirs, thereby gaining for your work author- ity and credibility. The first criterion for selecting a quotation is its suitability to your thesis. But carefully consider what your choice of sources says about you. Suppose you are writing a paper on the American work ethic. If you could use a line by comedian Jay Leno or one by the current secretary of la- bor to make the final point of your conclusion, which would you choose and why? One source may not be inherently more effective than the other, but the choice certainly sets a tone for the paper. The following two paragraphs conclude an essay examining the popularity of vulgar and insulting humor in television shows, movies, and other popular culture:

> But studies on the influence of popular culture suggest that cruel hu- mor serves as more than a release in modern society. The ubiquitous media pick up on our baser nature, exaggerate it to entertain, and, by spitting it back at us, encourage us to push the boundaries even fur- ther. As a result, says Johns Hopkins' Miller, "We're gradually erod- ing the kinds of social forms and inhibitions that kept [aggressive] compulsions contained."
>
> Before the cycle escalates further, we might do well to consider the advice of Roman statesman and orator Cicero, who wrote at the peak of the Roman empire: "If we are forced, at every hour, to watch or lis-

---

*Frances Wageneck, *Family Values in the Marketplace*, unpublished paper, 2000, 6. Used by permission.

ten to horrible events, this constant stream of ghastly impressions will deprive even the most delicate among us of all respect for humanity."*

The two quotations used here serve different but equally effective ends. The first idea provides one additional expert's viewpoint, then leads nicely into the cautionary note the writer introduces by quoting Cicero. The Roman's words, and the implied parallel drawn between Rome and contemporary culture, are strong enough that the author ends there, without stepping in and making any statements of her own. In other cases, quotations can be used to set up one last statement by the author of a paper.

Using quotations poses one potential problem: If you end with the words of another, you may leave the impression that someone else can make your case more eloquently than you. The language of the quotation will put your own prose into relief. If your prose suffers by comparison—if the quotations are the best part of your paper—spend some time revising. Avoid this kind of problem by making your own presentation strong.

QUESTION

Questions are useful for opening papers, and they are just as useful for closing them. Opening and closing questions function in different ways, however. The introductory question promises to be addressed in the paper that follows. But the concluding question leaves issues unresolved, calling on the readers to assume an active role by offering their own answers. Consider the following two paragraphs, written to conclude a paper on genetically modified (GM) food:

> Are GM foods any more of a risk than other agricultural innovations that have taken place over the years, like selective breeding? Do the existing and potential future benefits of GM foods outweigh any risks that do exist? And what standard should governments use when assessing the safety of transgenic crops? The "frankenfood" frenzy has given life to a policy-making standard known as the "precautionary principle," which has been long advocated by environmental groups. That principle essentially calls for governments to prohibit any activity that raises concerns about human health or the environment, even if some cause-and-effect relationships are not fully established scientifically. As Liberal Democrat MP [Member of Parliament] Norman Baker told the BBC: "We must always apply the precautionary principle. That says that unless you're sure of adequate control, unless you're sure the risk is minimal, unless you're sure nothing horrible can go wrong, you don't do it."
>
> But can any innovation ever meet such a standard of certainty—especially given the proliferation of "experts" that are motivated as much by politics as they are by science? And what about those millions of malnourished people whose lives could be saved by

---

*Nina J. Easton, "The Meaning of America," *Los Angeles Times Magazine* 7 Feb. 1993, 21.

> transgenic foods? [Is] the "precautionary principle" [really] so precautionary after all [?]*

Rather than ending with a question, you may choose to *raise* a question in your conclusion and then answer it, based on the material you've provided in the paper. The answered question challenges a reader to agree or disagree with you and thus also places the reader in an active role. The following brief conclusion ends a student paper entitled "Is Feminism Dead?"

> So the answer to the question "Is the feminist movement dead?" is no, it's not. Even if most young women today don't consciously identify themselves as "feminists"—due to the ways in which the term has become loaded with negative associations—the principles of gender equality that lie at feminism's core are enthusiastically embraced by the vast number of young women, and even a large percentage of young men.

SPECULATION

When you speculate, you ask about and explore what has happened or what might happen. Speculation involves a spinning out of possibilities. It stimulates readers by immersing them in your discussion of the unknown, implicitly challenging them to agree or disagree. The following paragraph concludes "The New Generation Gap" by Neil Howe and William Strauss. In this article, Howe and Strauss discuss the differences among Americans of various ages, including the "GI Generation" (born between 1901 and 1924), the "Boomers"(born 1943–1961), the "Thirteeners" (born 1961–1981), and the "Millennials" (born 1981–2000):

> If, slowly but surely, Millennials receive the kind of family protection and public generosity that GIs enjoyed as children, then they could come of age early in the next century as a group much like the GIs of the 1920s and 1930s—as a stellar (if bland) generation of rationalists, team players, and can-do civic builders. Two decades from now Boomers entering old age may well see in their grown Millennial children an effective instrument for saving the world, while Thirteeners entering midlife will shower kindness on a younger generation that is getting a better deal out of life (though maybe a bit less fun) than they ever got at a like age. Study after story after column will laud these "best damn kids in the world" as heralding a resurgent American greatness. And, for a while at least, no one will talk about a generation gap.†

Thus, Howe and Strauss conclude an article concerned largely with the apparently unbridgeable gaps of understanding between parents and children with a hopeful speculation that generational relationships will improve considerably in the next two decades.

---

*"Frankenfoods Frenzy," *Reason* 13 Jan. 2000, 17 Aug. 2000 <http://reason.com/bi/bi-gmf.html>.

†Neil Howe and William Strauss, "The New Generation Gap," *Atlantic Monthly* Dec. 1992, 65.

Credits

Graham: "The Future of Love: Kiss Romance Goodbye, It's Time for the Real Thing" by Barbara Graham, *Utne Reader*, January-February 1997, 20–23. Reprinted by permission of the author.

Wakatsuki: From *Farewell to Manzanar* by James D. Houston and Jeanne Wakatsuki Houston. Copyright © 1973 by James D. Houston. Reprinted by permission of Houghton Mifflin Company. All rights reserved.

Hetsroni: "Choosing a Mate in Television Dating Games: The Influence of Setting, Culture, and Gender" by Amir Hetsroni, Figures 1.1 and 1.2, and Table 1.1, *Sex Roles*, 2001, 42:1. Reprinted by permission of Plenum Publishing.

Feldman: "The (Un)Acceptability of Betrayal: A Study of College Students' Evaluation of Sexual Betrayal by a Romantic Partner and Betrayal of a Friend's Confidence" by S. Shirley Feldman, *et al.*, Figure 1, p. 511, *Journal of Youth and Adolescence*, 2000, 29:4, 498-523. Reprinted by permission of Plenum Publishing.

Solomon: "Landscape" in "The Western as Myth and Romance" from *Beyond Formula: American Film Genres*, 1st Edition, by Stanley Solomon, copyright © 1976 Heinle, a division of Thomson Learning, has been granted to Pearson Longman Publishers for class use. All rights reserved. Aside from this specific exception, no part of this book may be reproduced, stored in a retrieval system, or transcribed in any form or by any means—electronic, mechanical, photocopying, recording or otherwise—without permission in writing from the Thomson Learning Global Rights Group: www.thomsonrights.com. Fax 800 730-2215.

Critser: "Too Much of a Good Thing" by Greg Critser, *Los Angeles Times*, July 22, 2001. Copyright © 2001 by Greg Critser. Reprinted by permission of International Creative Management, Inc.

Staples: "Driving Down the Highway, Mourning the Death of American Radio" by Brent Staples, *New York Times*, June 8, 2003. Copyright © 2003 The New York Times Co. Reprinted with permission.

Naison: "Scenario for Scandal" by Mark Naison. Copyright 1982 by Commonweal Foundation. Reprinted with permission. For subscriptions call toll-free 1-888-495-6755.

Moss: "Important Word Meanings in Essay Assignments" from *Improving Student Writing: A Guide For Faculty In All Disciplines* by Andrew Moss and Carol Holder, 1988, University of California, Los Angeles. Reprinted by permission of UCLA Department of History.

Cohen: Excerpt from "Elements of an Effective Layout" from *Advertising* by Dorothy Cohen. © 1988. Reprinted by permission of Pearson Education, Inc. Upper Saddle River, NJ.

Collins: Excerpt from *Sociological Insight: An Introduction to Non-Obvious Sociology, 2e*, by Randall Collins, 1992, page 74.

Peselman: "The Coming Apart of a Dorm Society," by Edward Peselman. Reprinted by permission.

Winn: "Television and Addiction," from "Cookies or Heroin?" in *The Plug-In Drug, Revised and Updated 25th Anniversary Edition* by Marie Winn. Copyright © 1977, 1985, 2002 by Marie Winn Miller. Used by permission of Viking Penguin, a division of Penguin Group (USA) Inc.

Nestle Purina Pet Care: Fancy Feast: "The best the world has to offer now presents the best of the sea," 2003, Nestle Purina Pet Care. Reprinted by permission of McCann Erickson.

Birds Eye Foods: "Economize without Compromise," appeared in *Sunset*, February 1982. Birds Eye Foods. Reprinted with permission.

GE Monogram: GE Monogram appliance ad, appeared on back page of *New York Times Magazine*, August 24, 2003. Reprinted by permission of General Electric Appliances.

Marchand: Excerpt from "The Appeal of the Democracy of Goods" from *Advertising the American Dream: Making Way for Modernity 1920–1940*, by Roland Marchand. © 1985 The Regents of the University of California. Reprinted by permission.

Index